HOUSES OF THE DEAD?

Houses of the Dead?

Neolithic Studies Group Seminar Papers 17

Edited by

Alistair Barclay, David Field and Jim Leary

OXBOW | books
Oxford & Philadelphia

Published in the United Kingdom in 2020 by
OXBOW BOOKS
The Old Music Hall, 106-108 Cowley Road, Oxford, OX4 1JE

and in the United States by
OXBOW BOOKS
1950 Lawrence Road, Havertown, PA 19083

© Oxbow Books and the individual contributors 2020

Paperback Edition: ISBN 978-1-78925-410-5
Digital Edition: ISBN 978-1-78925-411-2 (epub)

A CIP record for this book is available from the British Library

Library of Congress Control Number: 2019957627

All rights reserved. No part of this book may be reproduced or transmitted in any form or by any means, electronic or mechanical including photocopying, recording or by any information storage and retrieval system, without permission from the publisher in writing.

Printed in the United Kingdom by Short Run Press

Typeset in India for Casemate Publishing Services. www.casematepublishingservices.com

For a complete list of Oxbow titles, please contact:

UNITED KINGDOM	UNITED STATES OF AMERICA
Oxbow Books	Oxbow Books
Telephone (01865) 241249	Telephone (800) 791-9354, Fax (610) 853-9146
Email: oxbow@oxbowbooks.com	Email: queries@casemateacademic.com
www.oxbowbooks.com	www.casemateacademic.com/oxbow

Oxbow Books is part of the Casemate Group

Front cover: The Cat's Brain site, Wiltshire under excavation. Adam Stanford Aerial-Cam Ltd.

Foreword

This book presents the proceedings of a seminar held in November 2018, organised by the Neolithic Studies Group (NSG) and hosted by the British Museum, that forms part of an ongoing series of NSG seminar papers.

The NSG is an informal organisation comprising archaeologists with an interest in Neolithic archaeology. It was established in 1984 and has a large membership based mainly in the UK and Ireland, but also including workers from the nations of the Atlantic seaboard. The annual programme includes two or three meetings spread throughout the year and includes seminars held in London and field meetings at various locations in north-west Europe.

Membership is open to anyone with an active interest in the Neolithic in Europe. The present membership includes academic staff and students, museums staff, archaeologists from government institutions, units, trusts and amateur organisations. There is no membership procedure or application forms and members are those on the current mailing list. Anyone can be added to the mailing list at any time, the only membership rule being that names of those who do not attend any of four consecutive meetings are removed from the list (in the absence of apologies for absence or requests to remain on the list).

The Group relies on the enthusiasm of its members to organise its annual meetings and the two co-ordinators to maintain mailing lists and finances. Financial support for the group is drawn from a small fee payable for attendance of each meeting.

Anyone wishing to contact the Group and obtain information about forthcoming meetings should contact the co-ordinators at the following addresses:

TIMOTHY DARVILL	KENNETH BROPHY
Department of Archaeology and Anthropology	Department of Archaeology
Bournemouth University	University of Glasgow
Poole	Glasgow
Dorset BH12 5BB	G12 8QQ

Alternatively, visit the NSG website at: http://www.neolithic.org.uk.

Dedicated to Richard Bradley

Contents

Foreword *by Timothy Darvill and Kenneth Brophy* v
Preface and acknowledgements *by Alistair Barclay, David Field and Jim Leary* ix
List of contributors xi

1. Schrödinger's Cat: Houses for the living and the dead 1
   Jim Leary, David Field and Alistair Barclay

2. Hypogea and the clubhouse: Neolithic Malta's houses of the living
   and houses of the dead 15
   Robert P. Barratt, Caroline Malone, T. Rowan McLaughlin and Eóin W. Parkinson

3. Houses of the living, houses of the dead: A view from the Polish lowlands 39
   Joanna Pyzel

4. 'Cicéron c'est Poincaré'. Dealing with geometry: Neolithic house plans
   and the earliest monuments 47
   Philippe Chambon

5. The dead and the Linearbandkeramik longhouse 59
   Penny Bickle

6. The long and short of it: Memory and practice in the Early Neolithic
   of Britain and Ireland 79
   Alasdair Whittle

7. Measuring up: Longhouses, enclosures or mounds? 91
   Roy Loveday

8. Houses foundational: Gathering histories at Dorstone Hill, Herefordshire 107
   Keith Ray and Julian Thomas

9. New work on long barrows in Lincolnshire 121
   Denise Drury and Tim Allen

10. A dialogue with the dead? The relationship between an Early Neolithic
    rectangular timber building and a chambered tomb on Holy Island,
    Anglesey, north-west Wales 135
    Jane Kenney

11. House of the living, house of the dead: An open and
    shut case from Ballyglass, Co. Mayo? 145
    Jessica Smyth

12. Shaky foundations: Romantic nationalism and the development
    of the 'Irish model' of Neolithic settlement 159
    Andrew Whitefield

13. Structure, metaphor and funerary practices in Neolithic Scotland 177
    Alison Sheridan

14. The state of play 191
    Frances Healy

Preface and acknowledgements

Despite the chronological disjuncture, Linearbandkeramik longhouses have widely been considered to provide ancestral influence for both rectangular and trapezoidal long barrows and cairns in Britain and Ireland, but with the discovery and excavation of more houses in recent times it may be possible to observe evidence of more contemporary inspiration. What do the features found beneath long mounds tell us about this and to what extent do they represent domestic structures? Indeed, can we distinguish between domestic houses or halls and those that may have been constructed for ritual purposes or ended up beneath mounds? Do so-called 'mortuary enclosures' reflect ritual or domestic architecture and did side ditches always provide material for a mound or for some other purpose, such as building construction? If doubt exists over what is found beneath the mounds, then what of the long barrows in finished form? Do we know what long barrows were actually for?

The idea for the seminar and volume stems from a discussion of the site of Cat's Brain and its remarkable internal structure. What struck us was how similar the layout looked to other buildings more commonly referred to as houses. Does Cat's Brain bring any clarity to our current thinking regarding houses of the living and the dead, or does it simply blur and challenge our collective understanding?

This volume examines these issues and seeks to explore the interface between structures often considered for the living with those often considered for the dead, and what role they played in earlier Neolithic society. It originated from, and represents the proceedings of, the Neolithic Studies Group conference in 2018, organised by the editors of this volume and entitled 'Houses of the dead?'. Of the 14 papers given on the day, all but two are published here. Those by Tom Booth ('Houses of dead relatives?') and Bill Britnell ('Timber structures at Gwernvale and Dyffryn Lane') are due to be published elsewhere and we have asked Frances Healy, who acted as discussant on the day, to capture the essence of the concluding remarks in the end paper; she gladly obliged. As ever, opinions are those of the individual authors.

We would like to thank Tim Darvill and Kenny Brophy, the NSG Co-ordinators, as well as the British Museum, in particular Neil Wilkin from the Department of Britain, Europe and Prehistory, for allowing and facilitating the smooth running of the conference. The editors would also like to thank Elaine Jamieson for her enormous help and assistance with illustrations: similarly Julie Gardiner, Jessica Scott and Declan Ingram at Oxbow for support and aid in getting this volume into print.

Alistair Barclay, David Field and Jim Leary, September 2019

List of contributors

TIM ALLEN
Historic England
The Axis
10 Holliday Street
Birmingham
B1 1TF
England
United Kingdom
Email: Tim.Allen@historicengland.org.uk

ALISTAIR BARCLAY
Cotswold Archaeology
Building 11
Kemble Enterprise Park
Cirencester
GL7 6BQ
England
United Kingdom
Email: Alistair.Barclay@cotswoldarchaeology.co.uk

ROBERT P. BARRETT
School of Natural and Built Environment
Queen's University
Belfast
Northern Ireland
United Kingdom
Email: rbarratt01@qub.ac.uk

PENNY BICKLE
Department of Archaeology
University of York
The King's Manor
York
YO1 7EP
England
United Kingdom
Email: penny.bickle@york.ac.uk

PHILIPPE CHAMBON
CNRS UMR 7206
Éco-Anthropologie
Musée de l'Homme
17 Place du Trocadéro
75116 Paris
France
Email: philippe.chambon@mnhn.fr

PAUL COPE-FAULKNER
Archaeological Project Services
The Old School
Cameron Street
Heckington
Sleaford
Lincolnshire
NG34 9RW
England
United Kingdom
Email: paul.cope-faulkner@apsarchaeology.co.uk

DENISE DRURY
Heritage Trust of Lincolnshire
The Old School
Cameron Street
Heckington
Sleaford
Lincolnshire
NG34 9RW
England
United Kingdom
Email: denise.drury@heritagelincolnshire.org

DAVID FIELD
Wollaton
Nottingham
Nottinghamshire
NG8 2QX
England
United Kingdom
Email: DavidJField1950@gmail.com

FRANCES HEALY
Chipping Norton
Oxfordshire
OX7 3QA
England
United Kingdom
Email: frances@franceshealy.plus.com

JANE KENNEY
Gwynedd Archaeological Trust
Craig Beuno
Ffordd y Garth
Bangor
Gwynedd
LL57 2RT
Wales
United Kingdom
Email: jane.kenney@heneb.co.uk

DAVID KNIGHT
Historic England
37 Tanner Row
York
YO1 6WP
England
United Kingdom
Email: David.Knight@HistoricEngland.org.uk

JIM LEARY
Department of Archaeology
University of York
The King's Manor
York
YO1 7EP
England
United Kingdom
Email: jim.leary@york.ac.uk

ROY LOVEDAY
School of Archaeology and Ancient History
University of Leicester
University Road
Leicester
LE1 7RH
England
United Kingdom
Email: r.e.loveday@btinternet.com

CAROLINE MALONE
School of Natural and Built Environment
Queen's University
Belfast,
Northern Ireland
United Kingdom
Email: c.malone@qub.ac.uk

T. ROWAN MCLAUGHLIN
School of Natural and Built Environment
Queen's University
Belfast
Northern Ireland
United Kingdom
Email: r.mclaughlin@qub.ac.uk

DAVID MCOMISH
Historic England
4th Floor
Cannon Bridge House
25 Dowgate Hill
London
EC4R 2YA
England
United Kingdom
Email: David.McOmish@HistoricEngland.org.uk

List of contributors

MATTHEW OAKEY
Historic England
37 Tanner Row
York
YO1 6WP
England
United Kingdom
Email: Matthew.Oakey@HistoricEngland.org.uk

NEIL PARKER
Archaeological Project Services
The Old School
Cameron Street
Heckington
Sleaford
Lincolnshire
NG34 9RW
England
United Kingdom
Email: neil.parker@apsarchaeology.co.uk

SEAN PARKER
Archaeological Project Services
The Old School
Cameron Street
Heckington
Sleaford
Lincolnshire
NG34 9RW
England
United Kingdom
Email: sean.parker@apsarchaeology.co.uk

EÓIN W. PARKINSON
Department of Archaeology
University of Cambridge
Cambridge
England
United Kingdom
Email: ewp24@cam.ac.uk

JOANNA PYZEL
Institute of Archaeology and Ethnology
University of Gdańsk
ul. Bielańska 5
PL 80-851 Gdańsk
Poland
Email: joanna.pyzel@univ.gda.pl

KEITH RAY
School of History
Archaeology and Religion
Cardiff University
Cardiff
CF10 3EU
Wales
United Kingdom
Email: RayK1@cardiff.ac.uk

ALISON SHERIDAN
National Museums Scotland
Chambers St
Edinburgh
EH1 1JF
Scotland
United Kingdom
Email: a.sheridan@nms.ac.uk

CAROLINE SKINNER
Historic England
24 Brooklands Avenue
Cambridge
CB2 8BU
England
United Kingdom
Email: Caroline.Skinner@HistoricEngland.org.uk

JONATHAN SMITH
Archaeological Project Services
The Old School
Cameron Street
Heckington
Sleaford
Lincolnshire
NG34 9RW
England
United Kingdom
Email: jon.smith@apsarchaeology.co.uk

JESSICA SMYTH
School of Archaeology
University College Dublin
Belfield
Dublin 4
Ireland
Email: jessica.smyth@ucd.ie

JULIAN THOMAS
School of Arts, Languages and Cultures
University of Manchester
England
United Kingdom
Email: Julian.Thomas@manchester.ac.uk

ANDREW WHITEFIELD
School of Geography and Archaeology
NUI
Galway
Ireland
Email: andrew.whitefield@nuigalway.ie

ALASDAIR WHITTLE
School of History
Archaeology and Religion
Cardiff University
Cardiff
CF10 3EU
Wales
United Kingdom
Email: Whittle@cardiff.ac.uk

Chapter 1

Schrödinger's Cat: Houses for the living and the dead

Jim Leary, David Field and Alistair Barclay

The sheltered, low-lying landscape of the Vale of Pewsey situated between the distinctive chalk scarps of the Marlborough Downs and the Salisbury Plain in Wiltshire comprises swathes of low Greensand hills, with thin bands of clay alongside the respective flanking chalk escarpments from which tributaries of the River Avon emanate. The better-known chalk upland areas include the two components of the Stonehenge and Avebury World Heritage Site, but in comparison, the Vale of Pewsey has few earthwork monuments – the result of millennia of farming the rich landscape (Leary *et al*. 2013, 224). This has increased a sense of distinctiveness, so much so, in fact, that the well-known antiquarian Richard Colt Hoare felt able to describe the Vale as a 'grand separation' and 'a very singular and decided boundary between the Northern and Southern districts' (Hoare 1819).

Located on the lip of the northern escarpment around the edge of the Vale are several Early Neolithic monuments, including the causewayed enclosures at Rybury, Knap Hill and Crofton and three long barrows: Adam's Grave, Kitchen Barrow and Giant's Grave. In a similar manner to the distribution of long barrows on the Salisbury Plain which mainly seem to focus on valleys, spring lines and streams towards the south of the Plain (McOmish *et al*. 2002, 22–7), the monuments on the escarpments clearly reference the Vale and overlook the spring-line. Excavated long barrows on the chalk at South Street, Avebury and Easton Down (as well as Giants Hills, Lincolnshire) appear to have been placed towards the edge of cultivated areas and those on the escarpment may similarly mark the edge of cultivated lands below. By comparison, within the Vale of Pewsey itself, only one Early Neolithic monument is known; a plough-levelled long barrow situated in a field called Cat's Brain. This lies on a remnant of slightly raised Lower Chalk, south-east of Hilcott and set between two branches of the River Avon above North Newnton and Wilsford. The unusual place-name may refer to the banded chalk and clay geology of the field, perhaps invoking the markings on a cat's head.

'Cat's Brain long barrow' (Monument Number: 1483725, NMR Number: SU 15 NW 143, Location: NGR SU 11851 57891) was first identified as a cropmark on an aerial photograph taken in 1972, along with the cropmarks of three nearby probable Bronze Age ring ditches arranged along a line heading south-east (Carpenter and Winton 2011). The photograph depicted a U-shaped ditch defining an area approximately 26 m by 20 m and aligned east–west with the open-end facing east. It also showed the scant remains of a trapezoidal structure within the ditch, although absence of this element on more recent photographs led to the assumption that it had been ploughed away. Based on the ditch form, it was thought to be similar to the 'Cranborne Chase type' of long barrow identified by Ashbee and seen at Thickthorn Down, Cranborne Chase, Dorset (Ashbee 1970; 1984; Barrett *et al*. 1991, 36–7) and with widespread parallels including examples in the Thames Valley; *e.g.* Radley (Bradley 1992), but the feature within appeared more related to trapezoidal long barrows such as Fussell's Lodge (Ashbee 1966).

Not only does Cat's Brain represent the only known Early Neolithic monument in the Vale, but it is also an important example of one sited off the chalk downs, almost centrally within the landform and within easy reach of the River Avon, just 1.5 km to the south-west. As such, and with concerns over on-going plough damage, it was subject to targeted excavation in the summer of 2017 as part of the Vale of Pewsey Project, which aimed to investigate Marden henge and its Neolithic hinterland. The excavation at Cat's Brain had expected to reveal the U-shaped ditch seen in the aerial photographs and little else, however in the event, and to the delight of the team, the investigations exposed the footprint of the Early Neolithic trapezoidal structure, which comprised postholes and beamslots that looked strikingly similar to a longhouse in plan, along with two large, flanking ditches. Although analysis and post-excavation work is ongoing and a programme of scientific dating by Historic England has yet to begin, some preliminary observations can be made.

The building is aligned east–west, parallel to the Vale itself, and measured 19.2 m in length and at the front (to the east) was 10.2 m in width tapering to 6 m at the back. It is exceedingly robust in places with deeply cut foundation trenches and large postholes (the largest measuring up to 1.3 m in diameter) that would have once held colossal timbers. While traditional interpretation suggests that this represents a mortuary chamber or enclosure, there is little to back this up, no burials for example, and the detail recorded on site suggests that it could equally represent a house for the living. On the other hand, much like Schrödinger's thought experiment where the hypothetical cat may be simultaneously both alive and dead, it may represent a combination of both. Its size would have provided space for an appreciable number of people and there seems little to doubt, given the size of the postholes, that it was originally roofed (although see Loveday this volume). The monument has long been plough-razed; plough marks are clearly visible in the chalk (Fig. 1.1) and the old ground surface and probably a good amount of the natural chalk has been removed, so that what is left is only very partial. Despite this, the remains of a floor plan are discernible (Fig. 1.2), which indicates that it was tripartite; divided into three roughly equal sections, with a very clear internal partition marking the most narrow, back section, while the slight remains of a central posthole indicates the division between the first and second sections (note this tripartite arrangement occurs in some much earlier buildings *e.g.* Bickle this volume). This arrangement is also reflected in the sides of the building. An earlier ditch was clearly visible under the back of the building (a feature that, combined with the flanking ditches, gave the appearance of a U-shaped ditch on the aerial photographs), and therefore this back section may represent an extension (or annexe) to the structure. The beamslots along the front of the building are substantially deeper than the rest, suggesting that the fabric of the building's frontage was more substantial than elsewhere, perhaps monumentally so. A break halfway along this front beamslot indicates the threshold, 1.1 m wide, through which people would have entered the building. Two large postholes either side of the building's façade further monumentalised this area, although there was no indication that they formed part of a forecourt.

Fig. 1.1: Vertical view of Cat's Brain under excavation (photo: Andy Burns).

Generally, few finds were recovered from the building, no doubt in part due to the loss of the original ground surface, but none were noted in the pre-excavation test pit sampling of the topsoil either, which could suggest that the building did not contain many objects in the first place and had been kept clean. An exception to this dearth was the recovery of two decorated chalk blocks that had been deposited deep into a posthole on the southern side of the building during its construction (Fig. 1.3). The decoration comprises deliberately created depressions and incised lines that have wider parallels at other Early Neolithic sites, for example at the Cissbury flint mines or Windmill Hill causewayed enclosure (Smith 1965; Teather 2016, fig. 8). These chalk blocks will, no doubt have had motif and meaning to the Neolithic communities that created them. Substantial deposits of charcoal indicate that the façade and other parts of the building structure may have been burnt and not subsequently replaced.

Either side of the building are large crescent-shaped flanking ditches; the curving nature of the ditches noticeably contrasting with the straight lines of the building. A deeper, wider pit marks the easternmost terminal of these ditches. Whether this simply formed a marker, or had a more prominent role in events, flanking as it does the façade, cannot be determined. Both ditches conform to the same general plan and mirror each other, perhaps suggesting a deliberate design. If the flanking ditches are contemporary with the building, it could be that the ditch extension marked expansions in the building, however, molluscs provide evidence of some interesting contrasts between these elements (Martin

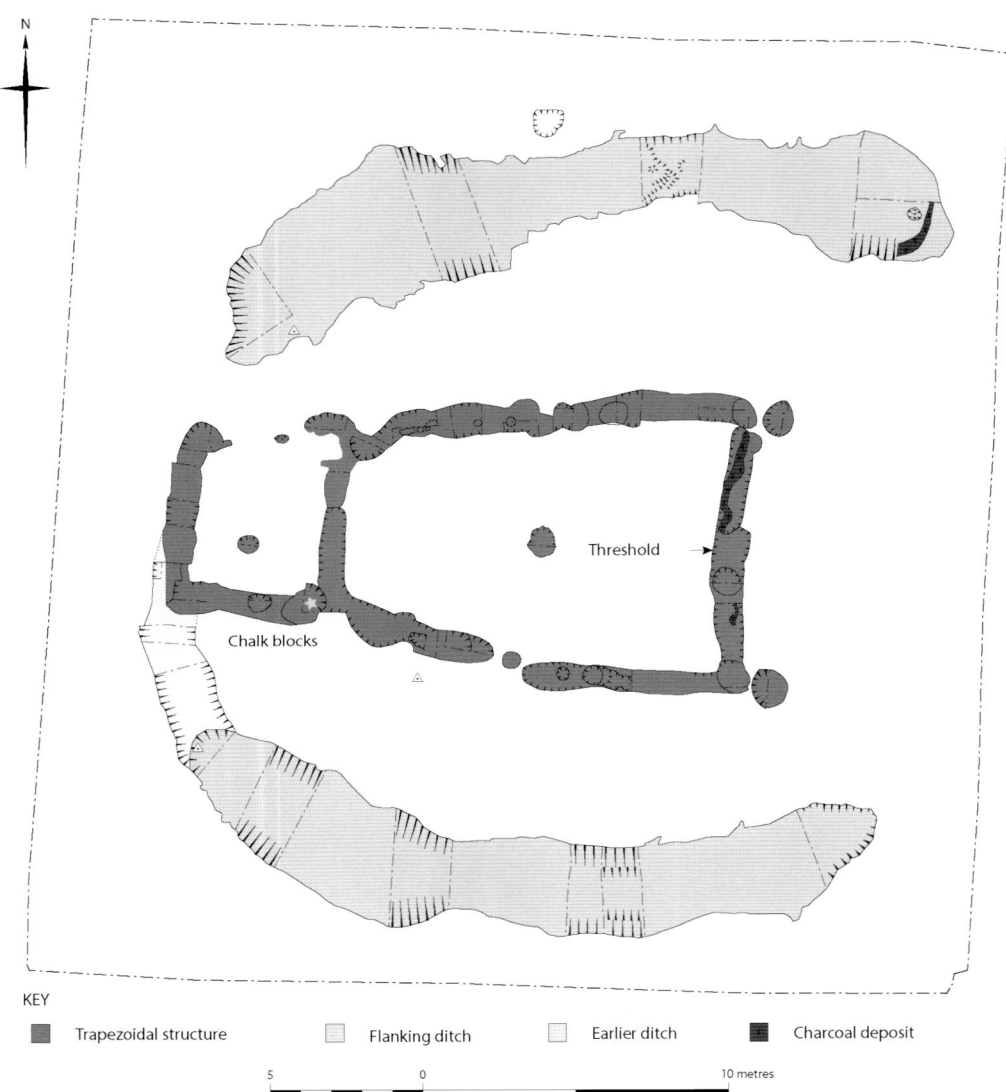

Fig. 1.2: Post-excavation plan of the Cat's Brain site (Elaine Jamieson).

Bell pers. comm.). In the samples examined so far, from the substantial postholes of the building façade, molluscs are very abundant and predominantly species of shady woodland conditions, though with more open areas. This contrasts with other long barrows subject to comparatively recent scientific excavation, which were often constructed in relatively open areas with a history of preceding activity (Ashbee *et al.* 1979; Saville 1990; Thomas 2013). Given the abundance of mollusca in some contexts one possibility that must be considered is that they were brought to the site perhaps in turves used as part of the building or in subsequent mound construction. By contrast the ditch sediments contain chalky primary fills with some fallen turves, but these contain very few molluscs and the secondary fills are decalcified. This contrast suggests a marked environmental change, relating to decalcification, and perhaps a significant time interval between the period of the structure and at least the final form of the flanking ditches. The decalcified secondary fill also points to a long period of stable environmental conditions, probably grassland, during which little or no chalk from the mound, or elsewhere, found its way into the ditch. Continuing post-excavation analysis and scientific dating will determine the nature and order of these events. Further up the profile of the southern flanking ditch, in a later fill, were pottery sherds representing about one third of a single Mortlake sub-style bowl decorated all over in a twisted cord herringbone motif. Peterborough Ware is commonly associated with the secondary fills of long barrow ditches, though here the presence of the only prehistoric pottery from the site, roughly mid-way along the south ditch, strongly suggests placed deposition rather than casual disposal (Michael Russell pers. comm.).

LONG BARROWS

Flanking ditches alongside long barrows are often seen as little more than quarries for the mound matrix, but whether this was their primary purpose remains unclear. Such ditches left entry points and access to the area around the barrow when they could easily have closed it off. Why so neat and why the causeways in the small end of some? Were these also barriers of the supernatural with proscribed entries or exit points? Clearly, continued access appears to have been important. Rarely were the ditches extended around the easternmost ends. Some of course were. At Holdenhurst the ditch extended around the larger east end, as does that at Fordingbridge 2, and in part at East Martin as well (Gill and Field 2019). Is this a regional trait? At Giants Hills 1 and 2 in Lincolnshire, the ditch encompassed both ends as it did at West Rudham in Norfolk (*e.g.* Kinnes 1992, 195–7). Curiously, the external ditch at both Giants Hills and West Rudham (Fig. 1.4; Field 2006, fig. 36) had an odd extension at the smaller end that is strangely reminiscent of the structure at both Cat's Brain and Fordingbridge 1. Further, it is curious that in the case of the eastern England examples it is the ditch that took this form, while in the two from the south it is the building or mortuary structure. For the moment, we must presume, following precedent, that the ditch material served to form a mound and there is no doubting that elsewhere that occurred, but worth recalling that some much earlier European longhouses had ditches alongside from which building material was obtained (*e.g.* Kinnes 1992, 66). Given the apparently designed ditch digging at Cat's Brain, it might be argued that it too was intricately related to construction. Could the ditch have provided material for cob walling? If

Fig. 1.3: Two incised chalk blocks recovered from a posthole within the Cat's Brain structure (photo: Jim Leary).

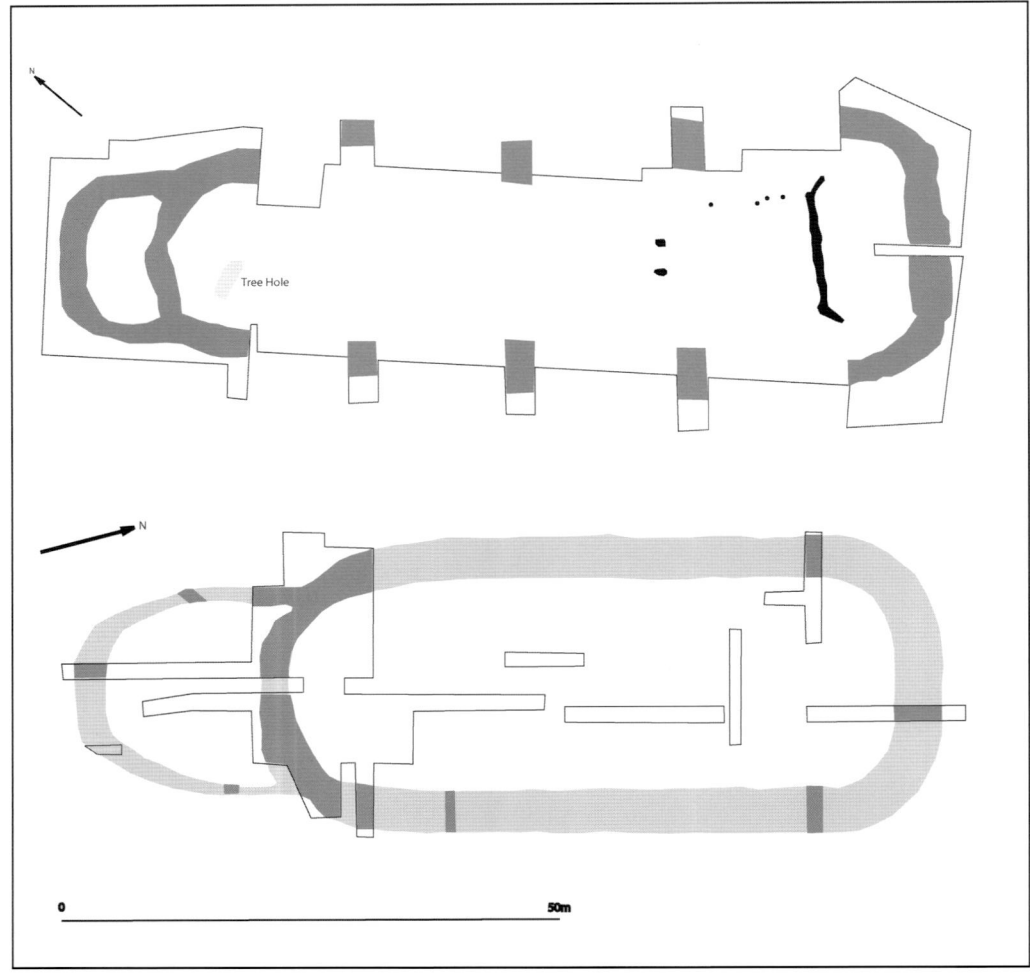

Fig. 1.4: Plan of Giants Hills 2, Skendleby Lincolnshire (redrawn from Evans and Simpson 1991) and West Rudham, Norfolk (redrawn from Hogg 1940). Note the lateral extension defined in each case by a ditch.

so, there was no trace on site and contrasting crescentic format and molluscan data suggest that there was more to it.

The nature of such mounds themselves can be briefly considered (for comprehensive analysis see Kinnes 1992). Some are vast, the mound at East Kennet reaches 6.6 m in height while others are so small you could almost leap over them. The long mound amongst the Normanton Down cemetery, near Stonehenge, for example is less than a metre in height. At 19 m in length, the latter is also among the shortest, whilst in contrast Old Ditch, Tilshead reaches an enormous 120 m. There is variety in form as well, trapezoidal, rectangular and ovoid (RCHME 1979); the trapezoidal examples, in particular, have invited comparisons with continental precursors (*e.g.* Kinnes 1975). The size and in particular the length is far beyond what is needed to cover a burial or two. If not to commemorate a specific person exactly what *was* their purpose? Do the different sizes simply reflect the size of the local workforce? It is often considered that the mound was used to put the underlying features beyond reach, perhaps because of a change of ideas or belief, perhaps to keep supernatural elements in, or out. But if so, why are some mounds so large?

The process of digging into the earth is one that essentially defines the British Neolithic. It seems to encapsulate a belief system that spread across northern Europe in the later fifth millennium with the digging of deep shaft flint mines. There appears to have been little practical purpose to this as flint was easily obtained from surface exposures, but the practice of excessive digging continued with the engraving of causewayed and other enclosures on the land and into the Later Neolithic with the deep ditches at some henges, such as Avebury, along with grand constructions such as Silbury Hill. In no instance do these appear to have been the result of entirely practical needs, and the tradition only started to lose its relevance with the introduction of Beaker related culture. Long barrow diggings form an integral part of this long-standing tradition and, attached to house-like structures, may have bound practical needs with the supernatural.

HOUSES FOR THE DEAD?

Long barrows are familiar monuments in the British landscape, and tradition often prevails in suggesting that they are for the burial of the dead. Less well considered, however, is the limited evidence for human remains from these monuments, suggesting that we may be missing the main point of them. Cat's Brain is a case in point since it failed to produce any human remains allowing suggestions that it may therefore have been a structure of another kind, a meeting place or even 'house for the living'. While remembering the adage that absence of evidence is not evidence of absence, how can we describe this long barrow, with its lack of human remains, as a burial monument? It therefore has provided something of a launchpad for a broader discussion on how we might begin to rethink long barrows.

The tradition of burial function is entrenched and can be traced at least as far back as John Aubrey who, familiar with the long mounds not far from his Wiltshire home, considered them 'sepulchres' (Fowles 1980). This was evidently a widely held belief and common received knowledge 'much as antients agree' (Defoe 1724, 201) possibly enhanced by the occasional diggings of shepherds and others. William Stukeley (1740, 38) considered them the burial place of archdruids and the tradition seemed to be confirmed by the excavations of William Cunnington who found a large number of skeletons in Bolesbarrow, Wiltshire (Cunnington mss, Devizes Museum). However, the warning signs were there – his excavations at other mounds, Knook Down and Sherrington, revealed no burials, and in others just one or two, in which case the sheer size of the long mound that covered them was simply put down to the importance of the person buried beneath. Modern excavation has encountered the same range. Stuart Piggott encountered no burials at Holdenhurst, Bournemouth or Thickthorn Down, Dorset (Drew and Piggott 1933), nor Ashbee *et al.* at Beckhampton Road and South Street at Avebury (Ashbee *et al.* 1979), nor Hogg at West Rudham, Norfolk (Hogg 1938). Yet some examples, such as Fussell's Lodge (Ashbee 1956) where the remains include infants, suggest those of a community even if the event was one of narrow chronological horizon.

Beneath some mounds, for example South Street, Beckhampton Road, and Giants Grave 1 and 2, Lincolnshire (Phillips 1936; Evans and Simpson 1991) longitudinal fence lines with divisions at right-angles were encountered that created bays or cells and indicated that other factors were at play. These were similar to examples in stone, to the stalled cairns of Orkney on the one hand and the fundamental components within some Cotswold-Severn long cairns on the other. Alan Saville (1990) considered the bays in the Cotswolds examples as purely a structural element, although others (Grimes 1960) could see no need for it, as other mounds required no such bracing. Those at South Street were each filled with slightly different material and it is conceivable that the cells could even represent social units or calendrical events (Field 2006, 149).

Some mounds, Wor Barrow, Fussell's Lodge, Willerby Wold and Kilham among them, had elongated palisade trenches beneath them, usually termed mortuary enclosures, sometimes interpreted as revetment for a mound, but alternatively as defining a mortuary precinct (Kinnes 1992, 88–90; see Loveday this volume). Holdenhurst revealed a similar feature in turf. There are clear similarities with examples not covered by a mound such as that on Normanton Down. Both Wor Barrow and Normanton Down had porches at one end, a feature that might be expected in domestic architecture. Dilwyn Jones (1998) used a more neutral term, oblong enclosures, in his study of these structures in Lincolnshire and demonstrated just how widespread they are. They too have little evidence of burial and, like long mounds, are extraordinarily long for the function; they could equally have served some other purpose altogether. Surely, Jones was right to leave the received baggage behind.

Many mounds (for example King Barrow, Old Ditch, Boles barrow and others) just had a platform or pavement of flints or other stones beneath them (Eagles and Field 2004), sometimes with a skeleton or two on it, sometimes several and sometimes none. Others had chambers or timber house-like structures. West Kennet is well known with five sarsen cave-like chambers (Piggott 1962), as is Fussell's Lodge, with burials set between postholes that are thought to have supported a pitched roof. At Nutbane, Hampshire (Fig. 1.5), an initial four-post mortuary house with sub-rectangular chamber set at the east end of the mound was rebuilt as a rectangular structure 6.7 m × 5.5 m comprising post bedding trenches with an entrance to both north and south in the west wall (Morgan 1959). It is worth comparing this with the easternmost element of the Cat's Brain building. An adjacent 'chamber' at Nutbane was also rebuilt forming a post and log enclosure 6.1 m × 5.5 m. This is one of the most house-like structures found beneath a long barrow and the complexity of the remains would stand a fresh analysis. It is these examples, if anything, that has led to the view that these are houses of the dead. However, while a large number of disarticulated bones were recovered at Fussell's Lodge, neither the original nor rebuilt mortuary house at Nutbane contained such burials. The extension or chamber to the west of the mortuary house, however, did, though in great contrast to Fussell's Lodge, just two adults and a child. The chamber was also rebuilt and this second structure contained a single adult burial. Set at right angles to the axis of the barrow, the mortuary house at Nutbane is probably the closest parallel to Cat's Brain and with the lack of burials in both phases of the mortuary house a similar question can be asked of it, what was the mortuary house for?

As excavations at Cat's Brain were taking place, further excavations at Dorstone Hill in Herefordshire by Keith Ray and Julian Thomas encountered three house-like structures subsequently mounded over (Ray and Thomas this volume).

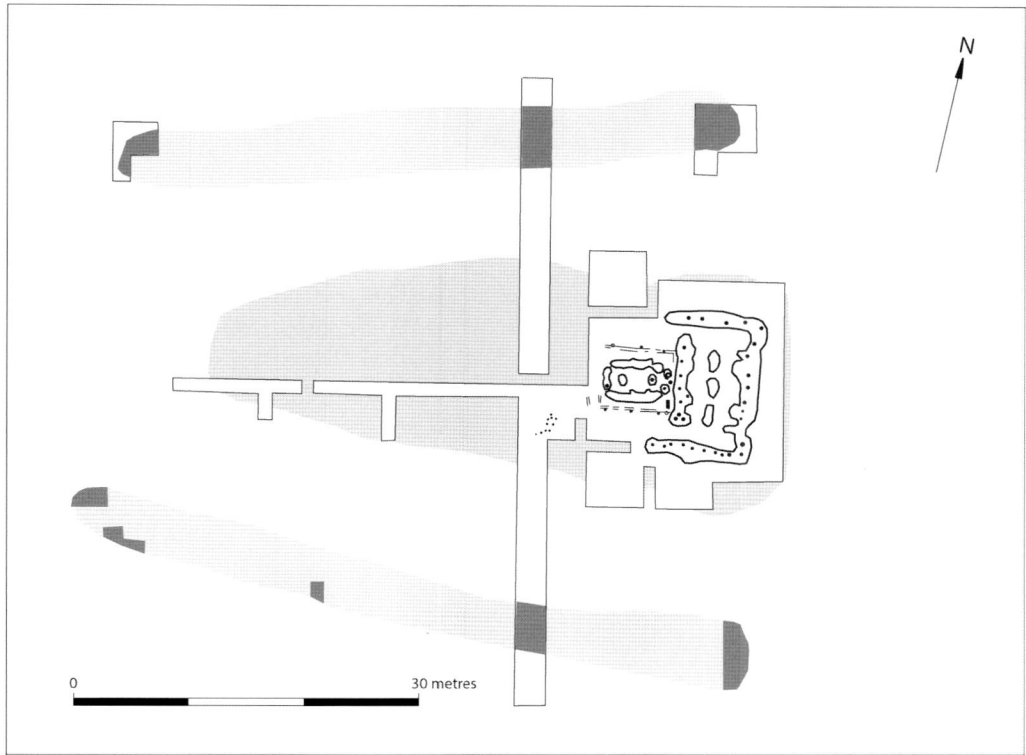

Fig. 1.5: Plan of Nutbane, Hampshire (redrawn from Morgan 1959).

HOUSES OF THE LIVING?

The resemblance between the houses of the living and those for the dead is quite striking in parts of central and eastern Europe (see Pyzel this volume; Hodder 1990, 145) and, while fully aware of the huge time gap, the similarity between some British long barrows and long cairns and the same continental houses has been much discussed (*e.g.* Ashbee 1966; 1970; Kinnes 1975; 1992 and references therein). In contrast, the difference between long barrows in their final state and British/Irish longhouses is quite markedly different. What then, if any, are the similarities between houses of the contemporary living with the dead? Some of the Cotswold Severn long cairns certainly had architectural elements of houses, most notably the false portals, and the gaps found in their timber equivalents, the so-called porched entrances (*e.g.* Wor Barrow and Fussell's Lodge) (Ashbee 1984, 34). Other long barrows were given timber façades that were notably inwardly bowed (Ashbee 1984, 37 and fig. 27) a feature that is also found in a few houses – two of the Horton houses (especially building 1: Chaffey and Brook 2012, fig. 14.4) and notably Newtown, Meath (Smyth 2014, fig. 3.5c). Axial pits for substantial posts are a feature of some Scottish halls with perhaps Warren Field, Crathes providing the clearest example (Murray *et al.* 2009, 52–3 and figs 26–7) and draws some comparison with the similar pits located within long barrow façades, mortuary houses and possible freestanding posts found beneath mounds. Whether such substantial posts, perhaps totemic or memorial, formed part of the contemporary structure is a moot point. However, such oversized structures could have been 'monster houses' built and used by the wider community. Although not intended as a parallel, some of the large houses documented during the early contact period of the North-west Coast of North America do perhaps illustrate what can be achieved in timber, including the setting of axial memorial posts, in terms of scale and breadth without the need for settings of central internal posts (Coupland 2013, 50–3 and fig. 4.3).

We should perhaps draw a distinction between the so-called mortuary house as perhaps typified by Fussell's Lodge (Ashbee 1984, 49–54) that were generally short, relatively narrow and possibly with a pitched roof. Some were positioned on the long axis of the barrow and behind the façade and connected to porch/portal structures, whilst others were arranged laterally and to the sides. Much the same variety of arrangements are encountered within long cairns. As such they may relate to just part of a house and perhaps elements that seldom survive.

It is perhaps those long barrows that had timber revetments and a façade that would have more readily resembled the houses of the living. As with the houses of the dead, these buildings are diverse in character but in England and Ireland broadly fall into two groups: post-built with walls probably of turf or wattle and daub, and those with more solid plank-built walls. Some structures, especially in Ireland, appear to combine both aisled post-settings and partitions. However, a considerable number of structures in both Ireland and southern England have little or no surviving trace of internal posts other than those that may have divided the structures into two or more rooms. Other buildings only have internal posts in one part of the structure indicating that additional structural support was needed in part rather than all of the buildings (*i.e.* to provide additional support for a raised floor or for a change in the roof construction). The two larger Horton buildings had little evidence for internal posts, and the same is true of many of the similar buildings in southern England and various structures in Ireland (Smyth 2014, fig. 3.5a–c). The point is significant for if we accept these buildings as roofed then what of the structure found at Cat's Brain?

The similarity of the Cat's Brain structure to the larger of the houses excavated at Kingsmead Quarry, Horton (Building 2) (Fig. 1.6), which also comprised posts and beam slots (Barclay and Harris 2017, 227 and fig. 15.3), was immediately apparent. Parallels can also be made with two of the structures recorded at Corbally, Ireland (Smyth 2014, fig. 3.5b: Corbally 1 and 2, in particular house 2). As with the structures found beneath long barrows, there is a degree of variability found in the ground plan, size and construction technique of the houses of the living. What is of interest here is the sharing of architectural cues between structures used by the living for domestic activities, ritual gatherings and for mortuary and spiritual purposes. Some structures, such as Cat's Brain, may appear ambiguous in this respect – betwixt and between what we would clearly classify as a house and a long barrow structure. Elsewhere, others have noted the interplay between the siting of houses and mortuary structures (see the papers by Kenny, Smyth, and Ray and Thomas this volume), which may be set close apart, in close proximity (overlapping) or as a composite construction – the extension of houses as seen at Lismore Field and White Horse Stone and at Dorstone Hill is perhaps mirrored in some structures of the dead. A small number of house-like structures and middens have been found beneath long barrows and cairns (see Whittle this volume). This interplay between what may be seen as more

Fig. 1.6: Early Neolithic house (building 2) Kingsmead Quarry, Horton (© Wessex Archaeology).

domestic activity or at the very least activities to do with habitation may be symbolised in later structures. Doorways require little explanation in terms of liminal thresholds, but what of the variety of box-like chambers that are sometimes found beyond the door or the porch-like arrangements that occasionally embellish such entrances?

The Cat's Brain structure did not just symbolise a building; it was one. It shares all the common themes of other known Neolithic timber halls – a similar orientation, and with an entrance at the broader 'business' end, while the trapezoidal format is well-known in much, much earlier LBK houses. In other words, Cat's Brain may not be a substitute for a house, but a real one. However, this is not necessarily to imply that it was a dwelling, associated with domesticity and privacy, but may, as Julian Thomas (2013) and others have pointed out, have represented society more broadly, a 'corporate social group'. The timber building, therefore, was more likely a ceremonial house that perhaps acted as a gathering place or centre of coordination, or even a storehouse for sacred heirlooms. Whatever its purpose, it will, no doubt, have reproduced values, practices and cosmological understandings of the social group and therefore been replete with collective symbolism and meaning. In this context, the engraved chalk plaques placed in one of the postholes may have been of profound significance, perhaps imbuing the uprights with supernatural power and spiritual energy.

CONCLUSION

Schrödinger's celebrated imaginary experiment presented a paradox. This focus on the long barrow at Cat's Brain highlights a similar paradox in the interpretation of this and similar monuments, and it is too easy to uncritically utilise traditional explanations that simply serve to reinforce preconceptions. While there is a lack of domestic debris, there is equally a lack of evidence for burial. Part of the answer may lie in our use and association of the word 'house', implying domesticity, whereas the structures that we encounter could have all kinds of functions: halls, lodges, kivas, or see Barratt *et al*. this volume, who refer to temples on Malta as 'club houses'. The variety of features encountered beneath long mounds certainly encourages a view that there may have been a range of functions. It could be appropriate to think in terms of shrines into which human remains were sometimes later incorporated, rather than as 'cemeteries' or 'ossuaries'. The extension at the west end at Cat's Brain, the furthest darkest corner, could easily fit that bill, but the large areas encompassed particularly by 'mortuary enclosures' may in contrast have a function completely unconnected with death. The common denominator is that these various structures were often covered over with earthen materials. Increasingly though, thanks to air photography, we discover examples of similar structures with no covering mound, so not only do we need to explain function, but also procure the reason why they should be covered in the first place. The structure at Cat's Brain could, at the same or different times, easily have housed the dead and the living – after all, living with ancestral remains need not have been unusual and the mere presence of human remains does not turn it into a tomb.

ACKNOWLEDGEMENTS

The research at Cat's Brain was led by Jim Leary and jointly funded by the University of Reading and the AHRC (AH/M008304/1) in partnership with Historic England and The Wiltshire Museum. The project team, especially Amanda Clarke and Sarah Lambert-Gates and all the excavators, are thanked for their work on the project. As are Elaine Jamieson and Freya Sadarangani for their work during post-excavation. Martin Bell and Michael Russell kindly made unpublished data available and commented on the text. The AHRC are thanked for supporting the project and funding part of this publication. Figure 5.1 is reproduced courtesy of CEMEX UK and Wessex Archaeology.

REFERENCES

Ashbee, P. (1966) The Fussell's Lodge long barrow excavations, 1957. *Archaeologia* 100, 1–80.
Ashbee, P. (1970) *The Earthen Long Barrow in Britain: an introduction to the study of the funerary practice and culture of the Neolithic people of the third millennium BC*. London, Dent.
Ashbee, P., Smith, I.F. and Evans, J.G. (1979) Excavation of three long barrows near Avebury Wiltshire. *Proceedings of the Prehistoric Society* 45, 207–300.
Ashbee, P. (1984) *The Earthen Long Barrow in Britain*. Norwich, Geo Books.
Barclay, A.J. and Harris, O.J.T. (2017) Community building: houses and people in Neolithic Britain. In P. Bickle, V. Cummings, D. Hofmann and J. Pollard (eds) *The Neolithic of Europe. Papers in honour of Alasdair Whittle*, 222–33. Oxford, Oxbow Books.

Barrett, J., Bradley, R. and Green, M. (1991) *Landscapes, Monuments and Society: the prehistory of Cranborne Chase*. Cambridge, Cambridge University Press.

Bradley, R. (1992) The excavation of an oval barrow beside the Abingdon causewayed enclosure, Oxfordshire. *Proceedings of the Prehistoric Society* 58, 127–42.

Carpenter, E. and Winton, H. (2011) *Marden Henge and Environs, Vale of Pewsey, Wiltshire. National Mapping Programme Report*. Historic England, Research Department Report Series no. 76–2011 (ISSN 1749–8775).

Chaffey, G. and Brook, E. (2012) Domesticity in the Neolithic: excavations at Kingsmead Quarry, Horton, Berkshire. In H. Anderson-Whymark and J. Thomas (eds) *Regional Perspectives on Neolithic Pit Depositions: beyond the mundane*, 200–15. Oxford, Oxbow Books (Neolithic Studies Research Papers).

Coupland, G. (2013) Household Archaeology of Complex Hunter-Gatherers on the North-west Coast of North America. In M. Madella, G. Kovacs, B. Berzsenyi and I. Briz I Godino (eds) *The Archaeology of Household*, 45–66. Oxford, Oxbow Books.

Defoe, D. (1724) *A Tour Through the Whole Island of Great Britain*. (Penguin edn reprint 1979) Harmondsworth, Penguin Books.

Drew, C.D. and Piggott, S. (1936) Excavation of long barrow 163a on Thickthorn Down, Dorset. *Proceedings of the Prehistoric Society* 2, 77–96.

Eagles, B. and Field, D. (2004) William Cunnington and the long barrows of the River Wylye. In R. Cleal and J. Pollard (eds) *Monuments and Material Culture: papers in honour of an Avebury archaeologist, Isobel Smith*, 47–69. East Knoyle, Hobnob Press.

Evans, J.G. and Simpson, D.D.A. (1991) Giants Hills 2 long barrow, Skendleby, Lincolnshire. *Archaeologia* 109, 1–46.

Field, D. (2006) *Earthen Long Barrows*. Stroud, Tempus.

Fowles, J. (ed.) (1980) *John Aubrey's Monumenta Britannica*. Sherborne, DPC.

Gill, M. and Field, D. (2019) New long barrow discoveries in the vicinity of the middle Avon valley and Cranborne Chase. *PAST* 91, 5–7.

Grimes, W.F. (1960) Burn Ground, Hampnett, Gloucestershire. In W.F. Grimes *Excavations on Defence sites 1939–1945*, 41–128. London, HMSO.

Hoare, R.C. (1819) *Ancient Wiltshire*. London, Lackington, Hughes, Harding, Mavor and Jones.

Hodder, I. (1990) *The Domestication of Europe. Structure and contingency in Neolithic societies*. Oxford, Basil Blackwell.

Hogg, A.H.A. (1940) A long barrow at West Rudham. *Norfolk Archaeology* 27, 315–31.

Jones, D. (1998) Long barrows and Neolithic elongated enclosures in Lincolnshire: an analysis of the air photographic evidence. *Proceedings of the Prehistoric Society* 64, 83–114.

Leary, J., Field, D. and Campbell, G. (2013) *Silbury Hill: the largest prehistoric mound in Europe*. Swindon: English Heritage.

Kinnes, I. (1975) Monumental function in British Neolithic burial practices. *World Archaeology* 7, 16–29.

Kinnes, I. (1992) *Non-Megalithic Long Barrows and Allied Structures in the British Neolithic*. London, British Museum (Occasional Paper 52).

McOmish, D., Field, D. and Brown, G. (2002) *The Field Archaeology of Salisbury Plain Training Area*. Swindon, English Heritage.

Morgan, F. de M. (1959) The excavation of a long barrow at Nutbane, Hants. *Proceedings of the Prehistoric Society* 25, 15–51.

Murray, H.K., Murray, J.C. and Fraser, S.M. (2009) *A Tale of the Unknown Unknowns. A Mesolithic pit alignment and a Neolithic timber hall at Warren Field, Crathes, Aberdeenshire*. Oxford, Oxbow Books

Phillips, C.W. (1936) The excavation of the Giants Hills long barrow, Skendleby, Lincolnshire. *Archaeologia* 85, 37–106.

Piggott, S. (1937) The excavation of a long barrow in Holdenhurst parish, near Christchurch, Hampshire. *Proceedings of the Prehistoric Society* 3, 1–14.

Piggott, S. (1938) The Early Bronze Age in Wessex. *Proceedings of the Prehistoric Society* 4, 52–106.
Piggott, S. (1962) *The West Kennet Long Barrow: excavations 1955–56*. London, HMSO.
Piggott, S. (1971) An Archaeological Survey and Policy for Wiltshire Part III: Neolithic and Bronze Age. *The Wiltshire Archaeological and Natural History Magazine* 66, 47–57.
RCHME (1979) *Long Barrow in Hampshire and the Isle of Wight*. London, HMSO.
Saville, A. (1990) *Hazleton North: the excavation of a Neolithic long cairn of the Cotswold-Severn Group*. London, HBMC.
Smith, I.F. (1965) *Windmill Hill and Avebury: excavations by Keiller 1925–1935*. Oxford, Clarendon Press
Smyth, J. (2014) *Settlement in the Irish Neolithic. New discoveries at the edge of Europe*. Oxford, Oxbow Books (Prehistoric Society Research Paper 6).
Stukeley, W. (1740) *Stonehenge: a temple Restor'd to the British Druids*. London, Innys and Manby.
Teather, A. (2016) Building new Neolithic connections through chalk art: the value of the archaeological collections of John Pull and James Park Harrison. *World Archaeology* 48, 2, 296–310.
Thomas, J. (2013) *The Birth of Neolithic Britain: an interpretive account*. Oxford, Oxford University Press.

Chapter 2

Hypogea and the clubhouse: Neolithic Malta's houses of the living and houses of the dead

Robert P. Barratt, Caroline Malone, T. Rowan McLaughlin and Eóin W. Parkinson

INTRODUCTION

Houses are functional spaces that provide context to the life of the individuals that inhabited them and metaphorical space that forge and preserve their identity. They are also the background for activity, both individual and communal. In this paper, domestic spaces in Neolithic Malta are discussed, comparing and contrasting those functional spaces of living people with the more abstract 'houses' of the dead. With the grand temples and complex hypogea, the Neolithic culture in the Maltese Islands has been the focus of extensive research and writing. There is a plethora of works discussing the cultural sequence, use and significance of the prehistoric sacred architecture. These mostly revolve around the 'temples', which are large megalithic apsidal structures, and the hypogea, which are underground cave systems used for the burial of the dead. But little has been written with regards to domestic spaces (Malone *et al.* 1988; 2009, chapter 3; Grima 2008). This is mainly due to a lack of evidence, which is much less visible and more vulnerable to destruction than the upstanding megalithic structures found across Malta and Gozo. The sheer monumentality of the surviving structures has, for much of the twentieth century, resulted in a situation where the exploration of the temples was a higher priority for archaeology in Malta. The Cambridge Gozo Project, initiated in 1987, redressed this imbalance with the instigation of large-scale field survey, the scientific excavation of the second large burial hypogeum and excavation of one Late Neolithic house structure. Recent fieldwork under the aegis of the succeeding FRAGSUS ERC project has focused considerable resources upon unearthing evidence for domestic life, with the excavation of another Late Neolithic house at a complex, multi-period settlement site. The FRAGSUS project has been assessing how far environmental and cultural fragility and their sustainability over time in Neolithic Malta can be identified. The work involved comprehensive study of previously unexplored aspects of Maltese prehistory, including the creation of a detailed chronology, landscape analysis and palaeoenvironmental fieldwork geared towards understanding how and why the megalith-building society emerged, then flourished, but seemingly collapsed at the start of the Bronze Age (Stoddart 2013).

THE MALTESE NEOLITHIC

The Mediterranean Maltese Islands (Fig. 2.1) are among the most interesting centres of prehistoric culture in Europe, despite their relatively small size (only 316 square km). A viable environment is dependent on seasonal rainfall stored in perched aquifers and springs, and the islands sustained early occupation from the earlier sixth millennium cal BC. The limestone geology of the islands is comprised of a stratigraphy of Globigerina and Coralline limestone and blue clay. The Globigerina is especially workable and therefore used extensively in the islands' architecture and quarried for the construction of underground structures.

During Malta's first colonisation in the sixth millennium cal BC, the soils were rich and fertile with adequate properties of moisture retention and resistance to erosion, and a reasonable cover of scrub and trees. The islands were heavily exploited for Early Neolithic agriculture, but as discussed below, once this initial 'boom' was over by 4900 cal BC, the human population reduced to barely-detectable levels for a millennium. The apparently rich environment masked a much frailer landscape gradually manifesting in soil loss and increased aridity. Managing this fragile, eroding landscape must have been the central preoccupation for the Late Neolithic megalith-builders. Micromorphological and archaeobotanical evidence suggests careful soil management throughout the Late Neolithic period (French *et al.* 2018), but despite their best efforts, natural trends towards aridification eventually overwhelmed the Late Neolithic Maltese society and, by 2350 cal BC, it became markedly reduced in scale. The timetable of these environmental and social changes is a product of the FRAGSUS project's

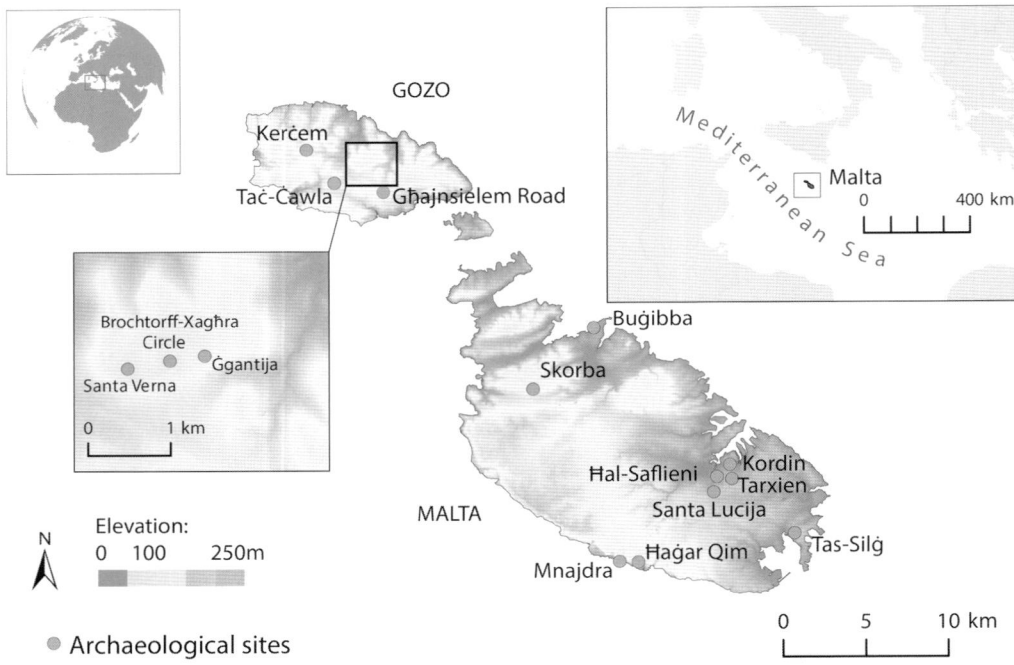

Fig. 2.1: Location map of Malta and Gozo and sites mentioned in text (R. McLaughlin).

extensive dating programme, resulting in the analysis of some 400 AMS radiocarbon samples applied to the Maltese environment, several prehistoric sites and human remains from Xagħra. David Trump's work had gathered about a dozen radiocarbon dates by the 1980s, and these were greatly increased by the Gozo Project (1987–94) to about 40 samples from burials. The sheer number and quality of the new findings have vastly improved the understanding of the so-called 'Temple Period' and its antecedents. The results have also helped push back the dating of early phases of occupation, which is now believed to have occurred $c.$5800 cal BC, based on cereal pollen analysis. However, the first cultural evidence dates to $c.$5500 cal BC, so unfortunately this earliest occupation phase still awaits more research and discovery. A period of depopulation seems to have taken place between $c.$4900–3800 cal BC, prior to a new arrival of population that can be identified as the so-called Żebbuġ phase, the first of several distinctive phases of the Late Neolithic Temple Period. Ceramic evidence suggests that this represents a fresh recolonisation of the archipelago from Sicily, and current work in the analysis of ancient DNA from Malta suggests a break from the preceding 'Cardial-Impressed' wave of Neolithisation (Ariano *et al.* forthcoming). The first 'temples' were constructed $c.$3700 cal BC and progressively increased in complexity until they evolved into the monumental megalithic structures that have become the emblem of this culture (Evans 1959). The best archaeological evidence dates to the final Tarxien phase, $c.$2900–2350, during which time some of the most elaborate megalithic complexes were built, as well as the two large hypogea burial sites, within which were interred a large quantity of human skeletal remains.

The insularity and small size of the Maltese landscape promoted the creation of a distinctive island culture, with no close parallels in adjacent southern Italy or Sicily. Despite some evidence of trade and cultural exchanges – especially of lithics, with Sicily and Lipari, the Temple people appeared relatively isolated (Stoddart *et al.* 1993) and their structures, beliefs and art were unique (but see Robb 2001; Grima 2002 for alternative views). Around 2400 cal BC the natural fertility of the soil had become depleted and probably compromised by fluctuating climatic conditions, which ultimately brought the end of the distinctive Temple culture. There is some evidence of abandonment of sacred sites, especially iconoclastic instances with the destruction of statues (for example, a smashed large figure overlying the final burials at Xagħra (Malone *et al.* 2009)). Until now, there was little evidence for this transitional phase, but it now seems that the so called 'Tarxien Cemetery' culture and its relative – the Thermi Culture – began to influence Malta during the later third millennium cal BC, manifested by distinctive pottery and funerary practices. This Early Bronze Age culture continued to 1700 cal BC, although in Malta we can be certain that the scale of society and its economy was much reduced. This is demonstrated by the archaeology, which is limited to sporadic re-use of megalithic sites and sparse cultural material evidence coupled with a lack of contemporary cereal pollen in sediments.

TEMPLES AND THE HYPOGEA

The 'temples' are the primary form of expression for the Temple Period. They are impressive megalithic structures, composed of high outer walls of large Globigerina stone slabs or rough Coralline boulders (depending on the local geology), that enclose a central corridor with niche or apse at the end and multiple lobed or apse-shaped rooms opening to the sides. External features include trilithon entrances, thresholds and steps, and usually a concave façade furnished with stone display benches, facing an open arena. Earlier temples were composed of single or trefoil apses, but later temples have as many as seven apses (Evans 1971). More than 30 temples, usually in groups of 2–3 remain, none complete with surviving roofs. We know from past and recent excavation that temple structures had long complex histories of modification. Unique architectural representations (models, sketched plans, see Fig. 2.2) provide insight into their appearance, although many details remain a matter for debate, such as the nature of the roofing (Clark 1998). Evidence from recent excavations at Tas-Silġ temple suggests that the temple structure was originally roofed with wooden and *torba* (crushed lime plaster) structures (Cazzella and Recchia 2012), whilst the construction of other sites is suggestive of corbelled stone roofing.

Entire complexes of these stone buildings were built, especially late in the Temple Period. They often share a façade and many internal connected rooms decorated with shelves, altars, display benches and carved art (Fig. 2.3). It's often difficult to phase these sites from architectural elements alone, but seriation of the pottery proposed by David Trump and John Evans has been used to establish site chronologies (Evans 1953). The primary function of the sites has mainly been defined as ceremonial (indeed often extravagant ideas of religion have been suggested) and, although some have questioned that assumption, the interpretation has dominated much of the Maltese Neolithic discourse (Gimbutas 2001).

Associated with temples are the few (at least three) hypogea known to survive in the Maltese Islands (Ħal-Saflieni and Santa Luċija on Malta and Xagħra on Gozo). These underground burial sites can be composed of many interconnected chambers with complex architecture and an abundance of skeletal remains and have antecedents in the form of various smaller rock-cut tomb cemeteries, which themselves evolved from a wider Central Mediterranean tradition (Whitehouse 1972; Malone 1996). The Ħal-Saflieni hypogeum is the main example, due to its size and preservation (Zammit 1912; Evans 1971). The skeletal remains within were unfortunately removed haphazardly in the early twentieth century, leaving only the remarkable subterranean structure and some artefacts as evidence of the funerary context. The Brochtorff-Xagħra Circle was excavated from 1987–1994 (Malone et al. 2009) and, although formed within a

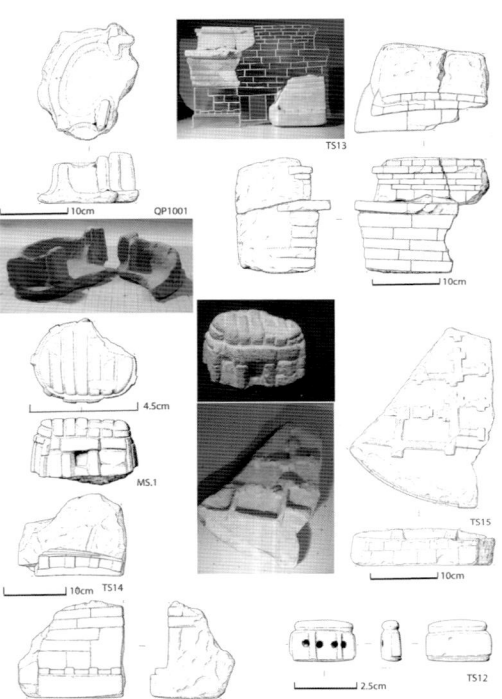

Fig. 2.2: Models of temple structures from Tarxien (TS12, TS13, TS14, TS15), Ħaġar Qim (QP1001) and Ta' Ħaġrat (MS.1) drawn at different scales (J. Gibbins) (photos C. Malone).

2. Hypogea and the clubhouse

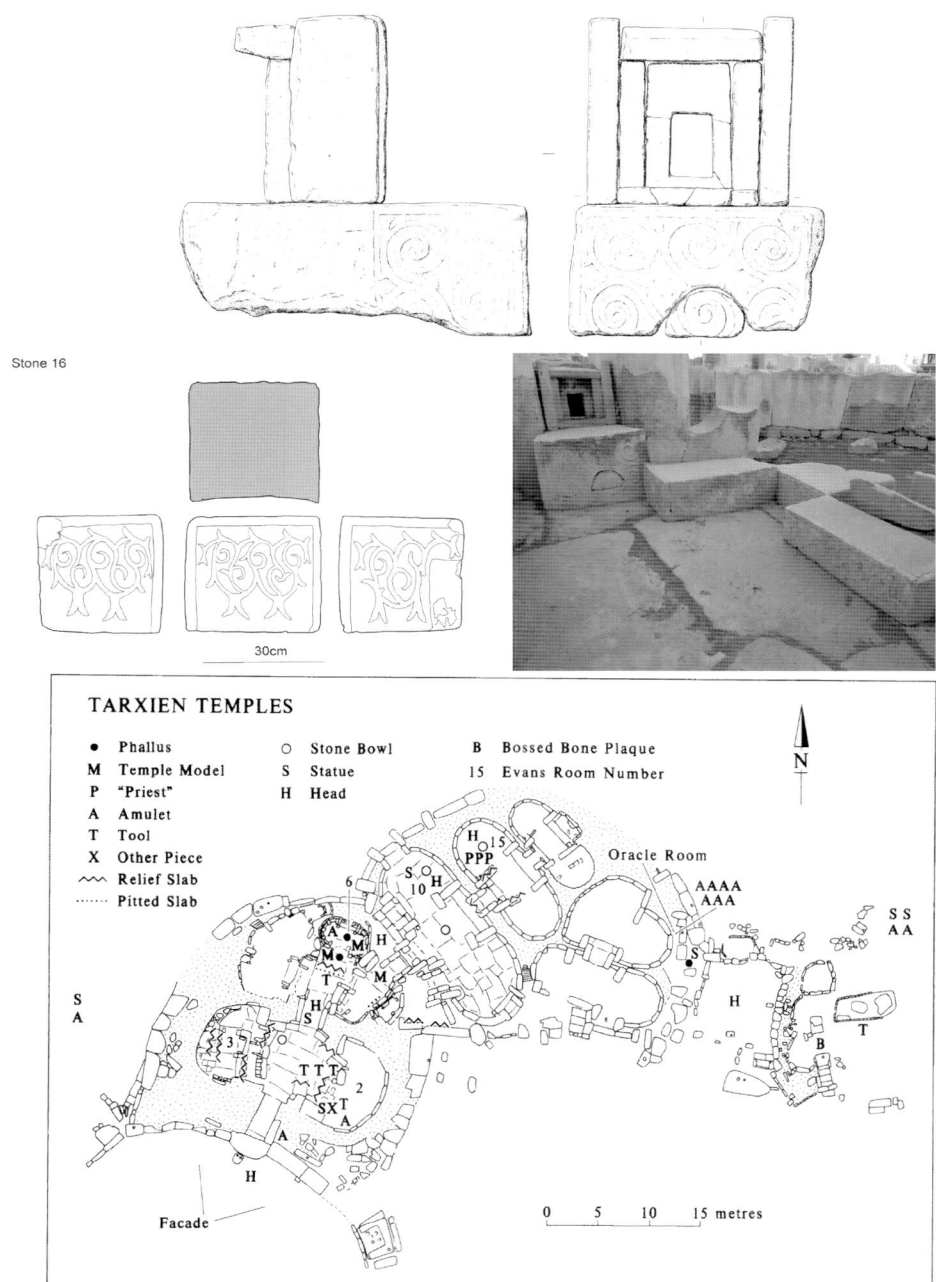

Fig. 2.3: Tarxien Temple Altar 'ß' with spirals in Room 1, drawing (J. Gibbins) and photo, Stone 16 placed at end of animal frieze 1 in Room 3 (C. Malone), Distribution of ritual objects discovered by Zammit at Tarxien (S. Ashley).

semi-natural collapsing cave system, the site retained a vast quantity of human remains. Although disturbed in the nineteenth century, and not yet fully explored, the material was exceptionally well preserved, and its excavation thus provided much needed information regarding burial practices in Neolithic Malta. Re-analysis of this skeletal assemblage using many current scientific approaches has also been one focus of the ERC FRAGSUS project.

DOMESTIC SITES

There is little evidence of purely domestic spaces on the Maltese Islands. This is due to the fragile and superficial nature of these sites, as the structures comprised less durable materials, and have been badly damaged by agriculture, terracing and building work. However, occasional sites have provided some clues on domestic activities. The most complete evidence is offered by the site of Għajnsielem Road (Gozo), which prior to FRAGSUS was the only house to have been fully excavated (Malone *et al.* 1988; 2009). Discovery was fortuitous, when foundation work for the construction of a modern house exposed successive plaster floors of a prehistoric house, but also removed half the structure entirely. The Għajnsielem Road house, dating to the Ġgantija phase of the 'Temple Period' (*c.*3300 cal BC) comprised two conjoined oval mud walls, the largest one measuring *c.*7 m in diameter; the smaller *c.*2 m across. The foundations were finely cut into the bedrock, and the walls were composed of shaped mud bricks or *pisè*. The centre of the main structure contained the remains of a mud brick pillar that may have been used as roof support. A recent 3D approximation of these structures has been created by one of the authors of this paper (Barratt), in an attempt to visualise what form they once took (Fig. 2.4). However, while the foundations and floors were well-preserved, there is little information regarding the above ground structure, such as height, roofing or external features. Therefore, it is difficult to formulate an understanding of the use of the site and the relationship between its various structural elements from archaeological data. Despite this lack of evidence, the visualisation approach provides some insight into the nature of domestic life in Late Neolithic Malta.

The FRAGSUS project enabled a detailed investigation of another Gozo settlement site at Taċ-Ċawla in Victoria-Rabat. This domestic site was discovered and partially explored some 25 years earlier when possible post structures were identified in several locations. The 2014 FRAGSUS project excavations exposed a substantial portion of the site, including the foundation walls of a 'house' and associated layers of midden material, floors and stone spreads, indicating the presence of multiple phases of occupation from earlier Neolithic to the Bronze Age and Roman periods. The dominant features were a series of plaster *torba* floors overlying a substantial rubble stone base and a modest encircling stone wall. The chronological sequence of the site is challenging due to its long history of agricultural use. Ceramic finds signalled occupation from the earliest Neolithic phases, but without structural context. Although most of the structural features dated to the Tarxien and Tarxien Cemetery phases, *c.*2900 to 2300 cal BC, thus spanning the end of the 'Temple Period', radiocarbon dating has demonstrated that the majority of the plant remains and animal bones recovered represents residual material from Early Temple Period phases (Żebbuġ-Ġgantija) *c.*3700 cal BC.

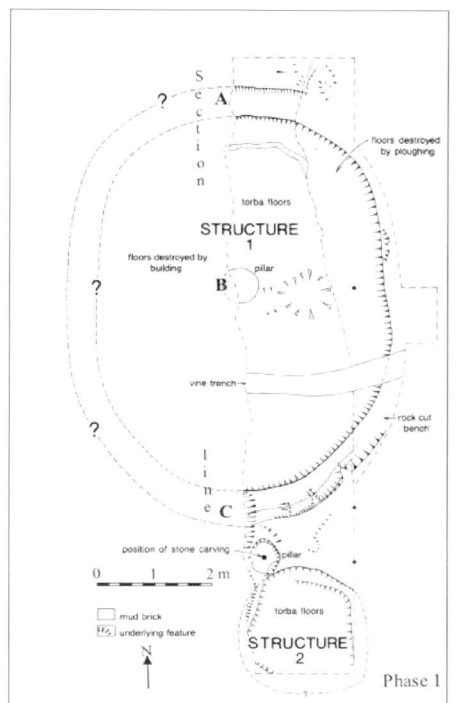

Fig. 2.4: The house excavated at Għajnsielem Road, Gozo in 1988, plan (S. Ashley), photograph (C. Malone) and digital reconstruction (R. Barratt).

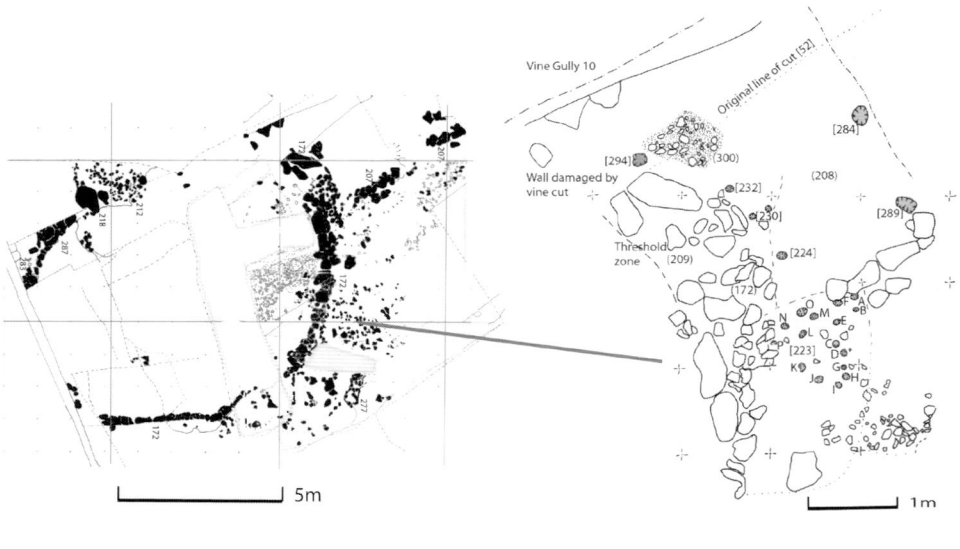
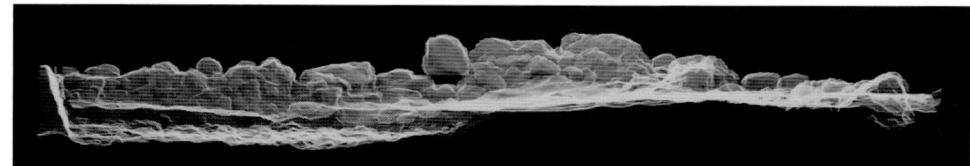

Fig. 2.5: Taċ-Ċawla Neolithic House under excavation, in plan, detail of postholes in north-east section (C. Malone), digital scan of structural wall (J. Meneely).

The Għajnsielem Road structures present a more congruous example of domestic space while Taċ-Ċawla is more incoherent. Taċ-Ċawla, however, has extensive superficial evidence, large-scale signs of re-working and of re-occupation, much of which was presumably formed from the material of former phases. While the 3300 cal BC Għajnsielem huts were made of shaped mud bricks, by 2500 cal BC the Taċ-Ċawla structure had low (0.7 m high) double skinned stone walls that related to stake holes, inside and outside, suggesting the presence of timber framework to support the roof, as well as evidence for an external porch-like structure. The structures were enveloped in rich soil containing evidence for a succession of prehistoric and later settlement phases (Fig. 2.5). Taċ-Ċawla was located on a south-eastern aspect of the Rabat central plateau, an area that offered protection from the cold north-westerly winds. The site overlay a significant aquifer-fed spring and was on some of the best agricultural soil on the island. Evidently, the spring had been accessed by a sloping bedrock ramp during the earlier Temple period, but it was then buried beneath part of the final Neolithic and Early Bronze Age walled structure, probably when the spring ceased to function. The domestic structures evolved through a number of phases, evidenced by several plaster floors and their rubble stone bases. From these two examples we can surmise that domestic structures in Neolithic Gozo were modest but functional. From the present sample, we can suggest domestic houses had oval rooms typically *c.*5–7 m in length, *torba* plaster floors formed of crushed limestone, clay and pot sherds, walls composed of a combination of timber frame, clay bricks with footings in the cut rock and low rubble walls. There is little evidence for roofing, but it seems the huts would have been covered in thatch, plaster and timber, although whether pitched or flat or domed is unclear. The location of the occupation centres was critical, as proximity to resources of water and soil were immutable constraints, which led to multi-phased uses of sites and the continuous occupation of specific areas for many centuries or even millennia.

DOMESTIC SPACES IN TEMPLES

Another large-scale excavation undertaken by FRAGSUS was the exploration of the Neolithic temple of Santa Verna on Gozo in 2015. The site had previously been explored by Thomas Ashby in 1911 (Ashby *et al*. 1913). The temple structure evolved through at least five phases, the best-resolved being the fourth phase, dating to the Ġgantija phase of the Temple Period. At that time, around 3300 cal BC, Santa Verna was similar to the homonymous temple complex found nearby. Unfortunately, Santa Verna has suffered great damage, both in recent times and in prehistory when the large megaliths may have been re-used for the late structural elaborations of the Brochtorff-Xagħra Circle nearby as well as for a medieval chapel on the site. Despite these destruction events, it is still possible to identify the plan of the site, and more importantly multi-phased occupational layers that lie beneath it. Radiocarbon samples show that the site was initially the location of a substantial Early Neolithic settlement dating to the mid-sixth millennium cal BC, the earliest date yet for human settlement on Malta (French *et al*. 2018). Even at that early stage, there was evidently a quite extensive site, comprising modest structures with plastered floors. Reoccupation of the site began *c.*3800 cal BC, confirmed by the overlying levels of Żebbuġ and Ġgantija material that signalled the temple structure (McLaughlin *et al*. forthcoming).

The changing form of domestic structures in prehistoric Malta provides an important link with our current understanding of the architectural changes seen in the temples and hypogea. It is likely that an architectural evolution resulting in the extraordinary megalithic 'temple' sites developed from domestic foci. The first settlers built structures in the Għar Dalam and Skorba phases (5500–5000 cal BC), most notably documented at Skorba temple in the form of an Għar Dalam wall and associated hut, and the pair of Red Skorba huts (Trump 1966). The Red Skorba huts were oval buildings, with cut and plastered floors with an apparent primary domestic use, even though Trump argued for a shrine-function on the basis of figurine fragments (Trump 1966; Lewis 1977). The original Skorba excavation also uncovered a complex sequence of settlement and monumental structures located beneath the later temples. They spanned from the sixth to the fourth millennium cal BC (Sagona 2015; Bonanno 2017) and provide the strongest sequence of gradual transformation from domestic to ceremonial (Bonanno *et al.* 1990). In 2016, FRAGSUS undertook a small-scale excavation to refine the chronology of the earlier occupational in particular, and to establish the construction of the megalithic buildings.

In the Żebbuġ phase (3800–3500 cal BC) the first 'temples' of Malta were constructed, based on connected single-lobed houses that formed trefoil plans, and conforming generally to the shape and size of the domestic houses described above. One interesting and largely ignored example is an oval room with a cut stone floor located within the East Temple of Ħaġar Qim (very similar in shape and scale to the Għajnsielem Road house), which was then enveloped within a more complex multi-roomed building. Its curious and somewhat awkward placement, almost within the main external approach to the main temple, might imply it was a foundational place, revered and retained as a historic memory within the ceremonial complex. By the later fourth millennium cal BC, the role of megalithic buildings appears to be as structured ceremonial spaces, and over time these buildings became ever more complex. In the Ġgantija phase (3500–3000 cal BC), the numbers of apses increased as did the scale of building, which then developed into the exceptional temple complexes of the Tarxien phase (3000–2350 cal BC), as seen at the phases type-site and Ħaġar Qim. The increased complexity is not only evident in the plans, but also in the internal divisions and fitments. Apsed rooms were separated by walls, screens and portholes, embellished with altars, oracle holes and niches that created a collection of closed spaces and hidden storage areas, some furnished with rich decorations. Through this long development of monumental and domestic construction, the landscape too filled up, as population grew (demonstrated by surface survey in Gozo (Boyle 2013)). In tandem with this expanding scenario, burial spaces also became progressively intricate, much larger in size and community focused. The number of chambers increased as did the complexity of embellishment and explicit internal spaces and external enclosure. This formalising process culminated in the impressive Ħal-Saflieni and Brochtorff-Xagħra Circle hypogea, and there is a clear association between the development of the temple and burial sites. It seems likely that the architecture reflected commonly-held ideas and a shared cosmology that prevailed throughout the islands. There are many elements in common in temple building and hypogea design, such as a predominant south-east orientation, the construction techniques and architectural devices, which in turn were mirrored in the domestic origins – the 'houses'.

We identify a recurring trend in the prehistoric architecture in Malta and pose that many sites of domestic occupation eventually led to the establishment of the monumental places.

The site of Skorba is a prime example of this tendency (Trump 1966). Originally excavated by David Trump in the 1960s, the Skorba megalithic complex played a pivotal role in the establishment of a chronology for the Maltese Neolithic, as well as for the understanding of Neolithic antiquity in the central and western Mediterranean (Trump 1966). The early chronological occupation (first Neolithic), provided Colin Renfrew with essential data for his anti-diffusion debate (Renfrew 1970; 1973).

TEMPLES AS DOMESTIC SPACES

From the first excavations of Themistocles Zammit in the 1910–30 period, through the work of subsequent scholars, the role of the megalithic buildings as 'temples' or ritual structures has remained undisputed: they have been interpreted as sacred places that were used as the background for ritual practices, popularly seen as focused on a Mother Goddess cult. But the architectural and material evidence, as well as the long succession of structural development, suggests their use was far from exclusively ritual. The structures contain compelling evidence for food preparation, feasting, rubbish disposal, ostentatious display, controlled access, ceremonial organisation and cosmological observations (Malone 2007; Lomsdalen 2010; Skeates 2017). Buildings of a more ephemeral nature were present around and often adjacent to the structures (Evans 1971) and may have had a much more explicit domestic function, perhaps in supporting ceremonial activities, residence and consumption. In many of the larger preserved sites there is strong evidence for continuity, enlargement and modification around the core foundation.

Although the exact activities that occurred in the megalithic buildings are unknown, the remains point to a mixture of the ceremonial, the performative and the domestic. So-called 'Oracle' holes, altars (or display tables), symbolic objects, statues and monoliths are primary examples of the attention-focusing devices that imply ritualised activities. At the same time there is an emphasis on creating clear internal division and areas of restricted access, possibly associated with particular locations of cult (Stoddart *et al.* 1993), which in the case of Tarxien, is partly borne out by the location of particular objects and installations. However, the seclusion offered by these areas and the large façade with display benches can also be linked to performance and 'theatre'. Raised platform stages and screens would be the perfect location for the entrance and exit of prominent players, providing ample opportunity for entertainment and communal moments. This would play an important part in sacred practices, but they may also serve a more mundane purpose of community building.

ANIMALS AND FEASTING

The communal aspect of the temples is emphasised by the presence of many food preparation locations (Malone 2007; Skeates 2008; Malone *et al.* 2019b). Hearths, shelves, grindstones, fire pits, benches and storage facilities all point to an extensive feasting tradition, focused on community but also the domestic. The presence of animal bone and horn can be found through many of the temple sites. One of the best examples is the complex at Tarxien, which is the most complex and best preserved (Zammit 1930) and, thanks to

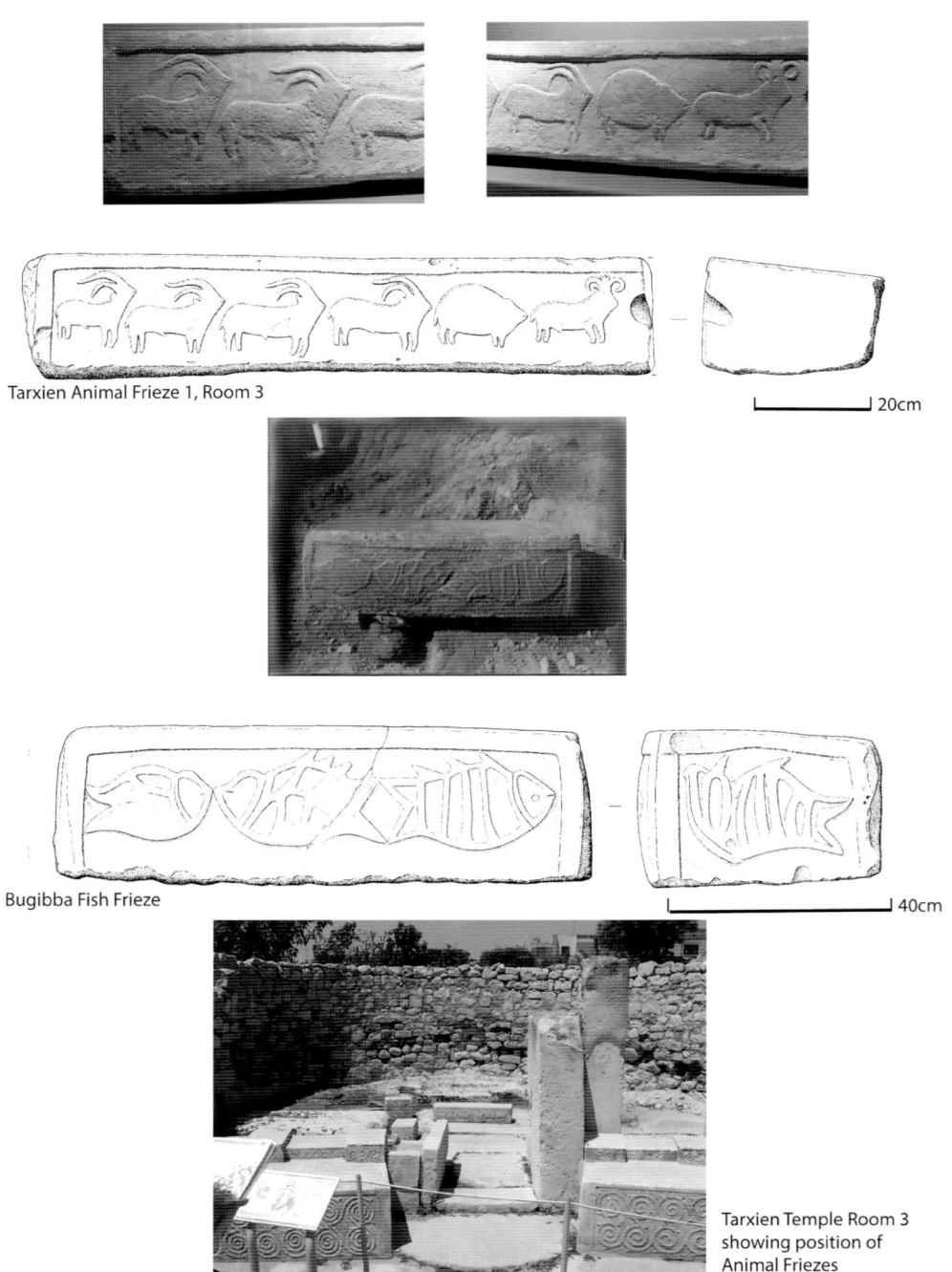

Fig. 2.6: Animal Friezes from Tarxien, Room 3 and Fish Frieze from Buġibba Temple (drawing J. Gibbins, photo C. Malone).

Zammit's detailed notes it is possible to identify the distribution of the animal remains (Malone 2018; Attard-Mallia 2018). Areas of particular density seem to be inner rooms, entrance areas, stairs and altars (Anderson and Stoddart 2007), areas that were well sealed beneath deposit before Bronze Age activities took place. In one instance, the bones are found behind and within a cupboard below an altar (Fig. 2.3) that contained flint blades and an assemblage of bones and horns. Evidently, prestigious animal body parts were displayed to viewers (skulls, frontals with horns), although arguably, also the least nutritious elements of the body. The ostentatious bone display and distribution suggests performative activities more akin to carnival and feast than to exclusive ritual.

The focus on prestigious animals is also evidenced by stones drilled for tie holes, prominently located in the forecourt areas at the main entrances to the buildings or in front of altars within them. The animals were therefore placed, butchered and cooked in very visible places, enabling communal participation in the drama. Since animals in prehistory were likely used as proxies for spirits or characters in ritual, and possibly emblematically as community identifiers, the Maltese data is compelling. Art objects from several megalithic sites (Fig. 2.6) appear to focus on different species, for example, at Ġgantija snake symbols predominate, at Santa Verna snails, at Buġibba fish and at Tarxien bulls and sheep (see Malone 2008 for discussion of animal categories).

LIVESTOCK

In Malta, agricultural stock was limited in number by the harsh summer environment, when water supplies were low. The bone age/sex distribution suggests that a typical assemblage would consist of a cow, a pig and a dozen sheep/goats, mostly killed either very young or in old age. The animals were slaughtered and eaten immediately, probably in the form of stew, given the preservation of the bones (see Malone *et al.* 2019b). However, certain animal parts were evidently retained for decorative and, doubtless, prestigious and symbolic display, particularly skulls and horns. Various anthropological studies have emphasised the value placed on animals in livestock-based societies. For example, in Tana Toraja in Sulawesi, Indonesia, households celebrate and record their feasting events by displaying buffalo skulls on the façade of the house as a record of successful feasts. In shamanic cultures in the Himalayas, temples are adorned with skulls and particularly with crania on posts to symbolise spirits. Similar practices may have been used in Maltese culture, and features such as 'libation' holes at thresholds may actually have held posts to display such objects. Tethering places were set in front of the temples for the public slaughter and likely ceremony of that act, and other smaller tethering holes were set within the buildings, usually associated with 'altars' and display areas. Archaeological evidence from Tarxien temple indicates that piles of bones, horns and skulls were located beside altars, which most likely displayed the outcomes of animal slaughter. This evidence, alongside wall carvings of two bulls represented together with a suckling pig and piglets in a hidden room, a cavalcade sheep, and a goat and pig in a more public space demonstrate the high value of these animals (see Fig. 2.6). From the FRAGSUS study of faunal remains at several sites, the diet was dominated by sheep, in contrast to the imagery of cattle. Our impression is that in prehistoric Malta bulls were the food of prestige, but their rarity and the need for a very large gathering to consume a single beast, meant infrequent but memorable feasts, symbolised later by the retention of horns and skulls.

The traditional misnomer of 'Temple' for Maltese megalithic buildings implies empty and silent religious spaces, but the archaeological data implies a highly sensory communal activity. The positioning of tie holes and animal bones suggest large groups would convene and partake in the butchery and consumption of meat in feasting events. Although these activities could have cult associations, it is clear that temples served more mundane purposes that go beyond ritual (Sagona 2015). They likely served communal, or 'domestic', functions associated with subsistence and daily life that reinforces the link between domestic and ceremonial space, rather than one of formal ritual.

HOUSES OF THE DEAD

The emphasis on communal activities is not solely present in the temples, since the funerary hypogea also offer an insight into the working of Neolithic Maltese society. Zammit and later scholars have named these underground burial sites the 'temples of the dead', suggesting similarities with the above-ground temples of the living (Ugolini 1934). Until the 1987–94 Gozo Project (Malone *et al.* 2009), the only example of an excavated burial hypogeum was Ħal-Saflieni, but its clearance in the early 1900s retained almost no organic material (human bones), whilst the modest chambers of Santa Luċija have not been recorded. The work at the Brochtorff-Xagħra Circle provided an exceptionally detailed record of the skeletal remains which were found intact and *in situ*, associated with artefacts and animal offerings, albeit, in a disarticulated co-mingled state, set within a natural cave system that was extended by additional quarrying. That work has been further assessed by the FRAGSUS Project through digitising the original excavation records and using these to reconstruct 3D models of the 5 m+ deep deposit (Fig. 2.7). Between 600 and 900 individuals were retrieved from various burial compartments, often organised by body part or age/sex, and even though early nineteenth century disturbance had damaged upper levels, the main bioanthropological knowledge of early Malta rests on this site. The compartments/chambers had been modified through the use of imported megaliths and screens, incorporating shelves, a huge bowl, display areas and passageways not dissimilar to the internal arrangement of temples. The burials represented two main episodes, possibly with a clearance phase between them, from the Żebbuġ-Ġgantija at the outset of the Temple Period *c.*3800 cal BC, and a finale in the Tarxien phase *c.*2400 cal BC. The latter saw major refurbishments of the interior space, using imported (and re-used) structural material. Overall, the site was in use for nearly 1,400 years. A third, much smaller burial 'cave' located at Kerċem in Gozo in the late 2000s also contained a few burials of the Tarxien period (Mercieca-Spiteri and Pace pers. comm.).

The development of burial in Neolithic Malta, much like the development of temple building, is characterised by a progressive increase in complexity from simple and single unit spaces, to multi-unit ones. There is little evidence of formalised burial in the earlier Neolithic (Stoddart 1999). By the fourth millennium cal BC, rock cut *a forno* tombs, consisting of 1–2 chambers, were in use, similar to those of contemporary Sicily and southern Italy, and were typified by collective burial rites often incorporating body parts of several

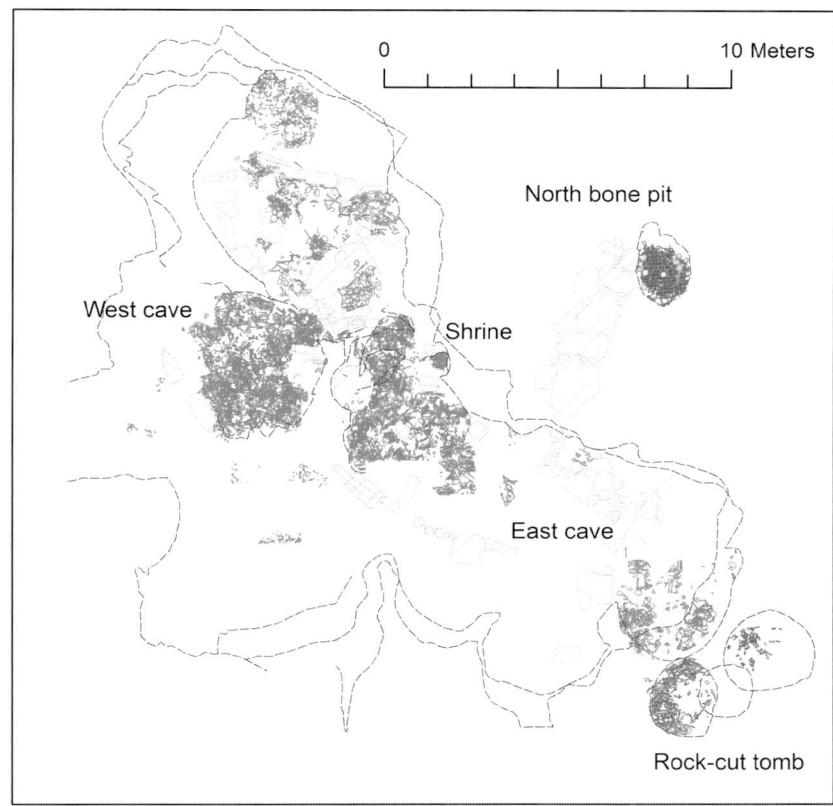
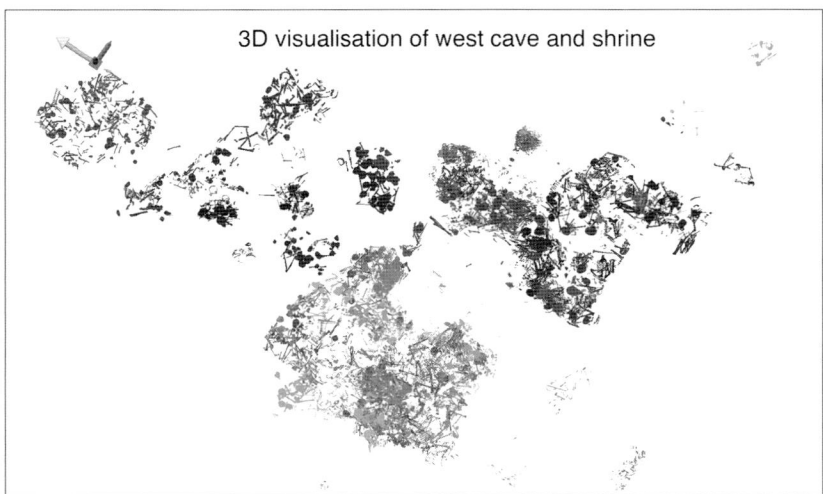

Fig. 2.7: Digitised plan of human bones from the Xagħra Circle (E. Parkinson and J. Thompson). 3D visualisation layout of the West Cave and Shrine area (R. Barratt).

individuals. By the Ġgantija phase in the mid-fourth millennium cal BC, burial practice became more complex, with multi-chambered tombs about 2 m in diameter and connected by a middle vertical shaft and many individual inhumations. The prime example of this form is Xemxija, where some tombs are composed of five interconnected chambers (Evans 1971; Zammit and Mayrhofer 1995). By the Tarxien phase burial sites increased in size and complexity through expansion and re-cutting, culminating in the two known large hypogea, and both sites show spatial expansion over time. Early (Żebbuġ) burials at Ħal-Saflieni were inserted into semi-natural chambers, later incorporated into the enlarging complex. Similarly, at the Brochtorff-Xagħra Circle, one subterranean twin-chambered tomb was found intact whilst other remnant and structurally incorporated 'tombs' were identified within parts of the expanded caves (Malone *et al.* 1995). The intact tomb contained parts of up to 64 individuals buried over a few generations (Malone *et al.* 2019a) with pottery, ochre, beads, shell pendants and carved bone pendants, a large shell, stone menhir marker, stone lamps and ochre palettes. The assemblage is a mixture of sacred and domestic material, and the two-chambered oval shape broadly resembles the house plans described above (Sagona 2015). Despite their smaller size, these rock cut tombs can be considered as 'houses for the dead'. Likewise, the multiple rooms of Ħal-Saflieni and the modified main cave system of the Brochtorff-Xagħra Circle can be identified as proxies for the 'temples of the dead' complexes during the Tarxien phase. The pattern of bone distribution and selection suggests that the journey towards an ancestral world did not terminate with the body's arrival at the hypogea, but progressed through stages of increasing disarticulation and anonymity as the skeleton was moved and rearranged. A similar, more direct, link between funerary and domestic spaces occurred in Sardinia, where the layout of elaborate rock-cut tombs dating to the Late Neolithic and Copper Age, the so-called *Domus de Janas*, mimic the floor plans and gabled roofs of house structures, alongside the inclusion of domestic furniture, such as hearths, benches and pilasters (Melis 2014). Adjacent areas of the central Mediterranean appear to have undergone similar broad changes in the fourth to third millennia cal BC, with the construction of rock-cut tombs and communal burial, although nowhere else reached the complexity and uniqueness of the Maltese examples. In peninsular Italy, the use of rock-cut tombs was commonly related to particular ceramic repertoires that consisted of flasks and drinking vessels, which also point towards a link between consumption, feasting and sacred space (Negroni-Catacchio 2004).

The archaeological evidence at Xagħra indicates superficial structures, altars and thresholds around the cave entrance, set within an encircling stone wall. Something similar may have existed at Ħal-Saflieni, although now lost and unrecorded. The notion of enclosed ceremonial space is suggested for these collective burial sites, whilst in contrast, the temple arenas, do not appear to have been physically enclosed. The main action of the burial sites was, however, below ground level and involved descent down steps to dark subterranean spaces set apart for ritual activities and display. The recorded evidence of stacks of skulls by the steps, screened and decorated space entered through restrictive porthole doors, enormous stone bowls, carvings, special artefacts and animal offerings evokes the Temple spaces above ground. Performance and theatrical display was similarly mirrored in both types of place, with controlled viewpoints through passages and doorways. Visibility analysis based on a 3D approximation of the Xagħra site shows

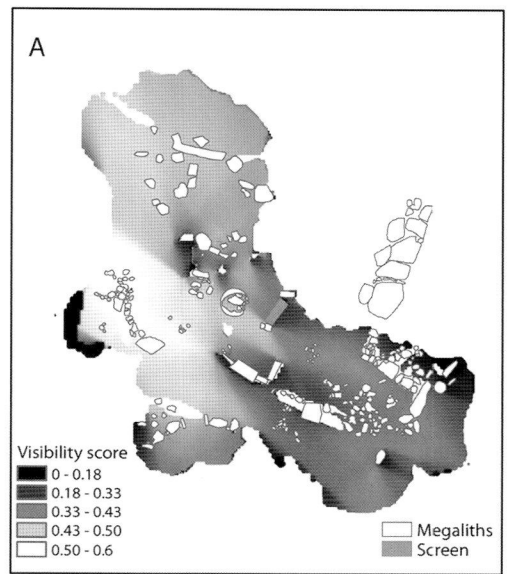 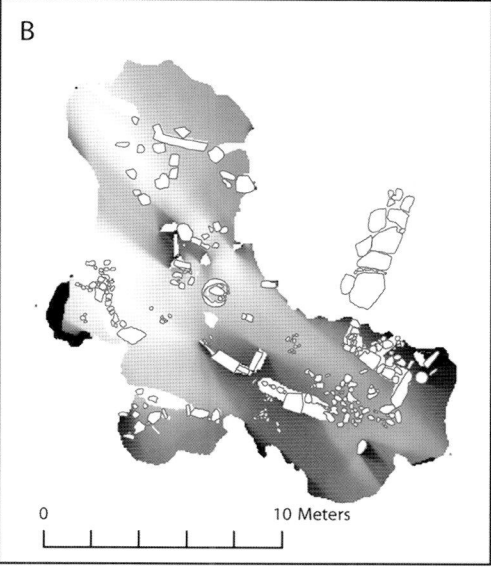

Fig. 2.8: Map of visibility scores within the Brochtorff-Xagħra hypogeum indicating the effect of (A) inserting and (B) removing a screen (R. Barratt).

how certain areas would have been highly visible and focused on a central deposition zone, referred to as the 'display zone' or 'Shrine' in the original publication (Fig. 2.8). This area featured some burials placed in plain view, perhaps to display the recently deceased. Another high visibility portion was a central corridor connecting the porthole entry via the 'Shrine Area' to a niche. This corridor of visibility is reminiscent of the central passage in the temples, with a far niche and apses either side (Malone 2008). The screens also impacted on the overall visibility and were clearly moved as the site evolved. Many megaliths belong to later stages of modification, set up above layers of earlier burial deposit, and changed both the view and circulation in the site. One particular later screen blocked visibility to the East Cave portion of the site. This blocking may be due to changing beliefs, making certain areas becoming more secret and sacred, much like selected apses in temples that become progressively more restricted. Alternatively, the screen may have a more functional explanation, as there are signs of roof collapse and deterioration in the East Cave with stones props inserted. The blocking thus covered up a dangerous collapsing zone. What is clear is that these funerary sites were designed, albeit in an organic manner, to provide a ceremonial setting and space that controlled movement, deposition and view.

Feasting associated with the funerary activities mainly took place, it seems, in the area above ground, although selected animal body parts were placed with burials (mainly heads and feet). Regular interaction with the remains of the dead seems to have been sustained over much of the use life of the Xagħra site, perhaps linked to funeral events and veneration of ancestors (Gregory 2013; Stoddart 2015). In particular, paths between piles of

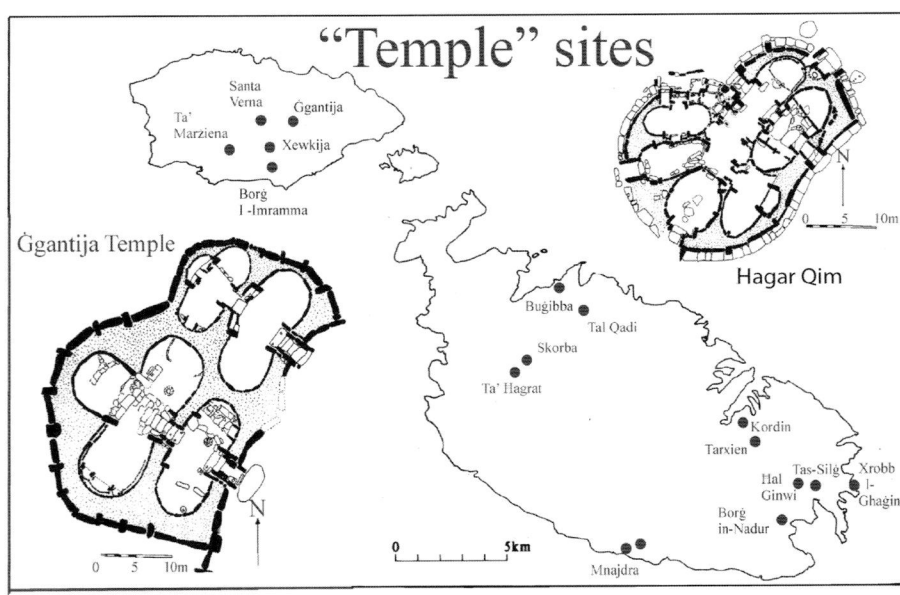

Fig. 2.9: 1. Ħaġar Qim Temple façade. 2. Hidden store and porthole in Mnaijdra Temple. 3. 'Holy of Holies' in Ħal Saflieni. 4. Temple plans for Ġgantija and Ħaġar Qim Temples and distribution map of the main known temple type structures (photos C. Malone).

bones mark the movement of people towards particular areas, perhaps to view statues or undertake rituals associated with the large stone bowl or altars. Limited and predetermined movement also allowed a metaphorical separation between the living and the dead and, the presence of thresholds, trilithons (in Ħal-Saflieni) and portholes, created a barrier or portal between these two worlds (Gregory 2013). To enter the house of the dead, visitors would cross thresholds and explore the predefined spaces of an ancestral home. Secret areas hidden behind screens recall rooms hidden behind closed doors. The separation between the visible and the invisible might also have imposed a sense of security, with the ever-dangerous dead confined to the underground world, away from the living above ground, and safely under control within the bounded space below and above.

Today, the cave roof has collapsed and been quarried away, forming an open-air setting that contrasts absolutely from its Neolithic appearance. Then, the darkness of the subterranean site would have added to the feeling of otherworldliness: the 3D approximation shows a dark and gloomy cave system. That cold echoing darkness would have accentuated the difference between the world of the living above and that of the dead below (Skeates 2017; Till 2017). For our study, light is particularly significant, both local and celestial, and there is evidence that the temples are aligned to certain cosmological alignments, such as solstices and equinoxes (Lomsdalen 2010). Although the outer stone circle has been destroyed, drawings of the site and 3D simulations suggest the entrance had an eastern alignment, which roughly coincides with the summer solstice or equinoxes (Barratt *et al.* 2018). The sun rose between the two large entrance pillars within the stone wall for most of the year, projecting shadows towards the centre of the circle and illuminating the entrance of the cave system. Standing at the cave entrance and looking down into the 'house of the dead', a visitor would also be looking to the setting sun in the west. That symbolism for both the cycle of life and the rising and setting of the sun is therefore fitting for the location in which living and dead meet (Fig. 2.9).

ĦAL-SAFLIENI

There are many similarities between Ħal-Saflieni and the Brochtorff-Xagħra Circle, both in architecture and in use. However, Ħal-Saflieni is deeper and more complex, carved by hand out of the soft Globigerina limestone. It is divided into three levels extending across intercommunicating spaces. The lowest level was dark and sunless, the middle area had scarce filtered light, while the upper layer would have been mainly in the open air, forming a quarried and architecturally built entrance zone off which small chambers opened. Today, it has suffered much damage due to natural deterioration and the construction of modern house foundations immediately above it. While most of the material evidence (especially bone) is lost from the complex, the original megalithic and carved elements are still intact, as well as the painted decorations (Evans 1971; Zammit and Mayrhofer 1995; Pace 2004). The numerous round-oval chambers are typically of 3–5 m in diameter, and roughly comparable to the above ground domestic spaces, and the larger *a forno* tombs. Two central rooms have stone carved corbelling to the roof and wall detail that bear striking similarities to the roof and detail of temple apses. Throughout the site the rooms are furnished with shelves, beams, trilithon and thresholds, comparable to Xagħra. Performance must have played a large part in the hypogea experience, exploiting the secluded and display areas, the oracle holes and interconnecting windows/doors between the spaces. Some areas (the central hall and the 'Holy of Holies') were difficult to access but remained highly visible through carefully cut openings, and presenting stage-sets for ritual events. A burial procession would have passed these areas advancing towards the deeper portions of the site and, as at Xagħra, similar installations (large stone bowl, altars, objects) were placed in strategically visible locations, probably in a formalised arrangement that conformed to notions of laterality and place, as mirrored in the temples (Malone 2007).

THE CLUBHOUSE

As the discussion above attempts to show, there is considerable connection between the architecture of Neolithic Maltese in domestic, communal ritual and burial sites. The rather limited evidence of the domestic spaces implies communal living arrangements, with individual huts associated with dispersed settlements. Alongside these modest places, and often emerging within them, the megalithic temple buildings still defy easy definition, but are undoubtedly part of the mundane domestic world, associated with communal activities, feasting and theatrical 'ritual'. Today in Malta, each parish has a Band Club, mainly comprised of the men who organise a succession of church festivities, processions, feast days and fireworks across the Christian calendar. Parallels could be drawn between the 'temples' and modern-day Band Clubs – community buildings that rivalled the neighbours, outcompeting in size, complexity, food, feast and festival. Perhaps such associations had restricted membership, and their navigation probably required special or secret knowledge, with only certain 'actors' controlling or accessing particular spaces or actions. In parallel to this notion of a community focus and competition, the subterranean burial sites may mirror the terrestrial houses and temples. They too incorporate aspects of domestic-ritual structures, using similar elements of the accepted canon of architectural form, but selected specifically for the ceremonial disposal of the dead. When the variations between our three categories of structure – the domestic hut, the megalithic temple and the subterranean hypogeum are compared, the temple becomes less of a *temple* and more a clubhouse of the living, while the hypogea can be seen as clubhouses of the dead. During life the individuals feasted and participated in group events, but once dead, they return to the ancestral pool where ongoing feasts maintained a close link with the cyclical festivities of the living.

ACKNOWLEDGEMENTS

This research is part of the FRAGSUS project, which is funded by the European Research Council (ERC Advanced) Grant 323727 FP7 (Ideas). This paper draws upon many stimulating discussions and collaborations with our FRAGSUS project colleagues. The fieldwork described here has been undertaken with the permission of the Superintendence of Cultural Heritage (Malta) and Heritage Malta. We are grateful to Sharon Sultana and Heritage Malta for permission to record museum objects at the National Museum of Archaeology, Valletta, illustrated here by C. Malone and Jason Gibbins.

REFERENCES

Anderson, M. and Stoddart, S. (2007) Mapping cult context: GIS applications in Maltese temples. In D. Barrowclough and C. Malone (eds) *Cult in Context*, 41–4. Oxford, Oxbow Books.

Ariano, B., McLaughlin, R., Power, R., Stock, J., Mercieca-Spiteri, B., Stoddart, S. Malone, C. and Bradley, D. (forthcoming) Chapter 10: aDNA and origins. In C. Malone, R. McLaughlin, R. Power and S. Stoddart (eds) *Revisiting the Xagħra Hypogeum*. Cambridge, McDonald Institute for Archaeological Research.

Ashby, T., Bradley, R.N., Peet, T.E. and Tagliaferro N. (1913) Excavations in various Megalithic Buildings in Malta and Gozo. *Papers of the British School at Rome* 6, 1, 1–126.

Attard Mallia, J. (2018) Beyond the structure: revisiting the Tarxien temples excavations. In N.C. Vella, A.J. Frendo and H.C.R. Vella (eds) *The Lure of the Antique: essays on Malta and Mediterranean archaeology in honour of Anthony Bonanno*, 161–75. Ancient Near Eastern Studies. Supp. 54. Leuven, Peeters.

Barratt, R.P. (2018) Recreating Neolithic Malta's Domestic Environment: 3D Reconstruction of the Ghajnsielem Road house. *Digital Applications in Archaeology and Cultural Heritage* 10, 1–6.

Barratt, R.P., Malone, C., McLaughlin, R. and Stoddart, S. (2018) Celebrations in prehistoric Malta. *World Archaeology* 50 (2), 1–14.

Bonanno, A. (2000) Early colonization of the Maltese islands: the status quaestionis. In V.M. Guerrero and S. Gomés (eds) *Colonización humana en ambientes insulares: Interacción con el medio y adaptación cultural*, 323–37. Palma, Universitat de les Illes Balears, Servicio de Publicaciones.

Bonanno, A. (2017) *The Archaeology of Malta and Gozo 5000 Cal BC–AD 1091*. Malta, Heritage Malta Publishing.

Bonanno, A., Gouder, T., Malone, C. and Stoddart, S. (1990) Monuments in an Island Society: The Maltese Context. *World Archaeology* 22 (2), 190–205.

Boyle, S. (2013) The Social and Physical Environment of Early Gozo: a study of settlement and change. Unpublished PhD Thesis, Queen's University, Belfast.

Cazzella, A. and Recchia, G. (2012) Tas-Silġ: The Late Neolithic megalithic sanctuary and its re-use during the Bronze Age and early Iron Age. *Scienze dell'Antichità* 18, 15–38.

Clark, D. (1998) Insular Monument Building: a cause of social stress? The case for prehistoric Malta. Unpublished PhD, University of Bristol.

Evans, J.D. (1953) The Prehistoric Culture-Sequence in the Maltese Archipelago. *Proceedings of the Prehistoric Society* 19, 41–94.

Evans, J.D. (1959) *Malta*. London, Thames and Hudson.

Evans, J.D. (1971) *The Prehistoric Antiquities of the Maltese Islands*. London, The Athlone Press.

French, C.A.I., Taylor, S., McLaughlin, T.R., Cresswell, A., Kinnaird, T., Sanderson, D., Stoddart, S. and Malone, C.A.T. (2018) A Neolithic palaeo-catena for the Xagħra Upper Coralline plateau landscape of Gozo, Malta. *Catena* 171, 337–58.

Gimbutas, M. (2001) *The Living Goddess*. Berkeley and Los Angeles, University of California Press.

Gregory, I.V. (2013) Tradition, time and narrative: Rethinking the Late Neolithic of the Maltese Islands. *Malta Archaeological Review* 11, 16–24.

Grima, R. (2002) Monuments and landscapes in Late Neolithic Malta. *Archaeology International* 6, 25–8.

Grima, R. (2008) Landscape, territories, and the life-histories of monuments in Temple Period Malta. *Journal of Mediterranean Archaeology* 21 (1), 35–56.

Lewis, H. (1977) *Ancient Malta: a study of its antiquities*. Gerards Cross, Colin Smythe Ltd.

Lomsdalen, T. (2010) Astronomy and intentionality in the Temples of Mnajdra. *Archaeoastronomy*, 1–14.

Malone, C. (2007) Ritual, space and structure – the context of cult in Malta and Gozo. In D. Barrowclough and C. Malone (eds) *Cult in Context*, 23–34. Oxford, Oxbow Books.

Malone, C. (1996) Cult and burial in the Neolithic and Early Bronze Age central Mediterranean: a study of the potential. In J.B. Wilkins (ed.) *Approaches to the Study of Ritual. Italy and the Ancient Mediterranean*, 31–54. Accordia Specialist Studies on the Mediterranean 2. London, Accordia Research Centre.

Malone, C. (2008) Metaphor and Maltese art: explorations in the Temple Period. *Journal of Mediterranean Archaeology* 21 (1), 81–109.

Malone, C. (2018) Manipulating the bones: eating and augury in the Maltese temples. In A.C. Renfrew, I. Morley and M. Boyd (eds) *Play, Ritual and Belief in Animals and Early Human Societies.* Papers of the Symposium held in Cambridge 2012, 187–208. Cambridge, Cambridge University Press.

Malone, C., Stoddart, S. and Trump, D. (1988) A house for the temple builders: recent investigations on Gozo, Malta. *Antiquity* 62, 297–301.

Malone, C., Stoddart, S., Bonanno, A., Gouder, T., Trump, D., Barber, G., Brown, C., Dixon, J., Duhig, C., Leighton, R. and Schembri, P. (1995) Mortuary Ritual of 4th Millennium BC Malta: the Żebbuġ Period Chambered Tomb from the Brochtorff Circle at Xagħra (Gozo). *Proceedings of the Prehistoric Society* 61, 303–45.

Malone, C., Stoddart, S., Bonanno, A. and Trump, D. (2009) *Mortuary Customs in Prehistoric Malta: excavations at the Brochtorff Circle at Xagħra (1987–94)*. Cambridge, McDonald Institute for Archaeological Research.

Malone, C., Cutajar, N., McLaughlin, R., Mercieca, B., Pace, A., Power, R., Stoddart, S., Sultana, S., Bronk-Ramsey, C., Dunbar, E., Bayliss, A., Healy, F. and Whittle, A. (2019a) Island questions: the chronology of the Brochtorff Circle at Xagħra, Gozo, and its significance for the Neolithic sequence on Malta. *Archaeological and Anthropological Sciences* 11 (8), 4251–306

Malone. C, McCormick, F., McLaughlin, T.R. and Stoddart, S. (2019b) Megaliths, people and palaeoeconomics in Neolithic Malta. In J. Müller, M. Hinz and M. Wunderlich (eds) *Megaliths, Societies, Landscapes: early monumentality and social differentiation in Neolithic Europe*, 753–769. Frühe Monumentalität und soziale Differenzierung 18. Bonn, Institut für Ur- und Frühgeschichte der CAU Kiel.

McLaughlin, R., French, C., Parkinson, E., Stoddart, S. and Malone, C. (forthcoming) Chapter 4: Santa Verna. In C. Malone, R. McLaughlin and S. Stoddart (eds) *Excavations in Maltese Prehistory*. Cambridge, McDonald Institute for Archaeological Research.

Melis, M.G. (2014) Sardinian prehistoric burials in a Mediterranean perspective: Symbolic and socio-economic aspects. In B. Schulz Paulsson and B. Gaydarska (eds) *Neolithic and Copper Age Monuments: emergence, function and the social construction of the landscape*, 7–21. Oxford, Archaeopress.

Negroni-Catacchio, N. (2004) La Cultura di Rinaldone, In N. Negroni-Catacchio (ed.) *Atti del Settimo Incontro di Studi: Pastori e guerrieri nell'Etruria del IV e III millennio a.C. La civiltà di Rinaldone a 100 anni dalle prime scoperte Vol. 1 (Viterbo – 21 Novembre 2003 Valentano (Vt) – Pitigliano (Gr), 17–18 Settembre 2004)*, 32–45. Milano, Centro Studio di Preistoria e Protostoria.

Pace, A. (2004) *The Ħal Saflieni Hypogeum, Paola. Insight Heritage Guides*. Santa Venera, Midsea Books.

Renfrew, C. (1970) New configurations in old world archaeology. *World Archaeology* 2 (2), 199–211.

Renfrew. A.C. (1973) *Before Civilisation*. Harmondsworth, Penguin Books.

Robb, J. (2001) Island identities: ritual, travel and the creation of difference in Neolithic Malta. *European Journal of Archaeology* 4 (2), 175–202.

Sagona, C. (2015) *The Archaeology of Malta: from the Neolithic through the Roman Period*. Cambridge, Cambridge University Press.

Skeates, R. (2008) Making sense of the Maltese Temple Period: an archaeology of sensory experience and perception. *Time and Mind* 1 (2), 207–38.

Skeates, R. (2017) Soundscapes of Temple Period Malta. *Time and Mind* 10 (1), 61–7.

Stoddart, S. (1999) Mortuary customs in prehistoric Malta. In A. Mifsud and C.S. Ventura (eds) *Facets of Maltese Prehistory*, 183–90. Malta, Prehistoric Society of Malta.

Stoddart, S. (2013) FRAGSUS: Fragility and sustainability in prehistoric Malta. *The European Archaeologist* 41, 20–4.

Stoddart, S. (2015) Mediating the dominion of death in prehistoric Malta. In C. Renfrew, M.J. Boyd and I. Morley (eds) *Death Rituals, Social Order and the Archaeology of Immortality in the Ancient World: 'Death Shall Have No Dominion'*, 130–7. Cambridge, Cambridge Archaeology Press.

Stoddart, S., Bonanno, A., Gouder, T., Malone, C. and Trump, D. (1993) Cult in an island society: prehistoric Malta in the Tarxien Period. *Cambridge Archaeological Journal* 3 (1), 3–19.

Till, R. (2017) An archaeoacoustic study of the Hal-Saflieni Hypogeum on Malta. *Antiquity* 91 (355), 74–89.

Trump, D. (1966) *Skorba: excavations carried out on behalf of the National Museum of Malta 1961–1963*. Oxford, Oxford University Press.

Trump, D. (2013) The prehistory. In G. Vella (ed.) *Ġgantija: The Oldest Free-Standing Building in the World*, 174–97. Malta, Heritage Malta.

Ugolini, L. (1934) *Malta. Origini della Civilta' Mediterranea*. Malta, Midsea Books.

Whitehouse, R.D. (1972) Rock cut tombs of the central Mediterranean. *Antiquity* 46 (184), 275–81.

Zammit, T., Peet, T.E. and Bradley, R.N. (1912) *The Small Objects and the Human Skulls Found in Hal-Saflieni Prehistoric Hypogeum at Casal Paula, Malta*. Malta, Government Printing Press.

Zammit, T. (1930) *Prehistoric Malta: the Tarxien temples*. London, Oxford University Press.

Zammit, T. and Mayrhofer, K. (1995) *The Prehistoric Temples of Malta and Gozo: a description by Sir Themistocles Zammit; design, photos, drawings, introduction, and additions by Karl Mayrhofer*. Malta, S. Masterson.

Chapter 3

Houses of the living, houses of the dead: A view from the Polish lowlands

Joanna Pyzel

Earthen long barrows occur in many regions of Europe in the fourth millennium (Midgley 2005; Müller *et al.* 2014), and it has long been discussed whether they belong to a much broader megalithic phenomenon or not. This controversy extends to the terms applied to their description: while some scholars, following taxonomic purity (recently Schulz Paulsson 2017), use the name 'non-megalithic long barrows' (Müller *et al.* 2014; Król 2017), others on the contrary interpret these unchambered tombs as an expression of 'megalithism' (Rzepecki 2011) or 'the megalithic idea' (Libera and Tunia 2006). The classification of long barrows can be a manifestation of either implicit or explicit estimation of their origin as well: whether they represent a common idea or even a single birthplace or not. The general acknowledged formal similarity with Danubian longhouses has been a focus of cultural inspiration, especially the Linear Pottery Culture (LBK), which found expression even in the call for papers for the conference that generated this volume (see Preface this volume). However, most of the vast long barrow area lies beyond the range of the LBK world and there are very few regions where the distribution of both phenomena really overlap (*e.g.* Hodder 1984). Special attention has always been paid to northern France where the presence of 'true' megaliths is unquestionable (see Chambon this volume); the eastern flank, represented by the Funnel Beaker Culture (further TRB), has been more neglected in interregional debates (notable exceptions: Bogucki 1988, 189; Midgley 2005; Rzepecki 2011) and despite the fact that V.G. Childe had noticed the similarity between long barrows and Late Danubian Lowland longhouses from Brześć Kujawski (Childe 1949). These quite spectacular buildings lasted longer than in other post-LBK regions, which was pointed out by, among others, A. Sherratt, who interpreted long barrows as a local, Mesolithic adaptation and transformation of the Danubian idea of monumentality (Sherratt 1990). In the light of new data on the Danubian and TRB communities in the Polish Lowlands, and from the perspective of post-LBK communities, this paper again addresses this issue.

LONG BARROWS AND THE POLISH LOWLANDS

Neolithic long barrows in the Polish lowlands belong to the Eastern Group of the TRB. So-called Kuyavian tombs are the most prominent example of these monumental structures (Chmielewski 1952): trapezoidal stone kerbs over 100 m long, east–west oriented, with an

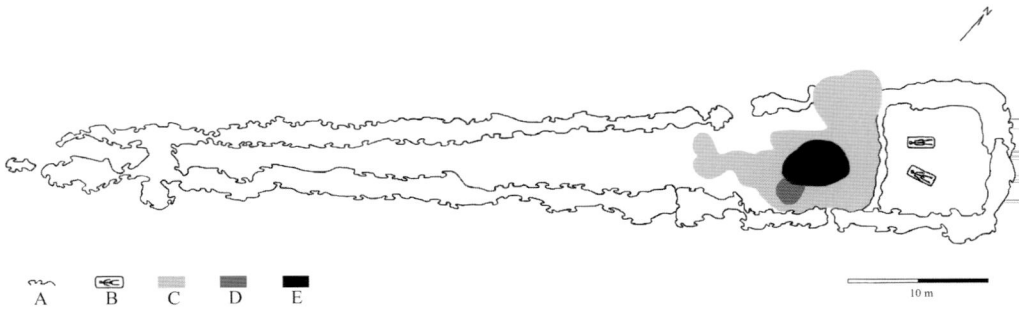

Fig. 3.1: An example of a TRB long barrow from the Polish lowlands. Sarnowo, site 1, Comm. Lubraniec, tomb 8. A – limits of trenches; B – burials within the 'annexe'; C – cultural layer; D – pit no. 1; E – pit of the central grave. After Wiklak 1980 and Rzepecki 2014.

earthen barrow over individual inhumation burials (Fig. 3.1). These monuments are, however, only the tip of the iceberg. Societies of the Eastern Group of the TRB built much smaller stone structures as well as wooden constructions, sometimes called *megaxylons* or recently Niedźwiedź type tombs (Rzepecki 2011). They are widely distributed within the loess area (of the South-Eastern TRB group and Baalberge), where stone building material is not easily available, but they also occur in the Lowlands, parallel to stone constructions.

In fact, the distribution of long barrows must have been much broader than the famous southern Kuyavian core concentration (Chmielewski 1952) as old maps and toponymy refer to already levelled monuments (Pospieszny 2010). These sources both demonstrate the enormous extent of destruction due to modern agriculture, although lidar scanning of forest areas is now detecting many previously unknown tombs (*e.g.* Matuszewska 2017). These evidences give a vague impression of how much is left from the contemporary TRB landscape.

The biographic approach, so popular in archaeology of recent decades, drew attention to complex 'life histories of megaliths' (Holtorf 1998), not only in the Northern Group of the TRB, where long barrows had often been transformed into megalithic chambered tombs (Müller *et al.* 2014), but also in the Eastern Group, where some stages of monument construction and use by TRB societies can be distinguished (Rzepecki 2004; 2011).

The origin of long barrows in the Eastern Group of the TRB is very controversial, with highly disputable dating, while for the Northern Group nobody places it before 3800 cal BC (Müller *et al.* 2014); and for the Eastern Group some scholars suggest its beginning around 4100–4000 cal BC or even earlier, about 4400 cal BC, contemporary with the equally debatable onset of the whole TRB phenomenon (Król 2017, further references therein). An hypothesis claiming the independent local development of long barrows exists, along with concepts stressing the western influence, transmitted from the megalithic tradition of France through the Michelsberg culture (Rzepecki 2004; 2011). Nowadays we are much more aware of the general possibility of such far-reaching interregional contacts in prehistory and a totally independent origin of the long barrow phenomenon in a similar time in different parts of Europe seems thus improbable but the weakness of this hypothesis is almost completely lacking in similar monuments (few examples so eagerly emphasised can be regarded as exceptions confirming the rule) in the Michelsberg culture. Without new investigations it is probably not possible to settle this dispute and it is definitely not the aim of this paper, which addresses the issue of the development of Lowland Danubian longhouses from the perspective of recent research.

DANUBIAN LONGHOUSES IN THE POLISH LOWLANDS

Large-scale rescue excavations conducted recently in numerous European countries as a result of the Venetta treaty demonstrate that longhouses of the LBK are a much broader phenomenon than previously assumed. They are not limited to the most fertile, core settlement upland areas, but can be found in every region occupied by the first farmers, even far beyond the loess belt. It is also the case for the Polish Lowlands, where the LBK inhabited many enclaves of fertile, heavy soils developed on clay ground moraine. Kuyavia, one of the best studied regions, is a good example of this with a recent survey identifying almost 400 sites (Pyzel 2006; 2010). Similar to other regions they cluster in small groups, however, not just arranged along water courses, but also lakes and postglacial valleys. Large-scale excavations of LBK sites took place in eastern Kujavia on the route of the A1 motorway, which runs alongside the Vistula river, on the edge of the Kuyavian Plateau, close to the Płock and Toruń Basins. Within the 78 km long strip 34 sites of the LBK were excavated in the early 2000s (Pyzel 2017). Boundaries of separate LBK settlements are very often difficult to estimate as their extensions do not necessarily overlap with multicultural archaeological sites: zones of more or less dense occupational concentrations could be detected instead. Postholes indicating longhouses were usually quite badly preserved. Despite this, various construction forms of different length could be distinguished, even though the division into longhouse types is not as straightforward as in the western part of the LBK (*e.g.* Moddermann 1986). However, traces of houses could often be determined by means of characteristic associating features placed on long sides of a house. Longhouses were oriented along the north–south axis, on some sites east–west rows of such constructions could be detected (site Wieniec 10: Maciszewski 2015). However, this was not a general rule as on other sites more clustered layouts occurred (site Smólsk 2/10: Muzolf *et al.* 2012). At Ludwinowo 7, which is the largest unearthed LBK settlement with at least 31 houses, both layouts existed in distinct parts of the site (Pyzel 2013; 2019). This site was settled during the whole Kuyavian LBK, with a minimum of six occupational phases with longhouses distinguished. On the basis of chronological analysis conducted for Ludwinowo (Pyzel 2006; 2010; 2013; 2019) we can assume that most single LBK houses in Kuyavia were not inhabited for very long. However, traces of houses overlapping occurred neither at Ludwinowo nor at any other long-lasting LBK site in this region. Furthermore, no other stratigraphic relations to LBK houses could be dated to the period of the Kuyavian first farmers. It means that the places of old houses were known and respected for much longer than the time of their occupation itself. We can even suppose that this knowledge was transmitted even beyond the LBK time.

The following post-LBK societies are separated from the LBK by a distinct typological and chronological hiatus, which indicates very deep cultural changes that took place on the Lowlands after the demise of the LBK (Czerniak *et al.* 2016; Czerniak and Pyzel 2016;

2019). We do not know if these transformations go hand in hand with a demographic hiatus on a regional scale as well, but settlement hiatuses could be observed on every single LBK site. The Polish Lowland societies of the first half of the fifth millennium belonged to the Late Stroke Band Pottery Culture (further SBK), known also as the Late Band Pottery Culture (Czerniak 2012). These societies did not continue the longhouse tradition of occupation of the LBK, which was followed by contemporary groups (*e.g.* SBK, Rössen) in other post-LBK regions. Excavations on the A1 motorway route provide again an excellent overview of the settlement system of this time. Traces of occupation were found on 15 sites, these are only shorter- or longer-lived clusters of pits left by much more mobile, smaller and scattered groups. The integration took place on special sites such as circular enclosures (roundels) known also from the Polish Lowlands (Czerniak and Pyzel 2019, further references therein).

Only one SBK site on the A1 motorway route was not previously inhabited by the LBK. It seems that a spatial vicinity to abandoned villages could have been somehow important by the settlement location, although traces of overlapping are much more rare. Some of them can be dated to the end of the SBK occupation. This is the time of increasing importance of references to the past, which reached its peak in the following Brześć Kujawski culture and which developed in its full form around 4400 cal BC (Czerniak *et al.* 2016). It is a time when in other regions of the vast post-LBK world longhouses become less important, tell settlement come to an end and a more mobile way of life gained significance. In the Polish Lowlands an opposite development took place: after a half millennium a system consisting of large, stable, long-lasting settlements appears again (Czerniak and Pyzel 2016; 2019). It resembles the LBK and this can be a reference to the past itself. Longhouses are a crucial, iconic element of this culture endowing sense and identity to its members. They constitute a final stage of the development of Danubian longhouses (the development which did not take place in the Polish Lowlands): they are trapezoidal in plan, with a foundation trench carrying not only walls, but also a roof construction (Fig. 3.2). This layout is almost identical with wooden unchambered long barrows of the TRB (best exemplified through the changing interpretation of the feature from Niedźwiedź – originally interpreted as a late Danubian house, now as a TRB tomb type (Rzepecki 2011, further references therein)). However, the orientation is different: while most of the TRB monuments follow the east–west axis, BKC houses are oriented north–south, exactly as older LBK buildings. In terms of their size and arrangement houses in the BKC seem much more standardised than in the LBK (Czerniak and Pyzel 2016) and they were very widespread indeed, which is evidenced not only by recent emergency excavations, but also aerial photos (Rączkowski and Ruciński 2015). This indicates the existence of a strong cultural norm regulating how a house had to look which influences our reception of the BKC as a very uniform entity. However, this norm did not rule the house succession practices, as they are much more varied with two prevailing models. Along the horizontal one, similar to the LBK, a vertical model resembling the tells existed and this discrepancy can be visible not only on different sites but also within them. This came to light not only due to the excavations on the A1 motorway route, where 15 sites of the BKC of different size and layout could be detected, but also when we compare these results with the neighbouring subregions of Brześć Kujawski and Osłonki (Grygiel 2008) with their outstanding central sites (Czerniak and Pyzel 2019). Both house foundation

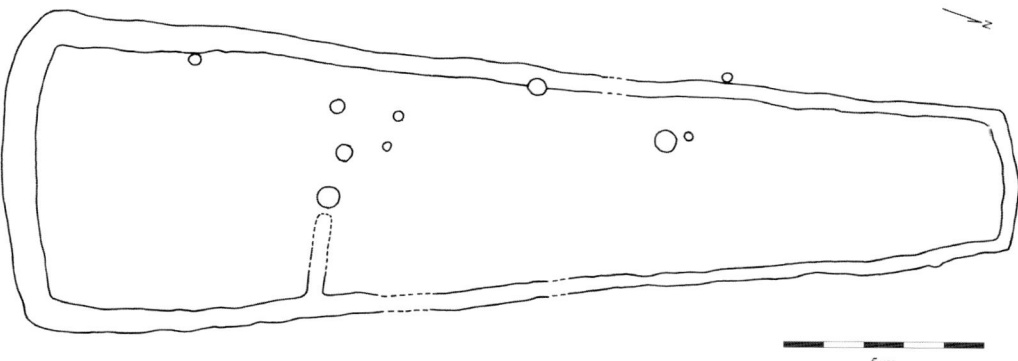

Fig. 3.2: An example of a Late Danubian longhouse from the Polish Lowlands. Brześć Kujawski, site 4, house 56. After Grygiel 2008, 126 fig. 103, modified.

practices make reference to the past. In fact, BKC societies not only referenced their own culture but also that of the considerably older LBK buildings, as exemplified on the different sites of the A1 route. At Bodzia 1 (Czerniak and Pyzel 2019, further references therein), Dubielewo 8 (Siewiaryn and Mikulski 2015) and Ludwinowo 3 (Marchelak 2017; Nowak 2017) places of singular LBK houses were left intact and became incorporated into a larger settlement. Unequivocal vertical relations, resembling the famous site of Bożejewice 22/23 in western Kujawia, where a BKC house plan perfectly overlaps a LBK building (Czerniak 1998; Midgley 2006, 9 fig. 5; Czerniak and Pyzel 2019, 79 fig. 3), could not be found, however it can be suggested for Ludwinowo 3, where a BKC house was erected above a LBK cluster of probably house associating features. Vertical relations are quite common on large BKC sites, sequences of up to five houses can be found there (Czerniak and Pyzel 2016, further references therein).

Old houses were also places of other memory practices such as deposits of various items. It is difficult to detect this in the case of the same uniform culture, but such offerings were also found on some LBK settlements on the A1 route (Nakonowo Stare 1, Bodzia 1, Ludwinowo 7; Pyzel 2019). Houses were foci of mundane and ritual activities for the BKC societies, they unified the world of the living with the world of the dead through the placement of burials in their vicinity, additionally expressed through the similarity in the orientation of long axis of both graves and buildings. No external cemeteries are known for the BKC, the number of burials, although different for various sites, seem to be altogether higher than for the LBK, even if not all members of society are represented (Czerniak and Pyzel 2013). It has usually been postulated that inhabitants were buried close to their houses, however, recent research demonstrates more complicated temporal relations. Due to Bayesian modelling for the BKC site at Racot in southern Greater Poland, the precise chronological order of separate features can be determined. A single grave detected at this site was located in the middle of a house, according to the radiocarbon model some 200 years after its abandonment (Czerniak *et al.* 2016). At Dubielewo 8 on the A1 motorway route more burials were found, dated either to the beginning or the end of the settlement (Siewiaryn and Mikulski 2015). The most astonishing discoveries were made at Ludwinowo

7 and Smólsk 2/10, where BKC burials were placed in pits associating LBK longhouses (Muzolf *et al.* 2012, fig. 4; Czerniak and Pyzel 2013). These findings shed new light on the large variability in the number of burials per house at BKC settlements (Czerniak and Pyzel 2019, 67, table 1): central sites with the highest values can possibly be regarded as burial places of people from outside the settlement, similar to Ludwinowo and Smólsk.

CONCLUSIONS

All these new data indicate that the Danubian idea of a longhouse found its proliferation in the Late post-LBK societies of the BKC on the Polish Lowlands: on the spatial and temporal frontier of the post-LBK world. Trapezoidal longhouses of this culture were both houses of the living and houses of their own and invented ancestors and a crucial mnemonic device that endowed sense and identity through reference to the past. This development marks an important step in the so often suggested transformation of houses of the living into houses of the dead. In the BKC, longhouses were both. TRB societies adopted and transformed them into long barrows, formally so similar to BKC houses and emphasised this change through a different orientation.

The tradition of erecting BKC longhouses lasted until *c.*4100 cal BC (Czerniak *et al.* 2016), up till now we do not have reliable radiocarbon dates for long barrows earlier than 4000 cal BC (Król 2017, further references therein), so they could have hardly been contemporary, but the temporal and ideological gap seems to be relatively small. Taking into account recent results of a DNA analysis of TRB groups in different parts of Europe indicating their Late Danubian origin (Skoglund *et al.* 2012; Chyleński *et al.* 2017), we must see the transformation of houses of the living into houses of the dead not as an abrupt change but as a further step in the gradual development of a long and pan-European Neolithic tradition.

REFERENCES

Bogucki, P. (1988) *Forest Farmers and Stockherders: early Agriculture and its consequences in North-Central Europe*. Cambridge, Cambridge University Press.
Childe, G.V. (1949) The origin of Neolithic culture in northern Europe. *Antiquity* 23, 129–35.
Chmielewski, W. (1952) *Zagadnienie grobowców kujawskich w świetle ostatnich badań*. Łódź, Biblioteka Muzeum Archeologicznego w Lodzi, Nr. 2.
Chyleński, M., Juras, A., Ehler, E., Malmström, H., Piontek, J., Jakobsson, M., Marciniak, A. and Dabert, M. (2017) Late Danubian mitochondrial genomes shed light into the Neolithisation of Central Europe in the 5th millennium BC. *BMC Evolutionary Biology* 17. doi.org/10.1186/s12862-017-0924-0.
Czerniak, L. (1998) The first farmers. Najstarsi rolnicy. In M. Chłodnicki and M. Krzyżaniak (eds) *Pipeline of Archaeological Treasures. Gazociąg pełen skarbów archeologicznych*, 23–36. Poznań, Poznańskie Towarzystwo Prehistoryczne.
Czerniak, L. (2012) After the LBK. Communities of the 5th millennium BC in North-Central Europe. In R. Gleser and V. Becker (eds) *Mitteleuropa im 5. Jahrtausend vor Christus. Beiträge zur Internationalen Konferenz in Münster 2010*, 151–74. Berlin, Lit.

Czerniak, L., Marciniak, A., Bronk Ramsey, C., Dunbar, E., Goslar, T., Barclay, A., Bayliss, A. and Whittle, A. (2016) House time: Neolithic settlement development at Racot during the 5th millennium CAL BC in the Polish lowlands. *Journal of Field Archaeology* 41 (5), 618–40.

Czerniak, L. and Pyzel, J. (2013) Unusual Funerary Practices in the Brześć Kujawski Culture in the Polish Lowland. In N. Müller-Scheeßel (ed.) *'Irreguläre' Bestattungen in der Urgeschichte Norm, Ritual, Strafe …?; Akten der Internationalen Tagung in Frankfurt a. M. vom 3. bis 5. Februar 2012*, 139–50. Bonn, Habelt.

Czerniak, L. and Pyzel, J. (2016) Being at home in the early Chalcolithic. The Longhouse phenomenon in the Brześć Kujawski culture in the Polish Lowlands. *Open Archaeology* 2 (1), 97–114.

Czerniak, L. and Pyzel, J. (2019) The Brześć Kujawski culture. The north-easternmost Early Chalcolithic communities in Europe. In R. Gleser and D. Hofmann (eds) *Contacts, Boundaries and Innovation: exploring developed Neolithic societies in central Europe and beyond*, 59–90. Leiden, Sidestone Press.

Grygiel, R. (2008) *Neolit i początki epoki brązu w rejonie Brześcia Kujawskiego i Osłonek. Tom II. Część I–III. Środkowy neolit. Grupa brzesko-kujawska kultury lendzielskiej*. Łódź, Wydawnictwo Fundacji Badań Archeologicznych Imienia Profesora Konrada Jażdżewskiego.

Hodder, I. (1984) *Burials, Houses, Women and Men in the European Neolithic*. In D. Miller and C. Tilley (eds) *Ideology, Power and Prehistory*, 51–68. Cambridge, Cambridge University Press.

Holtorf, C.J. (1998) The life-histories of megaliths in Mecklenburg-Vorpommern (Germany). *World Archaeology* 30 (1), 23–38.

Król, D. (2017) When, where and how long? A discussion around the questions on the chronology and origin of the TRB non-megalithic tombs in the Polish Lowlands. *Prace i Materiały Muzeum Archeologicznego i Etnograficznego w Łodzi, Seria Archeologiczna* 47, 421–41.

Libera, J. and Tunia, K. (eds) (2006) *Idea megalityczna w obrządku pogrzebowym kultury pucharów lejkowatych*, Lublin – Kraków, Wyd. IAE PAN Oddział w Krakowie, IA UMCS w Lublinie.

Maciszewski, I. (ed.) (2015) *Rozwój osadnictwa kultur wstęgowych na obszarze zlewni dolnej Zgłowiączki w rejonie Wieńca w gminie Brześć Kujawski. Autostrada A1*. Łódź, Warszawa, Archeologiczne Zeszyty Autostradowe Instytutu Archeologii i Etnologii PAN 17.

Marchelak, I. (2017) Osadnictwo grupy brzesko-kujawskiej kultury lendzielskiej. In I. Marchelak, A. Nierychlewska, I. Nowak and P. Papiernik (eds) *Ratownicze badania archeologiczne na stanowisku 3 w Ludwinowie pow. Włocławek, woj. kujawsko-pomorskie (trasa autostrady A-1)*, 35–83. Łódź, Wydawnictwo Fundacji Badań Archeologicznych Imienia Profesora Konrada Jażdżewskiego, Via Archaeologica Lodziensis VII.

Matuszewska, A. (2017) The Funnel Beaker Culture in the Szczecin Lowlands – looking back on the last 30 years. *Prace i Materiały Muzeum Archeologicznego i Etnograficznego w Łodzi, Seria Archeologiczna* 47, 131–47.

Midgley, M.S. (2005) *The monumental cemeteries of prehistoric Europe*. Stroud, Tempus.

Midgley, M.S. (2006) From ancestral village to monumental cemetery: the creation of monumental Neolithic cemeteries. www.jungsteinsite.de.

Modderman, P.J.R. (1986) On the typology of the houseplans and their European setting. In I. Pavlů, J. Rulf, M. Zápotocká (eds) Theses on the Neolithic site of Bylany. *Památky archeologické* 77, 383–94.

Müller, J., Dibbern, H. and F. Hage (2014) Non-megalithic mounds beneath megaliths: a new perspective on monumentality in North Central Europe. In M. Furholt, M. Hinz, D. Mischka, G Noble and D. Olausson (eds) *Landscapes, Histories and Societies in the Northern European Neolithic*. 171–82. Bonn, Habelt. Frühe Monumentalität und Soziale Differenzierung 4.

Muzolf, B., Kittel, P. and P. Muzolf (2012) Sprawozdanie z prac badawczych na wielokulturowym kompleksie osadniczym w miejscowości Smólsk, stanowisko 2/10, gm. Włocławek, woj. kujawsko-pomorskie. *Raport* 2007–2008, 43–64.

Nowak, I. (2017) Osadnictwo kultury ceramiki wstęgowej rytej. In I. Marchelak, A. Nierychlewska, I. Nowak and P. Papiernik (eds) *Ratownicze badania archeologiczne na stanowisku 3 w Ludwinowie pow.*

Włocławek, woj. kujawsko-pomorskie (trasa autostrady A-1), 19–31. Łódź, Wydawnictwo Fundacji Badań Archeologicznych Imienia Profesora Konrada Jażdżewskiego. Via Archaeologica Lodziensis VII.

Pospieszny, Ł. (2010) The Neolithic Landscapes of the Polish Lowlands. In A.M. Larsson and L. Papmehl-Dufay (eds) *Uniting Sea II. Stone Age Societies in the Baltic Sea Region*, 147–70. Uppsala, Uppsala University. Occasional Papers in Archaeology 51.

Pyzel, J. (2006) Die Besiedlungsgeschichte der Bandkeramik in Kujawien. *Jahrbuch des Römisch-Germanischen Zentralmuseums Mainz* 53 (1), 1–57.

Pyzel, J. (2010) *Historia osadnictwa społeczności kultury ceramiki wstęgowej rytej na Kujawach*. Gdańsk, Instytut Archeologii Uniwersytetu Gdańskiego(Gdańskie Studia Archeologiczne, Seria Monografie 1).

Pyzel, J. (2013) Different models of settlement organisation in the Linear Band Pottery Culture – an example from Ludwinowo 7 in eastern Kuyavia. In S. Kadrow and P. Włodarczak (eds) *Environment and Subsistence – forty years after Janusz Kruk's 'Settlement studies…'*, 85–93. Rzeszów, Bonn, Institute of Archaeology Rzeszów University; Dr. Rudolf Habelt GmbH. Studien zur Archäologie in Ostmitteleuropa/Studia nad Pradziejami Europy Środkowej 11.

Pyzel, J. (2017) Field survey versus excavation – compatibility of results illustrated by the example of selected sites from the A1 Motorway in the Włocławek Province, Poland. *Analecta Archaeologica Ressoviensia* 12, 285–97.

Pyzel, J. (ed.) (2019) *Ludwinowo, stanowisko 7. Osada neolityczna na Kujawach. Ludwinowo, site 7. Neolithic settlement in Kuyavia*. Pękowice, Gdańsk, Wydawnictwo Profil-Archeo, Wydawnictwo Uniwersytetu Gdańskiego.

Rączkowski, W. and Ruciński, D. (2015) Searching for hidden houses: optical satellite imagery in archaeological prospection of the Early Neolithic settlements in the Kujawy Region, Poland. In D.G. Hadjimitsis, K. Themistocleous, S. Michaelides and G. Papadavid (eds) Third International Conference on Remote Sensing and Geoinformation of the Environment (RSCy2015). *Proceedings of SPIE* 9535, 1–13 (doi: 10.1117/12.2195618).

Rzepecki, S. (2004) *Społeczności środkowoneolitycznej kultury pucharów lejkowatych na Kujawach*. Poznań, Wydawnictwo Poznańskie.

Rzepecki, S. (2011) *The Roots of Megalitism in the TRB Culture*. Łódź, Instytut Archeologii Uniwersytetu Łódzkiego, Fundacja Uniwersytetu Łódzkiego.

Rzepecki, S. (2014) Palimpsest, time perspectivism and megaliths. *Sprawozdania Archeologiczne* 66, 9–27.

Schulz Paulsson, B. (2017) *Time and Stone: the emergence and development of megaliths and megalithic societies in Europe*. Oxford, Archaeopress.

Sherratt, A. (1990) The genesis of megaliths: monumentality, ethnicity and social complexity in Neolithic north-west Europe. *World Archaeology* 22 (2), 147–67.

Siewiaryn, M. and Mikulski, P. (2015) Osadnictwo z okresu neolitu i wczesnej epoki brązu. In W. Kaczor and M. Żółkiewski (eds) *Dubielewo, gm. Brześć Kujawski, stanowisko 8. Archeologiczne badania ratownicze na trasie autostrady A1 w woj. Kujawsko-pomorskim*, 23–201. Poznań, Wydawnictwo Nauka i Innowacje.

Skoglund, P., Malmström, H., Raghavan, M., Storå, J., Hall, P., Willerslev, E., Gilbert, M.T.P., Götherström, A. and Jakobsson, M. (2012) Origins and Genetic Legacy of Neolithic Farmers and Hunter-Gatherers in Europe. *Scienc*e 336, 466–9 (doi: 10.1126/science.1216304).

Wiklak, H. (1980) Wyniki badań wykopaliskowych w obrębie grobowca 8 w Sarnowie w woj. Włocławskim. *Prace i Materiały Muzeum Archeologicznego i Etnograficznego w Łodzi. Seria Archeologiczna* 27, 33–83.

Chapter 4

'Cicéron c'est Poincaré'. Dealing with geometry: Neolithic house plans and the earliest monuments

Philippe Chambon

FROM CHILDE TO HODDER, OR FROM A STATEMENT TO A WHOLE SYSTEM

Considering what actually remains of most Neolithic features, ground plans are a critical and key source of data. Analogy being essential to archaeologists' methodology, it quickly became apparent that comparison between constructions for the dead and for the living would be unavoidable. Indeed, as soon as domestic features were identified for the Neolithic, parallels were drawn between them and the so-called megalithic monuments. Once described as analogous, the interpretation subsequently shifted towards one in which the origin of the megalithic monuments might be seen in the Early Neolithic longhouses.

Beyond the metaphorical assimilation of monuments to houses for the dead, the comparison of building techniques had been proposed by Sprockhoff as early as 1938. But it was Childe who underscored the similarity of the plans, using the houses of Brześć Kujawski and the burial spaces of Baltic barrows (1949, 135). The increasing discoveries of wooden architectural structures during the 1960s, be they houses or burials, led to an interpretation of mutual influence (Daniel 1965, 86). However, all burial monuments did not have a trapezoidal plan. A better understanding of the variability in form of Linear Pottery culture (LBK) domestic features came in handy to justify diversity of mound construction: rectangular shapes existed for the living as well as for the dead (Ashbee 1970). At this time, the hypothesis that the origin of megalithic forms derived from the domestic architecture of the Linear Pottery culture received greater clarity. Corcoran explicitly expressed the idea, perhaps for the first time, but confessed to having no idea of the mechanism (Powell *et al.* 1969, 77). Several years later, Whittle seemed to show some reluctance to embrace the same hypothesis, pointing out geographical missing links between houses and mounds: 'at any rate the possession of long-houses could in some areas have encouraged the acceptance of the long mound, if the sheer monumentality of long mounds were not sufficient attraction in itself' (Whittle 1977, 221). The 1980s provided the first strict and quantitative comparisons, for instance Marshall with house and monument measurements and proportions (Marshall 1981, 110). But it was Hodder who constructed a hypothesis that garnered real success (Hodder 1984), turning the argument into a whole system. He enumerated eight similarities (Hodder 1984, 59), some very general, like the use of trenches and postholes for construction (point 1), and others rather specific, like the tripartite division (point 6) or the internal decoration (point 7). If these criteria were not really discussed in detail thereafter, the filiation topic came out regularly, like a seasonal feature.

The mere designation of chambered tombs, as well as the number of individuals they accommodated, facilitated the transposition of houses for the living, and houses for the dead. But apart from the semantic point of view, what are the means of examining that issue? In fact, the origin of megalithic monuments, which remain the most impressive structures of the Neolithic, are still a subject of animated debate. This paper aims to explore three main axes. The first one deals with cultural origins of these monuments, their date of emergence and subsequently their roots within Mesolithic or Early Neolithic cultures. The second one is a tale of geometry: a strict comparison between house and monument plans beyond the selection of the most propitious examples to support correlation between the two. Finally, one cannot avoid the question of the meaning, and more precisely the link with ancestry that these monuments were supposed to express.

A MATTER OF DATES

Funerary monumentality is inseparable from the Neolithic of western Europe. Monuments have been known long before the invention of the Neolithic by archaeologists, one might even say since forever. Taking into account their distribution, the hypothesis of an autonomous development, apart from the spread of the Neolithic, has been regularly proposed. It must be said that the character of the Mesolithic in general and Mesolithic burials in particular, remain convenient arguments for scholars, thanks to the scarcity of data. In western Europe, Mesolithic sites dating to just before the Neolithic and in close connection with the first farmers are still quite rare. Knowledge of Mesolithic burial practices remain imprecise, but homogenous would not be an accurate way of describing them. Furthermore, there is no evidence of mounds surrounding burials or any other form of monument. Téviec and Hoëdic contain the only burials that might testify – from a distance – of such a desire (Péquart *et al.* 1937). In fact, monumentality did not appear to be a focus for western European hunters-gatherers. From a more ideological standpoint, could monumentality be regarded as an indigenous response to Neolithic colonisation? The latest populations of hunter-gatherers were not supposed to have disappeared before the earliest monuments were built. However, the first DNA analyses within monument-building populations have shown that a genetic contribution from late hunter-gatherers did exist, but was minor compared with that of earliest farmers (*e.g.* Deguilloux *et al.* 2011; Sánchez-Quinto 2019, 9470).

The Neolithic evidence is more suitable material for discussion. The quantity and the diversity of burial data makes it possible to consider a general pattern for evolution of these installations. Domestic features and burials are known for the first farmers, and in many cases sequences of funerary behaviour may be reconstructed. Thanks to the advances in Neolithic chronology, the absence of a close temporal connection between the houses of the first farmers and the earthen long barrows of Great Britain, or the long mounds of northern Europe is irrefutable. That the farmers of these regions would have recalled the appearance of domestic architecture from neighbouring regions dating to some 1,000 years before is simply nonsensical.

As it is home to some of the oldest megalithic burials, Brittany can be seen as the most suited location for a possible filiation. From Le Rouzic (1933), through L'Helgouach (1965), until Boujot and Cassen (1992) much concerted effort has been put into a chronological framework for the typology of megalithic architecture. However, one major point remains a matter of debate: whether the earthen long barrows, here the 'tertres armoricains', appeared first or not, or the earliest 'tombes à couloir' (passage graves) in parallel to the 'tertres armoricains'. In fact, repeated discoveries of long barrows in the heart of the

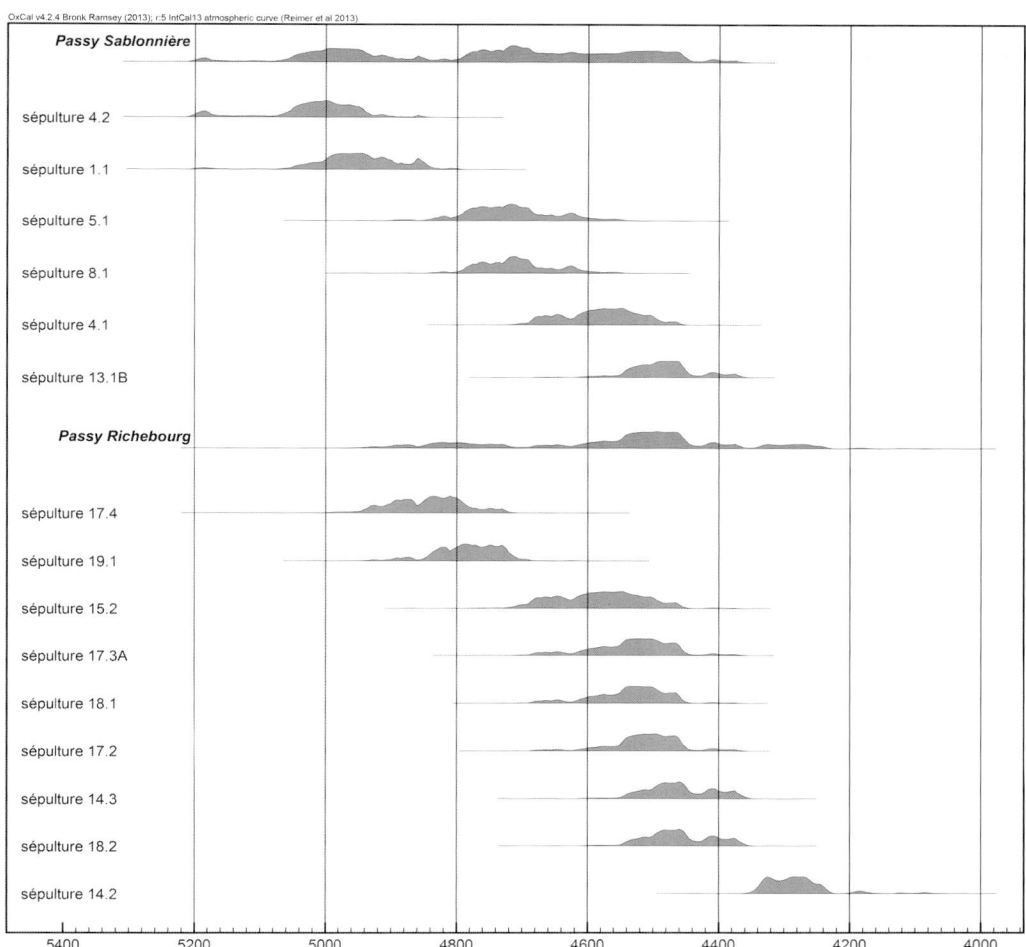

Table 4.1: Radiocarbon dates prior to 4500 BC from burials associated with Passy type monuments at the eponymous cemetery (data from Thomas 2011).

Paris Basin and then in Normandy have fundamentally changed the discussion (Carré *et al*. 1984; Chancerel *et al*. 1992; Delor *et al*. 1997). They were first connected with the later Cerny culture, that means shortly after 4500 BC. Considering the megalithic sequence, that seemed old enough to be placed at the very beginning. This did not consider the dates of Bougon F0 (Bougon, Nouvelle-Aquitaine). However, despite the conviction of their supporters, Bougon dates cannot be used in any reasoning. What had been first described as a unique middle Neolithic level (Mohen 1977) was eventually reinterpreted as two distinct periods of deposits (Scarre *et al*. 1993; Mohen and Scarre 2002), taking into account two sets of dates. However, in 1993, the presentation of the stratigraphy was wrong (it contradicted the one of 1977 and the field documents): without excluding the possibility of two phases of burials, there is definitely only one level for all of the Middle Neolithic. Furthermore, the details of which bones were sampled for dating is not clear (the dates from the Lyon laboratory correspond to bulk bone samples whose designation remained unspecified; Chambon 2003, 73), and, besides, grave goods did not support such a reading. Comparatively, the long barrow dates offer solid evidence. In Brittany, the modern excavation of the mound of Lannec er gadouer (Erdeven, Morbihan) provided dates and artefacts for the construction, coherent with the middle of the fifth millennium BC (Cassen 2000). In the Paris Basin, the dates of the Passy type monument are now numerous and consistent: they clearly indicate the beginning of this phenomenon soon after the Early Neolithic, about 4700 BC (Thomas 2011): in the eponymous cemetery, for instance, some may even span the passage between Early and Middle Neolithic (Table 4.1). However, at the present time, there is no evidence to support the hypothesis suggesting the first monuments occurred during the Rubané's direct successor period, the Villeneuve-Saint-Germain phase.

The dates of the Passy type monuments opportunely fill the gap between Early Neolithic domestic architecture and the first megalithic monuments. In comparison, the English and Welsh barrows appeared more or less one millennium after the end of the Linear Pottery culture (*e.g.* Bayliss and Whittle 2007); there was neither geographic nor chronological continuity between this culture and the beginning of real megalithic sequence in Atlantic areas of France. Long barrows, distributed both in the Paris Basin and Brittany, just after the spread of the Neolithic, proposed a passage from houses to burial monuments. If chronology and geography do not contradict the hypothesis, can it really be regarded as an argument for it?

THE GRAVES AS REFLECTION OF THE HOUSES?

Studies of the domestic architecture of the Neolithic consist mostly of dealing with Linear Pottery and its later development Mittelneolithikum, Lengyel cultures. In western Europe, discoveries concerning numerous cultures did not, for a long time, include house plans. By contrast, LBK farmers had left hundreds of them from central Europe to Brittany. Identification is made by the presence of postholes and trenches that correspond to house frame and walls. Ground plans show elongated, rectangular or trapezoidal features. The maximal width, of approximately 7–8 m, corresponded to the façade, and the length could vary between 20 to 60 m. Common proportions recur in the marked trapezoidal buildings of the LBK direct heirs, such as Brześć Kujawski or final Villeneuve-Saint-Germain. The façade, where the entrance is supposed to have always been located, faced east or south-east, depending on the region.

The architectural layout represents the major similarity highlighted by Hodder (1984). However, what is actually compared? On one side, there are houses, but on the other are there monuments or burial features? In the opinion of Childe (1949) and until Marshall (1981), it was the barrow that was reminiscent of the house. According to Hodder, however, it depends.

One can agree that the entrance in the case of Linear Pottery houses was located at the broader end, but the architectural evidence at Brześć Kujawski does not support such an obvious fact for the Lengyel houses (Grygiel and Bogucki 1981). On the other hand, what did Hodder mean by 'mound entrance' (1984, 56)? Not every mound contained a chambered tomb. When they did, a corridor that exited on the mound's border was far from systematic. That this entrance was located at the broader end remains a possibility, and nothing more. Furthermore, that some special feature has been dedicated to the entrance depends on our ability to identify it. When only the ground plan, but not the old ground surface, is preserved, revealing the entrance implies a degree of elaboration 'specifically with façades, antechambers, "horns", or activity concentrations' (Hodder 1984, 59). The case is different with burials, but it is hardly a matter of surprise that a grave entrance should be the place for ritual activity. As for the tripartite division of house and mound, there seems to be confusion between an entrance as a room or as a mere threshold.

To go back to the beginning of the story, what can be said of the shape of monuments? As far as Early Neolithic houses are concerned, monuments taken into consideration should be the oldest ones: Passy type in the Paris Basin and 'tertres armoricains' in Brittany. The former provides the biggest corpus. Passy (Bourgogne-Franche-Comté, Duhamel 1997), Fleury-sur-Orne (Normandy, Ghesquière *et al.* 2014) and Balloy (Île-de-France, Mordant 1997) provide a large range of shapes and dimensions, from less than 10 m long to 371 m (the largest to date). Duhamel and Midgley (2004, fig. 4A) have produced a sketch that summarises the diversity of shape. Generally speaking, some follow a strict rectangular outline, while others are rather more trapezoidal. But that is not all, from a geometrical standpoint, circular patterns clearly existed. Finally, it must also be said that some monuments simply cannot be reduced to single, regular geometric shapes. Indeed, some combine such shapes as the trapeze, the rectangle or the circle (Fig. 4.1).

Setting aside proportions that differ significantly from houses, round monuments appeared to contradict the filiation hypothesis. A solution to this conundrum was found by Duhamel, who connected these monuments with Middle Neolithic round buildings discovered in northern France (Duhamel and Midgley 2004, 225). This proposal did not solve the problem posed by the mix of geometric shapes.

A major issue relative to geometry is that there are few two-dimensional shapes. Among the simplest are the ellipse, the trapeze and the rectangle, including the circle as a specific case of the former and the square as an example of the latter. The triangle and the parallelogram, despite also being simple shapes, are less suitable for an inner layout. Furthermore, it should come as no surprise that Neolithic houses followed simple plans. Mounds had less architectonic constraints.

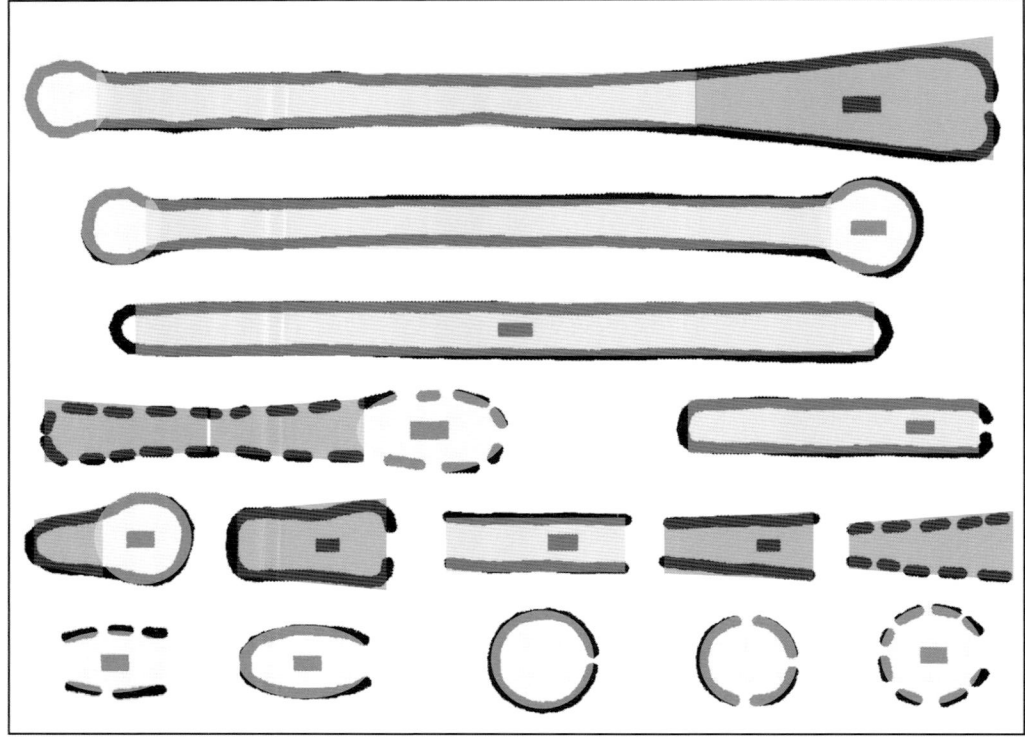

Fig. 4.1: The Passy type monuments reduced to geometrical shapes: they used and sometimes combined the trapeze, the rectangle and the ellipse (sketch of monuments after Duhamel and Midgley 2004).

Building techniques may also explain why burial chambers could have the same plan and even identical proportions as houses. The round plan of many chambers of 'tombes à couloir' may thus recall the one of Middle Neolithic buildings, sometimes with shared details, as Laporte and Tinevez (2004, 22) pointed out after Cassen (2001). Could the same house plan be used on the one hand to justify mound shapes and, on the other, the burial chamber layout? As a matter of fact, the problem with funerary monuments surpasses the comparison with houses. Indeed, should the inner feature be considered dependently or independently of the external aspect of the monument? Regardless, both must correspond to a geometric shape.

REFERENCE TO ANCESTORS?

Considering both the supposed identical shape, as well as the chronological succession of longhouses and long barrows, the underlying idea was that 'long barrow or megalith builders' had wished to emulate the first farmers of western Europe. If the previous houses

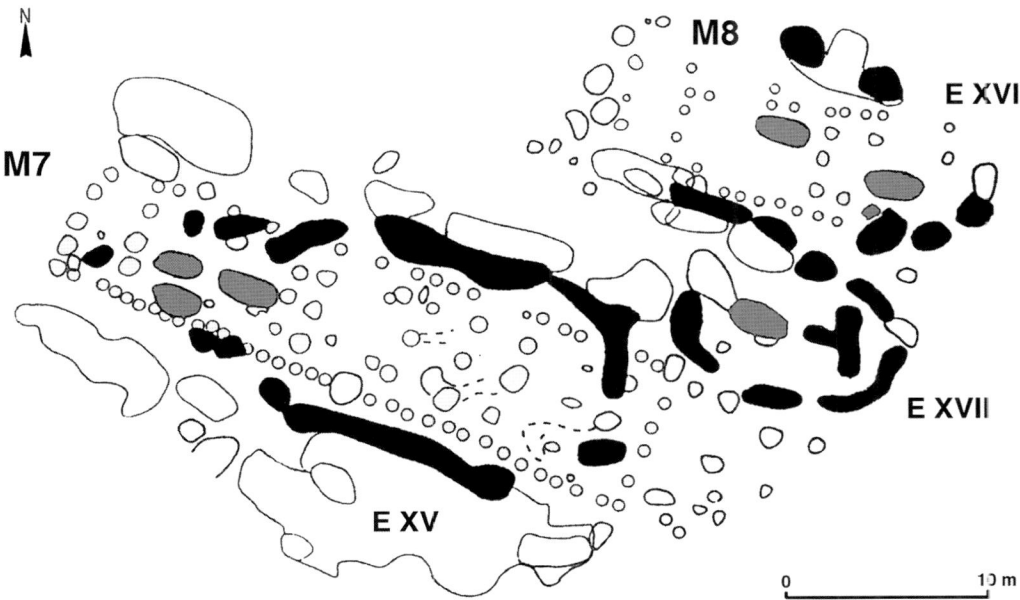

Fig. 4.2: Two monuments, at Balloy, overlapping Rubané houses: appropriation of the value attached to ancestor or practical use of the small mound caused by the ruins of the house? (after Mordant 1997).

were no longer in the spirit of the times, their design was transposed in burial context. By copying the ground plan of these houses, they gained the virtue of their predecessors and might thus lay claim to the land. In this perspective, the superposition of the burial layout over the ruins of the former house was an ideal outcome.

The discovery of three cases of Passy type monuments overlapping Rubané houses, from the cemetery of Balloy, in 1988 and 1993, quickly became famous (Mordant 1997). The sizes of monuments XV and XVI even seem to correspond exactly to those of the prior structures. They also conformed to their orientation. Some other arguments also deserve attention. First of all, monuments attributed to the Cerny culture did not follow immediately the Rubané houses; dwellings of the Villeneuve-Saint-Germain, intercalated between these two cultures, with more or less the same plan, were found a few hundred metres away, without any surrounding monuments. Additionally, at the location of the monumental burial ground, after the Rubané village, only burials occurred until the Iron Age.

As Mordant has suggested (Chambon and Mordant 1996, 398), the interpretation oscillates between two extremes. In the most symbolic one, it could be seen as a will to incorporate values attached to first inhabitants. But from a materialistic standpoint, it may correspond to a practical use of the pre-existing small mound resulting from the decay of the Rubané house, in order to obtain monumentality at little effort (Fig. 4.2). Of course, all intermediate scenarios may also be considered.

Without de-valuing this amazing case, you cannot see the woods for the trees. More than a hundred Passy type monuments have been excavated, as well as hundreds of Danubian houses in the Paris Basin. Taking them all into consideration, the case of Balloy remains unique. At Passy, Gron or Escolives-Sainte-Camille, monuments were set up not far from Rubané dwellings, even on the same plot in the case of Gron. There was, however, no superimposition. Even more surprising, in the Cerny non-monumental cemetery of Vignely (Île-de-France, Bostyn *et al.* 2018), burials were scattered amidst the ruins of the former Villeneuve-Saint-Germain village: nonetheless they most often managed to avoid the exact location of houses. It is only following the Cerny period, around one millennium after the village, that we find a small burial monument superimposed on the ruins of a house.

The issue is not so different for true megalithic monuments. For just one case of direct replacement of a Cerny house by a cairn including a 'tombe à couloir' at Cairon (Normandy, Ghesquière and Marcigny 2011), how many others with nothing of the sort? The question surpasses the simple overlapping of former houses by burial monuments. It is a matter of remembrance, or how people recalled what happened before and the way they positioned themselves in front of the past. Did they pay attention to the real identification of features, such as houses, or were they satisfied with the mere knowledge of the overall location of a former village? Nonetheless, one cannot deny a form of assignment to certain locations. In the Paris Basin, Rubané and Villeneuve-Saint-Germain burials occurred within villages. This pattern shifted with the arrival of the Cerny culture. By this time and afterwards, some places seem to have been dedicated to the dead or to religious purposes (with reservations that domestic settings remain, archaeologically speaking, very discrete for several periods).

Actually, proving the continuity, particularly in the symbolic domain, does not appear that easy. Although more recent, the case of the Bury 'allée sépulcrale' (gallery grave) is remarkable from this perspective. After a short use during the Late Neolithic, the grave was maintained for several centuries before being used again for burials (Salanova *et al.* 2017). There could hardly be a doubt about the meaning.

Ancestry is of real concern when it comes to talk about burial practices. However, the idea tends to be used in a very general way. As Hodder pointed out, 'any marker or inhumation cemetery could have functioned as a focus or as a symbol of the ancestors' (1984, 52). But, above all, predecessors cannot be seen systematically as ancestors. The process of becoming an ancestor is long and punctuated by ritual events (Hertz 1907). Ancestors, both real and mythical, are namely invoked. How could the builders of the first burial monuments have included amidst their religious patrimony anonymous predecessors, whose only remembrance would have been the ruins of theirs houses or villages?

CONCLUDING REMARKS

Undeniable similarities exist between plans of Early Neolithic houses and of later burial monuments. But these communal traits result mostly from the simple geometric forms used for the construction of structures across time. When considering a house or a burial chamber, a quadrilateral provides an easier space to organise than a triangle and the architectural constraints increase with more than four sides. In the case of mounds, an elongated form is the simplest way to suggest monumentality, and a trapezoidal shape allows for the installation of a real façade at one end, maintaining the elongated impression while reducing the work at the other end. The round shape appears more suitable when height was the main goal.

The concept of a house of the dead remains unclear. If it pertains to the type of burial, use of the term is excessive. It may be retained for chambered tombs: large vaults, passage graves, gallery graves, *etc.* It does not fit with individual burials included in the first long barrows. Monumental burials do not imply megaliths; furthermore, the most impressive ones, which were also the first ones and the closest to LBK houses, had no real inner architecture. And in a practical sense, a mound cannot be regarded as a house.

Metaphorically speaking, the question is quite different. A well identified location for the dead may be seen as the house of the dead, moreover in the case of a monumental one. Nowadays in the Occident, the dead person rests at the cemetery, and the living go there to visit them, as they do with living relatives. The dead place is organised, often with streets, districts and groupings. The word necropolis, literally city of the dead, first applied to the antic cemetery of Alexandria, though rare in English, is not a matter of misunderstanding. However, in the symbolic perspective, there is no place for a continuity or a transposition between Early Neolithic houses and later burial buildings. The investment in burial features implies firstly a separation of the dead and the living, secondly that some of the dead have been assigned a new social role.

The emergence of burial monumentality is often considered as being connected to the end of a colonisation phase (*e.g.* Renfrew 1976; Kinnes 1981). Regardless of locality this almost always corresponds to the Middle Neolithic. Does this then imply a constant recollection of early farmers?

Furthermore, if the link may appear logical, burial monumentality did not occur under the same conditions everywhere: in Mediterranean areas of Spain and France, evidence of monumentality is scarce before the Late Neolithic. Even putting the questions of houses and of later monumentality aside, the role of the Linear Pottery culture has been posited as crucial in this emergence. There have been, and there still are fierce debates over whether 'tertres armoricains' were connected to Rubané, but Villeneuve-Saint-Germain is now found up to Brittany lending credibility to this hypothesis. Unfortunately for the proponents of this hypothesis, monumental cemeteries, with Passy type monuments, have been recently discovered in areas never reached by LBK and its successors. The first case was in the Centre-Ouest, at Dissay, in a Chambon context (Pautreau *et al*. 2006) and more recently in the Rhône and the Ain valleys (Frascone 2008), east of Lyon, a context in which this period should correspond to Saint-Uze (Fig. 4.3). Both cultures were supposed to have further links with the Mediterranean Neolithic. Hardly anything is known of the first farmers domestic features in these regions.

Finally, the progression of longhouses to burial monuments corresponds to fluctuating investment over the course of the Neolithic. Periods with investment in domestic features differ from periods with monumental architecture for the dead. Remembrance of the dead is a token of perpetuation of the society. To argue that the souvenir included, somehow, the house shape of preceding populations, remains fully speculative; in the words of a bad classical French pun, first mentioned in *Le Croix* newspaper of 28th July 1893 – if it's round, it's not square!

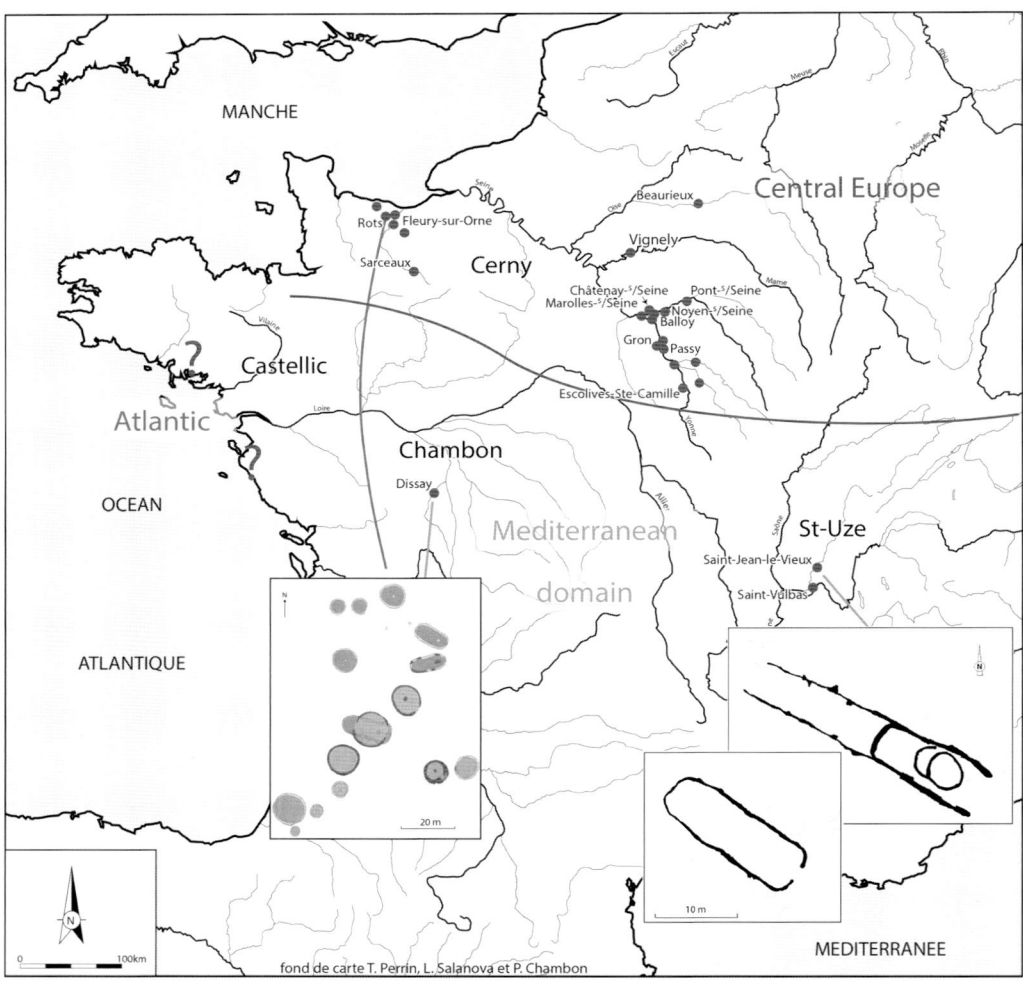

Fig. 4.3: Earthen long barrows from the second and the third quarter of the fifth millennium BC. Setting considering cultural spheres, most are located in the area previously under LBK influence, but recent discoveries concerned cultures related to the Mediterranean area. The question of the 'tertres armoricains' remains under discussion (Dissay after Pautreau et al. 2006; St-Jean-le-Vieux after Frascone 2008).

REFERENCES

Ashbee, P. (1970) *The Earthen Long Barrow in Britain*. London, Dent.
Bayliss, A. and Whittle, A. (eds) (2007) Histories of the dead: building chronologies for five southern British long barrows. *Cambridge Archaeological Journal* 17.1, supplement.
Bostyn, F., Lanchon, Y. and Chambon P. (ed.) (2018) *Habitat du Néolithique ancien et nécropoles du Néolithique moyen I et II à Vigneley « la Porte aux Bergers », Seine-et-Marne*. Paris, Société Préhistorique Française (mémoire 64).

Boujot, C. and Cassen, S. (1992) Le développement des premières architectures funéraires monumentales en France occidentale. In C.-T. Le Roux (ed.) *Actes du 17ᵉ colloque interrégional sur le Néolithique, Vannes 1990*, 195–211. Rennes, Suppl. 5 à la Revue Archéologique de l'Ouest.

Carré, H., Duhamel, P. and Fajon, P. (1984) Monuments et sépultures de Passy (Yonne), un ensemble funéraire du Néolithique moyen d'affinités danubiennes. In Colloque interrégional sur le Néolithique, Mulhouse, 5–7 act. 1984, résumé des communications, 23–5.

Cassen, S. (ed.) (2000) *Eléments d'architecture. Exploration d'un tertre funéraire à Lannec er Gadouer (Erdeven, Morbihan)*. Chauvigny, Association des Publications Chauvinoises.

Chambon, P. (2003) *Les morts dans les sépultures collectives néolithiques en France; du cadavre aux restes ultimes*. Paris, Suppl. 35 à Gallia Préhistoire.

Chambon, P. and Mordant, D. (1996) Monumentalisme et sépultures collectives à Balloy (Seine-et-Marne). *Bulletin de la Société Préhistorique Française* 93 (3), 396–402.

Chancerel, A., Desloges, J., Dron, J.-L. and San Juan, G. (1992) Le début du Néolithique en Basse-Normandie. In C.-T. Le Roux (ed.) *Paysans et bâtisseurs, Actes du 17ᵉ Colloque International sur le Néolithique, Vannes, 1990*, 153–73. Rennes, Suppl. 5 à la Revue Archéologique de l'Ouest.

Childe, V.G. (1949) The origin of Neolithic culture in northern Europe. *Antiquity* 23, 129–35.

Daniel, G.E. (1965) Editorial. *Antiquity* 39, 81–6.

Delor, J.-P., Genreau, F., Heurtaux, A., Jacob, J.-P., Leredde, H., Nouvel, P. and Pellet C. (1997) L'implantation des nécropoles monumentales au sud du Bassin parisien. In C. Constantin, D. Mordant and D. Simonin (eds) *La Culture de Cerny, Nouvelle économie, nouvelle société au Néolithique*, 381–396. Nemours, APRAIF (Mémoires du Musée de Préhistoire d'Ile-de-France, 6).

Deguilloux, M.-F., Soler, L., Pemonge, M.-H., Scarre, C., Joussaume, J. and Laporte L. (2011) News from the West: ancient DNA from a French megalithic burial chamber. *American Journal of Physical Anthropology* 144 (1), 108–18.

Duhamel, P. (1997) La nécropole monumentale de Passy (Yonne): description d'ensemble et problèmes d'interprétation. In C. Constantin, D. Mordant and D. Simonin (eds) *La Culture de Cerny, Nouvelle économie, nouvelle société au Néolithique*, 397–448. Nemours, APRAIF (Mémoires du Musée de Préhistoire d'Ile-de-France, 6).

Duhamel, P. and Midgley, M. (2004) Espaces, monumentalisme et pratiques funéraires des sociétés néolithiques en voie de hiérarchisation: les nécropoles monumentales Cerny du bassin Seine-Yonne. In L. Baray (ed.) *Archéologie des pratiques funéraires: approches critiques*, 211–48. Glux-en-Glenne, Bibracte (Bibracte; 9).

Frascone, D. (2008) *Saint-Jean-le-Vieux (Ain), occupations néolithiques et gallo-romaines*. Bron, Inrap Rhône-Alpes-Auvergne.

Ghesquière, E., Chambon, P., Giazzon, D., Hachem, L, Thevenet, C. and Thomas, A. (2014) Présentation liminaire de la fouille de la nécropole des Hauts de l'Orne à Fleury-sur-Orne (Calvados). *Internéo* 10, 179–81.

Ghesquière, E. and Marcigny, C. (ed.) (2011) *Cairon; vivre et mourir au Néolithique; la Pierre Tourneresse en Calvados*. Rennes, Presses universitaires de Rennes (Archéologie et culture).

Grygiel, R. and Bogucki, P.I. (1981) Early Neolithic Sites at Brześć Kujawski, Poland: Preliminary Report on the 1976–1979 Excavations. *Journal of Field Archaeology* 8, 9–27.

Hertz, R. (1907) Etude sur la représentation de la mort. *Année sociologique* 10, 48–137.

Hodder, I. (1984) Burials, houses, women and men in the European Neolithic. In D. Miller and C. Tilley (eds) *Ideology, Power and Prehistory*, 51–68. Cambridge, Cambridge University.

Kinnes, I. (1981) Dialogues with death. In R. Chapman, L. Kinnes and K. Randsborg (eds) *The Archaeology of Death*, 83–91. Cambridge, Cambridge University Press.

L'Helgouach, J. (1965) *Les sépultures mégalithiques en Armorique*. Rennes, Travaux du Laboratoire d'Anthropologie Préhistorique.

Laporte, L. and Tinevez, J.-Y. (2004) Neolithic houses and chambered tombs of western France. *Cambridge Archaeological Journal* 14 (2), 217–34.

Le Rouzic, Z. (1933) Morphologie et chronologie des sépultures préhistoriques du Morbihan. *L'Anthropologie* 43, 225–65.

Marshall, A. (1981) Environmental adaptation and structural design in axially-pitched longhouses from Neolithic Europe. *World Archaeology* 13, 101–21.

Mohen J.-P. (1977) Les tumulus de Bougon; 4000–2000 ans avant Jésus-Christ. *Bulletin de la Société Historique et Scientifique des Deux-Sèvres* 2/3, 5–48.

Mohen, J.-P. and Scarre, C. (2002) *Les tumulus de Bougon, complexe mégalithique du Ve au IIIe millénaire*. Paris, Errance.

Mordant, D. (1997) Le complexe des Réaudins à Balloy: enceinte et nécropole monumentale. In C. Constantin, D. Mordant and D. Simonin (eds) *La Culture de Cerny, Nouvelle économie, nouvelle société au Néolithique*, 448–79. Nemours, APRAIF (Mémoires du Musée de Préhistoire d'Ile-de-France, 6).

Pautreau, J.-P., Farago-Szekeres, B. and Mornais, P. (2006) La nécropole néolithique de la Jardelle à Dissay (Vienne). In R. Joussaume, L. Laporte and C. Scarre (eds) *Origine et développement du mégalithisme de l'ouest de l'Europe*, 375–9. Bougon, édition du Musée des Tumulus.

Péquart, M., Péquart, S.-J., Boule, M., and Vallois, H. (1937) *Téviec, station nécropole mésolithique du Morbihan*. Paris, Archives de l'Institut de Paléontologie Humaine (Mémoire n° 18).

Powell, T.G.E., Corcoran, J.X.W.P., Lynch, F. and Scott, J.G. (1969) *Megalithic Enquiries in the West of Britain*. Liverpool: Liverpool University Press.

Salanova, L., Chambon, P., Pariat, J.-G., Marçais, A.-S. and Valentin, F. (2017) From one ritual to another: the long-term sequence from the Bury gallery grave (Northern France, fourth-second millennia BC). *Antiquity* 91 (355), 57–73.

Sánchez-Quinto, F., Malmströma, H., Fraser, M., Girdland-Flink, L., Svensson, E.M., Simões, L.G., George, R., Hollfeldera, N., Burenhult, G., Noble, G., Britton, K., Talamo, S., Curtis, N., Brzobohata, H., Sumberova, R., Götherström, A., Storå, J. and Jakobsson, M. (2019) Megalithic tombs in western and northern Neolithic Europe were linked to a kindred society. *PNAS* 116, 9469–74.

Scarre, C., Switsur, R. and Mohen, J.-P. (1993) New radiocarbon dates from Bougon and the chronology of French passage-graves. *Antiquity* 67 (257), 856–9.

Thomas, A. (2011) Identités funéraires, variants biologiques et facteurs chronologiques: une nouvelle perception du contexte culturel et social du Cerny (Bassin parisien, 4700–4300 avant J.-C.). Unpublished thesis, Université de Bordeaux 1.

Sprockhoff, E. (1938) *Die Nordische Megalithkultur*. Berlin and Leipzig: De Gruyter.

Whittle, A.W.R. (1977) *The Earlier Neolithic of Southern England and its Continental Background*. Oxford: BAR Supplementary Series 35.

Chapter 5

The dead and the Linearbandkeramik longhouse

Penny Bickle

Houses and the dead share a persistent relationship in many regions of Neolithic Europe. Human remains can be found interred complete, located inside, beneath and alongside domestic structures, or disarticulated and distributed, across pits and other settlement features. However, rather than resting on a direct link between the dead and the house, Childe's (1949, 135) suggestion that longhouses were the inspiration for the long mounds of northern Europe ('to make the house of the dead'), was developed from the morphological similarities of long trapezoidal houses and mounds. He drew direct parallels between upright stones and wall timbers, and turfed mounds and thatched roofs (Childe 1949). With the concept of the house carried forward onto long mounds, the association between the dead, ancestors and houses has since travelled back in the reverse direction, informing interpretations of the Linearbandkeramik (LBK: Fig. 5.1) and post-LBK longhouses of

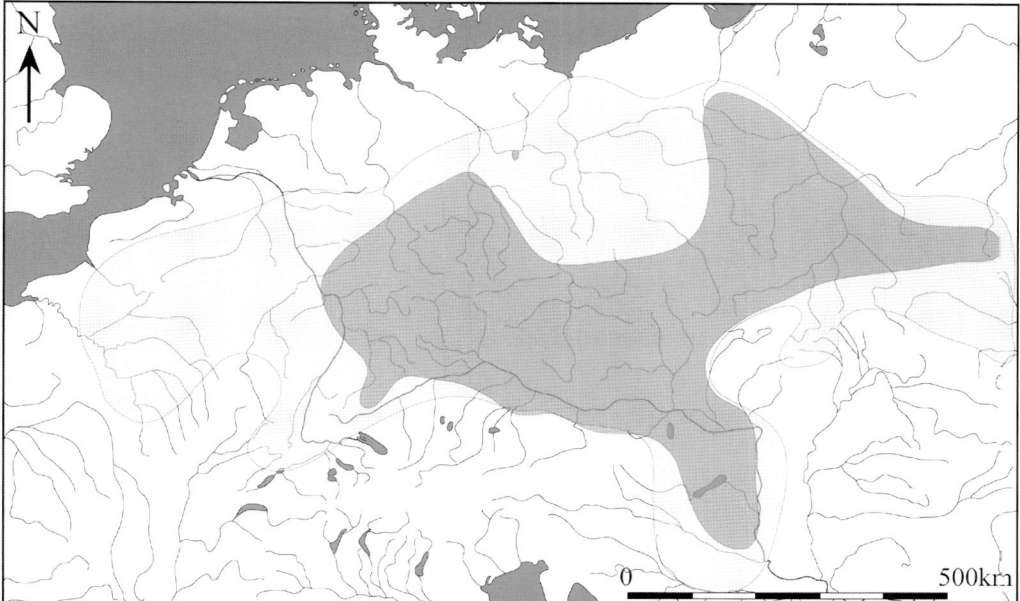

Fig. 5.1: Map of LBK distribution. The darker shading indicates phase one (c.5500–5300 cal BC), and the lighter shading, phase two (c.5300–5000 cal BC) (after Bickle and Whittle 2013, fig. 1.1).

central Europe (Bradley 2001; Turek 2014). Bradley (2001) is perhaps the best-known example of this approach, elegantly proposing that LBK longhouses were associated with ancestors through their orientation along the axis of migration from modern-day Hungary, perhaps representing a mythical homeland as the LBK spread through central Europe. His broader point was that the 'importance of the dead' had rarely been considered in terms of the longhouse evidence (Bradley 2001, 55), despite LBK settlement burials having been analysed as a phenomenon in their own right (*e.g.* Veit 1993; 1996).

A mostly implicit assumption has since persisted that it was appropriate to incorporate the dead into settlements because LBK longhouses 'reference[d] notions of ancestry and origin' (Jones 2005, 208). Despite attention to the symbolic and cosmological significances

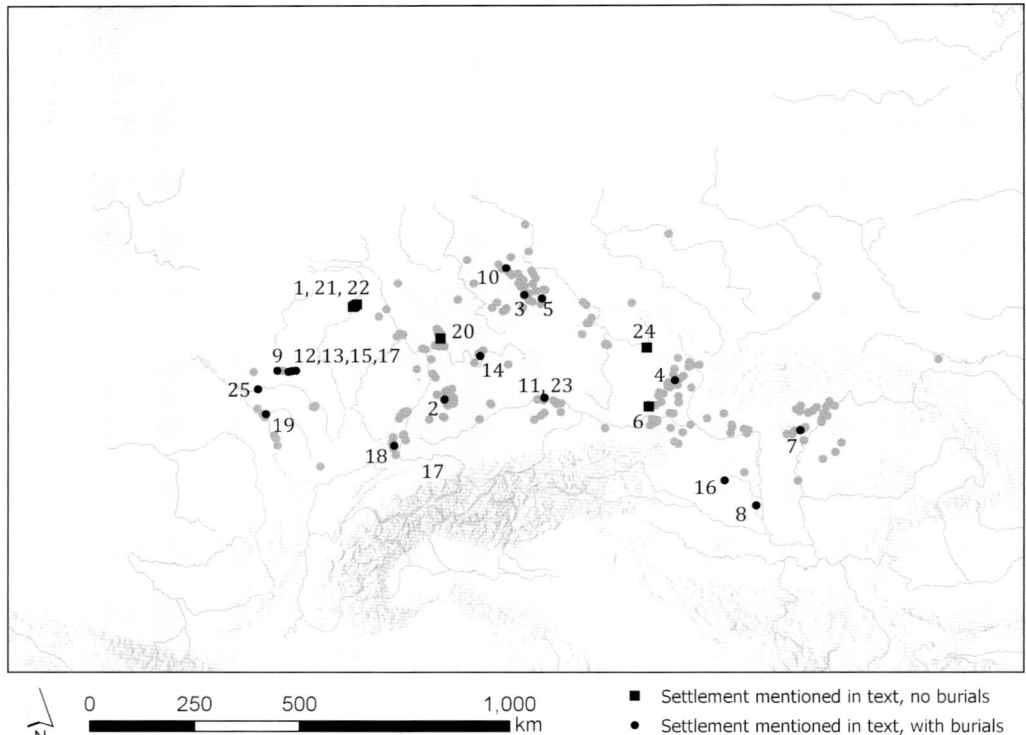

Fig. 5.2: LBK settlement sites mentioned in text. Numbered in the order they appear in the text: 1) Geleen-Janskamperveld, 2) Vaihingen, 3) Karsdorf, 4) Brno-Starý Lískovec, 5) Zauschwitz, 6) Mold, 7) Füzesabony-Gubakút, 8) Alsónyék-Bátaszék, 9) Bucy-Le-Long «La Fosselle», 10) Halberstadt, 11) Otzing, 12) Berry-au-Bac «Chemin de la Pêcherie», 13) Menneville, 14) Schwanfeld, 15) Cuiry-lès-Chaudardes, 16) Balatonszárzó, 17) Berry-au-Bac «Le Vieux Tordoir», 18) Ensisheim, 19) Vignely «la Porte aux Berges», 20) Bruchenbrücken, 2) Sittard, 22) Elsloo, 23) Mintraching, 24) Bylany, 25) Balloy. Sources: Esri, Airbus DS, USGS, NGA, NASA, CGIAR, N Robinson, NCEAS, NLS, OS, NMA, Geodatastyrelsen, Rijkswaterstaat, GSA, Geoland, FEMA, Intermap and the GIS user community. Made with Natural Earth.

central European longhouses shared (Hodder 1990; Bradley 2001; Jones 2005; Lüning 2009), and discussion of settlement funerary practices (Veit 1993; 1996; Hofmann 2009), there has been limited consideration of the specific relationships between the dead and the LBK longhouse. In a notable exception, Whittle (2012, 200–2) compared shared orientations, symbolisms and practices between the 'house and the grave', arguing that cemetery graves and longhouses could be regarded as a shared 'kaleidoscope', through which notions of living and death in the LBK world rotated. However, what is missing from this account, and other approaches to settlement burials, are the specific points in space and time when the dead and the longhouse met. LBK approaches and attitudes to the dead are thus treated as generalised, with the aspects of the house associated with the 'ancestors' (a term often used in a non-specific way) considered to be applicable across the geographical and chronological distribution of the culture. This paper, in contrast, asks whether there are particular patterns of association between the dead and houses in terms of spatial arrangement, temporal association and ritual practice. I do not claim to rethink living and dying in the LBK – nor aim to provide an account of what concepts long mounds were borrowing from longhouse – rather, I will explore how the dead were encountered around longhouse structure and chronology. Overall, in this paper, I aim to contribute to the understanding of why Neolithic houses were such a meaningful place for human burials by surveying the intersection of the dead and the longhouse (Fig. 5.2). Do such funerary practices arise in broader associations of the house and ancestors, in which the dead become incorporated into settlement and house memories, or are longhouses best regarded as places of transformation, in which the dead and their identities are redistributed?

THE LINEARBANDKERAMIK LONGHOUSE: A BRIEF OVERVIEW

Before considering the burial evidence, it is worth briefly exploring previous and current interpretations of central European longhouses and their households. For the sake of space, three different approaches to interpreting LBK longhouses are summarised here: (1) typological, which focus on explaining variation in architectural features; (2) symbolic or cosmological, which tend to regard shared features as representative of world views (*e.g.* origin myths); and (3) phenomenological, which have focused on how practice associated with buildings have shaped perception and social norms (*e.g.* how to participate in social life). Modderman's (1970) typology of the LBK longhouse set the tone for many later works. Length and internal post settings – such as the tripartite division from which he defined his three main house types, and the 'Y' and 'J' central post arrangements – have become the most important vectors for interpreting variation (*e.g.* Coudart 1998). Features such as different construction methods, loam pit fills (which flank the longitudinal walls), and life histories, also contribute to determining use and symbolic roles of various architectural elements (Hodder 1990; Bradley 1996; Coudart 1998; Stäuble 2005). The central section in Modderman's (1970; 1988) typology is thought to have been used for daily, domestic life and is always present. The north-western end of the house, which is sometimes found planked, has been hypothesised as a cattle stall (though phosphate analysis has since led to this hypothesis being rejected; Stäuble and Lüning 1999) or to have a special function such as a mortuary shrine (see below; Bradley 2001; Lüning 2009; please note that throughout the paper, the dominant house orientation of north-west–south-east is used, but across the LBK orientation of the house varies between west–east to north–south). The front or south-eastern end of the house is often considered to have been used for storage and is sometimes found with double sets of posts, perhaps suggesting an upper storey (*cf.* Rück 2009). Such features are made more complex by regional and chronological variations, and further refined typologies have been offered (*e.g.* Coudart 1998).

In contrast to typological approaches, interpretations based on cosmological or symbolic approaches have focused on the shared features of the house. For example, Hodder (1990) presents an all-encompassing cosmology for Neolithic houses, arguing they symbolised taming the wild, as part of negotiating the pervasive tension between the *domus* and *agrios*, which was at the heart of the spread of the Neolithic. Bradley (2001), as discussed above, has debated the symbolic dimensions of the houses, noting the shared orientation, which follow the direction of migration from the south-east, and patterns in the house lifecycle, to suggest strong ancestral associations. Elsewhere, Bradley (1996) has made comparisons between living and 'dead' houses, drawing comparisons between the pits excavated along both longhouses and tombs. This theme has been picked up recently by Turek (2014), who argues that these loam pits were excavated at the end of the house's use-life and part of the act of closing the house, before its use as a funerary structure. This is an interesting proposition, but it is challenging, based on current evidence, to argue that this was consistently the case across the LBK (Bickle forthcoming a). Vondrovský (2018) has suggested that the shared orientation of longhouses was associated with the cycle of the sun, raising the possibility of a cosmology in which the east and west became associated with life and death respectively.

Building on phenomenological perspectives, others, including myself, have argued that longhouses were unlikely to have passively represented cosmological or other aspects of social life and structure, but would have been active in mediating action in and perspectives on the world. Key themes have developed around notions of identity negotiation, emphasising flexibility and innovation (Whittle 2003; Hofmann 2013), kinship and social memory (Borić 2007; 2008), and time (Bickle 2013). Lévi-Strauss' (1982) model of 'house societies', in which the house has a social role through which kinship and inheritance are mediated, has also gained traction (*e.g.* Borić 2008). It is worth stressing here that for the most part, all the approaches sketched in outline above interpret longhouses as primarily 'homes' (excepting Soudský's 1969 proposal that the longest buildings were 'clubhouses'). Thus, variations in house layout and style between contemporary houses are thought to represent diversity between households, rather than in use or symbolic significance, and sometimes rendered as status differences between inhabitants (van der Velde 1979; 1990; Pechtl 2009), or as different economic strategies that framed social identity (Gomart *et al.* 2015). This assumption also contributes to supporting the notion that households were mostly autonomous, arranged in 'yards' or *Hofplätze*, with each generation building their longhouse next to the previous one (Boelicke 1982; Lüning 1988) and only loosely grouped into settlements of one, two (*e.g.* Geleen-Janskampervelt, Netherlands, Louwe Kooijmans *et al.* 2003) or more houses, or clans (*e.g.* Vaihingen, Baden-Württemberg Bogaard *et al.* 2016; *cf.* Rück 2007; 2009). On the whole then, longhouses have been interpreted as an external display of an independent household, who made decisions about building design based on a broad cosmological schema, layered with individual choices about status and identity.

Who this household was is relevant to the discussion here as burial alongside houses is often assumed (implicitly or explicitly) as a statement about belonging to certain houses.

Broadly, the LBK is envisioned as a patrilocal, if not patriarchal, society (Strien 2000; Bentley *et al.* 2012). Longhouses are thus generally thought to have had one kin-group per house, of six, or eight, to ten inhabitants (Lüning 1998, 38; Zimmermann *et al.* 2009, 13; Strien 2010). While assessing realistic household numbers is challenging, recent aDNA analysis may encourage us to think more critically about belonging and familial relationships in the LBK. At Karsdorf, Middle Elbe-Saale, central Germany, mtDNA profiles showed limited maternal lineages developing across its estimated 300-year span (Brandt *et al.* 2014, 100). While on the surface this seems to support patrilocal practices (paternal DNA was not assessed), for few maternal lineages to develop at the relatively substantial settlement (24 houses; Behnke 2012) is a surprise – *i.e.* that few brothers were setting up houses alongside each other – and suggests a 'dynamic and mobile' population (Brandt *et al.* 2014, 100). Burials alongside the same houses also suggested the same pattern, although the limited number of children interred made it difficult to reconstruct parent-child relationships, with individuals buried alongside houses demonstrating very few shared mtDNA lineages (Brandt *et al.* 2014, 100). With multiple numbers of men, women and children placed alongside houses at Karsdorf, this cannot just be explained away as women moving into households, as each person buried alongside houses would need to have a different mother and one person from each mother would need to have conveniently died and been placed alongside the house. To be clear, what these data challenge is a simple reading of family structure from those buried alongside individual houses, whilst acknowledging that this interpretation is based on mtDNA analysis from just one site. Further studies may yet produce other kin-based patterns. However, such data indicate that we should first make space for a more fluid and dynamic pattern of household membership than has perhaps been allowed for in the past and second, question whether inhabitants of houses were buried alongside the longhouse in which they lived.

BURIAL PRACTICES AT LBK SETTLEMENTS

The aim here is to consider the specific relationship between the longhouse and the dead, rather than debate the significance of burial on settlements more generally (as this has already been done, *e.g.* Veit 1993; Hofmann 2009). However, it is worth briefly dispelling some of the myths that persist about LBK settlement burial practices and setting out a perspective on how they fit into the wider landscape of LBK funerary practices. In bald summary, settlement burials in the LBK have been regarded as low status, but this is often framed in comparison to cemeteries. Settlement burials are considered to have received fewer grave goods, while women and children are over-represented in comparison to cemeteries (Pavúk 1972; Moddermann 1988; Häusler 1994; Nieszery 1995; Jeunesse 1997; Veit 1996; Röder 1998). There is also an implicit assumption that as settlement burials are interred in rubbish pits, they were therefore afforded less ceremony and effort than cemetery burials (*cf.* Hofmann 2009). The comparison to cemetery burials is salient here, as settlement burials are seen to deviate from the 'norm' provided by cemeteries, perhaps based on the familiarity of cemeteries to us in the modern world (Frirdich 2003). Veit (1996) even titled his major work on settlement burials *Studien zum Problem der Siedlungsbestattung im europäischen Neolithikum* [Studies on the problem of settlement burial in the European Neolithic], thus emphasising that settlement burials were the 'problem' to be explained [author's translation]. Given the widespread physical relationship between the Neolithic house and the dead elsewhere in Europe, LBK cemeteries should perhaps be seen as the more deviant practice, one which develops from the later phases of the culture (Whittle 2012). Besides, many of the assumptions that demographic differences, variance in grave goods and burial ritual represent status differences can be challenged (Hofmann 2009).

Although settlement burials are less well provisioned with grave goods than cemetery burials (50% of settlement burials, and 70% of cemetery burials, are accompanied by grave goods), men and women are equally likely to receive funerary objects at settlements (at a rate of 50%; Hedges *et al.* 2013, 374). Importantly, men and women are equally likely to be buried at settlements (Fig. 5.3). In some cases, the number of male burials can outnumber those of females. At Brno-Starý Lískovec (Moravia) all five adult burials were sexed as male, and no female burials were identified (Dočkalová and Čižmář 2008). When polished stone and flint are excluded from the comparison (30% of cemetery graves, 14% of settlement burials), other grave goods (such as pottery and *Spondylus* shell) actually have similar frequencies of prevalence, though overall the amount of grave goods is less at settlements (Hedges *et al.* 2013; Bickle forthcoming b). A wider range of body positions and orientations are found in settlement inhumations than those at cemeteries (*e.g.* 78% of burials are found in a left-crouched position at cemeteries, and only 58% at settlements: Hedges 2013). Child burials are more frequent at settlements, accounting for approximately half of all settlement burials, while the youngest age range is less well

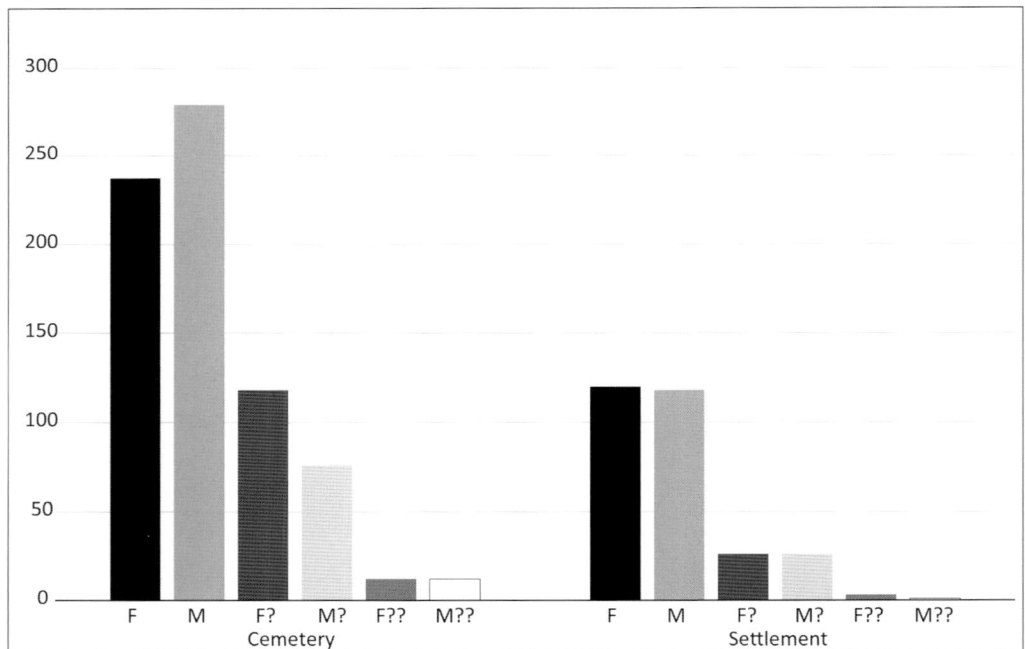

Fig. 5.3: Comparison of absolute count of male and female skeletons at LBK cemeteries and settlements (data from Hedges et al. 2013).

represented at cemeteries (Hedges *et al*. 2013; Bickle and Fibiger 2014). Bringing this data together, we can suggest that rather than status differences, we see greater variation in funerary practice and performance with settlement burials than we do at cemeteries (Hofmann 2009; 2015).

This variability is also seen in the location of burials at settlements. The dead found on settlements do not only appear in re-used rubbish pits, nor solely in the loam pits which flank the majority of longhouses. Veit (1993, 118–9; Fig. 5.4) identified approximately six locations on settlements where burials have been found, which range from graves apparently cut for the burial, to inclusion in a variety of settlement pits, not all of which are closely associated with houses. Spatial associations between houses and burials are therefore varied, and it can sometimes be challenging to assign burials to particular houses. Furthermore, the temporal relationship between burials and the history of a settlement is rarely certain. For example, a burial could have been made into an empty space of a settlement, only to have a house later built next to it, or burials could have been made alongside abandoned houses. Both cases have been argued for (see below). Settlement burials are also found in

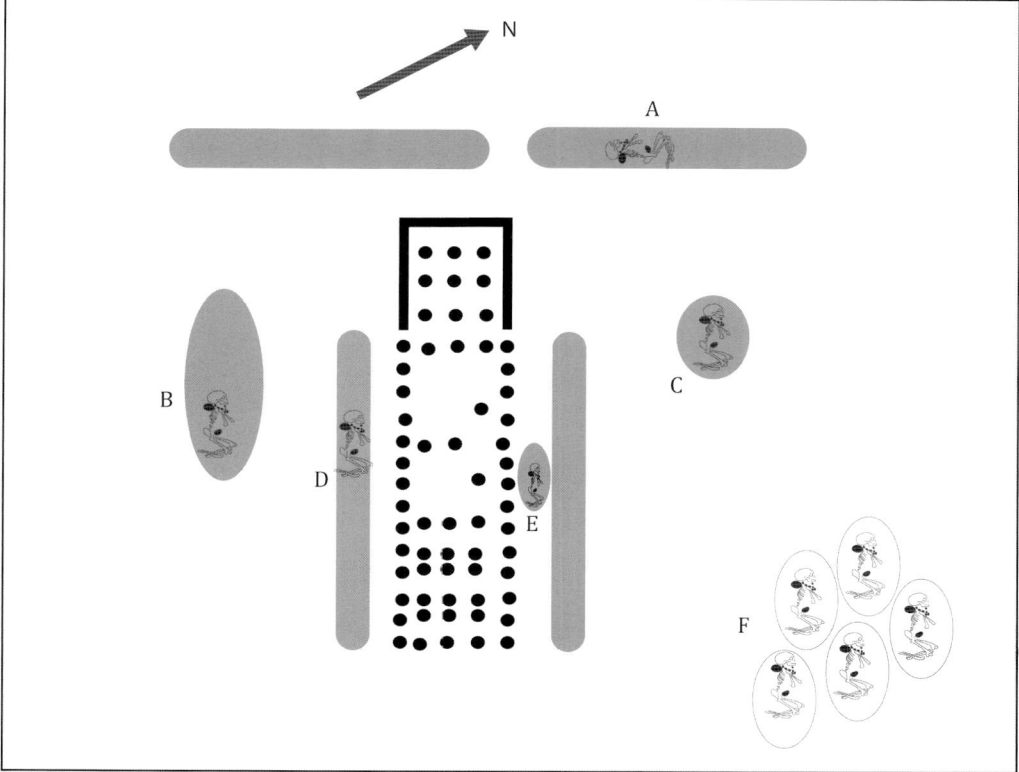

Fig. 5.4: Locations on settlements where LBK inhumations and disarticulated remains have been found. A) enclosure ditches, B) re-used settlement pits, C) isolated graves cut for the inhumation, D) loam pits, E) between house walls and loam pits, F) small groups of inhumations (after Veit 1993, 118).

small 'cemetery-like' groups, which in some cases may have subsequently developed into larger cemeteries. Clearly, not all settlement burials are related directly to individual houses.

Another less frequent assumption, but one that nevertheless persists, is that longhouses were abandoned on the death of the head of the household. Rarely does it appear that houses were burnt down on the death in the household, though there is one possible case at Zauschwitz (Saxony, Germany), where a two year old was found lying on its stomach and was described as 'significantly below' a patch of burning interpreted by the excavator as representing the remains of a burnt house (Veit 1996, 180). There remains disagreement over the extent to which houses were burnt (Kuper *et al.* 1973). As floor or walking surfaces are rarely preserved, 'burnt' houses are usually identified from burnt clay daub in postholes (thought to have made its way in as the posts were removed or rotted away: van der Velde 2008). In the case of house 12 from Mold, lower Austria, huge quantities of burnt clay daub were found in the loam pits (30 kg, 24 kg, and 22 kg, in comparison to the more usual 2–3 kg found in the site as a whole), which was interpreted by the excavators as an accidental fire (Lenneis 2004). The sheer quantities of daub in this case, discourage seeing smaller amounts as sufficient evidence for burning and may suggest burnt daub found in postholes may be from fireplaces or other clay settings (*e.g.* ovens) inside houses. In either case, the dead rarely appear directly related to burning events at houses, though cremations are found associated with both settlements and cemeteries indicating that burning after death was part of the repertoire of LBK funerary rites (Trautmann 2006). In summary, a great variety of practices are seen, and we should perhaps not exclude the possibility that some houses were deliberately burnt. However, the likelihood that a repeated pattern of burning houses on the occurrence of a death, and, by extension, regarding death as polluting, is low in the LBK.

THE DEAD AND THE LONGHOUSE

Here, I want to assess whether we can determine any repeated or regular spatial and chronological patterns associated with the dead and houses that may allow further insights into the relationship between the dead and the house. Some existing patterns have been proposed on the basis of single sites. At the Alföld Linear Pottery (AVK) site of Füzesabony-Gubakút (eastern Hungary), the excavator Domboróczki (2009), noted that burials appeared to be repeatedly placed in front of houses, but this does not appear to be replicated at other settlements, nor consistently practised at Füzesabony-Gubakút, only applying to seven from 12 burials. At Alsónyék-Bátaszék, (Trasndanubia, Hungary), burials were always dug into the western loam pits (Oross *et al.* 2013, 126). This pattern is repeated at Karsdorf, where there was a preference for the south-western side of houses (which are oriented northeast–south-west; Brandt *et al.* 2014). This is the side of the house that would have received the most sunshine (*cf.* Vondrovský 2018), but this is hardly a repeated pattern and we can see variation even between nearby settlements. For example, at Menneville in the Paris basin, France, all burials associated with houses were placed on the southern long side of the house (longhouses are oriented west–east in this region), but *c.*50 km further west, at Bucy-Le-Long «La Fosselle», burial on the north side of houses was favoured, with only one child burial placed south of a house (Hachem *et al.* 1998). At Paris basin sites, houses are distributed widely with wide spaces between houses (Bickle 2008). Similar patterns may be harder to see at sites with denser and multiple phases of occupation, where similar patterns may be obscured by subsequent building. Elsewhere, burials appear to cluster around certain houses, whilst avoiding others. For example, at Halberstadt, (Saxony-Anhalt, Germany) groups of six to eight graves were associated with one of the four houses excavated at the site (Oelze *et al.* 2011). There are also examples where burials are present on settlements but their association with particular houses is ambiguous. For example, at Otzing (Bavaria, Germany) only about five or six graves (including double burials) from 45, can be associated with a specific house, the others are either located away from the built areas of the settlement or placed between houses so their spatial association is unclear (Schmotz and Weber 2000). This diversity suggests that there are no clear regulatory rules associated with burial location, for example with the dead always associated with the north-western end of the longhouse, but that localised traditions could be created, varying even between nearby sites. Where the dead were placed in relation to the house could be a meaningful practice, perhaps arising out of specific local histories.

This consideration of the spatial layout of the burials around longhouses is complicated when the timing of the burial is considered. Due to the lack of grave goods in settlement burials, typological associations between burial and the contents of longhouse loam pits cannot be relied upon (Bickle forthcoming a). While few chronological relationships between specific burials and houses are therefore established with any certainty, by considering the depositional context of burial, a number of different chronological relationships can be proposed. Only in a rare number of instances can burials prior to or at the construction of the longhouse be proposed. For example, at Berry-au-Bac «Chemin de la Pêcherie» (Paris basin), two burials of young children aged 5–6 and 2–3 years appear closely associated with the walls of longhouses, to the extent that it would have been challenging to excavate the grave pit and place the burial inside without impacting on the structural integrity of the house, though no firm stratigraphic relationships could be discerned by the excavators (Fig. 5.5; *cf.* Farruggia and Guichard 1995, 164). Perhaps these burials took place as the house was being raised and carefully placed so the grave would not be cut by postholes. Lending some weight to the suggestion that these burials were prior to the construction of the house is burial 192 at Menneville (of an infant who died about 3 years), whose grave cut is described as 'under' a posthole of the southern wall of house 90, with the posthole destroying the infant's left foot (Farruggia *et al.* 1996, 125). There is a distinct trend to bury younger

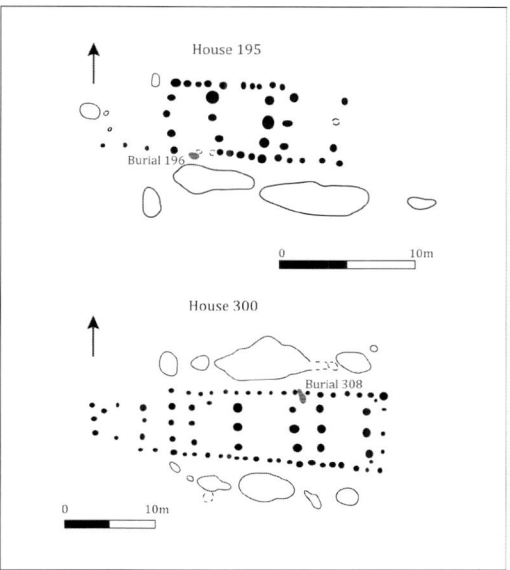

Fig. 5.5: The placing of the two infants buried in the walls of longhouses at Berry-au-Bac «Chemin de la Pêcherie» (after Farruggia and Guichard 1995; burial pits depicted in grey shading).

children close to the walls of houses in the Paris basin not repeated to the same extent elsewhere (Thévenet 2009), but as noted above, the denser agglomerations of buildings found on large settlements further east may obscure other such relationships.

It seems probable, therefore, that more burials were made while the house was occupied or after it had been abandoned, with these child burials as an exception. Here the disagreements about whether the loam pits were open during house occupancy are relevant, but a closer look at the burials themselves is also instructive. The well-known 'Schwanfeld hunter' burial is described as being placed at the 'bottom' of the loam pit he was found within (Lüning 2011), but this appears to be rare, with most loam pit burials (from an unsystematic search) appearing to be placed in the upper fills or subsequently dug in to the pit itself. Veit (1996, 178) classifies burials into those in settlement pits and those in their own graves, but sometimes finds it difficult to determine where burials were placed based on this criteria, suggesting a complex interplay of new pits cut and exploitation of existing pits. Four times as many burials are found in their own pits as in settlement pits (Veit 1993, 118) and even when burials are placed in loam pits, care is demonstrated. For example, at Cuiry-lès-Chaudardes, the burial of an infant was placed on ground sprinkled with ochre in a specially extended part of the loam pit associated with a house (Soudský *et al.* 1982). At Alsónyék and Balatonszárzó (both in Transdanubia, Hungary), burials were afforded their own grave cuts, dug into the top of the loam pit (Oross and Marton 2012, 259; Oross *et al.* 2013, 126). At Balatonszárzó, the excavators noted that skeletons lay on what they described as a 'dished, compact layer' which they interpreted as a 'hard-packed' surface suggesting preparation of the ground before burial and after the pit had gone out of use (Oross and Marton 2012, 259). Oross and Marton (2012, 263) hesitantly propose that at Balatonszárzó burials were made in areas of the settlement that had gone out of use based on the absolute dates and settlement chronology. It seems likely, therefore, that more burials took place after pits ended rather than at the start or during their use-life, but all possibilities seem to be represented in the archaeological record.

When settlement burials took place is rarely discussed, though they may not necessarily have been a constant practice across the life of the settlement. At Vaihingen (Baden-Württemberg, Germany), it is suggested that the settlement burials associated with houses dated to the earlier and final phases of the settlement, while other choices about funerary treatments were made in the intervening period, including placing inhumations in the ditched enclosure that surrounds the settlement (Bogaard *et al.* 2016). Disarticulated human remains found at Cuiry-lès-Chaudardes were associated with houses built in phase three and five (Parait 2007), two phases that share some architectural features, such as more trenched built north-western ends of houses, more 'rooms' in this section and the appearance of trapezoidal ground plans (Bickle 2008, 198). Alongside the suggested timing of burials at Balatonszárzó, these histories seem very site specific, rather than following a particular and repeated set of rules or ideals. Therefore, this discussion discourages the presence of a distinct funerary practice relating to a specific longhouse cosmology or associated with particular areas of their layout, with burial happening across the life of the house.

Death was not unfamiliar to LBK communities, nor were the dead seemingly avoided once buried. Thévenet (2004) identified a complex architecture for grave cuts at Berry-au-Bac «Le Vieux Tordoir», with the deceased placed in an overhung niche and grave goods placed on a 'banquette', while either the body or the body and banquette were closed with a removable cover that allowed continued access to the grave. Hofmann (2015) has argued that this is evidence that engagement with the body of the dead did not end on burial. This is supported by evidence from Alsace, where Boës (2003, 37 f) identified numerous incidents of decomposition in voids (the body was placed either in a niche or some form of organic container that kept it separate from the soil). In two occasions at the cemetery site of Ensisheim, bones were moved and placed in ways suggestive of human intervention (Boës 2003, 37). At the post-LBK site of Vignely «la Porte aux Berges» in the Paris basin, the excavators argued that a burial had been made in a house loam pit, only for the main bones to be retrieved at a later point, leaving behind disarticulated extremities (Thévenet 2018, 193). While this dates to later than the LBK discussed here, it may be a hint that in its western distribution at least, death did not mean the end of engagement with the body. This discussion is relevant to our consideration of the death and the house, as not only does it suggest a wide diversity of possible burial treatments associated with houses, but also concern with the decay and dissolution of death may have cross-cut the life of the house, with burial occurring before, during and after the house. I would argue, therefore, that for LBK communities there were no specific or codified, spatial or chronological relationships between the dead and longhouses.

THE LIFE AND DEATH OF THE LONGHOUSE

If the dead did not have a specific relationship with the house, were associations with death incorporated into the longhouse in other ways? We can return here, to some of the specific suggestions of Bradley (2001) that the house encompassed notions of ancestors through the north-west end of the house. Bradley further develops Coudart's (1998, 74) suggestion that the north-west end can sometimes be misaligned and therefore added at some point after the central section. These north-western sections were not only constructed from posts, but sometimes marked by trenches, interpreted as supporting plank, rather than wattle and daub walls. For Bradley (2001, 53), this indicates perhaps a more 'closed' section, which he proposes could have housed an ancestral shrine. Lüning (2009, 162) has explored this notion in more depth, demonstrating the distinctive architectural elements of this end of the house, including identifying instances where transverse ditched sections closed off almost the entirety of the north-western end of the house. In other cases, trenches and lines of posts suggest smaller enclosed spaces, perhaps with restricted patterns of movement and separate entrances (Lüning 2009, figs 20–28). Lüning (2009) emphasises the chronological nature of these features, appearing in middle and later phases of the LBK but analogous to the style of the earliest LBK longhouses, such as those at Bruchenbrücken (Hessen, Germany), where trenches rather than postholes mark the long walls of the house. Use of the trench construction method may hence recall earlier LBK building traditions, aligning with Bradley's (2001) association between the house and the origins of the LBK, and making the subsequent focus on trenching the north-west end of the house and a link with ancestors a rather neat interpretation. This practice continues to be elaborated across the length of the LBK, with late LBK houses at Sittard and Elsloo in the Netherlands entirely trenched (Waterbolk and Moddermann 1958/1959).

The north-west end can be, in some few cases, also elaborated through the addition of external rectangular enclosures, such as those attested at Mintraching (Bavaria, Germany; Stäuble 2005) and Bylany (Czech Republic; Soudský 1969). These enclosures are constructed

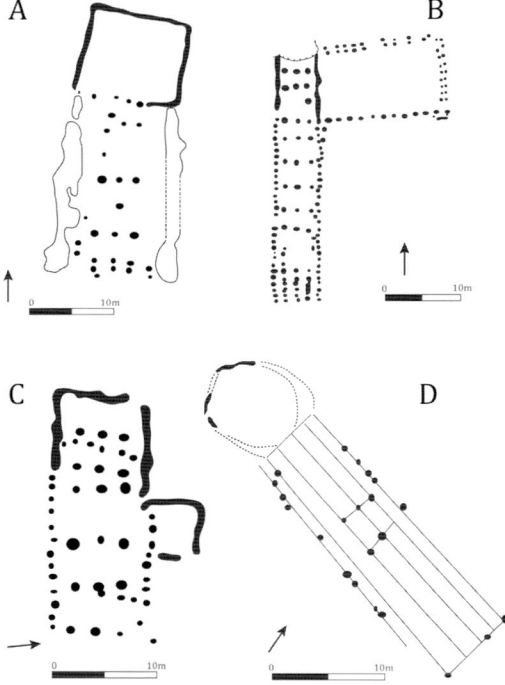

Fig. 5.6: Examples of the additional rectangular and circular enclosures added to the northwestern end of the longhouses. A) Mintraching; B) House 912, Bylany; C) House 16, Elsloo; D) House D, Immenhausen (after Lüning 2009, figs 6, 13, 14, and 17).

from both post settings and ditches akin to house trenches (Fig. 5.6). As the phosphate levels are lower inside these enclosed areas than they are outside, Lüning (2009, 154–6) rejects the suggestion they were livestock stalls, suggesting instead that these areas were places for formal social gatherings. At other sites, Lüning (2009) identifies rare palisaded circular features as part of similar 'cult complexes' on settlements, sometimes to the north or north-west of houses and sometimes isolated away from houses. Lüning (2009) argues that in contrast to the more intimate 'cult' spaces created inside the north-western end of the longhouse, these spaces were for the whole settlement. Overall, there is considerable variability between different forms of enclosure, in terms of size, orientation and construction methods. Lüning (2009) interprets these features as representing different scales of ritual activity taking place on settlements, with the north-western end reserved for house shrines to ancestral kin. Lüning (2009, 170) further supports the connection to ancestors through associations between the ceramic anthropomorphic and zoomorphic figurines (or 'idols'), which in the LBK are exclusively found on settlements, and that he has previously argued represent 'clan ancestors' (Lüning 2005). Lüning (2009) makes this link on the basis of calculating how much of the settlement is lost to erosion and then comparing the number of figurines found to the number of houses, finding a ratio of 1:1 at the sites of Schwanfeld, Frankfurt am Main-Niedereschbach, and Bruchenbrücken. A few bone figurines have been found in graves (*e.g.* Ensisheim, Alsace and Berry-au-Bac «Le Vieux Tordoir», Paris Basin; Bickle and Fibiger 2014), but mainly clay figurines are found fragmented on settlements (Petrasch 2002, 143). Hofmann (2014; 2017) has charted the variation found in LBK figurines, emphasising the fluid and ambiguous nature of their forms, arguing that they were created for small-scale and individual encounters, seemingly also represented by the varied and complex spaces created in the north-west end of the longhouse.

Both Bradley's (2001) and Lüning's (2005; 2009) interpretation of ancestral connections (real or fictive) place emphasis on attitudes and responses to the past, suggesting that it was a vivid part of interacting with the LBK longhouse. These ideas can be translated to the settlement more broadly, by considering the lifecycle of the longhouse. As discussed above, death as polluting does not seem to have been a concept widely adopted by LBK funerary practices, and this is paralleled in the treatment of longhouses after occupation (Bickle 2013). Longhouses appear to have been abandoned prior to the end of the life of their materials (Borić 2008, 127). Although the length of time houses stood for is debated (*e.g.* Rück 2009), recent Bayesian modelling of radiocarbon dates suggest shorter time spans of about 25 years or a generation at most (Jakucs *et al.* 2018). Newly abandoned longhouses appear to have been left to decay *in situ*, with many house plans not subsequently built upon, especially in the Paris Basin (Bickle 2013). Occasional finds from postholes suggest some posts may have been removed (Bradley 2001; Bickle 2013) and overlapping house plans suggest this was not always the case. However, the few instances where longhouses were later built directly over in the Middle Neolithic (such as at Balloy, Paris Basin, see discussion below; Mordant 1991; 1997), speak to houses remaining visible possibly as mounds for some time. Elsewhere, I have argued that unless attended to, such spaces would quickly have been the site of vegetation regrowth (Bickle 2013, 170–1, see particularly fig. 7.7). Therefore, while only some of the buildings would have ever been contemporary (Květina and Končelová 2013), after the first phase of houses were abandoned, LBK communities were living alongside the houses of the past generations.

Coupled with the evidence for LBK settlements being quite 'messy' places (see Wolfram 2008; Bickle forthcoming a), there would have many tangible reminders of the settlement's past inhabitants, present in the material on site (*e.g.* past ceramic styles from potsherds) and in its layout (*e.g.* pathways around former houses). This suggests, to me at least, that rather than generalised ancestors and imagined distant homelands, the past and dead associated with longhouses were rooted in timespans that were on a human scale and specific to site and/or house histories (Bickle 2008). As post-LBK cultures developed, the numbers of houses built together decreases. This can be seen particularly in the Paris Basin, where the average number of houses for LBK (RRBP) settlement is nine, but only four for the post-LBK (VSG culture), with a much larger standard deviation of eight for the LBK compared with 1.5 for the VSG (LBK 12 sites; VSG 15 sites: based on data from Bickle 2008). House architecture styles also change at this point, with far greater regional variation (Last 2013), seemingly losing key elements of the LBK house, such as the tripartite divisions, and shifting the focus for elaboration to the front of the house from the back (Bickle 2013, 162–3). LBK longhouse settlements would have lived on, however, in the landscape, if not always as visible mounds.

In a few rare occasions, there appears to be deliberate citation of these Early Neolithic pasts in the location of Middle Neolithic monuments and houses attributed to the Cerny culture (typically dated to 4600–4300 cal BC: Thomas *et al.* 2011). Midgley (2005) has previously written about the Middle Neolithic Passy monuments, linear ditch and possibly banked monuments up to 200 m long associated with burials, which at the site of Balloy (Paris Basin) are built directly over Danubian-style longhouses. A nearby palisaded enclosure at Balloy cuts the front of two VSG houses along its eastern edge (Mordant 1998), and a focus on the front of the house can also be seen in the siting of a possible Cerny house at Berry-au-Bac «Le Vieux Tordoir», where a Middle Neolithic house entrance is aligned directly along a LBK house, which, rarely for this region, also overlapped with another LBK house (Dubouloz *et al.* 1996). While these instances are admittedly rare, they are not insignificant engagements with the past. Yet, despite spans of several centuries, the postholes, pits, potsherds, lithics and so on, would not have been unfamiliar to Middle

Neolithic communities. Although pot styles had moved on, along with other changes in material culture, much encountered when digging into these sites, would have been familiar, recognisable and capable of being interpreted. I doubt, therefore, these were places of a distant mythological past. As for LBK communities, longhouses were sites of social engagement, worthy of sometimes being drawn on, in both activities associated with life (houses, enclosures) and death (burial).

CONCLUSION

This paper began by asking if burials occurred alongside LBK longhouses because of the broader associations between the house and ancestors, thus rendering it a suitable location for the dead? However, it has been concluded that there were no specific, codified relationships between the house and the dead. Rather, the evidence suggests continual engagement with the dead before, during and after the life of the house, in ways that make it challenging to separate out life and death as two distinct areas of social and material concern in the LBK. Rather than being regarded as 'polluting', the dead were actively part of engagement with the settlement, which along with other buried objects, may not have been regarded as inert or 'dead' (Bickle forthcoming a). The past inhabitants of the settlements and its history were, through older houses and possibly many aspects of material culture as well, always open to further engagement. I have argued here that this was not some distant or mythological past, but one that was specific, known and ever present to LBK communities. The variety of spatial, chronological and material relationships attested across the LBK distribution, alongside the aDNA evidence, requires that we adopt more fluid models of household membership, and the need for caution when applying a uniform or universal meaning to the dead on settlements. Rather than being representative of the past, I suggest that longhouses were regarded as places of transformation – a nexus of identity, among others – across which the living and the dead were variously distributed.

This has implications for how changes in architecture and the treatment of the dead across the sixth and fifth millennia cal BC are envisaged. The typical narrative is the breakdown of the house as an expression of uniform cultural identity as the LBK gives way to the various regional archaeological cultures that follow it, while enclosures and monuments increasingly take on this burden (*e.g.* Last 2013, 269). However, the discussion here cautions against over emphasising the unity of the house as represented by the Early Neolithic LBK longhouse at the expense of specific houses' and sites' histories. Conversely, the temporality and scale of the house may have changed into the fifth millennium cal BC in west and central Europe, but there were still moments and places where the house continued to be a meaningful way of engaging in both the past and the present. I would maintain that these were, as for the LBK, specific pasts that involved if not named individuals, then certainly a familiar and interpretable material presence in the landscape.

The aim here was not to present an account of burial and longhouses as the 'real' background or pre-history to long mounds, but to draw out some general threads relevant to the discussion of their relationship. First, the dead as representative of general concepts or ideals of the past (such as the 'ancestors') can be challenged. Instead, I argued that burial was part of an active engagement with the creation of specific histories for houses and settlements, arising out of local concerns and traditions. In this way, the dead do not passively reflect Neolithic attitudes to the past but (in their treatment) are rather active in shaping experiences of landscapes and houses, and in this sense they are as much about future intension as they are the past. Second, that a refined understanding of the 'past in the past' is possible, specific to different times and places, and this should not be treated as an area of study isolated from daily life. Finally, while the spread of the Neolithic and farming, which are synonymous throughout much of Europe, ushered in new socialities, we should continue to be alert to the emphasising of uniform mechanisms that reduce interpretive possibilities to central narratives. We should take seriously the diversity of practice in the past by acknowledging and charting variation as meaningful in its own right.

ACKNOWLEDGEMENTS

Many thanks to the editors for the invitation to speak at the conference and to prepare this paper. I am grateful to Alasdair Whittle, who commented on a draft of the paper, and Helen Goodchild, who prepared Figure 5.2. I am also indebted to the useful comments from the audience at the conference, which has helped me to clarify a number of points. All mistakes are my own.

REFERENCES

Behnke, H.J. (2012) Siedlungsgunst im Unstruttal bei Karsdorf, Burgenlandkreis: Ergebnisse der Grabungen 2006 und 2007. *Archäologie in Sachsen-Anhalt* 6, 35–70.

Bentley, R.A., Bickle, P., Fibiger, L., Nowell, G.M., Dale, C.W., Hedges, R.E.M., Hamilton, J., Wahl, J., Francken, M., Grupe, G., Lenneis, E., Teschler-Nicola, M., Arbogast, R.-M., Hofmann, D. and Whittle, A. (2012) Community differentiation and kinship among Europe's first farmers. *Proceedings of the National Academy of Sciences of the United States of America* 109, 9326–30.

Bickle, P. (2008) The Life and Death of the Longhouse: daily life during and after the Early Neolithic in the river valleys of the Paris Basin. Unpublished PhD thesis, University of Wales, Cardiff.

Bickle, P. (2013) Of time and the house: the Early Neolithic communities of the Paris Basin and their domestic architecture. In D. Hofmann and J. Smyth (eds) *Tracking the Neolithic House in Europe: sedentism, architecture, and practice*, 151–81. New York, Springer.

Bickle, P. (forthcoming a) The structure of chaos: decay and deposition in the Early Neolithic. In D. Hofmann (ed.) *Structured Deposition in the LBK*, 185–208. Leiden, Sidestone Press.

Bickle, P. (forthcoming b) Thinking gender differently: new approaches to identity difference in the central European Neolithic. *Cambridge Archaeological Journal*.

Bickle, P. and Fibiger, L. (2014) Ageing, childhood and social identity in the Early Neolithic of central Europe. *European Journal of Archaeology* 17, 208–28.

Boelicke, U. (1982) Gruben und Häuser: Untersuchungen zur Struktur bandkeramischer Hofplätze. In J. Pavúk (ed.) *Siedlungen der Kultur mit Bandkeramik in Europa. Internationales Kolloquium Nové Vozokany 17.–20. November 1981*, 17–28. Nitra, Archäologisches Institut der Slowakischen Akademie der Wissenschaften.

Boës, E. (2003) Comportements funéraires, modifications sociales et mentalités aux VIe et Ve millénaires avant J.C. en Alsace. In P. Chambon and J. Leclerc (eds) *Les pratiques funéraires néolithiques avant 3500 av. J.-C. en France et dans les régions limitrophes. Saint-Germain-en-Laye 15–17 juin 2001*, 33–43. Paris, Société Préhistorique Française.

Bogaard, A., Arbogast, R.-M., Ebersbach, R., Fraser, R.A., Knipper, C., Krahn, C., Schäfer, M., Styrung, A. and Krause, R. (2016) The Bandkeramik settlement of Vaihingen an der Enz, Kreis Ludwigsburg (Baden-Württemberg): an integrated perspective on land use, economy and diet. *Germania* 94, 1–60.

Borić, D. (2007) The house between grand narrative and microhistory: a house society in the Balkans. In R.A. Beck (ed.) *The Durable House: house society models in archaeology*, 97–129. Caarbondale, Southern Illinois University.

Borić, D. (2008) First households and 'house societies' in European prehistory. In A. Jones (ed.) *Prehistoric Europe: theory and practice*, 109–42. Oxford, Wiley-Blackwell.

Bradley, R. (1996) Long houses, long mounds and Neolithic enclosures. *Journal of Material Culture* 1, 239–56.

Bradley, R. (2001) Orientations and origins: a symbolic dimension to the longhouse in Neolithic Europe. *Antiquity* 75, 50–6.

Brandt, G., Knipper, C., Nicklish, N., Ganslmeier, R., Klamm, M. and Alt, K.W. (2014) Settlement burials at the Karsdorf LBK site, Saxony-Anhalt, Germany: Biological ties and residential mobility. In A. Whittle and P. Bickle (eds) *Early Farmers: the view from archaeology and science*, 95–114. Oxford, Oxford University Press for the British Academy.

Childe, V.G. (1949) The origin of Neolithic culture in Northern Europe. *Antiquity* 32, 129–35.

Coudart, A. (1998) *Architecture et société néolithique: l'unité et la variance de la maison danubienne*. Paris, Éditions de la Maison des Sciences de l'Homme.

Dočkalová, M. and Čižmář, Z. (2008) Neolithic settlement burials of adult and juvenile individuals in Moravia, Czech Republic. *Anthropologie* 46, 37–76.

Domboróczki, L. (2009) Settlement structures of the Alföld Linear Pottery Culture (ALPC) in Heves County (north-eastern Hungary): development models and historical reconstructions on micro, meso and macro levels. In J.K. Kozłowski (ed.) *Interactions Between Different Models of Neolithization North of the Central European Agro-ecological Barrier*, 75–127. Kraków, Polska Akademiai Umiejętności.

Dubouloz, J., Ilett, M. and Hachem, L. (1996) Berry-au-Bac «Le Vieux Tordoir». *Bilan Scientifique Picardie*, 18–9.

Farruggia, J-P. and Guichard, Y. (1995) Les sépultures. In M. Ilett and M. Plateaux (eds) *Le site néolithique de Berry-au-Bac «Le Chemin de la Pêcherie»*, 157–64. Paris, Centre National de la Recherche Scientifique.

Frirdich, C. (2003) Strukturen im Wandel: ein bandkeramisches Gräberfeld entsteht. In J. Eckert, U. Eisenhauer and A. Zimmermann (eds) *Archäologische Perspektiven: Analysen und Interpretationen im Wandel. Festschrift für Jens Lüning zum 65. Geburtstag*, 545–9. Rahden, Marie Leidorf.

Gomart, L., Hachem, L., Hamon, C., Giligny, F. and Ilett, M. (2015) Household integration in Neolithic villages: a new model of the Linear Pottery Culture in west-central Europe. *Journal of Anthropological Archaeology* 40, 230–49.

Hachem, L., Allard, P., Constantin, C., Farrugia, J.-P., Guichard, Y. and Ilett, M. (1998a) Le site néolithique Rubané de Bucy-le-Long «La Fosselle» (Aisne). *Internéo* 2, 17–27.

Häusler, A. (1994) Grab- und Bestattungssitten des Neolithikums und der frühen Bronzezeit in Mitteleuropa. *Zeitschrift für Archäologie* 28, 23–61.

Hedges, R., Bentley, R.A., Bickle, P., Cullen, P., Dale, C., Fibiger, L., Hamilton, J., Hofmann, D., Nowell, G. and Whittle, A. (2013) The Supra-Regional Approach. In P. Bickle and A. Whittle (eds) *The First Farmers of Central Europe: diversity in LBK lifeways*, 343–84. Oxford, Oxbow Books.

Hodder, I. (1990) *The Domestication of Europe*. Oxford, Blackwell.

Hofmann, D. (2009) Cemetery and settlement burial in the Lower Bavarian LBK. In D. Hofmann and P. Bickle (eds) *Creating Communities: new advances in central European Neolithic research*, 220–34. Oxford, Oxbow Books.

Hofmann, D. (2013) Intimate connection: bodies and substances in flux in the Early Neolithic of central Europe. In C. Watts (ed.) *Relational Archaeologies: humans, animals, things*, 154–72. London and New York, Routledge.

Hofmann, D. (2014) Cast in clay: Linearbandkeramik figurines and society. In C.-E. Ursu and S. Terna (eds) *Anthropomorphism and Symbolic Behaviour in the Neolithic and Copper Age Communities of South-eastern Europe*, 47–71. Suceava, Karl A. Romstorfer.

Hofmann, D. (2015) The burnt, the whole and the broken: funerary variability in the Linearbandkeramik. In Z. Devlin and E.-J. Graham (eds) *Death Embodied: archaeological approaches to the treatment of the corpse*, 109–28. Oxford, Oxbow Books.

Hofmann, D. (2017) Figurines and other bodies. A matter of scale? In V. Becker and H. Schwarzberg (eds) *Bodies of Clay: prehistoric humanised pottery*, 121–39. Oxford, Oxbow Books.

Jakucs, J., Oross, K., Bánffy, E., Voicsek, V., Dunbar, E., Reimar, P., Bayliss, A., Marshall, P. and Whittle, A. (2018) Rows with the neighbours: the short lives of longhouses at the Neolithic site of Versend-Gilencsa. *Antiquity* 92, 91–117.

Jeunesse, C. (1997) *Pratiques funéraires au Néolithique ancien: sépultures et nécropoles danubiennes 5500–4900 av. J.-C.* Paris, Éditions Errance.

Jones, A. (2005) Lives in fragments? Personhood and the European Neolithic. *Journal of Social Archaeology* 5, 193–224.

Květina, P. and Končelová, M. (2013) Neolithic LBK intrasite settlement patterns: a case study from Bylany (Czech Republic). *Journal of Archaeology* 2013 [no volume number] doi.org/10.1155/2013/581607.

Kuper, R., Löhr, H., Stehli, P. and Zimmermann, A. (1973) Struktur und Entwicklung des Siedlungsplatzes. In J.-P. Farruggia, R. Kuper, J. Lüning and P. Stehli (eds) Der bandkeramische Siedlungsplatz Langweiler 2, Gemeinde Aldenhoven, Kreis Düren. Köln/Bonn, Habelt. *Rheinische Ausgrabungen, Band 13*, 22–50.

Last, J. (2013) The end of the longhouse. In D. Hofmann and J. Smyth (eds) *Tracking the Neolithic House in Europe: sedentism, architecture, and practice*, 261–82. New York, Springer.

Lenneis, E. (2004) Ein unvollendet (?) abgebranntes Haus der Linearbandkeramik aus Mold bei Horn. *Archäologie Österreichs* 15, 16–8.

Lévi-Strauss, C. (1982) *The Way of the Masks* (translated by Sylvia Modleski). Seattle, University of Washington Press.

Louwe Kooijmans, L.P., Van de Velde, P. and Kamermans, H. (2003) The Early Bandkeramik settlement of Geleen-Janskamperveld: its intrasite structure and dynamics. In J. Eckert, U. Eisenhauer and A. Zimmermann (eds) *Archäologische Perspektiven: Analysen und Interpretationen im Wandel. Festschrift für Jens Lüning zum 65. Geburtstag*, 373–97. Rahden, Leidorf.

Lüning, J. (1988) Frühe Bauern in Mitteleuropa im 6. and 5. Jahrtausend v. Chr. *Jährbuch des Römisch-Germanischen Zentralmuseums Mainz* 35, 27–93.

Lüning, J. (2005) Bandkeramische Hofplätze und die absolute Chronologie der Bandkeramik. In J. Lüning, C. Frirdich and A. Zimmermann (eds) *Die Bandkeramik im 21. Jahrhundert. Symposium in der Abtei Brauweiler bei Köln vom 16.9.–19.9.2002*, 49–74. Rahden, Marie Leidorf.

Lüning, J. (2009) Bandkeramische Kultanlagen. In A. Zeeb-Lanz (ed.) *Krisen – Kulturwandel – Kontinuitäten: zum Ende der Bandkeramik in Mitteleuropa*, 129–90. Rahden, Marie Leidorf.

Lüning, J. (2011) Gründergrub und Opfergrab: Zwei Bestattungen in der ältestbandkeramik Siedlung, Schwanfeld, Ldkr. Schweinfurt, Unterfranken. In J. Lüning (ed.) *Schwanfeldstudien zur Ältesten Bandkeramik*, 7–99. Bonn, Habelt.

Midgley, M. (2005) *Monumental Cemeteries of Prehistoric Europe*. Stroud, Tempus.

Modderman, P.J.R. (1970) Linearbandkeramik aus Elsloo und Stein. *Analecta Praehistorica Leidensia* 3, 1–217.

Modderman, P.J.R. (1988) The Linear Pottery culture: diversity in uniformity. *Berichten van de Rijksdienst voor het Oudheidkundig Bodemonderzoek* 38, 63–139.

Mordant, D. (1991) Le site des Réaudins à Balloy (Seine-et-Marne): premiers résultats. In J. Despriée (ed.) *La région centre: carrefour d'influences? Actes du 15ème Colloque Interrégional sur le Néolithique, Châlons-sur-Marne*, 33–43. Châlons-sur-Marne, Éditions Associations Régionale pour la Protection et l'Étude du Patrimoine Préhistoire.

Mordant, D. (1997) Sépultures et nécropoles des VIème et Vème millénaires du Bassin Seine-Yonne. In C. Jeunesse (ed.) *Le Néolithique danubien et ses marges entre Rhin et Seine*, 135–55. Strasbourg, Cahiers de l'Assocaition pour la promotion de la recherche archéologique en Alsace.

Mordant, D. (1998) Émergence d'une architecture funéraire monumentale. In J. Guilaine (ed.) *Sépultures d'Occident et genèses des mégalithismes (9000–3500 avant notre ère)*, 73–90. Paris, Éditions Errance.

Nieszery, N. (1995) Linearbandkeramische Gräberfelder in Bayern. Espelkamp: Marie Leidorf.

Oelze, V.M., Siebert, A., Nicklisch, N., Meller, H., Dresely, V. and Alt, K.W. (2011) Early Neolithic diet and animal husbandry: stable isotope evidence from three Linearbandkeramik (LBK) sites in Central Germany. *Journal of Archaeological Science* 38, 270–9.

Oross, K. and Marton, T. (2012) Neolithic burials of the Linearbandkeramik settlement at Balatonszárszó and their European context. *Acta Archaeologica Academiae Scientiarum Hungaricae* 63, 257–300.

Oross, K., Osztás, A., Marton, T., Nyerges, É.Á., Kitti, K., Gallina, Z., Somogyi, K., Bánffy, E., Bronk Ramsey, C., Goslar, T. and Hamilton, D. (2013) Longhouse times: dating the Alsónyék LBK settlement. *Bericht der Römisch-Germanischen Kommission* 94, 123–50.

Pariat, J.-G. (2007) *Des morts sans tombe? Le cas des ossements humains en contexte non sépulcral en Europe tempérée entre les 6e et 3e millénaires av. J.-C.* Oxford, British Archaeological Reports.

Pavúk, J. (1972b) Zum Problem der Gräberfelder mit der Linienbandkeramik. *Alba Regia* 12, 123–30.

Pechtl, J. (2009) A monumental prestige patchwork. In D. Hofmann and P. Bickle (eds) *Creating Communities: new advances in central European Neolithic research*, 186–201. Oxford, Oxbow Books.

Petrasch, J. (2002) Fetisch, Idol oder Kultbild? Zu Terminologie und Interpretation anthropomorpher und theriomorpher neolithischer Satuatten. In R. Aslan, S. Blum, G. Kastl, F. Schweizer and D. Thumm (eds) *Mauerschau: Festschirft für Manfred Korfmann*, 861–83. Remshalden-Grunbach, Greiner.

Röder, B. (1998) Jungsteinzeit: Frauenzeit? Frauen in frühen bäuerlichen Gesellschaften Mietteleuropas. In B. Auffermann and G.-C. Weniger (eds) *Frauen – Zeiten – Spuren*, 241–69. Mettmann, Neanderthal-Museum.

Schmotz, K. and Weber, W. (2000) Untersuchungen in der linienbandkeramischen Siedlung von Otzing, Lkr. Deggendorf. In K. Schmotz (ed.) *Vorträge des 18. Niederbayerischen Archäologentages*, 15–37. Rahden, Marie Leidorf.

Soudský, B. (1969) Étude de la maison néolithique. *Slovenská archeológia* 17, 5–96.

Soudský, B., Bayle, A., Beeching, A., Biquard, A., Boureux, M., Cleuziou, S., Constantin, C., Coudart, A., Demoule, J.-P., Farruggia, J.-P. and Ilett, M. (1982) L'habitat néolithique et chalcolithique de Cuiry-lès-Chaudardes: Les Fontinettes – Les Gravelines (1972–1977). *Revue Archéologique de Picardie*, supplément 2, 57–119.

Stäuble, H. (2005) *Häuser und absolute Datierung der Ältesten Bandkeramik*. Bonn, Habelt.

Stäuble, H. and Lüning, J. (1999) Phosphatanalysen in bandkeramischen Häusern. *Archäologisches Korrespondenzblatt* 2, 169–87.

Strien, H.-C. (2000) *Untersuchungen zur Bandkeramik in Württemberg*. Bonn, Habelt.

Strien, H.-C. (2010) Demographische und erbrechtliche Überlegungen zur bandkeramischen Familienstruktur. In E. Claßen, T. Doppler and B. Ramminger (eds) *Familie – Verwandtschaft – Sozialstrukturen: sozialarchäologische Forschungen zu neolithischen Befunden*, 71–80. Kerpen-Loogh, Welt und Erde.

Thévenet, C. (2004) Une relecture des pratiques funéraires du Rubané récent et final du Bassin parisien: l'exemple des fosses sépulcrales dans la vallée de l'Aisne. *Bulletin de la Société Préhistorique Française* 101, 815–26.

Thévenet, C. (2009) Les sépultures rubanées du Bassin parisien: composition de l'échantillon funéraire et implantation sépulchrale. In A. Zeeb-Lanz (ed.) *Krisen – Kulturwandel – Kontinuitäten: zum Ende der Bandkeramik in Mitteleuropa*, 111–27. Rahden, Marie Leidorf.

Thévenet, C. (2018) Les sépultures et les os humains isolés de l'habitat néolithique ancien. In F. Bostyn, Y. Lanchon and P. Chambon (eds) *Habitat du Néolithique ancient et nécropoles du Néolithique moyen I et II à Vignely «La Porte aux Berges», Seine-et-Marne*, 177–95. Paris, Société préhistorique français.

Thomas, A., Chambon, P. and Murail, P. (2011) Unpacking burial and rank: the role of children in the first monumental cemeteries of western Europe (4600–4300 BC). *Antiquity* 85, 772–86.

Trautmann, I. (2006) The significance of cremations in Early Neolithic communities in central Europe. PhD thesis, Eberhard-Karls-Universität, Tübingen.

Turek, J. (2014) Houses of living and houses of dead in the Neolithic and Copper Age of Central Europe. *Préhistoires Méditerranéennes, Colloque 2014*, 1–22.

van de Velde, P. (1979a) On Bandkeramik social structure. *Analecta Praehistorica Leidensia* 12, 1–242.

van de Velde, P. (1990) Bandkeramik social inequality – a case study. *Germania* 68, 19–38.

van de Velde, P. (ed.) (2008) *Excavations at Geleen-Janskamperveld 1990/1991*. Leiden, Faculty of Archaeology, Leiden University.

Veit, U. (1993) Burials within settlements of the Linienbandkeramik and Stichbandkeramik cultures of central Europe: on the social construction of death in Early-Neolithic society. *Journal of European Archaeology* 1, 107–40.

Veit, U. (1996) *Studien zum Problem der Siedlungsbestattung im europäischen Neolithikum*. Münster, Waxmann.

Vondrovský, V. (2018) Let the sunshine in: the issue of Neolithic longhouse orientation. *European Journal of Archaeology* 21, 528–49.

Waterbolk, H.T. and Modderman, P.J.R. (1958/59) Die Grossbauten die BandKeramik. *Palaeohistoria* VI/VII, 163–71.

Whittle, A. (2003) *The Archaeology of People: dimensions of Neolithic life*. London, Routledge.

Whittle, A. (2012) Being alive and being dead: house and grave in the LBK. In A.M. Jones, J. Pollard, M.J. Allen and J. Gardiner (eds) *Image, Memory and Monumentality: archaeological engagements with the material world (a celebration of the academic achievements of Professor Richard Bradley)*, 194–206. Oxford, Oxbow Books.

Wolfram, S. (2008) *Die verzierte Keramik der bandkeramischen Siedlung Hanau-Klein-Auheim: Taphonomie, Chronologie, Siedlungsentwicklung*. Bonn, Habelt.

Zimmermann, A., Wendt, K.P., Frank, T. and Hilpert, J. (2009) Landscape archaeology in central Europe. *Proceedings of the Prehistoric Society* 75, 1–53.

Chapter 6

The long and short of it: Memory and practice in the Early Neolithic of Britain and Ireland

Alasdair Whittle

QUESTIONS

What were long barrows and long cairns? What were their connotations, roles and meanings in the Early Neolithic? Can they be confined to being seen as houses of the dead? Where did their inspiration come from? And should they be treated as some kind of class or form of practice in their own right, or should they be lumped, at a more general level, with other kinds of monumentality and memorialisation? For example, across even the relatively short transect of south Wales, there are both long cairns of the Cotswold-Severn – or Severn-Cotswold (and in this small matter of terminology hang several weighty tales) – tradition, and further west, portal dolmens of a kind most familiar around the Irish Sea; even within these long cairns there are plenty of differences, and there is a good case in particular for seeing the former Brecknockshire or Black Mountains group as markedly distinctive in terms of location, trajectory of development, architecture and depositional practice (Daniel 1950, 15–6; Lynch 2000, 69). North of this group, there is an enduring gap in the distribution of such constructions in central Wales (Daniel 1950, 27–8), despite reasonable (if mixed) evidence for Early Neolithic settlement. So can these varying monuments, which could all have been encountered across the Neolithic landscape of south Wales from say the 37th century cal BC onwards (Whittle *et al.* 2011, chapter 11), be seen as regional variations on one general theme, or do they reveal a multiplicity of ideas, attitudes and pasts?

These are complex questions, full answers to which would need a much longer account than this short paper can provide. A longer response (and from just the more recent literature, see for example Darvill 2004; Bradley 2007; Thomas 2013; Cummings 2017; Guilaine 2017; Ray and Thomas 2018) would have to deal with many aspects of community and social relations, balanced by attention to philosophical-religious beliefs (Carr 1995), senses of place, time and the past, attitudes to death and the dead, labour, monumentality, memory, and not least the particular historical contexts in which each and every generation found itself (Whittle 2018). My brief contribution here will therefore concentrate mainly on one dimension, that of the possible spans of memory at work in the Early Neolithic setting of Britain and Ireland, with a principal focus on long barrows and long cairns, but with an eye on wider, diverse practices in areas and times where these were less common. I will argue that longer-term memories are by no means impossible, and could have been one of the many threads in play in the worlds evoked by long barrows and long cairns, but that increasingly, as our understanding of chronological trajectories gradually improves, the evidence suggests shorter spans of both practice and memory in the Early Neolithic context. Single, big ideas have tended to dominate the past literature, a tendency which is still being repeated, for example in the recent interpretation of DNA evidence from megalithic constructions both rather sparse and widely scattered in time and space in terms of a single social form (Sánchez-Quinto *et al.* 2019). It is time to try out much more specific and particularising approaches.

THE LONG VIEW: SINGLE STRANDS

The legitimacy of the view that long barrows and long cairns could be linked to memory of the great timber longhouses of the Danubian tradition is itself bolstered by its venerable ancestry. This goes right back of course to none other than Gordon Childe (1949, in turn quoting the German scholar Ernst Sprockhoff; Darvill 2004, 75), and has been much discussed in the subsequent literature (detailed in Darvill 2004, 75–6). It is worth noting that Childe (1949, 135) referred in general terms to 'Danubian peasants', and quoted the example of Brześć Kujawski, which we would now understand as belonging to the Late Lengyel culture in the Polish lowlands of the later fifth millennium cal BC (Czerniak *et al.* 2017, and references). Subsequently the possible Danubian connection was reinforced by the specific, explicit and detailed points of formal comparison between LBK houses and long barrows (using the example of the Kilham long barrow from Yorkshire), as set out by Ian Hodder (1984). The putative link between longhouses and barrow mounds was further supported in a general way by Richard Bradley (2002, 29–32; *cf.* Midgley 2005), citing not only the Polish evidence but Balloy in northern France, closer to Britain, where long mounds or enclosures associated with single burials directly overlay longhouses, probably in Villeneuve-Saint-Germain and Cerny contexts respectively (Cassen *et al.* 2019, 577 and fig. 9).

All these suggestions have chronological implications, which in turn directly affect our view of practice and memory. The application of formal modelling (Bayliss 2009; Bayliss *et al.* 2016; Bayliss and Whittle 2015; 2018; Bánffy *et al.* 2018, and references) is now fundamental for the establishment of both robust and precise narratives. In the context of the LBK, this has thrown up surprises compared to the conventionally accepted estimates of date and duration, both at the start of the tradition (*e.g.* Jakucs *et al.* 2016) and in its aftermath (Denaire *et al.* 2017), but the end of the LBK remains plausibly in the 50th century cal BC (Denaire *et al.* 2017). Now if the Neolithic began in south-eastern Britain in the 41st century cal BC as proposed by Whittle *et al.* (2011), with the Coldrum monument in Kent probably dating from the 40th century cal BC onwards (Whittle *et al.* 2011, fig. 7.27; Wysocki *et al.* 2013) and long barrows and long cairns elsewhere in southern Britain probably generally not earlier than the 38th century cal BC (Bayliss and Whittle 2007; Whittle *et al.* 2011), then a gap of nearly a millennium emerges between the LBK proper and the first Neolithic things and practices in southern Britain and elsewhere in Britain and Ireland. (I note, of course, other views of the start of things, placed speculatively in one recurrent version for western Britain back into the later fifth millennium cal BC (Sheridan 2010a), and in another version involving a significant Mesolithic contribution (Ray and Thomas 2018, 91–4).) That seems an impossibly long span for direct social memory – way beyond the reach of the couple of centuries suggested by Richard Bradley (2002, 8 and references) as the normal limit for oral traditions before they alter or become corrupted. There are, it should be noted, counter examples with longer timescales, including Aboriginal myth relating to periods of lower sea level, European folk tales, and the transmission of Hindu sacred verse (Whittle 2018, 30–1 and references). Yet the likelihood of direct memory of the reality of longhouse living seems very slight.

Overlapping in time with the probable start of the British Neolithic were the last large longhouses in the Polish lowlands. These have been modelled as continuing in use until the beginning of the fourth millennium cal BC (Czerniak et al. 2017, fig. 7). These do not provide the specific points of comparison (for example in the lack of flanking ditches) with British long barrows and long cairns as noted by Hodder (1984), but they do offer general resemblance of the kind picked up by Childe. They were, however, at a considerable distance from Britain and Ireland (Bradley 2002, 30). And while recent and ongoing aDNA analyses have thrown up compelling evidence for extensive population replacement at the start of the Neolithic in Britain and Ireland (Cassidy et al. 2016; Olalde et al. 2018; Brace et al. 2019), there is no obvious sign yet of possible connections with the north European plain (and to the contrary some possibility, still requiring further analysis and explanation, of connections to Iberia).

Closer to home, but still distant in time, the last longhouses in the post-LBK or Danubian tradition of the Rhineland and surrounds appear to belong to the Rössen horizon, which in the upper Rhine has been formally modelled as ending in the 46th or 45th century cal BC (Denaire et al. 2017, fig. 21). I think it is safe to say that we do not yet have precise and robust chronologies for the sequence in northern France, but the Cerny mounds/enclosures at Balloy, overlying Villeneuve-Saint-Germain houses, could well date to somewhere between 4600–4300 cal BC (Dubouloz 2003; Thomas et al. 2011; see also Chambon this volume). As is well known, later house forms in this broad region also diverged somewhat from those of the LBK – with more trapezoidal shapes, fewer internal posts, and much less by way of flanking ditches, but sometimes of impressive length (among others see Hampel 1989; Bickle 2013; Hofmann 2013) – making any resemblance or possible connection between them and long mounds and long cairns less specific and more general.

Another obvious candidate as a prototype or point of reference and memory for the creation of long mounds and long cairns in the later context of the Early Neolithic of Britain and Ireland are other, but earlier long mounds! I still think there is much to unravel and precisely date in the fifth millennium cal BC sequence of the Paris basin and north-west France, but as our understanding gradually improves, there are at least three possible relevant exemplars to think about. Passy mounds – which might themselves reference longhouses – in the Paris basin and now as far north as Normandy (Chambon this volume) could date to somewhere between 4600–4300 cal BC, as already noted (Dubouloz 2003; Thomas et al. 2011). It is repeatedly asserted that the scarce, really big mounds of the Carnac area, the *grands tumulus* such as St Michel, could go back to the earlier fifth millennium cal BC, in a very early position within the Breton Neolithic sequence (Cassen et al. 2009; 2012; Schulz Paulsson 2017; 2019; Guilaine 2017, 69; Pétrequin et al. 2017; Wunderlich et al. 2019, fig. 1). I think it is still an open question whether the earliest dated material relates to construction rather than pre-mound activity (Scarre 2015, 79), and it is still a good question whether *tumulus carnacéens* are likely to have predated Passy mounds (Boujot and

Cassen 1993). Long mounds and cairns in Normandy, as a third possible precedent, also appear to date to the later fifth millennium cal BC (Scarre 2015, 81; Schulz Paulsson 2017; 2019 and references; Wunderlich *et al.* 2019, fig. 1), and thus offer, if they are relevant, a shorter span of memory, though potentially still one that would have been centuries-long. And how to choose between the competing possibilities of references to longhouses and venerably old mounds, both potentially still alive as ideas and themes in myth and story about a heroic, distant past? Perhaps *both* strands could have been at the back of people's minds when they came to build long barrows and long cairns in the varying contexts of Early Neolithic Britain and Ireland in the earlier fourth millennium cal BC.

THE SHORT VIEW: MULTIPLE STRANDS?

Childe's (1949, 135) original idea was framed as a question, and has very much the quality of a throwaway suggestion, albeit one that happened to resonate and stick (Darvill 2004, 75). A very different approach, now that we have much greater chronological precision within our grasp, is to concentrate on much shorter timescales and sequences of practice. A first important clue is the comparative scarcity of other, backward-looking references to the remote past in the Early Neolithic context as a whole. In three well known cases, Ascott-under-Wychwood, Hazleton and Gwernvale (Benson and Whittle 2007; Saville 1990; Britnell and Savory 1984), lateral chambered Cotswold-Severn monuments overlay later Mesolithic occupation, thus potentially spanning a gap of centuries, but in each case Early Neolithic activity also underlay the mounds and cairns, so that it is ambiguous whether the Neolithic constructions directly mark Mesolithic place (see further discussion in Gron *et al.* 2018, 116–17). Conversely, the modelled gaps between activity and middens on the one hand, and cairns on the other, appear to have been comparatively short (Benson and Whittle 2007; Meadows *et al.* 2007; *cf.* Griffiths 2017). The architecture of the West Kennet and Wayland's Smithy II long barrows appears remarkably similar, the latter perhaps deliberately built in a consciously archaising and backward-looking style; a gap of some two centuries has been modelled between them (Whittle *et al.* 2007, 133). In other formally modelled contexts in barrows and cairns, for all the talk of ancestors, there is little sustained sign of old, curated human remains (Whittle *et al.* 2007, 132–3). Skeleton 8 in the ditch at Wor Barrow appears to be an exception; previously shot in the chest by an arrow, this person could have been curated for getting on for two centuries (or more) before being deposited in a tightly wrapped bundle (Allen *et al.* 2016). Further afield, a previous possible explanation of the spread of dates from the Poulnabrone portal tomb in western Ireland was the long-term curation of human remains (Whittle *et al.* 2011, 604 and references), but the final publication comes firmly down on the side of deposition soon after death (Schulting 2014). An early date for the monument at Quanterness, Orkney, is based on human remains, which might have been curated until subsequent construction, but there are many uncertainties involved here (Schulting *et al.* 2010; Bayliss *et al.* 2017). (Other potential examples are discussed by Ray and Thomas (2018, chapter 6), but lack precise dating.)

As a final example, it is noticeable that very few causewayed enclosures are found with Mesolithic remains (Whittle *et al.* 2011, 888). It is surely the case that the examples of southern Britain are in some way derived from continental practice, in Michelsberg and further afield TRB, contexts. This raises the much debated question of the start date for the Michelsberg culture; using the more widely accepted (though largely informally estimated) date of *c*.4300 cal BC, there are Michelsberg enclosures from MKI onwards. Southern British examples probably from the late 38th century cal BC onwards could therefore have evoked much older memories of continental tradition, but the practice of enclosure construction continued to flourish widely across the late Michelsberg, TRB and Chasséen worlds in the first centuries of the fourth millennium cal BC (*e.g.* Whittle *et al.* 2011, 878–85 and references; Seidel *et al.* 2016; Gandelin *et al.* 2018). Once again, shorter rather than longer memory and referencing are implied.

To this general claim, we should add the evidence for diversity. In this perspective, long barrows and long cairns were just one element in a widening spectrum of architectural forms, depositional practice and sequences, and importantly, as that variability expanded, so potential points of reference correspondingly multiplied. If Danubian longhouses were in some people's minds, then so were many other potential ideas.

We know very little about early constructions. If the depositions in Coldrum date the initiation of that monument, probably from the 40th century cal BC onwards (Whittle *et al.* 2011, 381; Wysocki *et al.* 2013), the prominent construction is a stone-built chamber which has no obvious reference to Danubian or other longhouses, and perhaps some general resemblance to megalithic constructions in north-west France; we know very little about the accompanying mound, though there is a rectangular kerb setting (Wysocki *et al.* 2013; Scarre 2015, fig. 6.6). For reasons set out in detail in Whittle *et al.* (2011), I do not believe that there is yet any compelling evidence for other very early megalithic constructions in the west of Britain and in Ireland, as far north as Achnacreebeag in Argyll (Sheridan 2010a). It seems far more likely that portal dolmens and portal tombs belong to a more established phase of the Neolithic, and the probable date of Poulnabrone has already been cited; the date of Broadsands in Devon, however it is to be categorised, appears very similar (Whittle *et al.* 2011, 852), and could have general resemblance to megalithic constructions in north-west France (see also Scarre 2015, 85). Recently, Ray and Thomas (2018, 115; *cf.* Whittle *et al.* 2011, 872) have listed other potentially early constructions, including the Cotswold monuments of Burn Ground and Sales's Lot, the so-called banana barrow at Crickley Hill, and the earthen mound at West Cotton, Northamptonshire, but there are significant difficulties and uncertainties in each case (see Whittle *et al.* 2011), and these candidates need not date earlier than the 38th century cal BC or later.

The more reliably dated and modelled evidence therefore suggests the more widespread appearance of a range of architectural forms from around the start of the 38th century cal BC onwards. In mainland southern Britain there may have been a lag between the first Neolithic activity and the appearance of long cairns and long barrows. It is important to note the differing sequences of construction among long cairns and long barrows. The latter, as often commented, appear to have been closing constructions, that can follow prolonged, small-scale, earlier activity, for example at Fussell's Lodge (Wysocki *et al.* 2007, fig. 12; note models 1–3); there is little specific evidence for such closing mounds in southern Britain before the 37th century cal BC, in contrast to the long cairns probably initiated in the 38th century cal BC, as at Ascott-under-Wychwood, closely followed by Hazleton in the early 37th century cal BC (Bayliss and Whittle 2007). We should also note a tradition of 'diverse and small' non-megalithic monuments, probably starting in the 38th century cal BC (Whittle *et al.* 2011, 724, fig. 14.43; *cf.* Kinnes 1979).

Integrating Poulnabrone into the other evidence for the start of the Neolithic in Ireland (Schulting 2014; Whitehouse *et al.* 2014), there is a case now for something resembling model 2 of Whittle *et al.* (2011, 668), rather than their model 3: that is to say, little or no lag between the initiation of Neolithic activity and monument and indeed house construction. Though this needs further formal modelling, some portal tombs could have been part of this early scenario, to be joined from *c.*3700 cal BC by court tombs (Schulting *et al.* 2012; for a western variant see Jones 2019) and perhaps from soon after that by the first passage tombs (Bergh and Hensey 2013; Schulting *et al.* 2017). As part of this widening diversity, one should also note non-megalithic elements, including timber constructions, as at Dooey's Cairn, Ballymacaldrack, Co. Antrim, there preceding a court tomb (Sheridan 2006 and references), and round mounds, as at Rathdooney Beg, Co. Sligo, and Knockiveagh, Co. Down (Whittle *et al.* 2011, 613–14).

In Scotland, there is so far no clear evidence that Clyde cairns in the west date earlier than *c.*3700 cal BC. Robustly dated monuments on Orkney fall surprisingly late, with substantial stalled cairns in the 35th century cal BC, and possibly the first passage graves soon after (Griffiths 2016; Bayliss *et al.* 2017). North-eastern Carinated Bowl sherds from Vestra Fiold (Richards *et al.* 2013, 173–4), however, indicate an earlier presence, and none of the simplest tomb forms suggested as early by Davidson and Henshall (1989) has yet been properly dated and modelled. In lowland eastern Scotland, as at Pencraig Hill and Eweford West, East Lothian (Lelong and MacGregor 2007), mortuary activity does not appear to date earlier than *c.*3800 cal BC (Whittle *et al.* 2011, figs 14.152–3), and if construction ends with long barrow-like architecture, this was preceded by a welter of post and pyre arrangements. In the north-east mainland of Scotland, though dates for the area have not yet been formally modelled, the indications are of similar chronological trends (Davidson and Henshall 1991; Sheridan 2007). Round mounds in Scotland are again to be noted (Sheridan 2010b).

Although clearly selective and far from encyclopaedic, this brief survey should be enough to demonstrate that there was far more going on in terms of funerary practice and monumentality in the 38th, 37th and subsequent centuries cal BC than the construction of long barrows and long cairns. There was diversity, and many regional sequences suggest that diversity widened with time; given the likely circumstances of an extended process of the spread of Neolithic people and things across Britain and Ireland (*e.g.* Whittle *et al.* 2011), it was never to be expected that a single or unified set of practices should prevail. There was probably a correspondingly broad range of reference, citation and memory. So far, I have discussed potentially long memories of Danubian longhouses and early continental big mounds, as well as long cairns in Normandy and megaliths in north-west France as a whole, which were probably closer in time to the start of the Neolithic in southern Britain. The next obvious possible point of reference are British and Irish houses, the evidence for which at the time of Childe's initial paper (1949) was very sparse (*e.g.* Piggott 1954), but which is obviously now much more abundant, especially but not only in Ireland (Bradley 2007; Smyth 2014; Ray and Thomas 2018). Well dated examples appear early in the sequences for southern England, eastern Scotland and Ireland (Whittle *et al.* 2011), and these included substantial structures in all areas, which could have been good models for imitation and memorialisation, especially if they themselves were involved with lineage foundation (Ray and Thomas 2018, 306). But given the contrast between the wide distribution of timber houses and the regional diversity of barrow and cairn forms, we should not rely on any simple correlation between houses and monuments for a single, universal explanation. There may have been more pronounced but partial reference to the idea of the house in some areas compared to others. A significant but in its way under-interpreted feature of Cotswold-Severn tombs are the entrances and especially the 'false' entrances at the proximal ends of long cairns. For example at the proximal end of Penywyrlod, Talgarth, there was a substantial structure, with uprights and lintel, which appears to have been a monumental false entrance (Britnell and Savory 1984, fig. 4); much of the attention, however, is given to the lateral chambers here, including the impressive so-called Main Chamber, with their varying human contents. Perhaps it is more profitable to envisage a complex mix of ideas being played out in the Cotswold-Severn architecture: monumentalised entrances which could have evoked the doorways of houses, and long cairns, possibly some of them ridged (Saville 1990, 246), which could have provoked images of either the living or the dead house, or both; but also an obsession with layers, skins, openings and concealments along the sides of cairns (*cf.* Richards 2013, 16–23); the placing and replacing of human remains in cramped cists and small chambers, perhaps referring to storage of things in boxes, and in some cases a concern to block or fill up such containers; and a covering or gathering up of earlier activity including middens. This only partially maps on to what was going on in the sequence of activity at many earthen long barrows, and very different ideas may have been played out in the sequences and architecture of the other regional forms briefly sketched above, including large stones held up and tilted to the sky in portal dolmens/portal tombs (Whittle 2004), the enclosed assembly spaces of court tombs, and the varying linearities of Clyde chambers and Orkney stalls.

CONCLUSIONS

Much more could be said about any of the many possibilities canvassed in this short paper. I believe that we should keep as many of these open as possible, in our interpretation of early funerary practice and monumentality, rather than seek to reduce things to a single idea. As our understanding of chronology gradually improves – but with much still to be done to achieve rigorous and robust sequences everywhere – the range of possibilities perhaps comes into better focus. Far-reaching, backward reference to very old practices, in what would probably have been a mythic rather than directly remembered long past, could have been an element, but if so might have involved early forms of mound and cairn as much as Danubian longhouses. Within a shorter past, there could have been reference to the last, but geographically far-away, longhouses of the Danubian tradition, but also to long cairns and megalithic constructions on the adjacent continent in north-west France. Generally there appear to be rather few other instances within the Early Neolithic of Britain and Ireland of references to old practices, as seen for example in the scarcity of curation of ancestral human remains and in the story of enclosures in southern Britain, and so it seems reasonable to look around for more immediate points of reference in the architecture and practices associated with monumental tombs. There are many of these (especially as improving chronological resolution suggests an increasing diversity of practice from the 38th century cal BC onwards), and they include contemporary houses or parts of houses, such as doorways, but the house, though a powerful metaphor, does not constitute the whole frame of association and reference. Many, varying ideas of place, people and pasts may have been woven into the construction and use of the monuments we call long barrows and long cairns.

ACKNOWLEDGEMENTS

I should like to thank all those who helped with the dating projects referred to in this paper, including *The Times of Their Lives* (funded by the European Research Council: Advanced Investigator Grant 295412, 2012–2017), and especially Alex Bayliss and Frances Healy. I am grateful to Alistair Barclay, Penny Bickle, Bill Britnell, Seren Griffiths, Frances Healy, Peter Marshall, Colin Richards, Chris Scarre and Alison Sheridan for information and constructive criticism of an earlier draft of this paper.

REFERENCES

Allen, M.J., Smith, M., Jay, M., Montgomery, J., Bronk Ramsey, C., Cook, G. and Marshall, P. (2016) *Wor Barrow, Cranborne Chase, Dorset: chronological modelling*. Historic England Research Report 9/2016 (ISSN 2059-4453 Online).

Bánffy, E., Bayliss, A., Denaire, A., Gaydarska, B., Hofmann, D, Lefranc, P., Jakucs, J., Marić, M., Oross, K., Tasić, N. and Whittle, A. (2018) Seeking the Holy Grail: robust chronologies from archaeology and radiocarbon dating combined. *Documenta Praehistorica* 45, 120–36.

Bayliss, A. (2009) Rolling out revolution: using radiocarbon dating in archaeology. *Radiocarbon* 51, 123–47.

Bayliss, A., Beavan, N., Hamilton, D., Köhler, K., Nyerges, É.Á., Bronk Ramsey, C., Dunbar, E., Fecher, M., Goslar, T., Kromer, B., Reimer, P., Bánffy, E., Marton, T., Oross, K., Osztás, A., Zalai-Gaál, I. and Whittle, A. (2016) Peopling the past: creating a site biography in the Hungarian Neolithic. *Bericht der Römisch-Germanischen Kommission* 94, 23–91.

Bayliss, A., Marshall, P., Richards, C. and Whittle, A. (2017) Islands of history: the Late Neolithic timescape of Orkney. *Antiquity* 91, 1171–88.

Bayliss, A. and Whittle, A. (eds) (2007) Histories of the dead: building chronologies for five southern British long barrows. *Cambridge Archaeological Journal* 17.1, supplement.

Bayliss, A. and Whittle, A. (2015) Uncertain on principle: combining lines of archaeological evidence to create chronologies. In R. Chapman and A. Wylie (eds) *Material Evidence: learning from archaeological practice*, 213–42. Abingdon, Routledge.

Bayliss, A. and Whittle, A. (2018) What kind of history in prehistory? In S. Souvatzi, A. Baysal and E.L. Baysal (eds) *Problematising Time and History in Prehistory*, 123–46. Abingdon, Routledge.

Benson, D. and Whittle, A. (eds) (2007) *Building Memories: the Neolithic Cotswold long barrow at Ascott-under-Wychwood, Oxfordshire*. Oxford, Oxbow Books.

Bergh, S. and Hensey, R. (2013) Unpicking the chronology of Carrowmore. *Oxford Journal of Archaeology* 32, 343–66.

Bickle, P. (2013) Of time and the house: the Early Neolithic communities of the Paris basin and their domestic architecture. In D. Hofmann and J. Smyth (eds) *Tracking the Neolithic House in Europe: sedentism, architecture and practice*, 151–81. New York, Springer.

Boujot, C. and Cassen, S. (1993) A pattern of evolution for the Neolithic funerary structures in the west of France. *Antiquity* 67, 477–91.

Brace, S., Diekmann, Y., Booth, T.J., van Dorp, L., Faltyskova, Z., Rohland, N., Mallick, S., Olalde, I., Ferry, M., Michel, M., Oppenheimer, J., Broomandkhoshbacht, N., Stewardson, K., Martiniano, R., Walsh, S., Kayser, M., Charlton, S., Hellenthal, G., Armit, I., Schulting, R., Craig, O.E., Sheridan, A., Parker Pearson, M., Stringer, C., Reich, D., Thomas, M.G. and Barnes, I. (2019) Ancient genomes indicate population replacement in Early Neolithic Britain. *Nature Ecology and Evolution* 3, 765–71.

Bradley, R. (2002) *The Past in Prehistoric Societies*. London and New York, Routledge.

Bradley, R. (2007) *The Prehistory of Britain and Ireland*. Cambridge, Cambridge University Press.

Britnell, W.J. and Savory, H.N. (1984) *Gwernvale and Penywyrlod: two Neolithic long cairns in the Black Mountains of Brecknock*. Cardiff, Cambrian Archaeological Association.

Carr, C. (1995) Mortuary practices: their social, philosophical-religious, circumstantial, and physical determinants. *Journal of Archaeological Method and Theory* 2, 105–200.

Cassen, S., Boujot, C., Dominguez Bella, S., Guiavarc'h, M., Le Pennec, C., Prieto Martinez, M.P., Querré, G., Santrot, M.-H. and Vigier, E. (2012) Dépôts Bretons, tumulus carnacéens et circulations à longue distance. In P. Pétrequin, S. Cassen, M. Errera, L. Klassen, A. Sheridan and A.-M. Pétrequin (eds) *Jade. Grandes haches alpines du Néolithique européen. Ve et IVe millénaires av. J.-C*, 918–95. Besançon, Presses Universitaires de Franche-Comté; Gray, Centre de Recherche Archéologique de la Vallée de l'Ain.

Cassen, S., Chaigneau, C., Grimaud, V., Lescap, L., Pétrequin, P., Rodríguez-Rellán, C. and Vourc'h, M. (2019) Measuring distance in the monumentalities of the Neolithic in western France. In J. Müller, M. Hinz and M. Wunderlich (eds) *Megaliths–Societies–Landscapes: early monumentality and social differentiation in Neolithic Europe*, volume 2, 565–82. Bonn, Habelt.

Cassen, S., Lanos, P., Dufresne, P., Oberlin, C., Delqué-Kolic, E. and Le Goffic, M. (2009) Datations sur site (Table des Marchands, alignement du Grand Menhir, Er Grah) et modélisation chronologique du Néolithique morbihannais. In S. Cassen (ed.) *Autour de La Table: explorations archéologiques et discours savants sur des architectures néolithiques à Locmariaquer, Morbihan (Table des Marchands et Grand Menhir)*, 737–68. Nantes, Laboratoire de recherches archéologiques, CNRS and Université de Nantes.

Cassidy, L.M., Martiniano, R., Murphy, E.M., Teasdale, M.D., Mallory, J., Hartwell, B. and Bradley, D.G. (2016) Neolithic and Bronze Age migration to Ireland and establishment of the insular Atlantic genome. *Proceedings of the National Academy of Sciences of the United States* 113, 368–73.

Childe, V.G. (1949) The origin of Neolithic culture in northern Europe. *Antiquity* 23, 129–35.

Cummings, V. (2017) *The Neolithic of Britain and Ireland*. Abingdon, Routledge.

Czerniak, L., Marciniak, A., Bronk Ramsey, C., Dunbar, E., Goslar, T., Barclay, A., Bayliss, A. and Whittle, A. (2017) House time: Neolithic settlement development at Racot during the fifth millennium cal BC in the Polish lowlands. *Journal of Field Archaeology* 41, 618–40.

Daniel, G.E. (1950) *The Prehistoric Chamber Tombs of England and Wales*. Cambridge, Cambridge University Press.

Darvill, T. (2004) *Long Barrows of the Cotswolds and Surrounding Areas*. Stroud, Tempus.

Davidson, J.L. and Henshall, A.S. (1989) *The Chambered Cairns of Orkney*. Edinburgh, Edinburgh University Press.

Davidson, J.L. and Henshall, A.S. (1991) *The Chambered Cairns of Caithness*. Edinburgh, Edinburgh University Press.

Denaire, A., Lefranc, P., Wahl, J., Bronk Ramsey, C., Dunbar, E., Goslar, T., Bayliss, A., Beavan, N., Bickle, P. and Whittle, A. (2017) The cultural project: formal chronological modelling of the Early and Middle Neolithic sequence in Lower Alsace. *Journal of Archaeological Method and Theory* 24, 1072–149.

Dubouloz, J. (2003) Datation absolue du premier Néolithique du Bassin parisien: complément et relecture des données RRBP et VSG. *Bulletin de la Société Préhistorique Française* 100, 671–89.

Gandelin, M., Pons, F., Poirier, P., Dunbar, E., Reimer, P.J., Scharf, A., Bayliss, A., Healy, F. and Whittle, A. (2018) Datations radiocarbone et modélisation chronologique. In M. Gandelin and F. Pons (eds) *Le Rempart Chasséen de Château-Percin à Seilh (Haute-Garonne): une architecture monumentale de terre et de bois*, 83–121. Paris, INRAP et CNRS Éditions.

Griffiths, S. (2016) Beside the ocean of time: a chronology of Neolithic burial monuments and houses in Orkney. In C. Richards and R. Jones (eds) *The Development of Neolithic House Societies in Orkney*, 254–302. Oxford, Windgather Press.

Griffiths, S. (2017) We're all culture historians now: radiocarbon dating revolutions and archaeological theory. *Radiocarbon* 59, 1347–57.

Gron, K.J., Rowley-Conwy, P., Fernandez-Dominguez, E., Gröcke, D.R., Montgomery, J., Nowell, G.M. and Patterson, W.P. (2018) A meeting in the forest: hunters and farmers at the Coneybury 'Anomaly', Wiltshire. *Proceedings of the Prehistoric Society* 84, 111–44.

Guilaine, J. (2017) *Les Chemins de la Protohistoire: quand l'Occident s'éveillait (7000–2000 avant notre ère)*. Paris, Odile Jacob.

Hampel, A. (1989) *Hausentwicklung im Mittelneolithikum Zentraleuropas*. Bonn, Habelt.

Hodder, I. (1984) Burials, houses, women and men in the European Neolithic. In D. Miller and C. Tilley (eds) *Ideology, Power and Prehistory*, 51–68. Cambridge, Cambridge University Press.

Hofmann, D. (2013) Narrating the house: the transformation of longhouses in Early Neolithic Europe. In A.M. Chadwick and C.D. Gibson, *Memory, Myth and Long-Term Landscape Inhabitation*, 32–54. Oxford, Oxbow Books.

Jakucs, J., Bánffy, E., Oross, K., Voicsek, V., Bronk Ramsey, C., Dunbar, E., Kromer, B., Bayliss, A., Hofmann, D., Marshall, P. and Whittle, A. (2016) Between the Vinča and Linearbandkeramik worlds: the diversity of practices and identities in the 54th–53rd centuries cal BC in south-west Hungary and beyond. *Journal of World Prehistory* 29, 267–336.

Jones, C. (2019) The North Munster atypical court tombs of western Ireland – social dynamics, regional trajectories and responses to distant events over the course of the Neolithic. In J. Müller, M. Hinz and M. Wunderlich (eds) *Megaliths–Societies–Landscapes: early monumentality and social differentiation in Neolithic Europe*, volume 3, 983–1002. Bonn, Habelt.

Lelong, O. and MacGregor, G. (2008) *The Lands of Ancient Lothian: interpreting the archaeology of the A1*. Edinburgh, Society of Antiquaries of Scotland.

Lynch, F. (2000) The earlier Neolithic. In F. Lynch, S. Aldhouse-Green and J.L. Davies, *Prehistoric Wales*, 42–78. Stroud, Sutton.

Kinnes, I. (1979) *Round Barrows and Ring Ditches in the British Neolithic*. London, Department of Prehistoric and Romano-British Antiquities, British Museum.

Meadows, J., Barclay, A. and Bayliss, A. (2007) A short passage of time: the dating of the Hazleton long cairn revisited. *Cambridge Archaeological Journal* 17.1, supplement, 45–64.

Midgley, M. (2005) *The Monumental Cemeteries of Prehistoric Europe*. Stroud, Tempus.

Olalde, I., Brace, S., Morten E. Allentoft, M.E., Ian Armit, I., Kristiansen, K., Rohland, N., Mallick, S., Booth, T., Szécsényi-Nagy, A., Mittnik, A., Altena, E., Lipson, M., Lazaridis, I., Patterson, N., Broomandkhoshbacht, N., Diekmann, Y., Faltyskova, Z., Fernandes, D., Ferry, M., Harney, E., de Knijff, P., Michel, M., Oppenheimer, J., Stewardson, K., Barclay, A., Alt, K.W., Avilés Fernández, A., Eszter Bánffy, E., Bernabò-Brea, M., Billoin, D., Blasco, C., Bonsall, C., Bonsall, L., Allen, T., Büster, L., Carver, S., Castells Navarro, L., Craig, O.E., Cook, G.T., Cunliffe, B., Denaire, A., Egging Dinwiddy, K., Dodwell, N., Ernée, M., Evans, C., Kuchařík, M., Farré, J.F., Fokkens, H., Fowler, C., Gazenbeek, M., Garrido Pena, R., Haber-Uriarte, M., Haduch, E., Hey, G., Jowett, N., Knowles, T., Massy, K., Pfrengle, S., Lefranc, P., Lemercier, O., Lefebvre, A., Maurandi, J.L., Majó, T., McKinley, J.I., McSweeney, K., Balázs Gusztáv, M., Modi, A., Kulcsár, G., Kiss, V., Czene, A., Patay, R., Endrődi, A., Köhler, K., Hajdu, T., Cardoso, J.L., Liesau, C., Parker Pearson, M., Włodarczak, P., Price, T.D., Prieto, P., Rey, P.-J., Ríos, P., Risch, R., Rojo Guerra, M.A., Schmitt, A., Serralongue, J., Silva, A.M., Smrčka, V., Vergnaud, L., Zilhão, J., Caramelli, D., Higham, T., Heyd,

V., Sheridan, A., Sjögren, K.-G., Thomas, M.G., Stockhammer, P.W., Pinhasi, R., Krause, J., Haak, W., Barnes, I., Lalueza-Fox, C. and Reich, D. (2018) The Beaker phenomenon and the genomic transformation of northwest Europe. *Nature* February 21, 2018; doi:10.1038/nature25738.

Pétrequin, P., Gauthier, E. and Pétrequin, A.-M. (eds) (2017) *Jade: objets-signes et interprétations sociales des jades alpins dans l'Europe néolithique*. Besançon, Presses Universitaires de Franche-Comté; Gray, Centre de Recherche Archéologique de la Vallée de l'Ain.

Piggott, S. (1954) *Neolithic Cultures of the British Isles*. Cambridge, Cambridge University Press.

Ray, K. and Thomas, J. (2018) *Neolithic Britain: the transformation of social worlds*. Oxford, Oxford University Press.

Richards, C. (2013) Interpreting stone circles. In C. Richards (ed.) *Building the Great Stone Circles of the North*, 2–30. Oxford, Windgather Press.

Richards, C., Downes, J., Ixer, R., Hambleton, E., Peterson, R. and Pollard, J. (2013) Surface over substance: the Vestra Field horned cairn, Mainland, Setter cairn, Eday, and a reappraisal of late Neolithic funerary architecture. In C. Richards (ed.) *Building the Great Stone Circles of the North*, 149–83. Oxford, Windgather Press.

Sánchez-Quinto, F., Malmström, H., Fraser, M., Girdland-Flink, L., Svensson, E.M., Simões, L.G., George, R., Hollfelder, N., Burenhult, G., Noble, G., Brittong, K., Talamo, S., Curtis, N., Brzobohata, H., Sumberova, R., Götherström, A., Storå, J. and Jakobsson, M. (2019) Megalithic tombs in western and northern Neolithic Europe were linked to a kindred society. *Proceedings of the National Academy of Sciences* doi/10.1073/pnas.1818037116.

Saville, A. (1990) *Hazleton North: the excavation of a Neolithic long cairn of the Cotswold-Severn group*. London, English Heritage.

Scarre, C. (2015) Parallel lives? Neolithic funerary monuments and the Channel divide. In H. Anderson-Whymark, D. Garrow and F. Sturt (eds) *Continental Connections: exploring cross-Channel relationships from the lower Palaeolithic to the Iron Age*, 78–98. Oxford, Oxbow Books.

Schulting, R.J. (2014) The dating of Poulnabrone, Co. Clare. In A. Lynch (ed.) *Poulnabrone: an Early Neolithic portal tomb in Ireland*, 93–113. Dublin, Department of Arts, Heritage and the Gaeltacht.

Schulting, R.J., McClatchie, M., Sheridan, A., McLaughlin, R., Barratt, P. and Whitehouse, N.J. (2017) Radiocarbon dating of a multi-phase passage tomb on Baltinglass Hill, Co. Wicklow, Ireland. *Proceedings of the Prehistoric Society* 83, 305–23.

Schulting, R.J., Murphy, E. and Jones, C. (2012) New dates from the north, and a proposed chronology for Irish court tombs. *Proceedings of the Royal Irish Academy* 112C, 1–60.

Schulting, R.J., Sheridan, A., Crozier, R. and Murphy, E. (2010) Revisiting Quanterness: new AMS dates and stable isotope data from an Orcadian chamber tomb. *Proceedings of the Society of Antiquaries of Scotland* 140, 1–50.

Schulz Paulsson, B. (2017) *Time and Stone: the emergence and development of megaliths and megalithic societies in Europe*. Oxford, Archaeopress.

Schulz Paulsson, B. (2019) Radiocarbon dates and Bayesian modeling support maritime diffusion model for megaliths in Europe. *Proceedings of the National Academy of Sciences* doi/10.1073/pnas.1813268116.

Seidel, U., Stephan, E., Stika, H.-P., Dunbar, E., Kromer, B., Bayliss, A., Beavan, N., Healy, F. and Whittle, A. (2016) Die Zeit der großen Gräben: Modelle zur Chronologie des Michelsberger Fundplatzes von Heilbronn-Klingenberg „Schlossberg", Stadtkreis Heilbronn, Baden-Württemberg. *Praehistorische Zeitschrift* 91(2), 225–83.

Sheridan, J.A. (2006) A non-megalithic funerary tradition in Early Neolithic Ireland. In M. Meek (ed.) *The Modern Traveller to our Past: festschrift in honour of Ann Hamlin*, 24–31. Rathfriland, DPK.

Sheridan, J.A. (2007) From Picardie to Pickering and Pencraig Hill? New information on the 'Carinated Bowl Neolithic' in northern Britain. In A. Whittle and V. Cummings (eds) *Going Over: the Mesolithic-Neolithic transition in north-west Europe*, 441–92. Oxford, Oxford University Press for The British Academy.

Sheridan, J.A. (2010a) The Neolithisation of Britain and Ireland: the 'big picture'. In B. Finlayson and G.M. Warren (eds) *Landscapes in Transition*, 89–105. Oxford and London, Oxbow Books and Council for British Research in the Levant.

Sheridan, J.A. (2010b) Scotland's Neolithic non-megalithic round mounds: new dates, problems and potential. In J. Leary, T. Darvill and D. Field (eds) *Round Mounds and Monumentality in the British Neolithic and Beyond*, 28–52. Oxford, Oxbow Books.

Smyth, J. (2014) *Settlement in the Irish Neolithic: new discoveries on the edge of Europe*. Oxford, Oxbow Books.

Thomas, A., Chambon, P. and Murail, P. (2011) Unpacking burial and rank: the role of children in the first monumental cemeteries of western Europe (4600–4300 BC). *Antiquity* 85, 772–86.

Thomas, J. (2013) *The Birth of Neolithic Britain: an interpretive account*. Oxford, Oxford University Press.

Whitehouse, N.J., Schulting, R.J., McClatchie, M., Barratt, P., McLaughlin, T.R., Bogaard, A., Colledge, S., Marchant, R., Gaffrey, J. and Bunting, M.J. (2014) Neolithic agriculture on the European western frontier: the boom and bust of early farming in Ireland. *Journal of Archaeological Science* 51, 181–205.

Whittle, A. (2004) Stones that float to the sky: portal dolmens and their landscapes of memory and myth. In V. Cummings and C. Fowler (eds) *The Neolithic of the Irish Sea: materiality and traditions of practice*, 81–90. Oxford, Oxbow Books.

Whittle, A. (2018) *The Times of their Lives: hunting history in the archaeology of Neolithic Europe*. Oxford, Oxbow Books.

Whittle, A., Barclay, A., Bayliss, A., McFadyen, L., Schulting, R. and Wysocki, M. (2007) Building for the dead: events, processes and changing worldviews from the thirty-eighth to the thirty-fourth centuries cal BC in southern Britain. *Cambridge Archaeological Journal* 17.1, supplement, 123–47.

Whittle, A., Healy, F. and Bayliss, A. (2011) *Gathering Time: dating the Early Neolithic enclosures of southern Britain and Ireland*. Oxford, Oxbow Books.

Wunderlich, M., Müller, J. and Hinz, M. (2019) Diversified monuments: a chronological framework of the creation of monumental landscapes in prehistoric Europe. In J. Müller, M. Hinz and M. Wunderlich (eds) *Megaliths–Societies–Landscapes: early monumentality and social differentiation in Neolithic Europe*, volume 1, 25–9. Bonn, Habelt.

Wysocki, M., Bayliss, A. and Whittle, A. (2007) Serious mortality: the date of the Fussell's Lodge long barrow. *Cambridge Archaeological Journal* 17.1, supplement, 65–84.

Wysocki, M., Griffiths, S., Hedges, R., Bayliss, A., Higham, T., Fernandez-Jalvo, Y. and Whittle, A. (2013) Dates, diet and dismemberment: evidence from the Coldrum megalithic monument, Kent. *Proceedings of the Prehistoric Society* 79, 61–90.

Chapter 7

Measuring up: Longhouses, enclosures or mounds?

Roy Loveday

Evidence of wooden structures beneath earthen long barrows has long been the subject of discussion (*e.g.* Ashbee 1970: Kinnes 1992: Field 2006). This has largely focused upon those features bracketing burials, for which a range of labels have been coined as interpretations have changed. Here they will be referred to as mortuary chambers following Kinnes 1992, and Evans and Hodder 2006. Recent excavation of the Cat's Brain long barrow (Leary *et al.* this volume) where a mortuary chamber was absent has, however, forced closer consideration of the structural role of post lines recorded just within the skirts of some long barrows – in this discussion neutrally termed 'mound-edging structures'.

Such features were first recorded by Pitt Rivers at Wor Barrow, Dorset (1898) where post pipes 0.6 m high survived beneath the very substantial barrow (Bradley 1973, pl VII). They had been set in 'an oblong trench cut in the solid chalk, 1 ½–3 ½ feet *(0.45–1 m)* wide by 3 feet *(0.9 m)* average depth, enclosing an area 93 feet *(28 m)* long by 34 feet *(10 m)* wide with an opening on the south side 8 ½ feet *(2.6 m)* wide'. Since this structure lay some 4.5 m inside the surviving edges of the mound, Pitt Rivers considered it to be 'in all probability … a wooden version of the stone chambers so often found enclosing the interments in long barrows in other districts' (1898, 65). Piggott subsequently dismissed the idea on the grounds that the timbers were too small to have taken the thrust of a roof (1954, 54). Instead, it was incorporated in Atkinson's long mortuary enclosure group of sites, defined on the basis of Dorchester-on-Thames site VII (Atkinson *et al.* 1951).

These were rationalised as open enclosures intended for the excarnation of corpses prior to their placement in wooden mortuary chambers and the heaping up of sealing earthen mounds. Considerable confusion arose over this grouping, however, since the hypothesised sequence and *raison d'etre* permitted the incorporation of any rectangular-trapezoidal 'enclosure' of general long barrow proportions (Loveday 2006a, chapter 5). Importantly, that included both post-defined and lightly ditched sites (Atkinson 1951, 58) despite the fact that in southern Britain these displayed significantly different width norms: the former 10–12 m, corresponding to the unspread parameters of long mounds; the latter 20–30 m, corresponding both to platforms between long barrow ditches and to long enclosures revealed by aerial photography (Loveday 2006, fig. 32). The latter group appear to lie at the base of an emerging cursus series (Loveday 2006, chapter 3) so do not concern us here. The former group, however, have been given renewed prominence by questions arising over the remarkable structure revealed by excavation at Cat's Brain (Leary *et al.* this volume). What form did this wooden trapezoidal structure take? Was it an open enclosure, a house or were the post-lines simply revetment-embellishment for a former mound lying between its arc-like ditches?

In the two-dimensional world of the plough-razed sites that are the subject of excavation today, these are difficult questions to answer. Three approaches present themselves:

1. To compare the widths of timber enclosures under long barrows with those of Early Neolithic houses;
2. To consider the structural plausibility of roofing of such spaces using historical comparanda;
3. To look back at the three-dimensional world of earlier excavators (and at the remarkable survival at Haddenham) in order to assess the potential that recorded timbers had to stand independently.

LONG BARROW AND EARLY NEOLITHIC HOUSE WIDTHS

Developer-funded excavation has furnished a great windfall of Early Neolithic houses, particularly in Ireland. There Jessica Smyth's invaluable corpus (2014, appendix 1) demonstrates that they are overwhelmingly between 5 m and 7 m wide with a slight bunching around 5 m. Importantly, the sites overwhelmingly have evidence for internal, and often external, support posts (Smyth 2014, fig. 3.5). That sizing holds true for the British Isles as a whole, Gibson's recent plotting (2017, fig. 14) showing principal clustering between 4 and 6 m; sites above 7 m comprise primarily the Scottish 'hall' sites (see below).

When, however, we look at the greatest widths of long barrow edging structures, excluding forecourt horns, we find by contrast a remarkably consistent 10–12 m range (81%) in southern Britain, double that of houses (Table 7.1). This has long been evident (*cf.* Ashbee 1970, fig. 27), though being overshadowed by dramatic length variation (Ashbee 1970; Reed 1974) has gone largely unremarked.

In the north of Britain, sites are somewhat wider – notably the latter three in Table 7.1, of which Pencraig Hill and Eweford West are located only some 10 km from each other (Lelong and MacGregor 2008). This would appear to signal the operation of regional traditions. Such size clustering is difficult to ignore. Some form of compelling numerical template would appear to have been employed since it would be very difficult to consistently lay out structures 10–12 m wide by eye alone. Given the commonly assumed conceptual origin of long barrows in much earlier Linearbandkeramik (LBK) longhouses (*e.g.* Childe 1949: Ashbee 1970: Hodder 1990), is it possible that they might furnish answers?

Coudart (1998, annex A), however, records their width range as 5 to 7 m with a large majority measuring around 6 m; very occasional cases fall near 8 m. Bickle's 2008 survey of houses in the Paris Basin similarly recorded an average of 6–7 m (Bickle 2013). These figures are closely comparable to those of British houses but well short of long barrow widths. If long barrow palisade 'enclosures' were in fact 'houses of the dead' it seems they greatly exceeded the widths of LBK longhouses, that had the very considerable additional advantage of internal triple post arrays (*tierces*) to support their roofs.

House sites considerably above average width are on occasion encountered amongst the British evidence as at Horton where site 2 was some 7.71 m wide (P. Bradley pers. comm.). At Yarnton, a complex of postholes (Site 7, 3871) may have marked a slightly trapezoidal

Table 7.1: Long Barrow widths

Name	Max. distance between defined edges (exc. façade horns)
Wor Barrow (i)	10.6 m
Holdenhurst	10.6 m
Fussell's Lodge	10 m
Beckhampton Road	10 m
Catsbrain	10.2 m
Nutbane	12.5 m
Radley (i)	10 m
Redland Farm	10 m
Raunds long mound (gulley)	10 m
Haddenham	11.5 m
Giants' Hills 1	12 m
Giants' Hills 2	12 m
Willerby Wold	10 m
Kilham	10.7 m
East Heslerton	11 m
Street House	10 m
Garton Slack 37	12 m
Lochhill	11 m
Slewcairn	12 m
Pencraig Hill	14.5 m
Eweford West	14 m
Dalladies	17 m

house 11–15.5 m wide (see Hey *et al.* 2016, 52–60 and 466–8 for painstakingly thorough analysis). If so, it very significantly exceeded not only the widths of more convincingly aisled Early Neolithic examples (Hey *et al.* 2016, fig. 3.5) but also the twelfth century AD aisled hall of Oakham Castle; the closest twelfth century AD width equation in fact lies with the great hall of the royal palace of Clarendon (Wood 1965, 45) where advanced jointing using metal tools can be safely assumed. Post depths and diameters at Yarnton seem inadequate for the task whatever reconstruction is considered. Exceptions are posts considered to form a 'central, transverse corridor'. These were set at distances closely comparable to the separation of *longitudinal* aisle posts within confirmed Early Neolithic buildings (Hey *et al.* 2016, fig. 3.5) and alone returned early fourth millennium BC dates. Elsewhere a post hole of the curved western end produced an early third millennium BC date, pits on the southern and western edges of the inner complex, Grooved Ware, cremated bone registered an unusual and significant presence, and pig was the only identified animal bone. Rather than an exceptional house it may be better to regard this as a complex, multi-period structure, fenced at some point in its history.

Close concentration of sub-soil features within the 'house' contrasts with surrounding paucity (Hey *et al.* 2016, figs 12.37 and 12.45) but does find close parallel in a ring ditch (site 7056) some 500 m away on the same flood plain island (Hey *et al.* 2016, fig. 10.28). Since a former covering mound is probably implicated in survival, might this also explain

3871? Powell long ago (1969, 11) drew attention to the likelihood that Cotswold-Severn mound edging was a skeuomorph of turf walling. If so, progenitors are likely to have lain in the Upper Thames Valley to which Cotswold rivers run and where we are faced with a marked dearth of ditched long barrows. Might then the cluster of pits and post holes that comprise Yarnton 3871 witness an unditched turf mound (*cf.* Raunds long mound: Harding and Healy 2007) that covered an earlier house (*cf.* Gwernvale: Britnell and Savory 1984, 50–5) and incorporated or attracted a curvilinear structure (*cf.* Ty Isaf: Grimes 1939), subsequently becoming an obvious focus for later deposits and for a pit alignment that ran from a group of round houses some 2,000 years later in date (Hey *et al.* 2016, fig. 12.45)? In such a scenario rather than a deposit of fine Grooved Ware being made in the centre of a thousand year old former eastern room of unprecedented, unsupported size (8 × 10 m), it could be hypothesised to have been axially placed within some form of now invisible turf-built forecourt arrangement.

A consistently wider group of structures are the Scottish 'hall' sites (Brophy 2007). Unlike Yarnton 3871, they exhibit coherent evidence of multiple internal, transverse support structures based around aisle posts. Balbridie is the widest at some 11 m. Their distinction from the 4–6 m house norm is though reduced somewhat if, working from the example at Lockerbie Academy (Kirby 2011), we hypothesise turf walling linking the disengaged ends of internal partitions (Loveday 2006b). Significantly David Hogg's architectural study of Claish concluded that a roofed 'structure would function perfectly satisfactorily based purely on such uprights inside the apparent outer 'wall' (Hogg 2002). Rather than being awkward components of original designs then, that would have significantly complicated entry to these structures, the outer palisade at Claish and the outer gulley at Balbridie, could mark later phase commemoration or monumentalisation of former turf walled houses.

These structures would then group neatly at widths of around 6–7 m, wider than the 4–6 m of most Early Neolithic houses but with clear internal divisions that had the potential to act as aisle posts, either supporting longitudinal purlins or lateral tie beams (Hogg 2002). That is also true, in combination with axial posts, of the great Rössen houses (6–7 m wide: Coudart 1998, annex B), the unusually large (*c*.10 m wide) post Cerny structures at Mairy, Ardennes (Marolle 1998) and the Late Neolithic examples at Pelchatel, Brittany (Tinevez 2002). At a more obviously domestic scale, the general development from eastern France to Poland was away from transverse supports to a single axial post row, presumably supporting a ridge pole (Last 2013). In the Netherlands, Arnoldussen and Fontin (2006) have detailed movement from such single, axial lines of often irregularly spaced posts in the Late Neolithic, to regular double-post (three-aisled) form in the Middle Bronze Age. In the process, house width generally increased from 4 m to only 5 m. The same pattern has been recorded in southern Scandinavia (Boas 1991; Larsson and Brink 2013).

Within this European pattern of temporally occasional, internally strutted 'great houses' and axially supported domestic ones of limited width (Bradley 2013), some Bresz Kujavian trapezoidal houses are markedly anomalous in being 10 m or more in width *but lacking evidence of internal roof supports* (see below). Apart from an axial post hole at Cat's Brain, British long barrow edging structures similarly lack such evidence. A possible exception is the untested 33 m × 11 m structure recorded by the Stonehenge's Hidden Landscape Survey (Gaffney 2014) that recalls a continental house; even the antennae ditches can be paralleled as effectively at Plechatel (Tinevez 2002) as at Street House (Vyner 1984).

THE STRUCTURAL PLAUSIBILITY OF ROOFING THESE SPACES

Looking beyond the Neolithic evidence at wider but appropriate comparanda, a recent dendrochronological study of proven Medieval peasant houses in the Midlands demonstrated that those utilising crucks (for which there is no evidence in the form of gaps within post lines amongst Neolithic houses) cluster between 4.5 and 6 m in width, while for those of box frame construction the figures are 4–5.5 m (Alcock and Miles 2013, fig. 3.6). Aisle posts were seemingly a pre-requisite for halls over 7 m in width until developments in carpentry jointing from the fourteenth century allowed them to be omitted for high status halls (Wood, 1965, 49–51). The great hall of Stokesay Castle, built in the final decades of the thirteenth century, is an early example using base-crucks (Fig. 7.1). Measuring 9.5 m across it is a useful visual gauge of the required minimum span of roofing if long barrow edging structures (10–12 m across) are to be hypothesised as 'halls'.

The 4–6 m width range of medieval peasant houses not only closely accords with that of Neolithic houses, it is almost exactly prefigured by Anglo-Saxon houses. Marshall and Marshall (1991) note clustering of their widths at approximately 4.5 and 6 m, with most structures less than 7 m wide. At the date of their survey, only five excavated Anglo-Saxon sites had produced structures over 7 m wide. This they explain in terms of 'the lengths of timber available for use as a single (*tie*) beam to span the building, and by the strength of timber when used for this purpose'. In the absence of aisle posts such beams would have

Fig. 7.1: Stokesay Castle hall, Shropshire, late thirteenth century. Roofed with arch braces (base crucks). At 9.5 m wide it is a little narrower than long barrow edging structures (Table 7.1).

been essential to horizontally span the structures and prevent the roof pushing the walls outwards. To be effective, a tie beam needs to be notched as a lap joint to sit across and lock onto either opposing wall posts or onto beams, known as wall plates, fixed along wall tops. This notching, or presumably in more sophisticated Saxon structures, jointing, would inevitably have weakened the beam.

Young ash and silver birch can achieve slender, straight growths of 10 m or so in dense woodland situations but would present real handling problems. The weight of individual 10 m long rafters employed in the reconstruction of the Pimperne roundhouse are recorded as 4 cwts (203 kg) (Harding *et al.* 1993) and they, by virtue of conical construction, could be more readily raised from the ground tripod fashion. Setting the dead weight of a *horizontal* tie beam across a 10 m wide structure without internal support would present particular problems: too slender and the trunk would bow downwards pulling the walls in instead of stressing them against the roof's outward thrust; too substantial and it would place huge pressure on the wall posts/wall plate to which it was attached. Large posts that could have supported such tie beams are rarely closely paired in opposing wall lines of Saxon houses (*e.g.* Catholme; Losco-Bradley and Kinsley 2002). Nor is it possible, with the often irregular wall post lines of both Saxon and Early Neolithic houses, to easily envisage them being capped by continuous longitudinal timbers that would spread the weight; short sectional wall plates would fail to furnish the necessary rigidity. Turf walling (Loveday 2006b), for which light wall timbering conceivably furnished no more than internal cladding, may have eased that problem.

Those Anglo-Saxon structures over 7 m in width that furnished no evidence of aisle or ridge posts exhibit either substantial opposed posts (*e.g.* Cheddar West Halls where unsupported roofing has been ascribed to advances in carpentry jointing: Rahtz 1979, 384) or internal lobes in wall trenches that have been explained as footings for curving base-cruck blades acting as arches to support upper collar beams (*e.g.* Cowdery's Down: James *et al.* 1984). At the royal site of Yeavering, most structures were only some 6–7.5 m in width and described as 'little more than cottages' by Hope-Taylor (1977) yet overwhelmingly revealed evidence of aisle posts. The great hall (A4), ascribed to Edwin, was of a different order measuring 24 m × 11.6 m – comparable to the size of long barrow edging structures. It, however, had very substantial timbers set as aisle posts within and as raking buttress outside, features wholly missing from the Neolithic group. Additionally, its wall timbers were set in trenches that survived to depths of 2 m from the modern plough eroded surface (Hope-Taylor 1977, 60–2).

It is, of course, possible that the hall had been deliberately 'over engineered' as a demonstration of power and prestige (Ware 2005). Great Danish halls of Trelleborg type certainly demonstrate that spans of some 8 m could be achieved without recourse to aisle posts but the verandah posts so familiar from the 1940s reconstruction at the type site can, following excavation at Fyrkat, now be seen to have been raking buttresses comparable to those at Yeavering (Olsen *et al.* 1977). External posts set alongside wall lines appear to have been instrumental in Neolithic architectural developments post-LBK that witnessed removal or very significant reduction of the transverse triple post arrays that had characterised longhouse interiors (Coudart 1998, 83 and annexe B; Last 2013). They are also a feature of many of the much smaller Irish Neolithic houses (Smyth 2014, fig. 3.5). A structural role seems inescapable and their absence from long barrow edging structures is surely significant. The question of the often very substantial spans of Brześć Kujawski Culture (BKC) houses lacking both internal and external supports (Pyzel 2013) will be returned to below.

Evidence from the early medieval period then suggests that roofed wooden structures wider than about 6 m required either internal aisle posts or external raking posts. Edwin's great 12 m wide hall at Yeavering had both.

AN ETHNOGRAPHIC PERSPECTIVE – INDONESIA

Within Indonesian vernacular traditions elaborate roof structures that variously curve up and outwards like the prows of a ship or rise centrally to extravagant heights (Dawson and Gillow 1994) appear to belie the minimalist view of roof width-span advanced thus far. Since they are technologically appropriate to European Neolithic populations, they demand consideration. Note must, however, be taken of environmental context. In the rainforests of Indonesia, the roofs of vernacular structures – extravagant or otherwise – are largely constructed of lightweight materials: *e.g.* bamboo for purlins and rafters; palm leaves for thatching (Dawson and Gillow 1994; Schefold and Nas 2008). This has an obvious bearing on the load transmitted by a roof and the structural underpinning required.

Whatever their shape, roofs of Indonesian longhouses are almost invariably supported by a grid-like, hard wood framework of vertical piles and horizontal beams that takes the load straight to the ground (Schefold *et al.* 2004). This purely morticed and pegged framework, rising from stilts below a suspended floor, furnishes a rigid cellular skeleton within which rooms are created; walls simply comprise lightweight screens suspended from it. Significantly for the current discussion, horizontal elements of these frameworks rarely span widths in excess of 3–5 m. Thus, despite their extravagant roofs, origin/ancestor houses like the celebrated *tongkonan* of the Toraja of Sulawesi (Waterson 2000) are often small and cramped inside.

Communal longhouses are larger. For example, those on Siberut (*uma* belonging to 5–10 families and used for ritual and festive occasions) achieve widths of 10 m or so, and lengths sometimes in excess of 30 m (Schefold 2008). They are constructed around transverse post and beam variants of H frame construction that both divide the house into bays around 5 m in length and create longitudinal 'aisle' post lines. Resemblance to British Neolithic house plans is striking and significantly transverse beams rarely bridge gaps greater than 2–3 m (Schefold 2008, fig. 14). Similar measurements apply to Alas communal houses constructed on the more common grid framework, uprights being commonly spaced only 2.5–5 m apart (Nas and Iwabuchi 2008, 36–7, fig. 13).

Amongst these limited spans (comparable to, or even less than, the European examples discussed above) those of the great communal houses of the Karo Batak of Sumatra are an exception. Within an interior space uncluttered by partitions up to eight families can be accommodated (Dawson and Gillow 1994, 38–40, 49). An example at Lingga studied by Domenig (2008, 58–73) measured some 9 × 12 m between corner posts and typically for the tradition had a huge roof supported by 10 m tall ridge posts. These were seated on a central beam that was suspended some 2 m above the open living area of the house. While this beam received additional support from two slender posts resting on the house floor, companion beams at the eaves had free spans of some 10 m (Domenig 2008, 63–9, figs 15 and 16). Here it seems lies a measure of support for the hypothesis that long barrow edging structures could have been roofed. Note must be taken, however, of:

1. The lightweight nature of the rafters. These were set up in advance of erecting ridge posts and cross supports within them (Domenig 2008, 83). Opposed lines of bamboo lashed at the apex are quite readily self-supporting; dense birch and ash poles are not.
2. The solid base upon which the long, roof-supporting beams sit: horizontal logs mortised into corner posts and lap jointed onto others. The flanks of long barrow edging structures have revealed no evidence of large, opposed support posts regularly spaced to take such beams.

These are serious misgivings, but the possibility presents itself that the Karo Batak model furnishes a structural explanation for the Brześć Kujawski Culture (BKC) 'great houses', that in turn dimensionally and morphologically resemble long barrow edging structures.

BRZEŚĆ KUJAWSKI CULTURE HOUSES

Trapezoidal BKC houses in the Polish lowlands are defined by walls of whole or halved posts set in very deep trenches (1–1.5 m); internal post holes have rarely been recorded (Pyzel 2013, 186) and, when they have, are far shallower (*e.g.* some 0.25 m within house 56 at Brześć Kujawski: Grygiel and Bogucki 1986, fig. 6). Clearly the weight of the roof was borne by the outer walls. This presents limited structural problems since the majority of houses adhered to a modest size norm (Pyzel 2013, 186). Grygiel and Bogucki (1981, 15–16) note that house 55 at Brześć Kujawski measures 18 m × 6 m and was of 'more or less average dimensions when compared to other Late Lengyel long houses'. Spans in the order of 6 m are comparable to those Neolithic houses discussed above and may conceivably have been roofable without deeply grounded, internal support through the development of an A-form truss.

Amongst the large numbers of such houses, however, there stand a few of identical form that are 10 m or so in width (*e.g.* sites 2, 12, 22, 46 and 49 at Brześć Kujawski and 2, 3, 6 and 14 at Oslonki: Pyzel 2013, figs 8.2 and 8.3) (Fig. 7.2). Use of un- or minimally supported A-frames of such spans must be questioned particularly as thatched roofing requires a pitch of some 45°–50° to be efficiently waterproof (thatchingadvisoryservice.co.uk/roof-construction). Rafters at least 6 m long would therefore be required – extremely heavy and ungainly to raise whether as individual poles or as prefabricated roof trusses. While at the roof apex, 6 m above the ground, a ridge pole would need to be tied or jointed to each of the A-frames or paired rafters to ensure longitudinal stability.

The extravagantly long Rössen houses of central Germany and the Dutch Limburg advanced as the prototypes of BKC house, rarely achieve such widths (Coudart 1998, 199–126, records most as 6–7 m wide) and have the marked structural advantages of axial postlines, *tierces* (although widely spaced) and additional external posts (so-called pseudo-buttresses) along lateral, roof bearing, walls. It is possible that some of these elements were present in BKC houses but destroyed by plough erosion, although it is difficult to see why this should have applied almost exclusively to internal features; axial postholes and substantial transverse wall trenches survived in the equally large Michlesberg structures at Mairy, Ardennes (Marolle 1989).

7. Measuring up: Longhouses, enclosures or mounds?

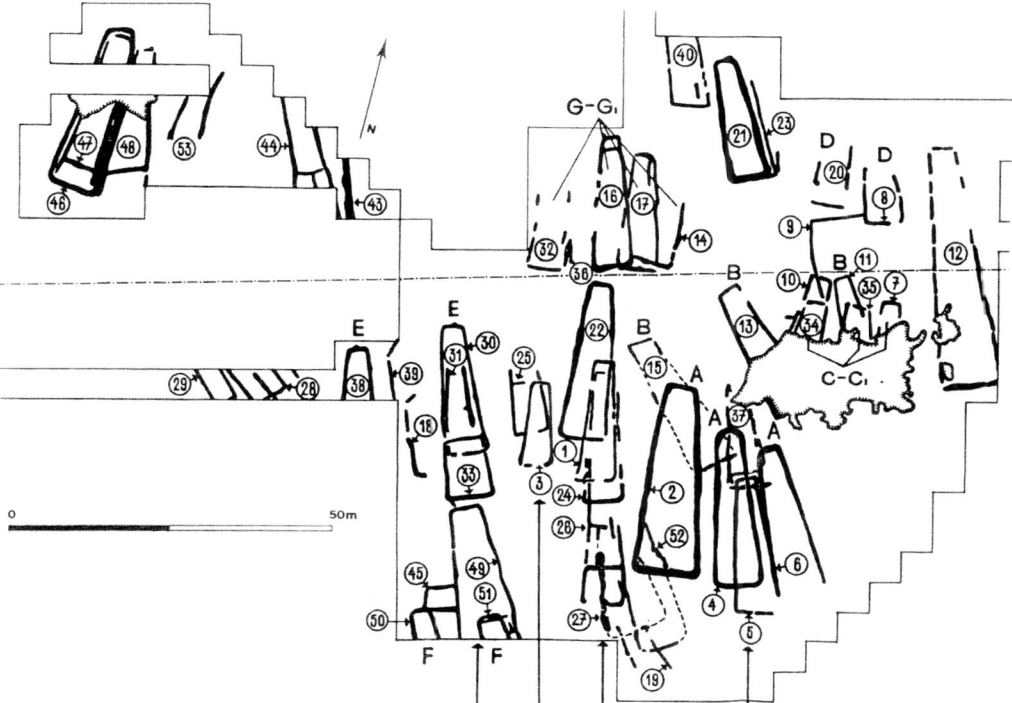

Fig. 7.2: Plan of Brześć Kujawski (after Midgley 1985).

Use of pad stones seems improbable: heavy rainfall, that would accelerate rot, is not a feature of the Polish lowlands, while raising a structure on pad stones presents major problems unless all the elements have previously been locked/bound together (*cf.* Indonesian vernacular architecture). Equally, sill beam construction for inner walls or post rows seems unnecessarily complex and wedging of roof or tie beam supports, unnecessarily precarious. Since elsewhere in Europe evidence of internal weight bearing structures appears ubiquitous, it seems we are presented with two possibilities.

The first is that the larger BKC sites were 'feat' constructions raised by competitive lineages (*cf.* Toraja origin houses) using extravagantly long tie beams. Their *raison d'etre* might then have been short-term event achievement rather than long-term functional stability. Even event construction would, however, appear to have necessitated spaced larger posts along lateral lines to hold tie beams or roof trusses, however temporarily. Such an ephemeral role would also sit uneasily with the idea that these houses were the progenitors of decidedly solid and enduring TRB long barrows (Midgley 1985).

The second possibility is one previously raised by Midgley (1985, 110–1, 208–10) – that some BKC houses may in fact have been plough-razed earthen long barrows. The close similarity of settlement and cemetery plans has been particularly remarked upon (Midgley 1985, 213–5; 2006, 8; Bradley 1998, 46–8) and note should be taken of the virtual equation of Kujavian long barrow widths (Midgley 1985, tab. 2a) with those of 'great' BKC houses. Elsewhere in northern Europe, with the exception of Denmark and a few scattered examples, long barrow widths are more limited: 4 to 7 m (Midgley 1985, tab. 2b–e). The cemetery at Stonowice exemplifies the interpretative problem: six long barrows with 'walls in the form of palisades built of timbers *c*.30 cm in diameter set in trenches up to 1 m in depth' that in form and plan could 'easily be mistaken for … a late Danubian settlement' (Midgley 2006, 8–9). The lessons of the Barkaer 'houses' (Madsen 1979) and Niedźwiedź (Midgley 1985, 110–1) are salutary.

Entertaining the idea that 'great' BKK houses were in fact long barrows would assist in explaining their breaking of an apparently tight house size-norm, as well as the classic pattern of house superimpositions of increasing size (*e.g.* at Brześć Kujawski 'great' house 46 over 47 and 48, and 33 over 30 and 31). Against it though, must be set the fact that superimpositions are not restricted to larger structures and that these, in any case, exhibit a low level of association with burials (Pyzel 2013, figs 8.2 and 8.3). Whatever the case, the validity of extrapolating a roofed hypothesis from these sites to British long barrows must be questioned. The extensive evidence reviewed above indicates we would be forced to conclude that in these two groups of sites, a form of roofing had been devised that was in advance of anything in Neolithic Europe or that followed for the next 5,000 years.

There is no doubt regarding the solidity of the walling of the BKC sites though, and that is also true of British sites like Wor Barrow, Fussell's Lodge, Kilham and Cat's Brain. But how safe is it to project that evidence on to the totality of British edge-defined long mounds?

COULD BRITISH LONG BARROW EDGING POSTS HAVE STOOD INDEPENDENTLY?

The sites discussed so far have all, with the exception of medieval cottages and Indonesian longhouses, come from the two-dimensional world of subsoil features. Their interpretation has necessarily been based upon *plan* matching. There are dangers in this approach: early Christian churches were legitimised by adoption of Roman basilican plan but had a very different function, while evidence of large structural edging need not equate to monumental height as the very substantial, but quite low, boulders edging north European long mounds demonstrate (Midgley 2010, fig. 2). To begin to understand the potential role of long barrow edging structures we need to add the third dimension – to look at evidence of their survival within upstanding mounds.

Pitt Rivers' photographs (Ashbee 1970, pl XIII) and section drawing (Bradley 1973) of his excavation at Wor Barrow show a post pipe of the underlying rectangular 'enclosure' surviving to a height of approximately 0.6 m within the later mound. Both also show that material had been banked up against the base of a post's outer face, leaving a buried turf line. The fact that a second turf line appeared to overlie this bank (that was interpreted as a toe bank supporting the freestanding timbers of an open enclosure) suggested to Richard Atkinson an open site with a history long enough for the upper turf line to have developed (Atkinson 1951). A toe bank on the *outside* of such a structure would though have had very limited utility. Since the prevailing south-westerly wind would hit the enclosure side on, it would have been an *internal* bank that was required. It is clear from Richard Bradley's work on Pitt Rivers' notebooks (1973) that the bank instead buttressed revetment posts against the *outward* pressure of an earlier mound, subsequently covered by the much larger second phase barrow.

A close parallel for the Wor Barrow toe bank was revealed during the excavation of the Beckhampton Road long barrow. It was similarly banked against the base of a barrow-edge post setting and similarly exhibited an upper turf line (Ashbee *et al.* 1973, fig. 18). In this case, however, it could be seen that the turfs were inverted. If laid that way to protect the toe bank they would have been ineffective – the grass would rot rather than grow and mesh the bank together. The gentle concavity of the upper profile of this bank is probably significant, as is its extension 2.5 m from the stake line. It suggests slippage from the mound, akin to the 'extra-revetment' material edging Cotswold-Severn long barrows (Darvill pers. comm. and 2004, 124; Mike Allen pers. comm.). Turf at both Wor Barrow and Beckhampton Road then is likely to have slipped from the barrow surface and lain where it fell, while lighter material ran further out. Collapse may have been quite rapid: the posts at Beckhampton Road were only some 5 cm in diameter and shallowly set – some failing to even penetrate below the base of the buried soil. They are unlikely to have stood independently. Rather, it seems, they closed bays within the mound as these were filled. This probably furnished short lived revetment or embellishment, although, given structurally unnecessary repetition of the bay pattern in stone within Cotswold-Severn mounds (Darvill 2004, 117–8), a primarily symbolic function is possible – they resemble rooms within a longhouse.

Spaced mound-edging posts revealed at Giants' Hills I are often referred to as defining a freestanding long mortuary enclosure but Phillips was clear that these posts were too shallowly set to have stood independently of the barrow: 'The side posts were set not very far into the old ground surface, but probably relied for some of their support on being partially buried in the edges of the mound … they cannot have remained in place very long' (1936, 49). They were probably tied into the hurdling bays, as seems likely at Beckhampton Road. At the adjacent Giants' Hills 2, chalk rubble walling (surviving just 2–3 courses high) appears to have fulfilled the same edging function. It certainly could not have stood to any height independently in order to define an earlier, open enclosure (Evans and Simpson 1991).

At the exceptionally well preserved Haddenham long barrow wattle fencing again edged a mound, and in like manner was considered to have been too shallowly set to have stood independently: 'There is no evidence that a free-standing timber enclosure occurred prior to the building of the mound … in any case, the revetment trenches is rather slight to have held timbers without the aid of the mound and banks' (Evans and Hodder 2006, 74).

No such considerations of structural fragility applied at Fussell's Lodge or at Kilham where enclosure posts were substantial timbers set in trenches 1–1.5 m deep (Ashbee 1966; Manby 1976). Like those of Wor Barrow, these could have stood independently. But neither site produced bone fragments from their respective preserved old land surfaces, outwith the burial chambers, as would have been expected had they defined open excarnation areas; in each case conditions for preservation were excellent. At Fussell's Lodge, Ashbee (1966, 14) was clear that: 'At no point did any layer over sail the bedding trench … in places straight edges, vertical in section, suggested retention of the mound by erstwhile timbers'.

The palisade of rectangular plan at Kilham (Fig. 7.3) is often advanced as an open pre-mound 'mortuary enclosure' (*e.g.* Kinnes 1992) but this interpretation is belied by the fact

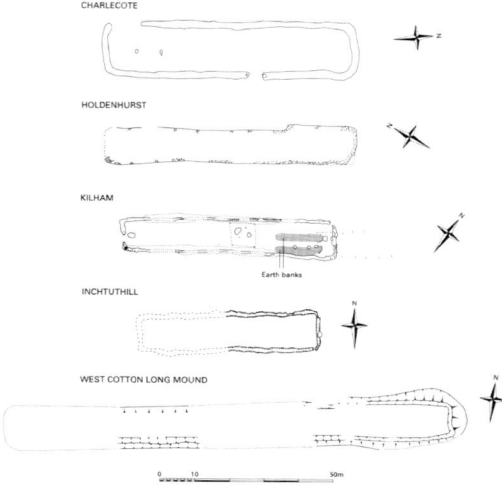

Fig. 7.3: Long barrow edging structures.

that its side trenches had been dug into the fill of earlier parallel ditches that almost certainly edged a low mound attached to the rear of the mortuary chamber. The interior, it seems, was already partially mounded when the palisade 'enclosure' was constructed. Only the area immediately around the burial chamber remained open for a period once quarry ditches for an enlarged mound were dug. That may also have been the case at Fussell's Lodge but unlike Kilham there were no breaks in quarry ditch lines to signal the fact.

Almost identical, but levelled, sites at Inchtuthill and Charlecote lacked quarry ditches and so have been more confidently claimed as open enclosures. Despite this, interruption of ridge and furrow sub-soil scarring across the Charlecote 'enclosure' points to the former presence of a mound that had lifted plough shares (Ford 2003), while at Inchtuthill it is the fill of the 1–1.7 m wide ditch either side of the posts that raises questions. This was notably loamy on the inside but gravelly on the outside (Barclay and Maxwell 1991), suggesting run-off from an enclosed turf or scrape mound. Inward collapse of the burning posts at some 45 degrees certainly doesn't support the idea that they revetted a large mound, but would be consistent with definition of a low, early mound, a role the Kilham enclosure probably fulfilled prior to its infilling; partial survival of a relict soil also points to the former presence of a mound.

Finally, Holdenhurst in Hampshire looks in plan to have been a turf walled – rather than wooden walled – freestanding enclosure later infilled from quarry ditches. But, unlike the even outer face of the turf wall, the inner side was very irregular with patches of brushwood incorporated and tied into the mound. Piggott (1937, 5–6) was clear that the building of mound and edging had proceeded concurrently.

So where earthwork survival has gifted us an above ground insight into long barrow edging, we find that most structures could not have stood independently. And of those that could, the evidence suggests construction in tandem with the mound that they revetted or embellished.

Undoubtedly the greatest potential for confusion lies with long barrows constructed entirely of turf or scraped-up material and so lacking clear defining ditches. The Raunds (or West Cotton) long mound defines the type (Harding and Healy 2007, 54–64). Once levelled by ploughing, palisade trenches that may have edged such mounds will present as either open enclosures or as exceptionally wide houses. Pencraig Hill – that bears a striking resemblance to Cat's Brain – is an example of the first. But the excavators' reference to the planks of its enclosure delimiting a redeposited till (Lelong and MacGregor 2008) strongly suggest the former presence of an internal mound, arguably from the outset. Early phases of the heavily damaged mound at Troelstrup – later delimited by a boulder kerb – paint the same picture and serve to remind us that ditchless barrows were widespread (Madsen 1979).

CONCLUSIONS

The case for reconstructing long barrow edging as the walling of roofed structures is hugely weakened by the evidence of limited beam spans from the Neolithic to early medieval period. It is also based on selective evidence: many sites have mound edging of very similar plan; only in a few cases could these have been weight bearing. In addition, suggestions of minimally grounded axial posts must take into account their necessary height if the 45°–50° pitch of thatch was to have been achieved: 6 m if walls 1.8 m high are hypothesised (*cf.* Fussell's Lodge; Ashbee 1970, fig. 32).

Interpretation of edging structures instead as open enclosures must similarly explain variation in their structural solidity and clear evidence, at Holdenhurst, for tandem construction of walling and mound (Piggott 1937). Commonality of plan argues against selectivity of evidence. Importantly, the hypothesised *raison d'etre* for such open enclosures has been eroded by excavations since the 1950s: Haddenham has demonstrated that wooden chambers could be accessed after mound construction, while bone fragments from the excarnation process have failed to materialise within 'enclosure' interiors protected by 'later' mounds (the lost 'human mandible' from within the wider, and demonstrably *open*, cursus-related, long enclosure Dorchester-on-Thames site VIII (Whittle *et al.* 1992, 148) is difficult to explain since, at adjacent Site I, an inhumation protected by a *covering* mound had been reduced almost to powder (Atkinson *et al.* 1951, 12; Loveday 1999, 50).

Rather it seems that edging-structures of posts, stakes, turf and even walling (*e.g.* Giants Hills II and Dalladies) were primarily architectural embellishments. Why these should have been dispensed with in some cases (*e.g.* Wor Barrow phase 2 barrow; Alfriston; North Marden (Kinnes 1992)) and what their close size grouping and morphology (excluding forecourts) signal, remain open questions. If they were simply facsimiles of houses, why were they consistently laid out to approximately twice house width? Why do even well-preserved barrows very rarely approach a collapse height commensurate with initial replication of a 45° roof pitch? Why were the mounds principally of a trapezoidal plan unrepresented by insular houses? And why do they overwhelmingly taper in profile to unusably low heights at their rear ends (even the emphatically rectangular Holdenhurst: Piggott 1937; RCHM 1979, 68–9)? Complex interaction and representation of archaic longhouse concepts (*cf.* basilican-style churches still built today) and Passy type monuments (Last 2013), coupled to a process of deliberate doubling of domestic dimensions, perhaps lies at their heart.

Seeking analogy for such apparently closed structures, edged in a range of materials and possessing very variable, or no, skeletal material, it is worth recalling the fifth to third century BC stupas of the Indian sub-continent: enlarged mounds, probably reflecting tent/house form, possibly influenced by burial mound traditions emanating from cultures to the west, incorporating apparently minute fragments of sacralised bone and subject to architectural and ritual embellishment.

ACKNOWLEDGEMENTS

I am very grateful to Pippa Bradley for sharing information about the dimensions of houses at Horton, to Tim Darvill and Mike Allen for their thoughts on the 'toe banks' at Wor Barrow and Beckhampton Road, and to David Field for discussion of numerous points.

REFERENCES

Alcock, N. and Miles, D. (2014) *The Medieval Peasant Houses in Midland England*. Oxford, Oxbow Books.

Arnoldussen, S. and Fontijn, D. (2006) Towards familiar landscapes? On the nature and origin of Middle Bronze Age landscapes in the Netherlands. *Proceedings of the Prehistoric Society* 72, 289–318.

Ashbee, P. (1966) The Fussell's Lodge Long Barrow. *Archaeologia* 100, 1–80.

Ashbee, P. (1970) *The Earthen Long Barrow in Britain*. London, Dent.

Ashbee, P., Smith, I.F. and Evans, J.G. (1979) Excavation of three long barrows near Avebury, Wiltshire. *Proceedings of the Prehistoric Society* 45, 207–300.

Atkinson, R.J. C (1951) The excavations at Dorchester, Oxfordshire. *The Archaeological Newsletter* IV, 4, 56–9.

Atkinson, R.J.C, Piggott, C.M. and Sandars, N.K. (1951) *Excavations at Dorchester, Oxon. First Report*. Oxford, Ashmolean Museum.

Barclay, G. and Maxwell, G. (1991) A long mortuary enclosure within the Roman legionary fortress at Inchtuthill, Perthshire. *Proceeding of the Society of Antiquaries of Scotland* 121, 27–44.

Bickle, P. (2013) Of time and the house: the Early Neolithic communities of the Paris Basin and their domestic architecture. In D. Hofmann and J. Smyth (eds) *Tracking the Neolithic House in Europe: sedentism, architecture and practice*, 151–82. New York, Springer.

Bradley, R. (1973) Two notebooks of General Pitt-Rivers. *Antiquity* 47, 47–50.

Bradley, R. (1998) *The Significance of Monuments*. London, Routledge.

Bradley, R. (2013) House of Commons, House of Lords: domestic dwellings and monumental architecture in Prehistoric Europe. *Proceedings of the Prehistoric Society* 79, 1–18.

Britnell, W.J. and Savory, H.N. (1984) *Gwernvale and Penywyrlod: two Neolithic long cairns in the Black Mountains of Brecknock*. The Cambrian Archaeological Association.

Brophy, K. (2007) From big houses to cult houses: Early Neolithic timber halls in Scotland. *Proceedings of the Prehistoric Society* 73, 75–96.

Childe, V.G. (1949) The origin of Neolithic culture in northern Europe. *Antiquity* 23, 129–35.

Coudart, A. (1998) *Architecture et société néolithique. L'unité et la variance de la maison danubienne*. 67 Documents d' Archéologie Francaise. Paris, Editions de la Maison des Sciences de l'Homme.

Darvill, T. (2004) *Long Barrows of the Cotswolds and Surrounding Areas*. Stroud, Tempus.

Dawson, B. and Gillow, J. (1994) *The Traditional Architecture of Indonesia*. London, Thames and Hudson.

Domenig, G. (2008) Variations in Karo Architecture. In R. Schefold and P.J.M. Nas, *Indonesian Houses Volume 2: survey of vernacular architecture in Western Indonesia*, 49–99. Leiden, Brill.

Evans, C. and Hodder, I. (2006) *A Woodland Archaeology: Neolithic sites at Haddenham. The Haddenham Project volume 1*. Cambridge, the McDonald Institute.

Evans, J.G. and Simpson, D.D.A. (1991) Giants' Hills 2 long barrow, Skendleby, Lincolnshire. *Archaeologia* 109, 1–45.

Field, D. (2006) *Earthen Long Barrows: the earliest monuments in the British Isles*. Stroud, Tempus.

Ford, W.J. (2003) The Neolithic complex at Charlecote, *Transactions of the Birmingham and Warwickshire Archaeological Society* 107, 1–39.

Gaffney, V. (2014) Stonehenge's hidden landscape. *Current Archaeology* 296, 10–3.

Gibson, A. (2017) Excavation of a Neolithic house at Yarnbury, near Grassington, North Yorkshire. *Proceedings of the Prehistoric Society* 83, 189–212.

Grimes, W.F. (1939) The Excavation of Ty Isaf long cairn, Brecknockshire. *Proceedings of the Prehistoric Society* 5, 119–42.

Grygiel, R. and Bogucki, P.I. (1981) Early Neolithic sites at Brześć Kujawski, Poland. Preliminary report on the 1976–1979 Excavations. *Journal of Field Archaeology* 13, 9–27.

Harding, D., Blake, I. and Reynolds, P. (1993) *An Iron Age Settlement in Dorset: excavation and reconstruction*. Edinburgh, Edinburgh University Department of Archaeology.

Harding, J. and Healy, F. (2007) *The Raunds Area Project: a Neolithic and Bronze Age landscape in Northamptonshire*. Swindon, English Heritage.

Hey, G., Bell, C. Dennis, C. and Robinson, M. (2016) *Yarnton: Neolithic and Bronze Age settlement and landscape. Results of excavations 1990–98*. Oxford, Oxford Archaeology (Thames Valley Landscapes Monographs 39).

Hodder, I. (1990) *The Domestication of Europe: structure and contingency in Neolithic societies*. Oxford, Blackwell.

Hogg, D.J. (2002) Aspects of the Claish structure. In G. Barclay, K. Brophy and G. MacGregor, Claish, Stirling: an Early Neolithic structure in its context. *Proceeding of the Society of Antiquaries of Scotland* 132, 111–4.

Hofmann, D. and Smyth, J. (2013) *Tracking the Neolithic House in Europe: sedentism, architecture and practice*. New York, Springer.

Hope-Taylor, B. (1977) *Yeavering: an Anglo-British centre of early Northumbria*. Department of Environment Archaeology Reports 7. London, HMSO.

James, S., Marshall, A. and Millett, M. (1984) An early medieval building tradition. *The Archaeological Journal* 141, 182–215.

Kinnes, I. (1992) *Non-Megalithic Long Barrows and Allied Structures in the British Neolithic*. London, British Museum (Occasional Paper 52).

Kirby, M (2011) *Lockerbie Academy: Neolithic and early Historic timber halls, a Bronze age cemetery, an undated enclosure and post-medieval corn-drying kiln in S.W. Scotland*. Scottish Archaeology Internet Reports 46 (www.sair.org.uk).

Larsson, L. and Brink, K. (2013) Lost and found: houses in the Neolithic of southern Scandinavia. In D. Hofmann and J. Smyth, *Tracking the Neolithic House in Europe: sedentism, architecture and practice*, 329–47. New York, Springer.

Last, J. (2013) The end of the Longhouse. In D. Hofmann and J. Smyth, *Tracking the Neolithic House in Europe: sedentism, architecture and practice*, 261–82. New York, Springer.

Lelong, O. and MacGregor, G. (2008) *The Lands of Ancient Lothian: interpreting the archaeology of the A1*. Edinburgh, Society of Antiquaries of Scotland.

Losco-Bradley, S. and Kinsley, G. (2002) *Catholme: an Anglo-Saxon settlement on the Trent Gravels in Staffordshire*. Nottingham, Department of Archaeology.

Loveday, R. (1999) Dorchester on Thames – ritual complex or ritual landscape? In A. Barclay and J. Harding (eds) *Pathways and Ceremonies: the cursus monuments of Britain and Ireland, Neolithic Studies Group Seminar Papers 4*, 49–66. Oxford, Oxbow Books.

Loveday, R. (2006a) *Inscribed Across the Landscape: the cursus enigma*. Stroud, Tempus.

Loveday, R. (2006b) Where have all the Neolithic houses gone? Turf – an invisible component. *Scottish Archaeological Journal* 28 (1), 81–104.

Madsen, T. (1979) Earthen long barrows and timber structures: aspects of the Early Neolithic practice in Denmark. *Proceedings of the Prehistoric Society* 45, 301–20.

Manby, T.G. (1976) The excavation of the Kilham long barrow, East Riding of Yorkshire. *Proceedings of the Prehistoric Society* 42, 111–60.

Marolle, C. (1989) Le village Michelsberg des Hautes Chanvières à Mairy (Ardennes), *Gallia Préhistoire* 31, 93–117.

Marshall, A. and Marshall, G. (1991) A survey and analysis of the buildings of Early and Middle Anglo-Saxon England. *Medieval Archaeology* 35, 29–43.

Midgely, M. (1985) *The Origin and Function of the Earthen Long Barrows of Northern Europe*. Oxford, British Archaeological Reports (BAR International Series 259).

Midgley, M. (2006) *From Ancestral Village to Monumental Cemetery: the creation of monumental Neolithic cemeteries*. www.jungsteinSITE.de.

Midgley, M. (2010) *Who was Who in the Neolithic?* www.jungsteinSITE.de.

Nas, P.J.M. and Iwabuchi, A. (2008) Aceh, Gayo and Alas house forms in the special region of Aceh. In R. Schefold and P.J.M. Nas, *Indonesian Houses Volume 2: survey of vernacular architecture in Western Indonesia*, 17–48. Leiden, Brill.

Olsen, O., Roesdahl, E. and Schmidt, H. (1977) *Fyrkat. En jysk vikingeborg I–II*. Copenhagen, Nordiske Fortidsminder.

Phillips, C.W. (1936) The excavation of the Giants' Hills long barrow, Skendleby, Lincolnshire. *Archaeologia* 85, 37–106.

Piggott, S. (1937) The excavation of a long barrow in Holdenhurst parish, near Christchurch. *Proceedings of the Prehistoric Society* 3, 1–14.

Piggott, S. (1954) *Neolithic Cultures of the British Isles*. Cambridge, University Press.

Pitt Rivers (1898) *Excavations on Cranborne Chase, IV*. Privately published.

Powell, T.G.E. (1969) Introduction to the field study of megalithic tombs. In T.G.E. Powell, J.X.W.P. Corcoran, F. Lynch and J.G. Scott, *Megalithic Enquiries in the West of Britain, A Liverpool Symposium*, 1–12. Liverpool, Liverpool University Press.

Pyzel, J. (2013) Change and continuity in the Danubian longhouses of lowland Poland. In D. Hofmann and J. Smyth, *Tracking the Neolithic House in Europe: sedentism, architecture and practice*, 183–96. New York, Springer.

Rahtz, P. (1979) *The Saxon and Medieval Palaces at Cheddar: excavations 1960–62*. Oxford, British Archaeological Reports (BAR British Series 65).

Reed, R.C. (1974) Earthen long barrows: a new perspective. *Archaeological Journal* 131, 33–57.

RCHME (1979) *Long Barrows in Hampshire and the Isle of Wight*. London, HMSO.

Schefold, R. and Nas, P.J.M. (2008) *Indonesian Houses Volume 2: survey of vernacular architecture in Western Indonesia*. Leiden, Brill.

Schefold, R. (2008) The house as group. Traditional dwellings on Siberut, Mentawai. In R. Schefold and P.J.M. Nas, *Indonesian Houses Volume 2: survey of vernacular architecture in Western Indonesia*, 145–74. Leiden, Brill.

Schefold, R., Domenig, G. and Nas, P. (2004) *Indonesian Houses: tradition and transformation in vernacular architecture*. Singapore, University Press.

Smyth, J. (2014) *Settlement in the Irish Neolithic: new discoveries on the edge of Europe*. Prehistoric Society Research Paper 6. Oxford, Oxbow Books.

Tinevez, J-Y (2002) The Late Neolithic settlement of La Heronnais, Pléchatel in its regional context. In G. Varndell and P. Topping (eds) *Enclosures in Neolithic Europe: essays on causewayed and non-causewayed sites*, 37–50. Oxford, Oxbow Books.

Vyner, B. (1984) The excavation of a Neolithic cairn at Street House, Loftus, Cleveland. *Proceedings of the Prehistoric Society* 50, 151–95.

Ware, C. (2005) The social use of space at *Gefrin*. In P. Frodsham and C. O'Brien (eds) *Yeavering. People, Power and Place*. Stroud, History Press.

Waterson, R. (2000) House, place and memory in Tana Toraja (Indonesia). In R.A. Joyce and S.D. Gillespie (eds) *Beyond Kinship. Social and Material Reproduction in House Societies*, 177–88. Philadelphia, University of Pennsylvania Press.

Whittle, A., Atkinson, R.J.C., Chambers, R. and Thomas, N. (1992) Excavations at the Neolithic and Bronze Age complex at Dorchester-on-Thames, Oxfordshire, 1947–1952 and 1981. *Proceedings of the Prehistoric Society* 58, 143–201.

Wood, M. (1965) *The English Medieval House*. London, Bracken Books.

Chapter 8

Houses foundational: Gathering histories at Dorstone Hill, Herefordshire

Keith Ray and Julian Thomas

One way to think about Neolithic monuments is to regard them as a form of material narrative, in the sense that they represented the tangible embodiment of a community's collective history. For pre-literate societies, architecture has often served as a reminder of a shared past, and in this way as a means of reaffirming and consolidating traditions, identities and social relationships (Duly 1979, 22). Houses, shrines, temples and tombs can all act as repositories of memory and foci of communal belonging (Helms 1998, 14). Across Neolithic Europe, however, the construction of some groups of monuments was both episodic and sequential in character, composed of a series of events which might individually have been of brief duration, but which were played out over a protracted period of time (*e.g.* Müller *et al.* 2014). Each of these events might have been connected with a significant happening in the life of its host community: the death of a leader, a memorable feast, an important marriage, a spectacular exchange of goods, or the creation of an alliance. Such structures and complexes therefore developed incrementally, as a series of material additions or transformations that corresponded with a kind of story, in which each new element responded to, and potentially transformed the significance of, whatever had come before. The outcome was a tangible accumulation, and an intricate layering of activity across time, that embodied a shared past, and in doing so facilitated future acts of remembering and telling.

A case in point is provided by Dorstone Hill in Herefordshire, located just inside the English border with Wales, on a spur extending from a narrow upland watershed between the rivers Wye and Dore. Here, we have been conducting excavations over the past eight years (Fig. 8.1), on a site that has long been known for surface concentrations of Mesolithic and Neolithic flintwork, and which had been subjected to small-scale investigations by Roger Pye and Christopher Houlder in the 1960s (Pye 1967; 1968; 1969). More recently, measured analytical field survey conducted by English Heritage drew attention to a low bank that ran across the modern field, at the narrow point where the hilltop becomes linked with the escarpment (Oswald *et al.* 2001, 64). At that time, it was conjectured that a ditch might complement that bank on its northern side, and it seemed possible that Dorstone Hill had been closed off by a continuous rampart. Arguably, such a site might have been comparable with the final phase of the Early Neolithic enclosure at Crickley Hill in Gloucestershire, where a series of phases of interrupted ditch were eventually replaced by a more substantial set of defences (Dixon 1988). At Crickley Hill too, an enclosed promontory overlooked an expanse of lowland. However, the lidar plots for the Dorstone area reveal that the 'bank' was not a

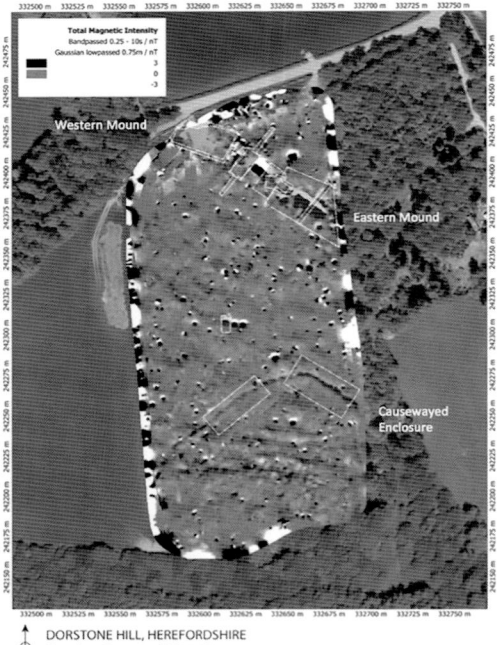

Fig. 8.1: Dorstone Hill, Herefordshire: areas excavated, 2011–18, superimposed on magnetometer survey (background plan courtesy Martin Roseveare, TigerGeo).

continuous feature, but was interrupted in two places, leaving three separate linear mounds, arranged end to end. Excavations since 2011 have demonstrated that no ditch exists, while local residents have reported that the mounds were substantial upstanding features until bulldozing took place during the 1940s, when land was being taken in for ploughing under wartime conditions.

Our own investigations have demonstrated that these structures were Neolithic long barrows, and the arrangement of linear monuments in alignment is not without precedent, whether in the case of the long mounds associated with the Dorset Cursus (Barrett *et al.* 1991, 50), or that of the cursus monuments and mortuary enclosure at Manor Farm, Old Wolverton (Hogan 2013, 2). The status of the mounds as three separate features is emphasised by the distinctiveness of the construction of each. What they have in common is that each mound has as its core a mass of brightly orange-coloured clayey material, much of which appears to have consisted of daub (including some form of binding agent, most likely cow-dung: Mike Allen pers. comm., July 2014). This seems to have been burned at a temperature in excess of 600°C, to judge from the resulting thermo-remanent magnetism. The burning shows up vividly as distinct patches on both magnetometer and magnetic susceptibility survey, again emphasising the discreteness of the three mounds. This intensely burned material was found to contain numerous lengths of charred, apparently structural, timbers. This provided a first clue that the burnt clay and daub might represent the debris of a number of former buildings. The material had in each case apparently been shovelled up to form a narrow, rectangular heap and this had been cut back on each of the long sides to a regular vertical face. The spade cut from this operation could be observed in section, descending into the underlying subsoil. Turf had then been stacked against the cut face, encapsulating the daub core and forming the bulk of each long mound.

THE TIMBER BUILDINGS

We consider that the best explanation for this evidence is that each of the three long barrows was raised on the footprint of what had previously been a timber-framed building, and which had in each case been deliberately destroyed by fire. The suite of 11 radiocarbon dates that has been acquired for the site so far places the construction of the long mounds in the middle of the 38th century BC, and the buildings somewhat earlier, perhaps in the late 39th or early 38th century. It is anticipated that the acquisition of further dates and the construction of Bayesian models for the site will further enhance the precision of this chronology. However, in this temporal horizon substantial wood and daub structures are most likely to belong to the halls or houses which represent a distinctive feature of the primary Neolithic on the British mainland, and which in a number of cases appear to have been deliberately destroyed by fire (Barclay and Harris 2018). Aside from the surface lithic concentrations noted above, there is as yet no evidence for any significant activity on the hilltop before the construction of these buildings, and it seems likely that this represented a powerful statement of inception or foundation. This might in each case have involved the coalescence and binding together of a new community, or the establishment of a new and powerful leader, with whom the house or hall concerned might have been associated. Elsewhere, we have emphasised the connection between 'housebuilding' and the formation of new social units at a time of fundamental change in the opening centuries of the Neolithic (Ray and Thomas 2018, 105). Our argument here will be that the social implications of such an event lent Dorstone Hill an enduring importance, tied to the origins and identities of specific descent groups.

The construction of tombs and barrows over the remains of 'houses' (broadly defined) is a recurring theme in the archaeology of Neolithic Europe. For instance, Rzepecki (2011, 208) describes the way that Linearbandkeramik longhouses in Poland were transformed after they fell into decrepitude into rectilinear enclosures containing graves. Similarly, at Balloy on the Seine, a cluster of longhouses of the Villeneuve-St-Germain group were replaced on the same locations by long mortuary enclosures in the succeeding Cerny phase. Nearby was a causewayed-ditched enclosure, also of Cerny date, and the similarity of this complex with that at Dorstone will soon become apparent (Chambon and Mordant 1996, 396). In Ireland, a rectangular timber house was revealed beneath the dual-court tomb of Ballyglass in Co. Mayo (Ó Nualláin 1972, 54), while closer to Herefordshire, at Gwernvale in the Black Mountains of Wales, a rectilinear structure composed of postholes and beam-slots was found beneath the forecourt of a long cairn (Britnell and Savory 1984, 50–4; figs 13 and 14). At each of these sites, a 'house of the living' was replaced by or converted into a 'house of the dead'. Such a process necessarily involves a combination of continuity and change. Houses and halls are structures that are often associated with a founding personage or group, and that become freighted with memory through the accumulation of both significant events and habitual, everyday conduct. Such a building achieves a status as a 'place of the ancestors' as it continues to be dwelt in or visited over the generations. When a house is replaced by (or converted into) a tomb, it remains a place at which people gather for acts of remembrance, but the focus may narrow toward the explicit veneration of the past and/or the dead (Kirch 2000, 104). Physical changes, in which structures become more durable and conspicuous, but less practicable, may reflect this transformation.

At Dorstone Hill, what remained to the present day of the three timber buildings had been damaged by their destruction, the subsequent construction of the long barrows on top of them, the robbing of the site for stone in the medieval or early modern period, and the bulldozing of the site mentioned above. As a consequence, their traces were somewhat fragmentary. However, enough remained for us to be able to demonstrate that although all three had been treated in similar ways, they had not been architecturally uniform to begin with. The westernmost structure revealed traces of substantial load-bearing post-rows, outer walls, internal partitions and a linear depression down the central axial line of the building. This had perhaps been worn into an earthen floor by repeated footfall, going to and from the entrance. In terms of size (at approximately 20 m × 14 m), internal organisation and orientation this structure is considered to be closely similar to the Early Neolithic building at Yarnton in Oxfordshire (Hey *et al.* 2016, 51). If anything, however, the Dorstone example is somewhat more massive and 'overengineered' than that at Yarnton, with the major postholes being particularly large.

By contrast, the traces of the eastern building involved few subsoil features. The burnt daub deposit had been neatly squared off and contained eight surviving pieces of charred planks. These pieces covered an area approximately 9 by 3 m and, given that the clearly-visible grain of the timber in each case shared the same east–west orientation (in line with the deduced roof-line of the former standing building), are interpreted as the vestiges of a massive (probably) oaken floor. Individual uprights were found set within and perpendicular to the timber flooring slabs, descending into cut sockets. These may have framed divisions within the structure or may have supported the planking as a suspended wooden floor. The extent of the burning and daub debris east–west indicates that this building was at least 18 m long, but its exact width could not be determined. Given the absence of definite earth-fast posts the building had possibly been an entirely box-framed structure held in place by the combined weight of the timber of its superstructure and floor. However, the precise character of the superstructure of this building was difficult to ascertain, since in this part of the excavated area the topsoil gave way immediately onto the perhaps deliberately levelled sandstone bedrock, and any cut features may have been lost to erosion.

Between these two buildings a third hall or house had been raised. This comprised a central aisle defined by paired aisle-posts spaced around 8 m apart, with two flanking aisles each of around 2 m width, with the outer side of each apparently marked by a post-in-trench wall. Traces were found of at least two internal partitions (represented by carbonised vertical stakes) marking out bays within the aisles. This building was approximately 18 m long from gable to gable. The interiors of the burnt timbers sealed within the daub matrix of this structure had mineralised, but the charred outer surfaces enabled details such as the forms of primitive cruck members or braces, rafter-poles and at least one mortice-hole in a larger timber to be recorded.

The construction and ostentatious destruction of these three buildings, in a highly conspicuous location, must have had a strongly performative character. The summit of Dorstone Hill is visible over a very wide area, ranging from the Clee Hills of Shropshire in the north to the Black Mountains to the south-west. These were events that would have been witnessed by significant numbers of people, particularly when we consider that the structures must have burned through the night and featured as smouldering smoke-producing remains perhaps over several days. Such dramatic episodes would likely have entered into the oral traditions of the local social groups. When the burnt residues of the buildings were shovelled together and formed into the nuclei of the long mounds, it is arguable that what was being celebrated was not just a group of dead ancestors but the 'houses' themselves, not only as former physical structures of a novel kind, but as the familial descent groups whose corporate identity had been brought into existence with and through those structures. In this sense, we might say that each mound was a 'tomb of the house', encapsulating both the remains of a structure and the history that it embodied. For this reason, the architectural diversity of the Dorstone halls is potentially of considerable significance. If each represented a different set of constructional conventions, it is conceivable that they were created by different social units, or different elements within a single society. It may indeed be proposed relatedly that the markedly different forms of construction of the three buildings was a deliberate manipulation of built form specifically in order to signal differentiation between these distinct social entities. Moreover, if, from the start of the Neolithic, Dorstone Hill was a place where a number of communities were periodically coming together to form a greater unity, this might have anticipated the presence of the causewayed enclosure on the hilltop, generations later.

THE LONG MOUNDS

The distinctiveness of the build forms of each of the three houses appears to have been carried over to the sustaining of difference in the form of the successor barrows constructed over the building footprints. The turf of the central mound was found to have been revetted by a timber palisade, which contained a series of distinct post-pipes, and which plausibly may have re-used the former wall-line of the underlying building. This palisade then rotted and collapsed before a loose stone cairn was mounded over the remaining barrow, into which a number of stone cists were later inserted. The cairn extended beyond the ends of the original turf mound, and appeared to join the three mounds together, creating an unbroken envelope, although one within which three distinct mounds would still have been discernable. The cists were concentrated on the northern side of the mound, facing toward the Wye Valley, and generally did not encroach on the area containing the burnt building debris. One of the cists contained a fine leaf-shaped flint arrowhead, which appeared to have been made on a flake from an axe, and which had a missing tip and a clear impact fracture. The soil in this part of the site is highly acidic, and unburned bone does not survive, but it is possible that the arrowhead had entered the cist in a human body, or fragment thereof.

The western mound, by contrast, was contained within an upright dry-stone wall, onto which a series of cellular stone buttresses were attached (Fig. 8.2). On the southern side of the mound this wall was missing, and a massive rob trench demonstrated that the stone had been removed, presumably in medieval or early modern times. A series of nebulous stone features in this part of the site appear to have been connected with this later activity. The buttresses were concentrated on the eastern end of the mound, and at the terminal two separate 'loops' of walling can be discerned. This has the effect of enhancing the trapezoidal form of the mound, echoing the layout of the underlying building. The cellular character of these buttress structures is remarkably similar to the internal architecture of some Cotswold-Severn long cairns, such as Hazleton North in Gloucestershire (Saville 1990, 32). Yet rather than forming the stabilising internal skeleton of the mound, the walls of the Dorstone western mound were added around the periphery, perhaps again emphasising that the burnt daub core was the heart of the structure and was to be left undisturbed. Significantly, a group of these long cairns are located not far from Dorstone, in the Black

Fig. 8.2: The western mound, Dorstone Hill, under excavation in 2014 (photo: Adam Stanford, Aerial-Cam).

Mountains, while the tomb of Arthur's Stone, with its massive capstone, also probably belongs to this tradition (Corcoran 1969, 21; Darvill 2004, 86; Ray 2015, 55). Despite these evident affinities, the western mound had no orthostatic chamber set in its terminal, nor did it have cists deep in the mound, accessed by megalithic passages. Instead, a small stone chamber was set immediately into the side of the monument, keyed into the outer wall, its vertically-set slab-like orthostats that defined the rear of the chamber having been visibly truncated by the action of the bulldozer. Once again, it appears that the deposit of burnt building debris was deliberately being conserved, for no chamber was allowed to cut into it.

The eastern mound was different again (Fig. 8.3). Here there was neither a palisade-like revetment nor a retaining stone wall, and the burnt building deposit represented a clearly defined rectangle surrounded by turf. The mound was capped by a cairn of substantial stones, and a terrace had been cut along the northern side of the mound to receive this cairn. At the western end of the barrow a linear timber mortuary structure had stood, bracketed by two massive postholes. This means that the eastern and western mounds faced toward each other, and it is possible that the central mound (which had no primary chamber, only the cists added at a later stage) was the last to be built, filling in the space between the two. The postholes were positioned on the axis of the barrow, but again quite separate from the burnt building deposit. Between the posts was a shallow slot, paved with flat stones, and a dense rectangle of charcoal represented what had apparently been a covering 'lid' sealing the chamber (Fig. 8.4). The form of this mortuary structure suggests an affinity with the

Fig. 8.3: The eastern mound, Dorstone Hill, under excavation in 2016 (photo: Adam Stanford, Aerial-Cam).

eastern, lowland tradition of earthen long barrows, rather than with the long cairns of the west (Kinnes 1992, 81). The well-preserved example from the Foulmire Fen long barrow at Haddenham in Cambridgeshire demonstrates the probable character of such a chamber: a simple timber box set in a linear defile (Evans and Hodder 2006, 89). It is quite possible that this wooden structure had stood for some period beside the timber building, before the destruction of the latter. So activities involving the manipulation of human remains may have coincided with the use of the buildings. The chamber was contained within its own U-shaped ditch and following its decommissioning had been covered by a small mound, which was stratified below the main long barrow mound. Although unburned bone did not survive in this part of the site, large quantities of cremated remains had been thrown into the southern side of the U-shaped ditch, and then covered over with a dense mass of stone. One possibility is that this bone had been retrieved from the mortuary structure, burned, and deposited in the ditch when the mound had been raised. This would imply that the timber chamber had been conceived less as a place of repose for the remains of the dead, and more as a place of transformation, in which fleshed bodies had been allowed to rot down. When the ditch was dug and the mound created, the chamber went out of use and was emptied.

Fig. 8.4: The linear mortuary structure beneath the eastern mound at Dorstone Hill, with its surrounding ditch, filled on the southern side by a stone cairn sealing a mass of cremated bone (photo: Adam Stanford, Aerial-Cam).

Some while after the construction of the eastern long mound (and presumably also after the encapsulation of the three formerly distinct mounds into a single monument with a monumentalised north-facing façade), a series of intrusive features were cut through stone and turf capping of the barrow from above. Four large pits were inserted, each lined with settings of concentrically arranged stone slabs, onto which the cremated remains of humans and cattle were placed. All four pits were dug so as to expose, but not intrude into, the remains of the underlying burnt building, another example of the reverence with which these traces continued to be treated. A fifth feature was a small cylindrical pit, dug close beside the location of the now buried timber chamber. This contained one fine polished flint axe, a polished stone axe and a bifacially worked flint blade (Fig. 8.5). This latter was exceptionally fresh, and some of the debitage from its manufacture was found in the pit alongside it. This suggests that the object had never been in circulation, but had been made specifically for deposition, in what arguably amounted to an act of veneration and remembrance. Immediately to the north-east of the timber chamber, a further example of the intrusive stone cists identified in the central mound was discovered. This truncated the socket for a massive post, which may conceivably have stood beside the chamber, before being enclosed within its encircling ditch.

Fig. 8.5: Bifacial flint knife from the small cylindrical pit located beside the mortuary structure in the eastern mound at Dorstone Hill (photo: Adam Stanford, Aerial-Cam).

Taken together, these intrusive features suggest the persistence of a detailed memory of what lay beneath at least the eastern-most of the mounds, and a desire to connect past and present through acts of reference and citation.

THE CAUSEWAYED ENCLOSURE

Around two centuries after the construction of the long mounds, a small single-circuit causewayed enclosure, roughly 150 m in diameter, was created on the southern tip of Dorstone Hill, directly overlooking the Golden Valley (Fig. 8.6). Ironically, the fieldwork that revealed the mounds and their underlying buildings had been designed to investigate a Neolithic enclosure, but the presence of such an enclosure was only revealed when a magnetometer survey was conducted across the entire hilltop. The monument was located approximately 120 m south of the line of long mounds, and it is striking that it was clearly flattened in plan along its north-east side, in a way that is comparable with other causewayed enclosures such as Robin Hood's Ball in Wiltshire (Thomas 1964). The straight run of ditch segments in this part of the site stands in marked contrast with the curvature of the rest of the perimeter. Significantly, this section of the ditch runs precisely parallel with the arrangement of long barrows. This is a further example of the way that each new development on Dorstone Hill

Fig. 8.6: The causewayed enclosure ditch at Dorstone Hill under excavation in 2017 (photo: Adam Stanford, Aerial-Cam).

was keyed into the emerging pattern by citing and harking back to earlier events and structures. The long mounds were constructed over the buildings; the cists and pits were cut into the long mounds; the layout of the enclosure echoed that of the mounds.

Some of the materials and practices manifested at the enclosure were new, such as the occurrence of flakes from Group VI stone axes. But there is also striking evidence of continuity from the buildings and long mounds. For instance, blades of rock crystal are found amongst the mounds, and debris from the working of this material were recovered from a pit located beside the western mound and sealed by material derived from the decomposition of the structure. Further examples of worked rock crystal occur in the causewayed enclosure ditches. Similarly, the plain carinated bowl pottery with developed rims found beneath the long mounds continued in use at the causewayed enclosure, although here it was complemented by thicker, bag-shaped vessels.

In the unstable clay subsoil of Dorstone Hill it seems that the enclosure ditches silted up very rapidly indeed, and it is possible that an attempt to retard this process was made by revetting the dump banks with stone walling, much of which later tumbled into the ditch on the inner side. However, there was also extensive recutting activity in the ditches, including the digging of a series of bowl-shaped features, some of which were lined with stones, and some of which contained deposits of cultural material. Yet many of these recut features, particularly in the shallower ditch segments toward the eastern and western extremities of the enclosure, were enigmatically empty. These may have contained ephemeral materials that have not survived, but it is also possible that the action of repeatedly cutting holes along the perimeter of the enclosed area was more important than placing items in them (Bailey 2018, 29). On the northern edge of the enclosure, the notoriously capricious Herefordshire subsoil includes a stratum of 'corn stone', a calcareous conglomerate, and in a restricted area unburned bone is preserved. Thus, some of the stone-lined recuts contain animal bone alongside large slabs of pottery: elements from the meat-rich body-parts of cattle, and fragments of sheep suggesting butchery as well as consumption on site. These recuts surely echo the intrusive stone-filled pits in the body of the eastern mound. At one point, a more massive recut appears to have removed the causeway between two ditch segments, and this was filled with a dense concentration of much larger stones, which seem to have entered the feature from the inside of the enclosure. Large slabs of stone had also been thrown into the ditch in various places, particularly at the butt-ends of ditch segments on either side of what may have been entrances. Massive sandstone boulders also featured in what may have been one of the final structures on Dorstone Hill, a tight cluster of three stones in the interior of the enclosure, a little way back from the ditch circuit. At least one of these had a clear socket containing packing-stones, suggesting that at one time these represented a setting of standing stones. Individual standing stones, and groups of stones are not uncommon in the immediate region of Dorstone (Ray 2007, 69), and it has sometimes been noted that settings of stones may represent 'closing statements', either commemorating the activity that has taken place on a given site, or explicitly bringing it to an end (Bradley 2011, 169).

A HISTORY OF GATHERINGS

The sequence of construction and deposition at Dorstone Hill can justifiably be claimed to constitute a story or narrative. Each constitutive act performed at the site drew upon a detailed understanding of past events, while contributing to the gathering accretion of material traces. Ultimately, the entire complex referred back to the moment of 'coming into being', the foundational activity constituted by the construction of the three timber halls or houses. It may not be beyond the bounds of possibility that for successive generations of Neolithic people Dorstone Hill represented an 'origin place', to which it was important to retain a connection. Starting from this constitutive moment, the ensuing pattern of burnings, buildings and burials provided the fixed points within a narrative history of people and place, something that could be reconstructed and recounted over the following generations. Neolithic history, we might say, was vested in material things and their dispositions.

The sequence of Early Neolithic timber halls/houses replaced by revetted long mounds with mortuary associations at the site is so far extremely rare in the British context. One further curiosity of this particular site, however, within the so-far understood 'canon' of Neolithic practices is the close association of structures in a line and associated with a post-framed mortuary structure that belongs early in the sequence and was also oriented along the same axis. One explanation derives also from the diversity of styles not only of the rectangular timber structures, but also of the successor mounds. This diversity may perhaps represent the coming together at this site of three distinct lineages, bringing with them contrasting traditions of building and commemoration. The concept of 'gathering together' has long been understood in the context of causewayed enclosures (and the faunal remains from the enclosure at the upper part of the Dorstone Hill site indicate the likelihood that feasting was a prominent aspect of activity there). However, the idea that houses and long mounds might also represent the co-presence of different lineages in the same location has not until now been explicitly considered, despite the fact that it has long been known that long mounds (for example in the Cotswold-Severn tradition in Gloucestershire and the Black Mountains) also occur in pairs.

We want to close this account by referring directly to the title that we have chosen for this contribution. The 'foundational houses' are, in the literal sense, the timber and daub house or hall structures that initiated the sequence. But as we have already implied, the 'houses' concerned are at one and the same time also figurative. They represented the descent-groups both united by, and possibly also differentiated by, lineage. In other words, while the group of structures represents corporate descent, the deliberately different styles of structure may reflect, for example, distinct lineage segments that themselves may well be an amalgam of indigenous and incoming populations. The houses or halls are therefore foundational in both a material and an historical sense. The subsequent acts of commemoration that we have documented reinforce the sense in which the primary activity and its monumentalisation were foundational events, enabling the construction of the lineage history of the founding people, or each of the foundational clan-segments and their descendants.

The building of the halls and collective burial chamber and the subsequent raising and defining of the mound structures necessitated and celebrated the gathering-together of newly Neolithic people on the hilltop. The hilltop and its monumentalised structures therefore represented a history of gatherings at this important foundational location. In this way, Dorstone Hill became historicised for the communities who felt that they had a stake in its past. Through time it served as an accumulating material record or mnemonic for origins and assembly, which marked it as a place appropriate – at least through the fourth millennium – for further gatherings.

REFERENCES

Bailey, D. (2018) *Breaking the Surface: an art/archaeology of prehistoric architecture*. Oxford, Oxford University Press.

Barclay, A.J. and Harris, O.J.T. (2017) Community building: houses and people in Neolithic Britain. In P. Bickle, V. Cummings, D. Hofmann and J. Pollard (eds) *The Neolithic of Europe: papers in honour of Alasdair Whittle*, 222–34. Oxford, Oxbow Books.

Barrett, J.C., Bradley, R.J. and Green, M. (1991) *Landscape, Monuments and Society: the prehistory of Cranborne Chase*. Cambridge, Cambridge University Press.

Bradley, R.J. (2011) *Stages and Screens: an investigation of four henge monuments in northern and north-eastern Scotland*. Edinburgh, Society of Antiquaries of Scotland.

Britnell, W. and Savory, H. (1984) *Gwernvale and Penywyrlod: two neolithic long cairns in the Black Mountains of Brecknock*. Cardiff, Cambrian Archaeological Association.

Chambon, P. and Mordant, D. (1996) Monumentalisme et sépultures collectives à Balloy (Seine-et-Marne). *Bulletin de la Société Préhistorique Française* 93, 396–402.

Corcoran, J.W.X.P. (1969) The Cotswold-Severn group. 1: Distribution, morphology, and artifacts. In T. Powell, J. Corcoran, F. Lynch and J. Scott, *Megalithic Enquiries in the West of Britain*, 13–72. Liverpool, Liverpool University Press.

Darvill, T. (2004) *Long Barrows of the Cotswolds and Surrounding Areas*. Stroud, Tempus.

Dixon, P. (1988) The Neolithic settlements on Crickley Hill. In C. Burgess, P. Topping, C. Mordant and M. Madison (eds) *Enclosures and Defences in the Neolithic of Western Europe*, 75–88. Oxford, British Archaeological Reports s403.

Duly, C. (1979) *The Houses of Mankind*. London, Thames and Hudson.

Evans, C. and Hodder, I. (2006) *A Woodland Archaeology: Neolithic sites at Haddenham*. Cambridge, McDonald Institute.

Helms, M.W. (1998) *Access to Origins: affines, ancestors and aristocrats*. Austin, University of Texas.

Hey, G., Bell, C., Dennis, C. and Robinson, M. (2016) *Yarnton: Neolithic and Bronze Age settlement and landscape*. Oxford, Oxford Archaeology Unit.

Hogan, S. (2013) Manor Farm cursus complex: floodplain investigations on the River Great Ouse, Milton Keynes. *Past* 73, 2–4.

Kinnes, I. (1992) *Non-Megalithic Long Barrows in the British Neolithic*. London, British Museum.

Kirch, P.V. (2000) Temples as 'holy houses': the transformation of ritual architecture in traditional Polynesian societies. In R.A. Joyce and S.D. Gillespie (eds) *Beyond Kinship: social and material reproduction in house societies*, 103–14. Philadelphia, University of Pennsylvania Press.

Müller, J., Dibbern, H. and Hage, F. (2014) Non-megalithic mounds beneath megaliths: a new perspective on monumentality in North Central Europe. In M. Furholt, M. Hinz, D. Mischka, G. Noble and D. Olausson (eds) *Landscapes, Histories and Societies in the Northern European Neolithic*, 171–82. Bonn, Dr Rudolf Habelt GmbH.

Ó Nualláin, S. (1972) A Neolithic house at Ballyglass, near Ballycastle, Co. Mayo. Journal of the Royal Society of Antiquaries of Ireland 102, 49–56.

Oswald, A., Dyer, C. and Barber, M. (2001) *The Creation of Monuments: Neolithic causewayed enclosures in the British Isles*. London, English Heritage.

Pye, W.R. (1967) Dorstone Hill. *Transactions of the Woolhope Naturalists Field Club* 39, Part 1, 157.

Pye, W.R. (1968) Dorstone Hill. *Transactions of the Woolhope Naturalists Field Club* 39, Part 2, 362.

Pye, W.R. (1969) Dorstone Hill. *Transactions of the Woolhope Naturalists Field Club* 39, Part 3, 475.

Ray, K. (2007) The Neolithic in the West Midlands: a review. In P. Garwood (ed.) *The Undiscovered Country: the earlier prehistory of the West Midlands*, 51–78. Oxford, Oxbow Books.

Ray, K. (2015) *The Archaeology of Herefordshire: an exploration*. Eardisley, Logaston Press.

Ray, K. and Thomas, J.S. (2018) *Neolithic Britain: the transformation of social worlds*. Oxford, Oxford University Press.

Rzepecki, S. (2011) *The Roots of Megalithism in the TRB Culture*. Łódź, Fundacja Uniwersytetu Łódzkiego.

Saville, A. (1990) *Hazleton North, Gloucestershire, 1979–82: the excavation of a Neolithic long cairn of the Cotswold-Severn Group*. London, English Heritage.

Thomas, N. (1964) The Neolithic causewayed camp at Robin Hood's Ball, Shrewton. *Wiltshire Archaeological Magazine* 59, 1–25.

Chapter 9

New work on long barrows in Lincolnshire

Denise Drury and Tim Allen with David Knight, David McOmish, Matthew Oakey and Caroline Skinner, and Paul Cope-Faulkner, Neil Parker, Sean Parker and Jonathon Smith

INTRODUCTION

The long barrows of the Lincolnshire Wolds are only one component in a highly complex multi-period landscape, and as with any typological grouping, categorisation throws up its own questions when one looks at the variations and themes in the material. The diagnostic characteristics of long barrows that allow them to be formally differentiated from other features may lead one to prioritise them and other diagnostic features over contemporary less typo-chronographically distinct remains. Simple boundary divisions or stock and homestead enclosures are hard to pick apart in a multi-period landscape without excavation and structured scientific dating. Notwithstanding those caveats, features which are readily assigned by period provide a starting point to broader landscape analysis and their relationships to overlapping or juxtaposed features are an important focus of this project. If these are houses for the dead, they do not appear from this narrowly focused programme of air photographic and geophysical work to be co-located with the houses of the living. We are not seeing domestic activity directly adjacent to funerary monuments nor do they appear to come with appurtenances of former homes transformed to tombs. We suppose therefore that contemporary dwellings lay in those areas of higher ground reoccupied over subsequent millennia or in valley bottoms beneath later colluvium. Evans and Simpson (1991) infer a field edge location for their Giant Hills II barrow (from environmental evidence perhaps leading us to a model of the houses of the dead as sentinels on the margins of communal lands (*cf.* Bradley 1993)).

Barrows make up around 15% of the assets on the Historic England at Risk register (Historic England 2019). Of these, the earliest and most important group, are long barrows since frequently they appear to structure subsequent episodes of land division and monument making. These Early Neolithic monuments form key elements in the prehistoric landscape which are subsequently sometimes 'remade' and re-interpreted by succeeding communities and frequently structuring later landscapes. In this context the possible long barrow identified by Willis (2013) at Mount Pleasant emerges from a tangle of later features. There are clear concentrations in central southern England (Salisbury Plain, Dorset and Cranborne Chase, Cotswold-Severn groupings, for example) and the Wolds of Lincolnshire and East Yorkshire (Ashbee 1970; Kinnes 1992; Field 2006). Evidence of Early Neolithic activity other than long barrows is still sparse in Lincolnshire with only one causewayed enclosure securely identified (at Barholm on the Fen Edge at the south of the county) and a possible Cursus at Thorganby

(Jones 1998), but no Early Neolithic house has yet been confirmed in Lincolnshire. Landscape scale work by Chown (1994) on the Bain Valley demonstrates activity but we still struggle to identify discrete domestic sites in the Early Neolithic on the Wolds. Interventions on the chalk Wolds have been dominated by pipeline and cable projects which may have inherent methodological limitations in addressing features that are non-diagnostic in air photos or geophysics. Current developer-funded infrastructure projects seek to advance methods in these areas and this issue is the focus of curatorial efforts to better target Early Neolithic features in evaluation. This remains a very partial Early Neolithic landscape in comparison to the fen edge when one moves into Cambridgeshire (*e.g.* Tabor *et al.* 2016). As on the East Yorkshire Wolds (Roskams and Whyman 2005), the Lincolnshire Wolds remains perhaps a landscape of the houses of the dead and the fields of the living.

To curate this resource effectively requires a robust dataset to inform protection and future management: the better our knowledge about the location, condition and context of these monuments of national importance, the easier it becomes to communicate their significance to landowners, tenant farmers and wider communities of interest. In turn, Historic England and other agencies are then better placed to ensure their conservation within the wider productive landscape. The long barrows of Lincolnshire are a group of monuments particularly at risk from cultivation because they mostly sit within an arable setting, and often on the shoulders of the rolling chalk landscape as this project has confirmed.

Approximately 100 sites were identified from Scheduled Monument (National Heritage List for England), National Record of the Historic Environment, and local Historic Environment Records for assessment, the majority of which are located on the Lincolnshire Wolds, a range of hills in the north-eastern quarter of the county of Lincolnshire, midway between Lincoln and the coast. They run roughly parallel with the North Sea coast, from the Humber in the north-west to the edge of the Lincolnshire Fens in the south-east. They are the highest area of land in eastern England between Yorkshire and Kent. In 1973, the main area of the Lincolnshire Wolds, extending to 558 square kilometres (216 square miles), was designated an Area of Outstanding Natural Beauty (AONB). Following the completion of aerial photographic analysis phase by Historic England, Heritage Lincolnshire/ Archaeological Project Services began fieldwork on the assessment programme in 2017 and this component is due to be completed in 2019. This fieldwork stage will produce an initial project report, but further synthesis is planned by Historic England's National Aerial Investigation and Mapping team (Historic England forthcoming).

LINCOLNSHIRE LONG BARROWS

Whittle *et al.* (2011, 839 and 869) propose a *c.*3800 cal BC date for the spread of Neolithic 'things and practices' into the Wolds (but they stress this is outwith the area modelled in their study). Dating of the Giants Hills 2 barrow at Skendleby (from human bone and antler) suggests the monument originated in the mid-fourth millennium cal BC (Evans and Simpson 1991, 40–3) whilst the adjacent barrow, Giants Hills 1 has a later fourth millennium cal BC date (Barker *et al.* 1969, 287). Sadly, all but one of the human bones from the 1930s work at Giants Hills are lost (probably in the bombing of the Royal College of Surgeons in the Second World War), which may explain why the early radiocarbon dates from Giant

Hills I are from antler. The human remains from Giants Hills II are in Lincolnshire County Museum but have not been subject to further study since publication.

As with all type categories applied to monuments such as long barrows, their grouping together and distinction from other features (*e.g.* mortuary enclosures *cf.* Loveday 2006) is problematic given the heterogeneous character of the sites, as will be illustrated below. These issues of typology are further complicated by the multi-phase development of monuments and the attritional effects of later cultivation by which phases of elaboration are added and stripped. There are strong cohesive themes in this monument class in terms of form, placement and apparent absence of domestic activity, thus we argue their grouping remains a valid starting point to their discussion and analysis. Whilst the present project targets long barrows rather than mortuary enclosures *per se*, this only appears to have excluded one scheduled monument on the Lincolnshire Wolds (due to the dominant use of 'long barrow' as a descriptor in schedule entries). We are content that this site (*Neolithic long mortuary enclosure and two Bronze Age bowl barrows immediately north of Otby Top Farm*) is well located and does not require re-plotting. All associated archaeological features appearing alongside the possible long barrows were mapped from the air photographs. In particular, features more akin to 'mortuary enclosures' have been highlighted in the study as targets for potential designation and management input.

Long barrows have long been recognised as special (or remarkable places) in the Lincolnshire landscape as indicated in evocative names such as Giants' Hills, Deadmen's Graves and Spellow Hills, articulating both notions of the distant past and their status as landmark venues for public discourse (*spell – low* or 'assembly mound'); the earliest recorded mention of the name is in the early twelfth century (Pantos 2001a and b). In terms of antiquarian interest, Spellow Hills was first noted by Stukeley (cited Phillips 1932, 193–6), and as Phillips observed, 'More stories are told about this long barrow than of any other in the county' in testimony to its prominence. However, the visibility of upstanding sites such as Spellow was not reflected in further structured antiquarian investigation of sites in the Lincolnshire Wolds (Phillips 1932; 1933) the few very basic accounts of intervention sit, in sharp contrast, in terms of the depth or recording and analysis to the pioneering work undertaken on the Yorkshire Wolds (Greenwell 1877; Mortimer 1905), the Wessex Downs (Colt Hoare 1812) or the Peak District (Bateman 1848; 1861). There is therefore not a significant *corpus* of antiquarian work upon which to draw when studying the long barrows of the Lincolnshire Wolds.

The long barrows of Lincolnshire were first systematically recorded in the 1930s by C.W. Phillips working for the Ordnance Survey (with some previous suggestions from O.G.S. Crawford), and revealed a group of sites focused tightly on the Wolds with 15 examples ultimately identified (Phillips 1932; 1933; 1934; 1936) including upstanding as well as recently lost features. Phillips undertook substantial and detailed excavation of Giants' Hills at Skendleby in 1933–4 (Phillips 1936) revealing the complex internal structure of these features with partitioned bays within the mound and a paved mortuary structure bearing human skeletal remains (Phillips 1936). The debate on the structural phasing and architectural form of these internal structures cannot be advanced beyond where Ashbee (1984) and Kinnes (1992) left it, except to stress the diversity of form and proportion in the Lincolnshire air photo sites within which these structural elements may have been only one element in a wider grammar of components. To really move forwards on the specifics of how these sheds/chambers functioned would probably require the excavation of one of the remaining larger extant mounds rather than further reconsideration of previous work. The quality of Philips' work was, in many respects, well ahead of many of his contemporaries and revealed the structural complexity of the monument as well as a long history of significance for local communities with subsequent activity at the site extending into the Iron Age. Phillips' work also formed the basis for an initial group of designations under the Ancient Monuments Acts.

The number of identifiable long barrows largely remained static until the 1980s when detailed aerial survey by Paul Everson of the Royal Commission on the Historical Monuments of England (RCHME) identified additional sites as crop mark features (Everson 1980; 1983; Everson and Hayes 1984). Targeted survey and intrusive investigation by Patricia Phillips in the1980s (Phillips 1989) focused on site identification and assessment of survival. This theme was echoed in the rescue excavation work by Evans and Simpson funded by the Department for the Environment of Giants' Hills 2 – a ploughed barrow lying adjacent to that dug by C.W. Phillips in the 1930s (Evans and Simpson 1991). The Giants Hills excavations remain the only extensive investigations of long barrows in Lincolnshire. Since that time, some limited work has also been done on pipeline projects at the Neolithic long barrow 940 m north-north-west of Mount Pleasant (Bonner and Griffiths 1993).

The National Mapping Programme carried out by the RCHME in the 1990s highlighted the existence of many more long barrows/funerary enclosures and this survey work was published by Dilwyn Jones in his important *Proceedings of the Prehistoric Society* article (Jones 1998). Also in the 1990s, English Heritage carried out the Monuments Protection Programme (MPP) which increased the number of sites afforded protection as Scheduled Monuments. This work, however, proceeded largely in parallel with the National Mapping Programme and thus neither work was able to wholly benefit from the assessed results of the other. The outcome was that the body of sites mapped from aerial photographs remained only partly integrated with those afforded statutory protection. In 1999 the RCHME was merged with The Historic Buildings and Monuments Commission (then known as English Heritage). Since 2015, the statutory record and advice functions of HBMCE have been carried out under the new name Historic England and the English Heritage Trust has been formed as a charity to manage historic properties in State care.

Lincolnshire's long barrows are mostly located on the chalk ridge of the Lincolnshire Wolds and lie within a designated Area of Outstanding Natural Beauty (AONB). They are particularly at risk due to the large-scale reconversion of pasture to intensive arable cultivation in the years following the Second World War and, more broadly, from earlier episodes of cultivation from the medieval period and through the agricultural improvements of the eighteenth and nineteenth centuries. There is much scope to examine the development of the Wolds landscape in more detail and to situate the survival of these sites within that account. In the mid-2000s the English Heritage *Scheduled Monuments at Risk* programme revealed that of 48 long barrows designated as Scheduled Monuments, 36 were highly at risk, making the long barrows of the Lincolnshire Wolds the East Midland's most at Risk category. Working with Natural England, through agricultural stewardship schemes, the number of scheduled sites at Risk has been greatly reduced and now only 20 Lincolnshire long barrows remain on the Register (Historic England 2019). Further positive outcomes are in negotiation or underway (using the results of the present study) and these should reduce this total further. The need for greater spatial accuracy and interpretive confidence in defining areas of national importance on the ground has become clear as negotiations with landowners have proceeded under the more archaeologically focused agri-environment schemes set in place since 2005.

The Lincolnshire Long Barrows Assessment project is an Historic England initiative designed to better understand and manage Neolithic long barrows in the historic county of Lincolnshire. Since the completion of the Lincolnshire National Mapping Programme and through the aerial analysis phase of the Lincolnshire Long Barrows Project, 14 new long barrows were identified. In addition to locating these new sites, recent work resulting from reconnaissance recording, established that some of the scheduled areas for known barrow sites did not accurately reflect the true position of the monument and scope for better alignment between features and arable reversion to grassland was recognised so as to deliver better protection to buried remains. Using modern methods of photo rectification, it was decided to remap the barrows of Lincolnshire in order to ascertain true location which will reflect on the listing element. The principal aim of the project is to provide a robust dataset to inform protection and future management of this group of monuments. The majority of the identified long barrows are located in the Wolds, a particularly important group of sites which are at risk from the pressures of modern cultivation. As part of this project some 100 sites have been identified for review in the field, and Heritage Lincolnshire/Archaeological Project Services were commissioned in 2017 to undertake the fieldwork assessment.

AERIAL PHOTOGRAPHIC ASSESSMENT

Underpinning the fieldwork is Historic England's review and analysis of known scheduled and undesignated long barrows and the production of mapping, drawn from new aerial photographic transcription to current standards. This work reassessed all long barrow sites within the historic county of Lincolnshire and included any site currently scheduled or recorded on the National Record of the Historic Environment (NHRE) or Historic Environment Record (HER) as a long barrow. The sources employed for the transcription included all available vertical and oblique aerial photographs (prints and digital) from the 1930s to 2013 (some 4,000 images), lidar data were available, and further digital elevation models (DEMs) derived from gridded height data. In addition, bespoke reconnaissance flights were undertaken by Historic England (in winter 2016) over scheduled long barrows to capture imagery to create DEMs through the digital photogrammetry process of Structure from Motion (SfM).

The mapping produced a detailed record of the current condition of each barrow, as well as any associated features (archaeological and non-archaeological. The mapping included all features identified in the same land parcel, including both archaeological and natural features such as palaeochannels) and was a key resource in guiding the field visits and subsequent research relevant to the understanding and management of the long barrows.

FIELDWORK PROGRAMME

One hundred and thirty-five sites recorded as long barrows were subject to aerial photographic assessment. A number of these were dismissed as non-barrows, most often due to a confusion in the appearance of cropmarks and soilmarks on historic aerial photographs where chalk pits or geological features of a similar shape and size were confused with a barrow. As a result,

94 sites were put forward for field assessment. The fieldwork programme comprised three main stages: an initial site visit, data gathering and reporting, selection of sites for geophysical survey and targeted small-scale trench excavation at a small subset of the surveyed sites.

Contacting and visiting the individual landowners formed a key part of the project in order to talk to owners about the monuments on their land, establish site conditions and current management regimes and identify any issues. Establishing that relationship was important as the fieldwork surveys could only be undertaken with the co-operation and permission of the landowners. The information from the site visit and available background material on each site was drawn together to produce a data report for each long barrow which is returned to Historic England's Listing Advice team.

Whilst a few long barrows have upstanding earthwork remains, most sites are known from cropmarks and have been much reduced by cultivation, a number surviving, now as below-ground features only but in many cases the scheduled monuments were revealed through SfM as low relief earthworks. Many of these 'flat' sites remain in cultivation and some are under grass or in reversion from arable to pasture. These sites were the focus of the geophysical survey programme which targeted sites where aerial photography was unclear or inconclusive, or where there was some question on the form or interpretation of the cropmarks. In most instances the geophysical survey was, of necessity, tightly focused on the barrow and immediate surrounding area. However, in some cases the opportunity was also taken to examine the wider setting, and potentially the relationship, of individual long barrows set in close association with each other or where they lay within more extensive cropmark complexes. There were several logistical issues that were encountered during this work, chief amongst these was finding a window of opportunity within the intensive cropping cycles for each site in which it might be possible to undertake fieldwork.

In the main, magnetometer survey was employed as the preferred geophysical technique and was found to be particularly effective on the chalk uplands. In some cases, resistivity was used in addition where magnetometry proved inconclusive on other geologies. The project allowed for approximately half the sites to be subject of geophysical survey and, in total, 43 long barrow or potential long barrow sites have been surveyed. Selected based on the geophysical survey results, the small-scale trench excavation was targeted to establish the presence of the enclosing ditch, the survival of mound material and investigation of potential associated features. Individual trenches were typically 10 m by 1 m or equivalent area. Six individual sites were examined by means of trench excavation.

Of the sites included in the field programme, some 80 individual sites are thought to represent, or are likely to represent, the remains of long barrows whilst others were found to represent chalk pits or apparently natural glacial striations. Although the majority of long barrow sites lie on the Lincolnshire Wolds (Fig. 9.1), mainly located on the uplands, a small number of sites lie outside the Wolds area and are discussed separately below. It should be noted that for the purposes of the project, the term 'long barrow' was maintained throughout and during the fieldwork classification by type was not attempted although there is a wide range of forms and dimensions.

In the Wolds, many of the long barrow sites are found on valley sides or at the head of valleys and where on a slope are located below the crest and frequently aligned along the contours; the orientation reflecting the topographical location. It is interesting to note that several long barrows lie between palaeochannels, perhaps suggesting that they respect these features or were placed close to streams and spring lines.

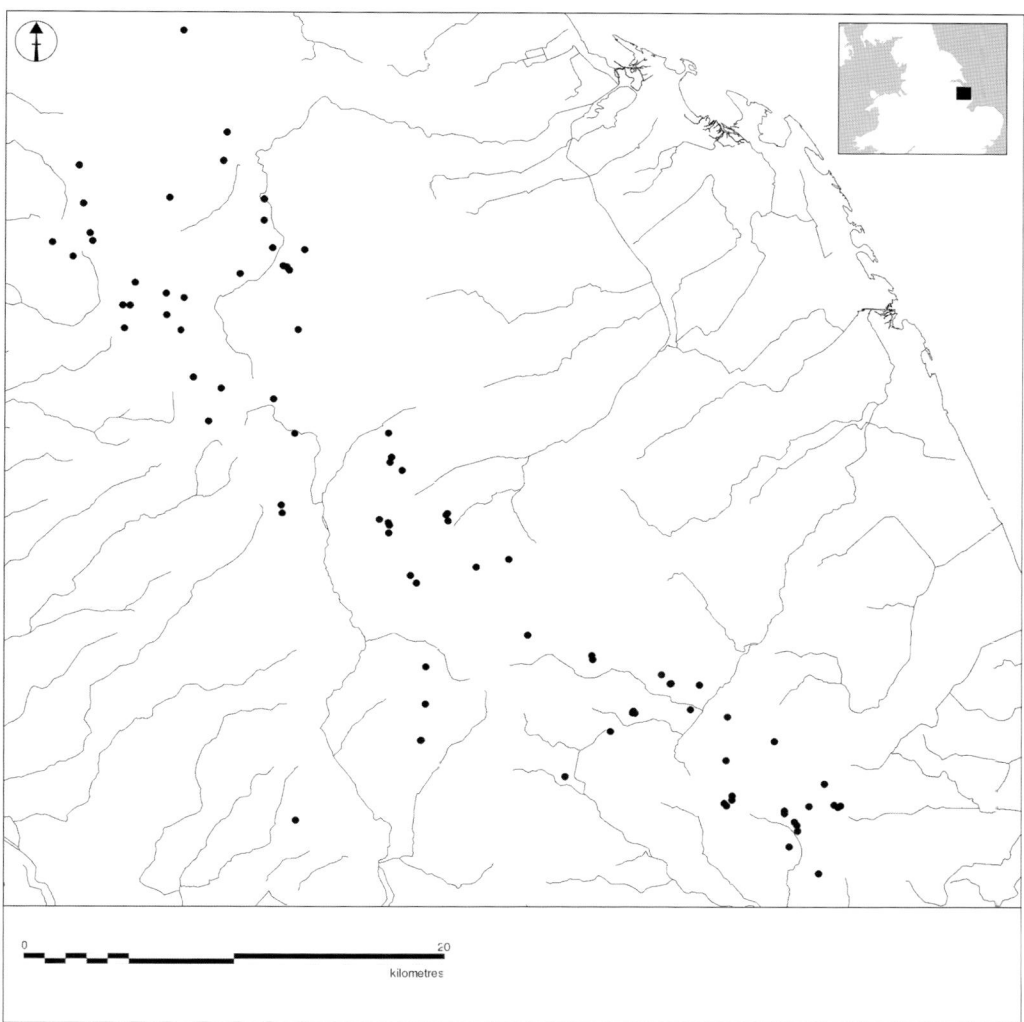

Fig. 9.1: Distribution of sites in the Lincolnshire Wolds included in the Lincolnshire Long Barrows Project. © Historic England (aerial photographic data) Heritage Trust of Lincolnshire/Archaeological Project Services (geophysical survey data). © Crown Copyright and database right 2018. All rights reserved. Ordnance Survey Licence number 100024900.

The diverse character of the Lincolnshire sites (ranging from ovoid or kidney shaped to strictly linear, and from slight ditches likely to have produced only a small mound to substantial standing features) have previously been grouped (see Jones 1998) on the basis of form, described as oval, trapeziform (subdivided by straight/convex terminals), and oblong and those illustrated here (Figs 9.2 and 9.3) reflect that range. What we find in the field may represent only an end point in a sequence of site development and different sites may have taken different paths or drawn upon different elements from a pallet of components

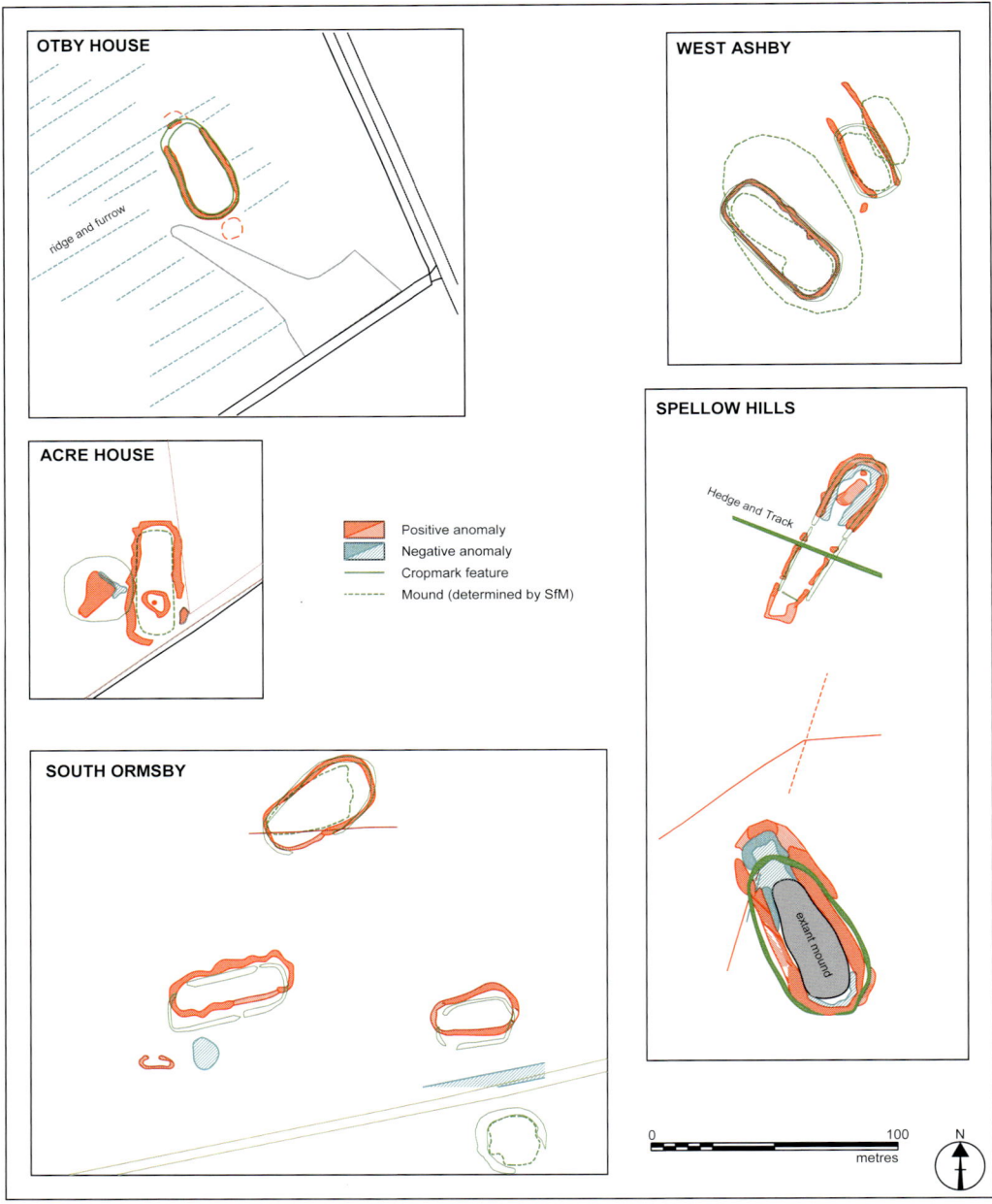

Fig. 9.2: Combined aerial photographic data and geophysical survey interpretation – selected sites, Lincolnshire Long Barrows Project. © Historic England (aerial photographic data) Heritage Trust of Lincolnshire/ Archaeological Project Services (geophysical survey data). © Crown Copyright and database right 2018. All rights reserved. Ordnance Survey Licence number 100024900.

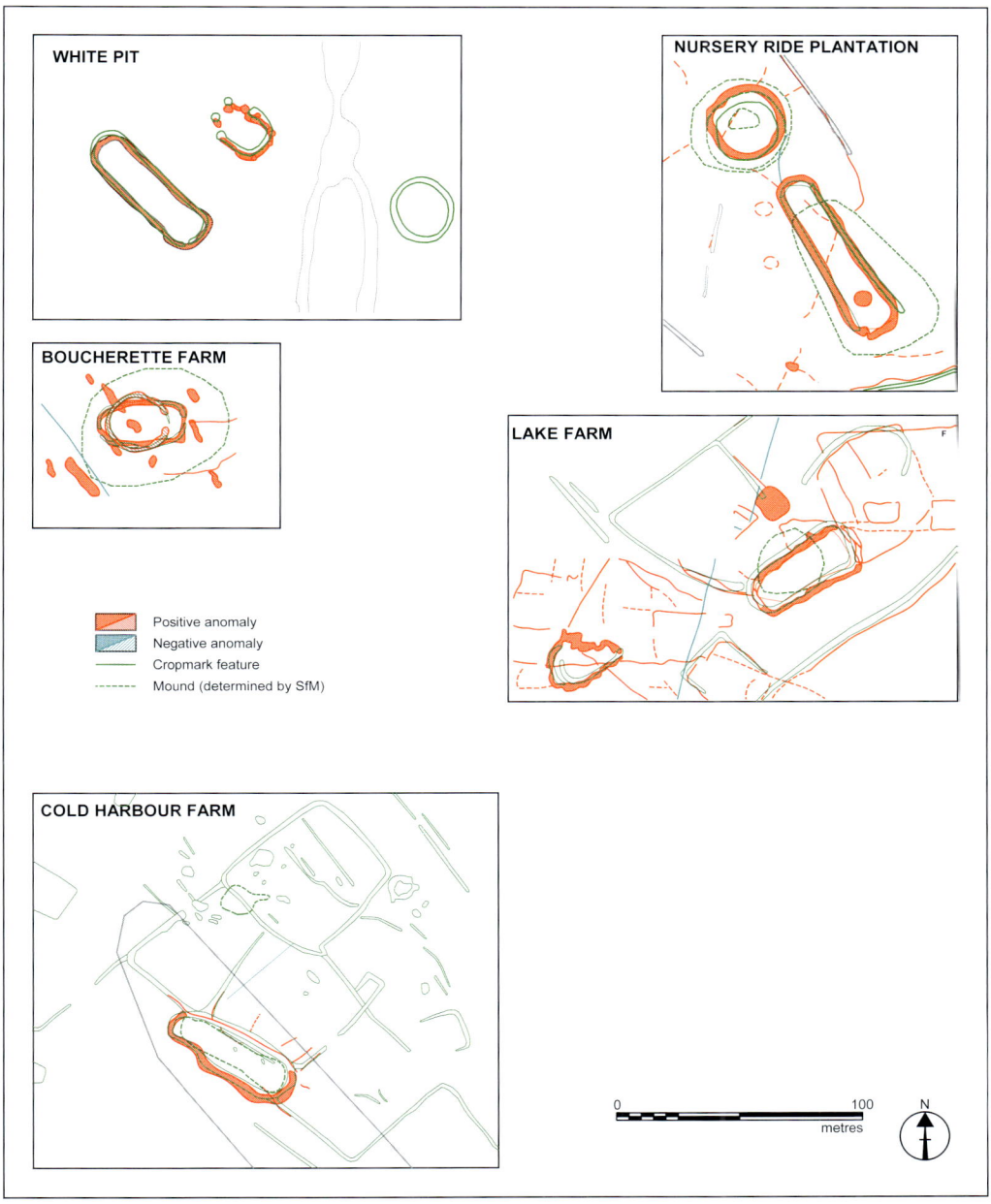

Fig. 9.3: Combined aerial photographic data and geophysical survey interpretation – selected sites, Lincolnshire Long Barrows Project. © Historic England (aerial photographic data) Heritage Trust of Lincolnshire/ Archaeological Project Services (geophysical survey data). © Crown Copyright and database right 2018. All rights reserved. Ordnance Survey Licence number 100024900.

(Barrett 1993). The attritional effects of cultivation tend to strip away phases of activity, leaving as at Otby House (Fig. 9.2) only the shadow of a mound in the un-weathered chalk within the ditch, from which the protective effect of a now lost mound can be inferred. Dimensions of the enclosures tend to range from 40 m to 80 m in length and between 20 m to 30 m in width, but there is a wide variation with examples outside the range, both smaller and larger. The enhanced mapping and geophysical surveys have identified an increased number of sites where the enclosure ditch is complete with limited evidence for openings or entrances across the range of forms.

The majority of the enclosing ditches appear to be relatively narrow (3 m or less in width) and survive up to about a metre in depth where tested by excavation which contrasts sharply with the wide, deep ditches recorded in the limited excavated examples around prominent earthwork mounds (such as Giants Hills 1 and 2 and Hoe Hill). The aerial photographic assessment has, through digital elevation modelling, greatly extended the number of sites with mound material within or spreading over the enclosing ditches. However, given the apparent size of the enclosing ditches these mounds are unlikely to have been of any great height. This adds a significant dimension to the record for sites where there is no discernible evidence for mounds at ground level. Un-ploughed mound material was neither detected in any of the magnetometer surveys nor in the limited cases where small scale excavation was carried out despite mound material (modified by ploughing) being evident as discrete low earthworks on SfM and in direct field observation. This was a very limited programme of excavation and thus undisturbed mound material may well survive in ploughed mounds with greater standing height or a more gentle history of cultivation. From the evidence of both the aerial photography and the geophysical surveys, it is noted that few of the enclosures appear to have internal features.

There are only a few examples of substantive upstanding earthwork remains in the modern landscape, however, the longevity of long barrows in the landscape can be seen in a number of sites that lie in close proximity to round barrows (such as Nursery Ride Plantation, Fig. 9.3), whilst a few long barrows have round barrows superimposed (for example at Boucherette Farm, Fig. 9.3) indicating a continuation or developing funerary tradition. A number of the long barrow sites lie in association with or within cropmark complexes, some of which are extensive and represent intensive Romano-British settlement (as seen at Stenigot). The later enclosures frequently appear to respect the alignment of the long barrow and to incorporate or reuse the enclosure ditches (for example at Cold Harbour Farm, Fig. 9.3). Although dating evidence has yet to be obtained, the relationship of a long barrow at Lake Farm, (Fig. 9.3) with a later Roman period enclosure has been demonstrated through excavation. At Cold Harbour the wider complex includes two long barrows, in proximity to round barrows, which appear to have been incorporated into a Late Iron Age/Roman field system and in the post-medieval period incorporated into the boundary.

The Lincolnshire Wolds long barrows are found as single examples, closely associated 'pairs' or groups of three (within 100 m), and larger 'groups' where up to four long barrows lie within 900 m of each other. Three groups of barrows lie at the southern end of the Wolds, the upstanding earthwork remains are the well-known Spellow Hills, Giants' Hills and Deadmen's Graves mapped by C.W. Phillips in the 1930s. Spellow and Giants' Hills lie in the same valley, with Spellow at the head of the valley and Giants' Hills positioned further down the valley, on a south-west facing slope. Deadmen's Graves lies in the adjacent valley with the barrows positioned closely together on the south facing slope (see Field 2006, 106 and fig. 52 for a plot of these).

Phillips recorded five mounds across these three groups; two each at Deadmen's Graves and Giants' Hills (the latter now excavated) and one at Spellow Hills. Evidence from aerial photographs has added another six long barrows to that total; a further three at cropmarks at Spellow Hills, two cropmarks found in a similar topographic position along the valley side to the north-west of Giants' Hills earthworks and a cropmark in close proximity to one of the Deadmen's Graves.

The Spellow Hills earthwork was thought prior to Phillips' (1932) work to be a series of conjoined round barrows due to the extremely uneven profile and is depicted as such on the 1888 Ordnance Survey mapping. There are references to antiquarian investigations and finds from Spellow, but no firm evidence survives, although heavily disturbed ground along the spine of the monument hints at past digging. Recent geophysical survey has shown that the mound (measuring 55 m in length) is enclosed by a ditch with overall dimensions of 90 m by 30 m (Fig. 9.3). The ditch (up to 10 m wide) extends some 25 m beyond the northern end of earthwork suggesting that mound material may have been lost in this area, or that it was not covered in the same way.

A further three elongated ditched enclosure cropmarks are found around the Spellow earthwork, between 100 m and 400 m distant. The closest, to the north, is trapezoidal, measuring 80 m by 20 m, tapering to a flattened southern terminal (Fig. 9.2). Geophysical survey has indicated that there may possibly be some bank or mound material at the northern end where the enclosing ditch is 4 m wide; however, it narrows considerably to the south. The two long barrows to the south of Spellow Hills are elongated oval and oblong enclosures, 69 m and 51 m in length with enclosing ditches. Mapping has recorded the presence of a low spread mound at each site.

Excavation has generally supported the results of the geophysical surveys, including the presence, or absence, of remains. At Otby House (Fig. 9.2), on the western edge of the Wolds, geophysical survey suggested that an elongated oval enclosure had a double ditch at the northern end and a small circular feature adjacent to the southern, slightly broader end. Excavation confirmed their presence and revealed a notable variation in the profile of the southern section of the enclosing ditch and the narrower, double ditches at the northern end. No mound material had been recorded from the aerial data, although a slight variation in the pattern of ridge and furrow cultivation may suggest that there may have been a greater depth of cover here, however, no surviving surfaces or mound material was identified in the excavation areas.

Similarly, trench excavation on a site where mound material was recorded through DEM (at West Ashby, Fig. 9.2), did not have undisturbed mound material (visually separable from the general chalky plough soil), or surviving surfaces in section despite the mass of cultivated mound material still extant over the feature in the SfM model. It appears that in these cases mound material remains broadly in place but is modified by the action of cultivation through its profile. A long barrow site, located in proximity to other cropmark features at Lake Farm, was shown by geophysical survey to be incorporated into a much more extensive complex of enclosures, thought to represent a Romano-British field system. Excavation targeting the relationship of the barrow ditch with the later enclosure demonstrated the relationship of the long barrow ditch with a later boundary which has been dated to the

Roman period. None of the small-scale excavations have produced ceramic material which can be definitively dated to the Neolithic. However, samples recovered from the ditches may provide potential for dating/environmental evidence and await further analysis.

There are a small number of long barrow sites recorded outside the Lincolnshire Wolds, for example sub-rectangular enclosures recorded in the south of the county at Harlaxton and South Rauceby. These have long barrow characteristics but appear to have a rather different form to the features seen on the chalk uplands. They appear to be more rectangular and are shorter and wider. In both cases the sites are located on valley floors and are associated with extensive cropmark complexes which include pit alignments and round barrows. At Harlaxton the enclosure ditch, prominent on aerial photographs, was not located by magnetometry but study of air photographs inaccessible at the time of the current analysis may allow this issue to be explored further in the future. Follow up resistivity survey identified a possible ditch and suggested the presence of some mound or bank material. Excavation revealed a very shallow, narrow ditch and there is some uncertainty on the form and nature of the remains, although scientific dating and environmental evidence may provide further information.

INITIAL OUTPUTS AND NEXT STEPS

This project represents a unique opportunity to review all the recorded Neolithic long barrows in Lincolnshire. It is providing an up to date and robust dataset to inform future protection and management and thus ensure their long-term survival. The new aerial photographic mapping has provided an extremely accurate map base, identified previously unknown features and shown that very shallow earthworks or buried mound material survive at a much greater number of sites which appear to be flat. Geophysical survey has confirmed the high degree of accuracy achieved by the new mapping using latest techniques and contributed a significant body of new evidence on the detail of individual sites and their immediate context. The excavation, although small scale, has provided information on the survival of buried remains. Evidence from sampling undertaken during the project may yet provide further evidence on dating, which is currently very limited for this class of monument in the county. In thinking about these places as houses for the dead our interpretation is heavily framed by the few fully excavated sites, which as discussed may only represent aspects of the long barrow vocabulary deployed by Early Neolithic people on the Lincolnshire Wolds. They seem on this limited and highly focused study to be places set to a degree apart from the living but in closely articulated relationships to the micro-topography of the Wolds. These appear to be monuments made by people with a close experience of place and a desire to reference one monument with another in architectural tension. There is structural complexity within these monuments beyond the formation of chambers/deck-house like sheds and façades at the high or blunt end. The apparent annexes at the lower or sharper end of these features visible at Otby House, Giants' Hills and Spellow (Fig. 9.2) suggest a need to mediate or annexe the story already told. Only through further extensive excavation can we start to look at how the varied elements of long barrow architecture (for instance mound partitions) appear and are associated across the variety of feature forms outlined above, but we hope the present study would allow such a project to be framed.

The work undertaken to address the specific aims of the long barrows project has highlighted further questions (beyond the scope of the current programme) such as the link between form, function and date, whether all had mounds, their place in the wider landscape and relationship with farmed land and settlement and their relationship with palaeochannels (and the potential for environmental and dating evidence). The project has demonstrated the great importance of re-mapping with current air photographic analysis techniques and has highlighted the potential for further work through detailed lidar analysis, particularly in terms of understanding these monuments in their wider landscape setting. Further opportunities will emerge as current lidar survey for the Environment Agency completes nationwide coverage at 1 metre sample resolution. It is hoped the new, enhanced project dataset will make a significant contribution to our knowledge and understanding of Neolithic funerary monuments as well as to future studies, research and debate.

ACKNOWLEDGEMENTS

The Lincolnshire Long Barrows Project is initiated and funded by Historic England and this paper represents the combined efforts of staff at Historic England and Heritage Lincolnshire. Our research builds public value in the understanding and positive management of the sites. This work would not have been possible without the assistance of numerous private landowners and colleagues in Natural England, the Historic Environment Record Officers at Lincolnshire County Council, North Lincolnshire and North East Lincolnshire unitary authorities and The Lincolnshire Wolds AONB Countryside Service.

REFERENCES

Ashbee, P. (1984) The Earthen Long Barrow in Britain (2nd edn). Norwich, Geo Books.
Barker, H. Burleigh, R. and Meeks, N. (1969) Natural Radiocarbon Measurements VI. *Radiocarbon* 11 (2), 278–94.
Barrett, J. (1994) *Fragments from Antiquity: an archaeology of social life in Britain, 2900–1200 BC*. Oxford, Blackwell.
Bateman, T. (with Glover, S.) (1848) *Vestiges of the Antiquities of Derbyshire, and the Sepulchral Usages of its Inhabitants*. London, John Russell Smith.
Bateman, T. (1861) *Ten Years' Digging in Celtic and Saxon Grave Hills, in the counties of Derby, Stafford, and York, from 1848 to 1858; with notices of some former discoveries, hitherto unpublished, and remarks on the crania and pottery from the mounds*. London, John Russell Smith.
Bewley, R.H. and Jones, D. (1992) Aerial archaeology in Lincolnshire: 1991 and beyond. *Lincolnshire History and Archaeology* 27, 41–3.
Bonner, L.D. and Griffiths D.W. (1993) Skitter to Hatton 4050 mm diameter pipeline, 1993. Unpublished report in Lincolnshire Historic Environment Record.
Bradley, R. (1993) *Altering the Earth*. Edinburgh, Society of Antiquaries of Scotland Monograph 8.
Chowne, P. (1994) The Bain Valley survey. In M. Parker Pearson and R.T. Schadla-Hall (eds) *Looking at the Land: archaeological landscapes in eastern England, recent work and future directions*, 27–32. Leicester, Museums, Arts and Records Service.
Colt Hoare, R. (1812) *The Ancient History of Wiltshire, Volume 1*. London, William Miller.
Evans, J.G. and Simpson, D.D.A. (1991) Giants' Hills 2 long barrow, Skendleby, Lincolnshire. *Archaeologia* 109, 1–45.

Everson, P. (1980) North Lincolnshire, aerial reconnaissance (in 1979). *Lincolnshire History and Archaeology* 15, 80.
Everson, P. (1983) Aerial photography and fieldwork in north Lincolnshire. In G.S. Maxwell (ed.) *The Impact of Aerial Reconnaissance on Archaeology*, 14–26. London, Council for British Archaeology Research Report 49.
Everson, P. and Hayes, T. (1984) Lincolnshire from the air. In N. Field and A. White (eds) *A Prospect of Lincolnshire*, 33–41. Lincoln, privately published.
Field, D. (2006) *Earthen Long Barrows: the earliest monuments in the British Isles*. Stroud, Tempus Publishing.
Jones, D. (1998) Long barrows and Neolithic elongated enclosures in Lincolnshire: an analysis of the air photographic evidence. *Proceedings of the Prehistoric Society* 64, 83–114.
Greenwell, W. (1877) *British Barrows, a Record of the Examination of Sepulchral Mounds in Various Parts of England*. Oxford, Clarendon Press.
Historic England (2019) *Heritage at Risk Register*. https://historicengland.org.uk/advice/heritage-at-risk/search-register/advanced-search.
Kinnes, I. (1992) *Non-Megalithic Long Barrows and Allied Structures in the British Neolithic* (British Museum Occasional Paper 52). London, British Museum.
Loveday, R. (2006) *Inscribed Across the Landscape: the cursus enigma*. Stroud, Tempus Publishing.
Mortimer J.R. (1905) *Forty Years' Researches in British and Saxon Burial Mounds of East Yorkshire, including Romano-British Discoveries, and a Description of the Ancient Entrenchments on a Section of the Yorkshire Wolds*. London, A. Brown and Sons.
Pantos, A. (2001a) Lincolnshire Assembly-Places. No 15 (unpublished) cited in Lincolnshire Historic Environment Record https://www.lincstothepast.com/SPELLOW-HILLS-LONG-BARROW/227212.record?pt=S.
Pantos, A. (2001b) The Meeting Place of Langoe Wapentake. *SLHA Journal: Lincolnshire History and Archaeology* 36, 66–9
Phillips, C.W. (1932) The long barrows of Lincolnshire. *Archaeological Journal* 89, 174–203.
Phillips, C.W. (1933) The present state of archaeology in Lincolnshire, part 1. *Archaeological Journal* 90, 106–49.
Phillips, C.W. (1934) Some new Lincolnshire long barrows. *Proceedings of the Prehistoric Society of East Anglia* 7, 423.
Phillips, C.W. (1936) The excavation of Giants' Hills long barrow, Skendleby. *Archaeologia* 85, 37–106.
Phillips, P. (ed.) (1989) *Archaeology and Landscape Studies in North Lincolnshire*. Oxford, British Archaeological Report 208.
Phillips, P. and Probert, S. (1989) Hoe Hill Long Barrow. Stratigraphy of Excavation Across Quarry Ditch. In P. Phillips (ed.) *Archaeology and Landscape Studies in North Lincolnshire*, 7–19. Oxford, British Archaeological Report 208.
Roskams, S.P. and Whyman, M. (2005) Yorkshire archaeological research framework: a resource assessment. Report 2936 for YARFF and English Heritage.
Tabor, J. Billington, L. Healy. F, and Knight, M. (2016) Early Neolithic pits and artefact scatters at North Fen, Sutton Gault, Cambridgeshire. *Proceedings of the Prehistoric Society* 82, 161–91.
Whittle, A., Barclay, A., Bayliss, A., McFadyen, L., Schulting, R. and Wysocki, M. (2007) Building for the dead: events, processes and changing worldviews from the thirty-eighth to the thirty-fourth centuries cal. BC in southern Britain. *Cambridge Archaeological Journal* 17:1 (supplement), 123–47.
Whittle, A. Richardson, W., Healy, F. and Bayliss, A. (2011) *Gathering Time: dating the Early Neolithic enclosures of southern Britain and Ireland*. Oxford, Oxbow Books.
Willis, S. (2013) *The Roman Roadside Settlement and Multi-Period Ritual Complex at Nettleton and Rothwell, Lincolnshire*. The Central Lincolnshire Wolds Research Project, 1. Pre-Construct Archaeology Limited and University of Kent, https://kar.kent.ac.uk/40748/11/Nettleton%20final%20version.pdf.

Chapter 10

A dialogue with the dead? The relationship between an Early Neolithic rectangular timber building and a chambered tomb on Holy Island, Anglesey, north-west Wales

Jane Kenney

This paper explores the relationship between an Early Neolithic timber building and a Neolithic chambered tomb on Holy Island or Ynys Gybi off the west coast of Anglesey, north-west Wales (Fig. 10.1). Trefignath chambered tomb, which has featured in the literature since the mid-seventeenth century (Smith 1987, 3–5), was recorded in 1874 by a local antiquarian (Stanley 1874). The tomb was fully excavated in the late 1970s by Christopher Smith for the Welsh Office in advance of consolidation of the monument (Smith 1987). The tomb is a scheduled monument (An011) and in Cadw guardianship. The existence of an Early Neolithic timber building was completely unsuspected before the excavation of a large development site known as Parc Cybi, on the southern outskirts of Holyhead. The excavations were carried out by Gwynedd Archaeological Trust between November 2006 and July 2008, with a second season September 2009 to February 2010, funded by the Welsh Government as the developer (Kenney *et al.* 2019). Between May and October 2007, the remains of a timber building were excavated and recorded, constituting postholes, foundation trenches and other features. The importance of the relationship of the building to the tomb was evident at the time of excavation so the outline of the consolidated tomb was surveyed as part of the same survey used to locate the excavation features. This was carried out using a Geodometer total station theodolite and was fixed to OS National Grid coordinates using a survey quality Global Positioning System to locate survey stations.

The building measured approximately 15.5 m long and 6 m wide and was aligned east-north-east to west-south-west (Fig. 10.2). Five pairs of posts formed two parallel rows arranged symmetrically about the long axis of the building, representing a central aisle. A slightly more irregular pattern of posts and plank slots formed the side and end walls of the building. The structure had three bays defined by the locations of the aisle posts, with an additional compartment at the eastern end. There were a small number of features around the building, mostly of minor significance except for a posthole about 9 m to the north, which contained a large, unfinished cannel-coal bead. Radiocarbon dates from the posthole showed that it was contemporary with the use of the building.

Features within and forming the plan of the building contained numerous artefacts including many sherds of Early Neolithic Irish Sea Ware pottery and lithics, particularly local black chert. These finds were suggestive of domestic waste, an impression supported

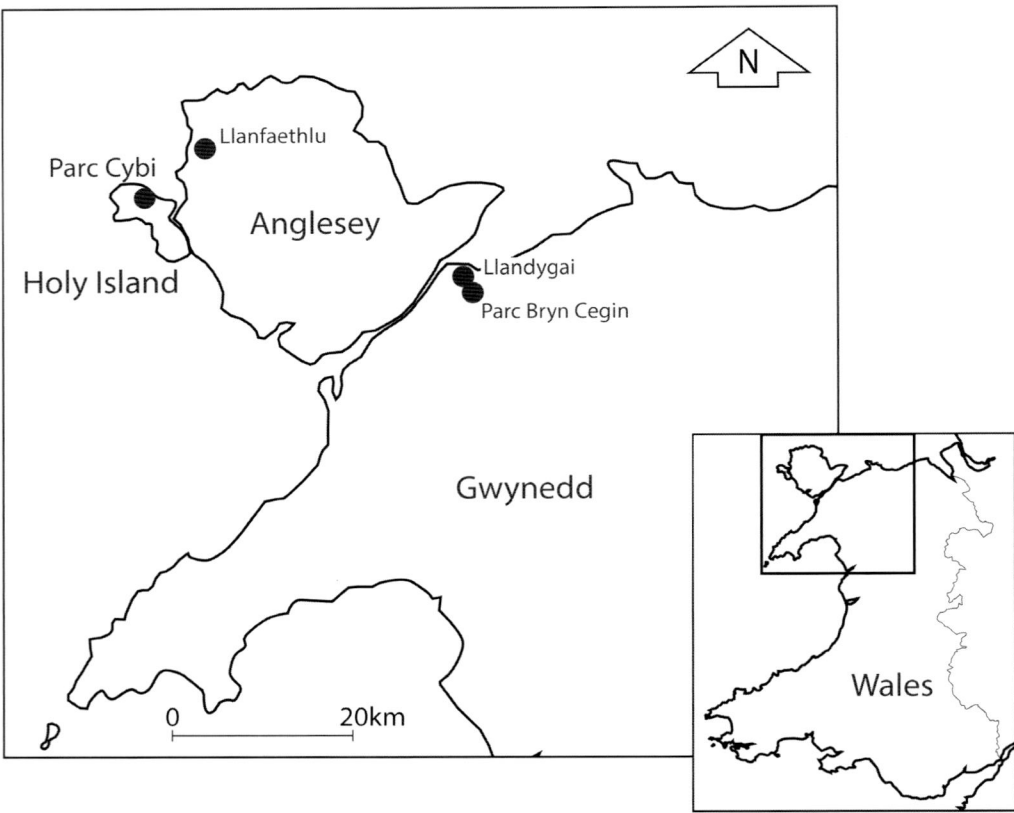

Fig. 10.1: Location of Parc Cybi and other sites in north-west Wales with Early Neolithic rectangular timber buildings.

by the recovery of fragments of burnt animal bone (unburnt bone did not survive due to soil conditions) and two saddle querns. There were also tiny flakes of knapped colourless crystal quartz and occasional flakes of Group VII stone, some of which had polished areas indicating that they originated from ground stone axes.

Although at least one posthole had a postpipe suggesting the post had rotted *in situ* it appears that the building was largely demolished and activity involving the repeated use of pit hearths occurred shortly after. The location of pit hearths cutting the remains of structural elements of the building demonstrates that these were used after the building had been demolished, but the radiocarbon dates from the pit hearths are indistinguishable from those of the use of the building. The pit hearths also contained the same pottery as was used in the building. While the pottery might possibly have originated from the building's use, the dated charred material was from burnt layers that represented the use of the pit hearths. It is concluded that the activity occurred very soon after the abandonment and demolition of the building, so soon that it is not possible to distinguish this from the occupation by radiocarbon dating. The pit hearths may have been part of a closing ritual for the building.

Nine radiocarbon dates were obtained from single short-lived items (charred hazel twigs, hazelnut shells and cereal grains) from a variety of features across the building. When the results of these dates are placed with a Bayesian model they indicate that the building was used from *3725–3655 cal BC (95% probability)*, and probably *3710–3665 cal BC (68% probability)*, until *3655–3610 cal BC (95% probability)*, and probably *3645–3625 cal BC (68% probability)*, with a duration of use of probably *30–75 years (68% probability)* (Hamilton 2019).

The Trefignath chambered tomb is a complex monument with three phases of development, which are fortunately well-understood due to its complete excavation (Smith 1987). Prior to the construction of the first tomb on the site, there was activity resulting in a scatter of lithics and Irish Sea Ware pottery on the ground surface preserved by the subsequent cairn. Irish Sea Ware is a type of Early Neolithic pottery, identified by Frances Lynch in Wales, consisting of undecorated fines wares in a vesicular fabric; the vessel forms include both shouldered and unshouldered bowls

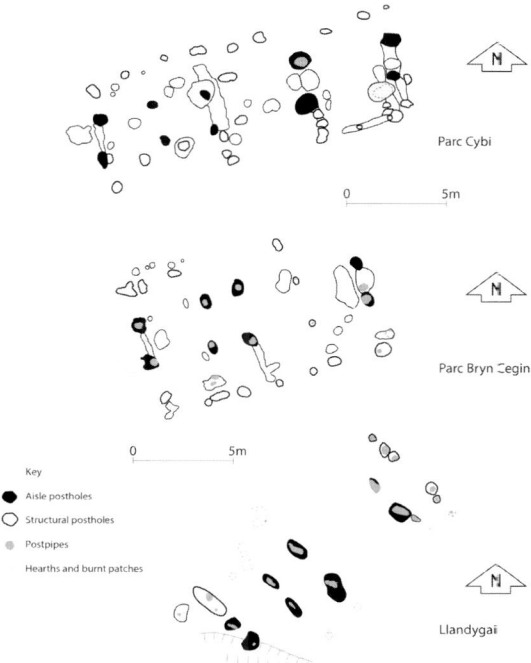

Fig. 10.2. Plan of the rectangular timber building at Parc Cybi compared to those from Llandygai and Parc Bryn Cegin (partly after Kenney 2008, fig. 7, reproduced with kind permission of the Cambrian Archaeological Association).

(Lynch 1976). This activity may have been related to the building of the monument but, it could indicate earlier activity. Four features were found under the cairn, which are interpreted as intercutting postholes that could all have been in use together. These were quite substantial and may hint at a timber structure pre-dating the tomb, though there was insufficient evidence to suggest the plan of such a structure. The first tomb had a small chamber opening to the north and probably had a small circular cairn. Smith suggests that this was a simple Passage Grave (Smith 1987, 14). The cairn was then extended into a long cairn and a new chamber built to the east. This new tomb had a new alignment, east-north-east to west-south-west, with the chamber opening to the east where there was a forecourt. The cairn was then further lengthened and a third chamber built with a new forecourt (Fig. 10.3).

A radiocarbon date of 3977–3695 cal BC (HAR–3932) (95.4% confidence, calibrated using OxCal 4.3; 5050±70 BP) was obtained on charcoal from the ground surface under the first cairn (Smith 1987, 45). The date was on a bulk charcoal sample from a mixed context, so it can only give a very general *terminus post quem* date for the building of the tomb. Sherds of Peterborough Ware and a possible Grooved Ware sherd from the forecourt of

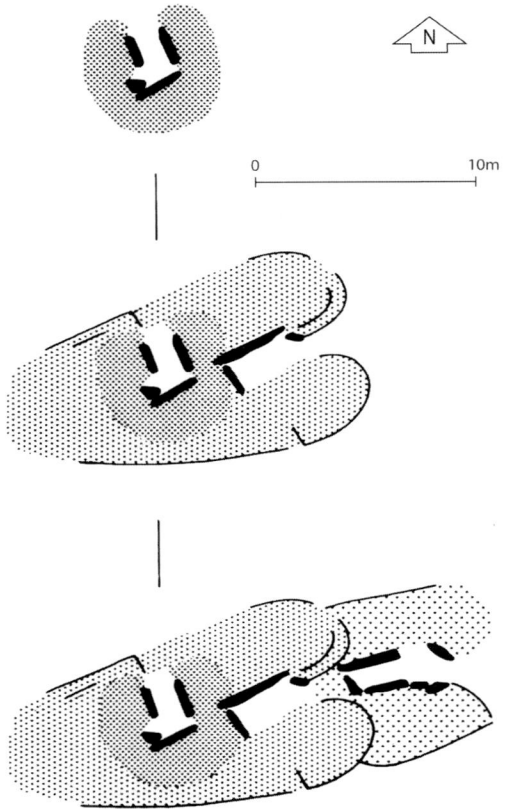

Fig. 10.3. The development of the Trefignath Chambered Tomb, from Smith 1987, fig. 21 (reproduced with kind permission of C.A. Tolan-Smith and the Cambrian Archaeological Association)

the third chamber indicate the use of the tomb, or at least the forecourt, into the mid and possibly late Neolithic. Peterborough Ware from the Parc Cybi excavation dated from *3390–3165 cal BC (68% probability, start of Mortlake style)* to *3060–3000 cal BC (68% probability, end of Fengate style)* (Hamilton 2019).

The tomb is located on a rocky outcrop on top of a locally prominent rise at 19–20 m OD. To the east of the tomb, the ground falls away steeply and there is a long view over the sea to Anglesey. To the south, if there were no trees, as there are at present, there would be a view to the mountains of Snowdonia, and to the north-west is the prominent form of Holyhead Mountain, though the tomb does not seem to reference this (contra Cummings 2004, 34). From the north-west the tomb would have been visible on the skyline to someone standing near the base of the gentle slope. The rectangular timber building was located about 97 m west-south-west of the tomb, at 17 m OD, also close to the top of the same rise. The building was situated where a broadening of the ridge would have made it less visible from a distance than the tomb and was immediately north of a rocky outcrop, which also would have made the building less obvious and would have largely hidden it from the south. The building was positioned so that the tomb would be visible past the edge of the outcrop, as if visibility of the tomb was important. The tomb was at a slightly higher level than the building and the western end of the tomb would have been on the skyline from the building. There was almost certainly clear visibility between the two features in the Neolithic as pollen analysis from the buried soil under the tomb showed that the immediate landscape was open grassland (Greig 1987, 43). The survey of the two monuments shows that they were on the same alignment.

The date of the tomb is too uncertain to be sure of the sequence in relation to the timber building. If the radiocarbon date from the buried soil can be taken to give a very rough *terminus post quem* date for the first phase of the tomb it would suggest this could have been built shortly before or during the life of the building. The pottery shows that the later phases of the tomb were in use after the building was abandoned but the second phase could have been built during the life of the building.

The following sequence is proposed for the building and the various phases of the tomb (Fig. 10.4). It is suggested that the small passage tomb was built first. This opened to the

10. A dialogue with the dead?

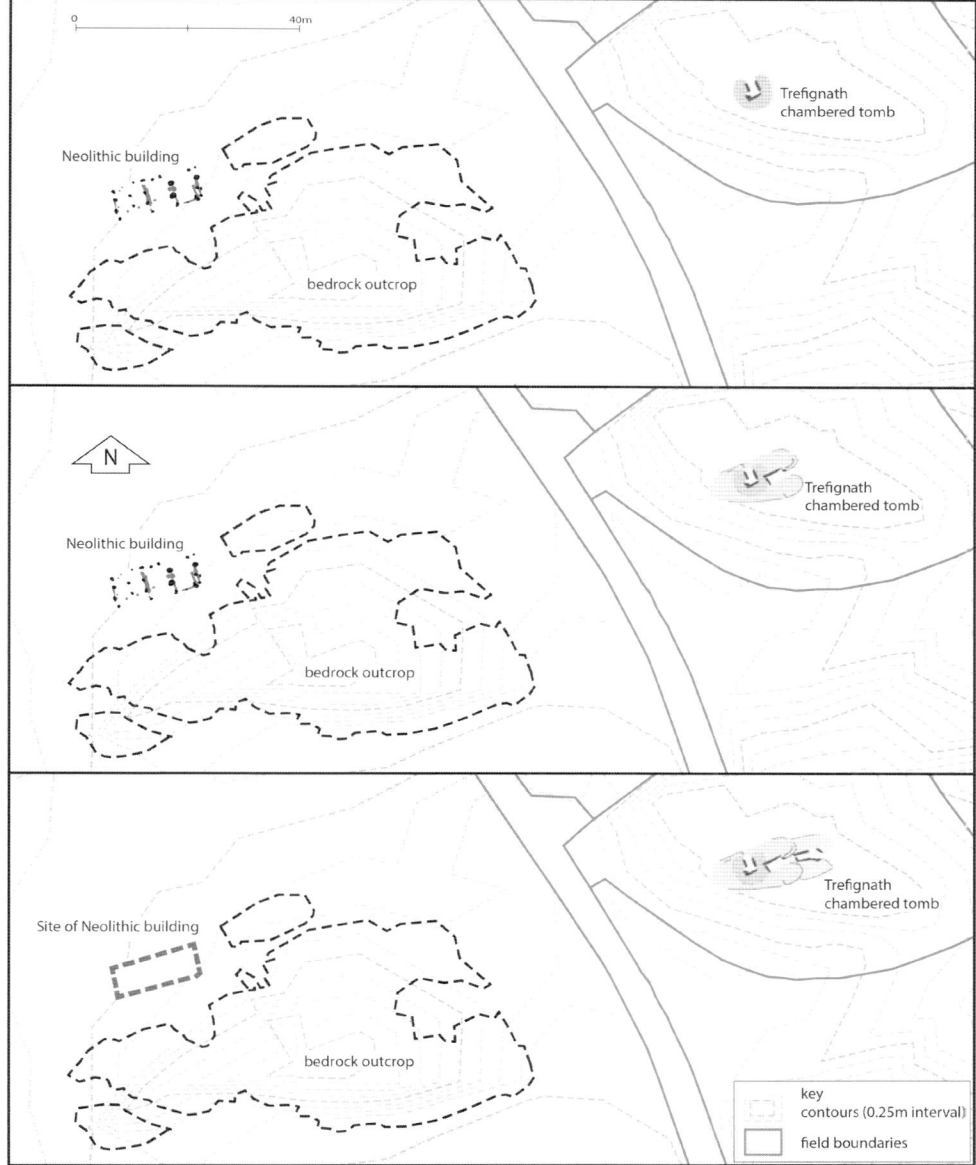

Fig. 10.4. Relationship of the Early Neolithic building and the tomb at the three stages of the tomb's development.

north and does not appear to have influenced the alignment of the subsequent phases of the tomb. The timber building was then constructed orientated on the tomb, that is, the building was aligned so that its long axis was pointing towards the tomb. It is suggested that the tomb may have provided a foresight for an alignment on the sunrise in spring. The second phase of the tomb then seems to have followed this alignment, so that it opened towards the sunrise. The third phase continued and extended this alignment, even though the building is likely to have been abandoned and demolished long before the third phase of the tomb was built.

The change of alignment of the tomb in its second phase indicates a relationship between the tomb and the timber building. Rather than the simple dichotomy of the building being for the living and the tomb for the dead, there appears to have been a dialogue between the two.

The relationship between the timber building, the tomb, and the rising sun needs to be examined further. The azimuth of this alignment is about 80 degrees from OS grid north, and the relevant sunrise would have fallen in April, shortly after the equinox. This falls within the range of approximately west-south-west to east-north-east alignments studied by Loveday (2012). He considers these alignments (between 67–84°) as potentially of significance over a long duration in prehistoric cultures; as seen in the large Mesolithic postholes excavated in the Stonehenge carpark, the Greater Stonehenge Cursus, many classic henges, and some stone circles (Loveday 2012). Two of the henges that Loveday considers are those at Llandygai, near Bangor, Gwynedd (Lynch and Musson 2001), and the duration of this alignment might be pushed forwards by considering the early medieval burials on the same site, the majority of which are on this same alignment. It is highly unlikely that the burials followed the alignment of the henges, even if traces of their banks could still be seen, but they were possibly influenced by a solar alignment in a similar way. Longley (2001) considered that the Llandygai burials and most early medieval burials in north-west Wales were aligned on the sunrise at Easter. As Easter is a movable feast, this is not sunrise on a single day but on a range of days from March 21st to April 25th, giving a range of alignments within a tight arc. The date of Easter is basically fixed by the first full moon after the spring equinox. Ruggles (1999, 148–9, 150–1) considers that prehistoric societies would be unlikely to recognise the equinox as an event of significance and would probably have been unable to fix it with any degree of accuracy. The equinoxes are not marked as special by the rising and setting of the sun, unlike the solstices, when the daily progression of the sunrise and sunset along the horizon stops and then reverses. The solstices are relatively easily recorded by observing from a fixed point and noting a feature on the horizon that indicates the point at which the sun stops before reversing its progress. Loveday suggests that the solstices could be used with the lunar months to provide a timetable for prehistoric festivals that did not drift with the lunar cycle. Counting a set number of full moons from the winter solstice could provide a marker for a spring festival that would fall at about the same time as the Christian Easter but might be used by societies of very different traditions at different periods. Loveday (2012, 347) points out that west-south-west to east-north-east alignments might be read in both directions and refer to sunsets as well as sunrises, so that the full range of events covered might be sunrises in April and then mid-August to mid-September, or sunsets from early February to early March and then October. However, he suggests that the April and October alignments might be the most significant, marking respectively the reawakening of nature or the start of winter. At Parc Cybi the alignment appears to refer specifically to the sunrise and therefore it seems most likely that a spring festival was being marked by the alignment of the timber building and the tomb.

There is currently little evidence that a west-south-west to east-north-east alignment was of general importance to Early Neolithic timber buildings. Smyth (2014, 22–23) has considered the orientation of these structures in Ireland and does not record one on a west-south-west to east-north-east alignment, although 21 are on a north-east to south-west alignment. In Scotland the structures at Claish and Lockerbie Academy were close to north–south, while that at Balbridie was almost exactly east–west (Barclay *et al.* 2002, illustration 25; Kirby 2011). However, the building in Warren Field, Crathes, Aberdeenshire did have a west-south-west to east-north-east alignment, with the east-north-east emphasised (Murray *et al.* 2009, 30). Darvill looked at the buildings from England and Wales known in 1996 (Darvill 1996) and his fig. 6.4 suggests that Structure A from Lismore Fields, Derbyshire and Structure 1 from Clegyr Boia, Dyfed fall within this alignment range. Of more recently discovered buildings, that found at Kingmead Quarry, Horton, Berkshire was aligned west-south-west to east-north-east (Chaffey and Brook 2012, 204), but there is no suggestion that this was an important alignment for English structures. However, an Early Neolithic rectangular timber building found at Parc Bryn Cegin, Llandygai, Gwynedd (Kenney 2008) was on the same alignment (Fig. 10.2). A nearly contemporary building, about 500 m away and excavated in advance of the Llandygai Industrial Estate, was aligned north-east to south-west (Lynch and Musson 2001). These two buildings were very similar in plan to the Parc Cybi building, with the exception that the latter had the additional compartment on the eastern end. This similarity perhaps indicates a coherent building tradition in the region. The site of Llanfaethlu near the north coast of Anglesey provides both contradiction and support for this regional tradition. All four Early Neolithic buildings on this site have a different layout and orientation, though House 1 has similarities to the Llandygai buildings and is aligned west-south-west to east-north-east. House 4 is probably aligned south-west to north-east at a similar angle to Llandygai I (Rees and Jones 2017). It is probably best not to draw conclusions until this site is fully published.

A relationship of this sort with a tomb is also rare. There are a few sites where Neolithic buildings have been found under tombs, most famously at Ballyglass, County Mayo (Ó Nualláin 1972) but also Gwernvale, Powys (Britnell and Savory 1984). There are other examples, such as Hazleton North (Saville 1990), where postholes have been found under tombs, though not certainly part of rectangular buildings. Buildings near tombs are just as rare. Remains interpreted as a domestic settlement were found about 40 m north of the tomb of Caravat Barp at Bharpa Carinish, North Uist, but this site was dated to the latter part of the fourth millennium (Crone *et al.* 1993), later than the Early Neolithic rectangular timber buildings. While not aligned on a tomb the Early Neolithic building at White Horse Stone and probable Early Neolithic building at Pilgrim's Way, Kent, were close to an Early Neolithic megalithic tomb, two megalithic chambers and other possible megalithic structures and might possibly have influenced the location of those monuments (Garwood 2011, 86–8).

The scarcity of Neolithic structures near tombs may partly be due to the rarity of excavations near these monuments, as well as the destruction of tombs leaving no upstanding remains. Although Anglesey has many surviving tombs even more are mentioned in antiquarian accounts, showing that many have been destroyed (Smith 2003). The scarcity of tombs on the mainland opposite Anglesey is notable and may be due to their destruction by improving landlords; Kelly (1974) lists 11 probable chambered tombs in Caernarvonshire, mentioned by antiquarians but no longer visible. Early Neolithic buildings are difficult to find except where extensive stripping of ploughsoil has taken place under archaeological control in advance of development. It may be that the coincidence of suitable archaeological investigation with a surviving tomb is sufficiently rare that this relationship is hardly ever noted.

As the building at Parc Bryn Cegin was on the same alignment as that at Parc Cybi it raises the question of whether this was related to a tomb or had some other feature as a foresight. Any foresight would have been on top of the ridge to the north-east of the building, but this area was not excavated during the archaeological works on that site (Kenney 2008). A geophysical survey was carried out over this area and revealed a large circular anomaly (Sabin 2005) but the lack of excavation meant that this was not tested and could possibly be an artefact of the geology.

If the alignment of the Parc Cybi building did mark a spring festival this could hint at its use. The artefacts recovered were suggestive of normal domestic activity, though how such activity could be distinguished from seasonal feasting is not obvious. Lipid analysis may provide some evidence. Sherds of pottery from the Parc Cybi building were analysed for lipid residues and all samples, where lipids were preserved, proved to be of dairy fats (Dunne and Evershed 2019a). Although dairy fat is common in Early Neolithic assemblages it is unusual for no traces of other fats to be found. This might suggest that dairy products were considered as the only appropriate food to be held by pottery vessels or it could mean that the building was used only at a time of year when young livestock had recently been born and milk was particularly plentiful. The latter suggestion would support the connection with a spring festival, but this interpretation should be used with some caution. Sherds from an area of temporary occupation, roughly contemporary with the building but 490 m away, also showed that vessels were only used for dairy products. This tradition may have been common to occupation and activity sites of all types in the Early Neolithic of Holy Island, and not unique to the rectangular timber building. Sherds analysed from the building at Parc Bryn Cegin, Llandygai did show that while pots mainly contained dairy products some had been used for the processing or cooking of animal body fats (Dunne and Evershed 2019b).

It has been argued that the evidence from Parc Cybi indicates a relationship between the rectangular timber building and the tomb which influenced the location of the building, and subsequently the re-alignment of the tomb. It is also suggested that the alignment may have marked a spring festival. The scarcity of similar alignments within Britain and Ireland, suggests that this may have been a tradition of only local significance. However, the relationship between the building and the tomb does support the contention that similar Neolithic timber structures may not have been purely domestic in function but also had ritual or ceremonial connections.

ACKNOWLEDGEMENTS

The excavation and post-excavation analysis of the Parc Cybi site was funded by the Welsh Government. The author would like to thank Frances Lynch and Andrew Davidson for their comments on this paper. Thanks also to Roy Loveday for making the author aware of his work on solar alignments.

REFERENCES

Barclay, G.J., Brophy, K. and MacGregor, G. (2002) Claish, Stirling: an Early Neolithic structure in its context. *Proceedings of the Society of Antiquaries of Scotland* 132, 65–138.

Britnell, W.J. and Savory, H.N. (1984) *Gwernvale and Penywyrlod: two Neolithic long cairns in the Black Mountains of Brecknock*, Cardiff, Cambrian Archaeological Association (Cambrian Archaeological Monographs 2).

Chaffey, G. and Brook, E. (2012) Domesticity in the Neolithic: excavations at Kingsmead Quarry, Horton, Berkshire. In H. Anderson-Whymark and J. Thomas (eds) *Regional Perspectives on Neolithic Pit Deposition: beyond the mundane*. Oxford, Oxbow Books, 200–15.

Crone, A., Armit, I., Boardman, S., Finlayson, B., MacSween, A., and Mills, C. (1993) Excavation and survey of sub-peat features of Neolithic, Bronze and Iron Age date at Bharpa Carinish, North Uist, Scotland. *Proceedings of the Prehistoric Society, 59*, 361–82.

Cummings, V. (2004) Connecting the mountains and sea: the monuments of the eastern Irish Sea zone. In V. Cummings and C. Fowler, *The Neolithic of the Irish Sea: materiality and traditions of practice*, 29–36. Oxford, Oxbow Books.

Darvill, T. (1996) Neolithic buildings in England, Wales and the Isle of Man. In T. Darvill and J. Thomas (eds) *Neolithic Houses in Northwest Europe and Beyond, Neolithic Studies Group Seminar Papers 1*, 77–112. Oxbow Monograph 57, Oxford, Oxbow Books.

Dunne, J. and Evershed, R.P. (2019a) Organic residue analysis of Neolithic and Bronze Age Pottery from Parc Cybi. In J. Kenney, N. McGuinness, R. Cooke, C. Rees and A. Davidson, Multi-period Excavations at Parc Cybi, Holyhead, Anglesey. Unpublished Gwynedd Archaeological Trust Report, volume 3.

Dunne, J. and Evershed, R.P. (2019b) Organic Residue Analysis of Early Neolithic Pottery from Parc Bryn Cegin, Llandygai, near Bangor, Wales. Unpublished report of Organic Geochemistry Unit, School of Chemistry, University of Bristol.

Garwood, P. (2011) Chapter 3: Early prehistory. In P. Booth, T. Champion, S. Foreman, P. Garwood, H. Glass, J. Munby and A. Reynolds, *On Track: the archaeology of High Speed 1, Section 1 in Kent*, 37–150. Oxford, Oxford Wessex Archaeology (Monograph No. 4).

Greig, J.R.A. (1987) Pollen and plant macrofossils. In C.A. Smith and F.M. Lynch, *Trefignath and Din Dryfol, the excavation of two megalithic tombs in Anglesey*, 39–44. Cardiff, Cambrian Archaeological Monographs No. 3.

Hamilton, D. (2019) The Radiocarbon Dates. In J. Kenney, N. McGuinness, R. Cooke, C. Rees and A. Davidson, Multi-period Excavations at Parc Cybi, Holyhead, Anglesey. Unpublished Gwynedd Archaeological Trust Report, volume 3.

Kelly, R.S. (1974) The probable sites of some disappeared chambered tombs in Caernarvonshire in the light of antiquarian references. *Archaeologia Cambrensis* CXXIII, 175–9.

Kenney, J. (2008) Recent excavations at Parc Bryn Cegin Llandygai near Bangor, North Wales. *Archaeologia Cambrensis* 157, 9–142.

Kenney, J., McGuinness, N., Cooke, R., Rees, C. and Davidson, A. (2019) Multi-period Excavations at Parc Cybi, Holyhead, Anglesey. Unpublished Gwynedd Archaeological Trust Report (this report will be available to download from the Archwilio and Coflein websites (search for Parc Cybi)).

Kirby, M. (2011) *Lockerbie Academy: Neolithic and Early Historic timber halls, a Bronze Age cemetery, an undated enclosure and a post-medieval corn-drying kiln in south-west Scotland*. Scottish Archaeological Internet Report 46, https://archaeologydataservice.ac.uk/archives/view/sair/contents.cfm?vol=46 (accessed 16/09/2019).

Longley, D. (2001) Early Medieval Cemetery. In F. Lynch and C. Musson, A prehistoric and early medieval complex at Llandegai, near Bangor, North Wales. *Archaeologia Cambrensis* 150, 106–15.

Loveday, R. (2012) The Greater Stonehenge Cursus – the Long View. *Proceedings of the Prehistoric Society* 78, 341–50.

Lynch, F. (1976) Towards a chronology of megalithic tombs in Wales. In G.C. Boon and J.M. Lewis (eds) *Welsh Antiquity*, 63–79. Cardiff, National Museum of Wales.

Lynch, F. and Musson, C. (2001) A prehistoric and early medieval complex at Llandegai, near Bangor, North Wales. *Archaeologia Cambrensis* 150, 106–15.

Murray, H.K., Murray, J.C. and Fraser, S.M. (2009) *A Tale of the Unknown Unknowns: a Mesolithic pit alignment and a Neolithic timber hall at Warren Field, Crathes, Aberdeenshire*. Oxford, Oxbow Books.

Ó Nualláin, S. (1972) A Neolithic house at Ballyglass near Ballycastle, Co. Mayo. *Journal of the Royal Society of Antiquaries of Ireland* 102, 49–57.

Rees, C. and Jones, M. (2017) Wales' earliest village? *Current Archaeology* 332, 18–26.

Ruggles, C. (1999) *Astronomy in Prehistoric Britain and Ireland*. New Haven and London, Yale University Press.

Sabin, D. (2005) Geophysical Survey Report: Parc Bryn Cegin, Llandegai, Bangor. Stratascan unpublished report No. J1963.

Saville, A. (1990) *Hazleton North, the Excavation of a Neolithic Long Cairn of the Cotswold-Severn group*. London, HBMCE (English Heritage Archaeological Report no 13).

Smith, C. (1987) The excavation of the Trefignath burial chambers – 1977 to 1979. In C.A. Smith and F.M. Lynch, *Trefignath and Din Dryfol, the excavation of two megalithic tombs in Anglesey*. Cardiff, Cambrian Archaeological Monographs No. 3.

Smith, G. (2003) Prehistoric Funerary and Ritual Monument Survey: West Gwynedd and Anglesey. Unpublished Gwynedd Archaeological Trust Report No. 478.

Smyth, J. (2014) *Settlement in the Irish Neolithic, New Discoveries at the Edge of Europe*. Oxford, Oxbow Books (Prehistoric Society Paper No. 6).

Stanley, W.O. (1874) Cromlech at Trefigneth. *Archaeological Journal* 31, 1–2.

Chapter 11

House of the living, house of the dead:
An open and shut case from Ballyglass, Co. Mayo?

Jessica Smyth

The Early Neolithic court tomb at Ballyglass is the larger of two such monuments (Ma. 13 and Ma. 14 in the national inventory of megalithic monuments) in Ballyglass townland and one of a group of 30 court tombs forming a dense concentration on the carboniferous sandstones around Bunatrahir Bay in north Mayo. The tomb is situated on level ground at the western edge of a narrow area of lowlands between the sea and higher peat-covered ridges to the south-west, with the Ballinglen and Bellananaminnaun rivers lying 500 m to the east and west, respectively (Fig. 11.1). Ballyglass Ma. 13 seems to have been first noted in the early nineteenth century by cartographer William Bald. In a letter postmarked 'Castlebar 1825' to

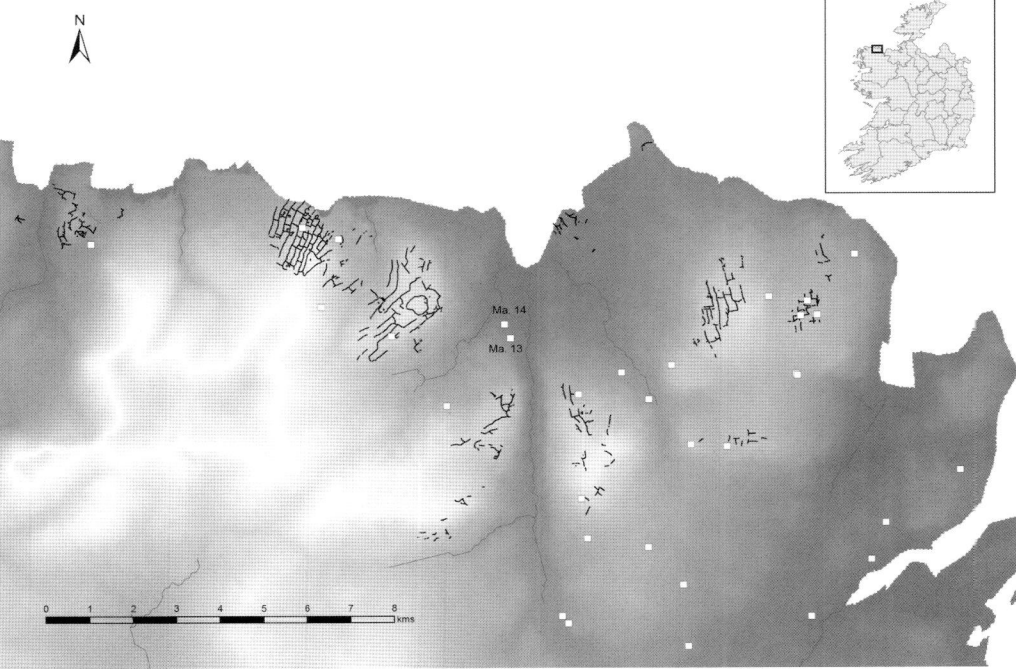

Fig. 11.1: Location of Ballyglass Ma. 13 and Ma. 14 court tombs, north-west Mayo, showing density of court tombs (white squares) and the extent of sub-bog field walls (part of the Céide Fields complex) in the surrounding area.

Fig. 11.2: Post-excavation plan of the court tomb and underlying house at Ballyglass, showing the extent of cuttings. The postholes and section of foundation trench uncovered beneath the kerb during the 1969 field season is also marked.

a Miss Clendening in Dublin, Bald provided a simple sketch of the monument, describing it as 'a druidical place of worship having two cromlechs' (Hayes 1965, 110). The dual gallery and central court features of Ballyglass Ma. 13 were subsequently confirmed in the modern megalithic surveys of the mid-twentieth century onwards (de Valera 1951; 1960, 94 and plate VI; de Valera and Ó Nualláin 1964). These surveys recorded a north-west–south-east orientation and a large elliptical central court measuring 11.50 m (north-west to south-east) × 7.25 m (north-east to south-west) with a lateral entrance to the north-east and two segmented galleries running off the court in opposite directions (Fig. 11.2). The sandstone and granite orthostatic structure had survived almost entirely intact, along with a number of corbels and a single sandstone lintel in position above the galleries. Two large sandstone slabs lying at either end of the court were interpreted as displaced gallery capstones.

As one of only eight known central court tombs in Ireland, Ballyglass Ma. 13 has received more attention than most (*e.g.* Ó Nualláin 1976) and remains the only central court tomb to have been excavated. Excavation took place over three 8-week seasons in July and August 1969–71 and were directed by Seán Ó Nualláin, Archaeological Officer to the Ordnance Survey of Ireland. Prior to excavation, the original form of the surrounding cairn was unclear, although sections of surviving kerb suggested a long elliptical-shaped cairn, 35 m in maximum length and 15 m in maximum width. Due to the symmetrical nature of the tomb, the main baseline was set up to divide the court and the galleries along their long axes with a site grid laid out along this baseline and ten cuttings marked out. Additional cuttings were opened in subsequent years to expose the full extent of the Early Neolithic house, and a large area to the south of the tomb and house was opened to investigate the extent of cultivation evidence revealed outside the kerb. In the final season of fieldwork, the area north of the tomb was opened in a series of adjoining cuttings. Cuttings were also opened in fields to the east and west of the tomb (Fig. 11.2). An interim report was published soon after excavations finished (Ó Nualláin 1972), although the site awaits full publication. In collaboration with the University College Dublin School of Archaeology, this work was at an advanced stage prior to Ó Nualláin's death in 2006. The archive remains in University College Dublin and the publication project has seen renewed effort in recent years, with specialist reports and additional radiocarbon dates commissioned. I am grateful to my University College Dublin colleagues for permission to reproduce components of the Ballyglass monograph currently in preparation.

TOMB-HOUSE STRATIGRAPHY

Clear stratigraphic evidence for the tomb-house sequence emerged over Ó Nualláin's three fieldwork seasons. The first season in 1969 focused on the north-western end of the tomb, and excavation just outside the western section of the kerb revealed two postholes and

Fig. 11.3: Pre-excavation photograph (facing north-east) of Ballyglass house, showing the south-western section of the court tomb kerb overlying part of the foundation trench.

a short section of a narrow trench containing dark soil (Fig. 11.2). Removal of the cairn material and overlying strata in this area in 1970 revealed the foundations of a rectangular timber building, which was excavated in 1971 (Fig. 11.3). The postholes and trench uncovered in 1969 were then recognised as forming the southern corner of the building, overlain by the line of the kerb at this point. This earlier timber building, while described in the interim report as running north-west to south-east (Ó Nualláin 1972, 54), the same orientation assigned to the court tomb above (Ó Nualláin 1976, 103), is very definitely on a different, more north-north-west to south-south-east orientation, a point that will be returned to below.

HOUSE OF THE LIVING?

From the time of its discovery, the Ballyglass timber building was recognised as belonging to an emerging corpus of Neolithic rectangular houses across Ireland and Britain (Ó Nualláin 1972, 55). In the early 1970s, there were very few direct comparisons from the island of Ireland: the discovery at Ballynagilly, Co. Tyrone a couple of years earlier (ApSimon 1969) and the rectangular houses uncovered at Lough Gur, Co. Limerick 20–30 years previously (Ó Ríordáin 1954). Nearly 50 years later and with over 100 Irish Neolithic timber buildings now documented (Smyth 2014), Ballyglass can be seen to belong to a very recognisable style of timber architecture in use in the early fourth millennium BC. Measuring approximately 13 m × 6 m and defined along three sides by a continuous slot trench with associated postholes, Ballyglass bears a particularly close resemblance to houses uncovered at Corbally, Co. Kildare and Tankardstown, Co. Limerick (Smyth 2014, fig. 3.8). Charcoal from the postholes and wall trenches of the Ballyglass house, identified as oak and hazel with some willow or poplar (McKeown n.d.), indicate a mix of sturdier post and planking and lighter structural elements and align well with wider island-wide patterns (Smyth 2014, 34–6).

Domestic spaces are of course defined as much by function as by form, and there is ample additional evidence for Ballyglass serving as a 'house of the living'. Pottery sherds representing up to 18 Early Neolithic Carinated Bowls were recovered from contexts such as the foundation trenches, postholes and the area outside the house, and the assemblage has close affinities with pottery from other Irish Early Neolithic houses (Roche n.d.). These pots were certainly used for processing food: carbonised matter and sooting was visible on a number of exterior and interior surfaces and ruminant dairy fats have been identified in vessels recently selected for organic residue analysis, well documented in assemblages from other Early Neolithic houses (Fig. 11.4; Smyth and Evershed 2016). The small lithic assemblage is also characteristic of house sites: a few fine re-touched pieces such as leaf-shaped arrowheads and a plano-convex knife with some tool maintenance and use but few cores and little production evidence (Smyth 2014, 54–5), although the area to the east of the house may have been used for chert working (Warren n.d.).

Fire-reddened areas of clay were revealed within the eastern and south-eastern end of the house, with the largest of these occurring in the south-eastern end of the central compartment, comprising a spread of oxidised clay underneath a dense charcoal deposit. It may indicate the presence of a hearth, although the charcoal deposit appeared to radiate outwards from the plank footing in the south-eastern partition wall and could also be the

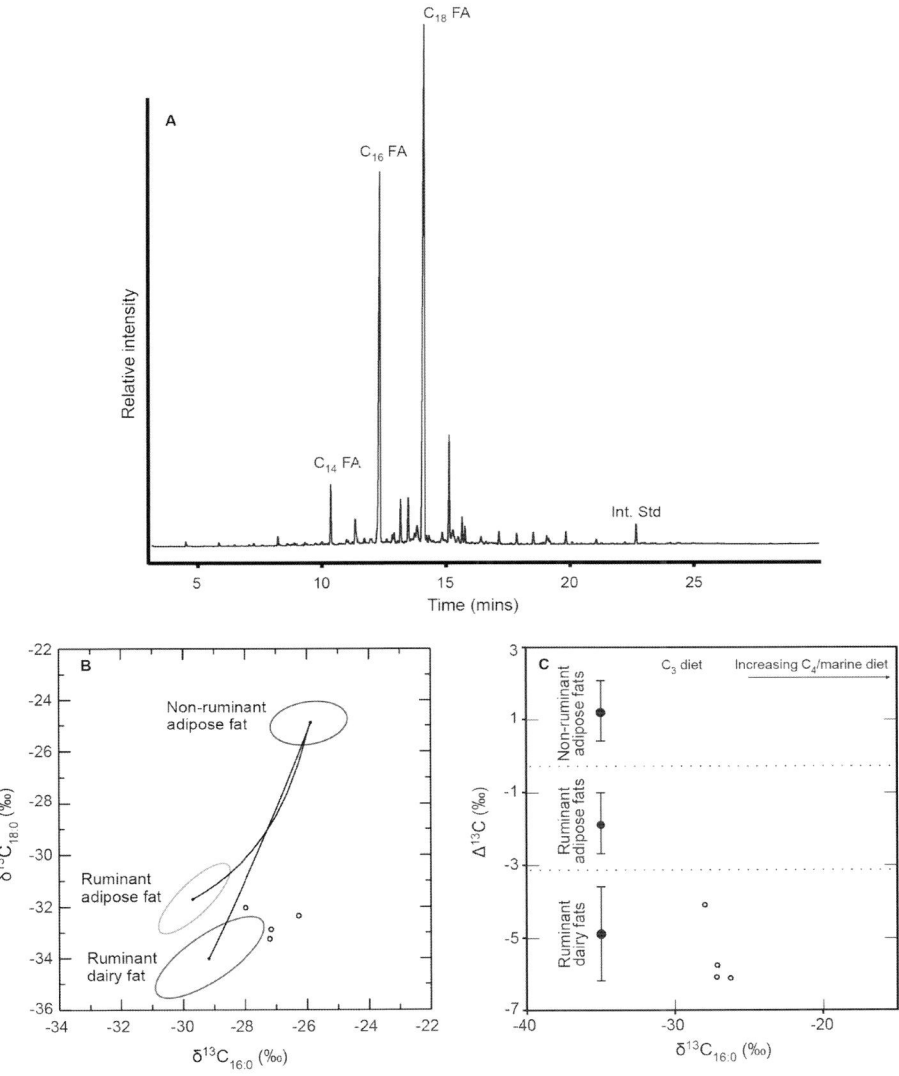

Fig. 11.4: Partial gas chromatogram of lipid extract from BGS-4, a sherd of Early Neolithic Carinated Bowl from Ballyglass house (Vessel 5 in Fig. 11.5), showing a lipid distribution characteristic of a degraded animal fat. Cx FA are free fatty acids of carbon length x; Int. Std is the internal standard (C_{34} n-alkane); b) Scatter plot showing $\delta^{13}C$ values determined from $C_{16:0}$ and $C_{18:0}$ fatty acids preserved in Carinated Bowl pottery from the Ballyglass house. Ellipses show 1 standard deviation confidence ellipses from modern reference terrestrial species from the UK (Copley et al. 2003). Archaeological and modern data are corrected for the addition of a methyl carbon during derivatisation using a mass balance equation (Rieley 1994) and the reference fats are corrected for the contribution of post-industrial carbon (Friedli et al. 1986); c) the same data with $\Delta^{13}C$ values (=$\delta^{13}C_{18:0}$–$\delta^{13}C_{16:0}$) plotted against $\delta^{13}C_{16:0}$ values. Ranges of the $\Delta^{13}C$ values are based on a global database comprising modern reference animal fats from the UK, Africa, Kazakhstan, Switzerland and the Near East.

burnt remains of structural timbers and wattle screens. Episodes of intense burning are not uncommon in Irish Early Neolithic houses and arguments for accidental or deliberate burning can vary from site to site (Smyth 2014, 65–7). Either way, it provides further evidence that the house beneath the court tomb at Ballyglass was functioning similarly to other houses across the island.

Where Ballyglass may diverge from the wider corpus is in the so far unique recovery of a human cremation associated with the house. As is common on Irish sites, no unburnt bone was recovered from the excavation but analysis of the cremated material identified 97 fragments of poorly cremated bone (weighing a total of 14.5 g) found with a quartz chip within the charcoal spread in the south-eastern part of the house. Eight of these fragments were identified as human skull (Delaney n.d.). There was no further contextual information recorded, but Early Neolithic pottery recovered from a posthole (F32) in this area had a fragment of unidentified cremated bone adhering to it (Roche n.d.; Fig. 11.2), making this deposit more likely to be associated with the house than the later tomb. Deliberate deposits of burnt bone have been recorded at two other houses: Tankardstown South, Co. Limerick and Cruicerath, Co. Meath, the former identified as animal bone and the latter unidentifiable (Smyth 2014, 58). It is tempting to suggest that this human cremation at Ballyglass had some role in the site's trajectory and the subsequent construction of the court tomb. However, with so many poorly preserved and unidentifiable bone assemblages from Early Neolithic houses their association with human remains is far from being fully understood.

DATING BALLYGLASS HOUSE AND COURT TOMB

Dating evidence is another consideration in assessing the 'specialness' of the Ballyglass house and the relationship between house and tomb. There have been three phases of radiocarbon dating since the site was excavated, involving the Smithsonian Institute (1974), Centrum voor Isotopen Onderzoek, Groningen (1999), and Queen's University Belfast (2008). Four bulk samples of unidentified charcoal from the house wall trenches and one oak sample from a posthole in the south-eastern wall of the central house compartment were dated by the Smithsonian Institute (Ó Nualláin 1976, 114). A sample of oak charcoal from an ashy deposit east of the house and underlying the cairn was dated by Groningen. More recently, hazelnut shell from an external corner posthole and cereal rachis fragments from the eastern wall trench of the house have been dated at Queen's University Belfast (Table 11.1).

The Smithsonian measurements, while all statistically consistent, cluster in the latter half of the fourth millennium BC (the Middle Neolithic) and are considered anomalously recent for their contexts. A similar error or offset has been noted for other Smithsonian dates on samples from nearby Ballyglass Ma. 14 and the Céide Fields (see Cooney *et al.* 2011). In contrast, the most recent dates on short-lived samples from the Ballyglass house, within the range 3950–3650 BC at 95% probability, fit well with current Bayesian models for the Irish Early Neolithic house horizon (*starting 3730–3660 cal BC* at 95% probability, Cooney *et al.* 2011 or *starting 3720–3680 cal BC* at 95% probability, Whitehouse *et al.* 2014; Table 11.1).

Table 11.1: Radiocarbon dates from the house and tomb at Ballyglass

Lab code	Material	Context	BP determination	Calibrated date range BC (2σ)	$\delta^{13}C$	Sample id
SI-1452	Charcoal (unidentified)	House, east wall trench	4480±90	3380–2910 (94.5%)	–	E83:446-8
SI-1453	Charcoal (unidentified)	House, eastern partition wall trench	4530±95	3520–2920	–	E83:442-5
SI-1451	Charcoal (unidentified)	House, south wall trench	4575±90	3630–3580, 3540–3020	–	E83:436-8
SI-1454	Oak charcoal	House, posthole F62	4575±105	3640–3560, 3540–3010, 2980 2960, 2950–2940	–	E83:456
SI-1450	Charcoal (unidentified)	House, north wall trench	4680±95	3660–3310, 3300–3260, 3240–3100	–	E83:432/3
GrN-24989	Bulk charcoal (hazel, willow/poplar, oak)	Pit F72, back chamber of west gallery in tomb	2350±80	760–340, 320–200	–	E83:293
GrN-24891	Oak charcoal	Ash spread F63 beneath cairn east of house	4990±110	4040–4010, 4000–3620, 3590–3530	–	E83:468
UBA-8570	Hazelnut shell	House, posthole F43	5005±42	3950–3690	–14.5	E83:153
UBA-8571	Cereal rachis fragments	House, eastern end of east wall	4948±32	3790–3650	–29.5	E83:475

Measurements calibrated using measurements calibrated using OxCal v4.3.2 (Bronk Ramsey 2017) and IntCal13 atmospheric curve (Reimer et al. 2013).

The amount of time that elapsed between the house being demolished and the court tomb being constructed is more difficult to determine. The court orthostats were never lifted and the underlying deposits not excavated, thus no primary dating material was retrieved. The 1999 date from the ash spread beneath the cairn, together with two house dates above, provide *termini post quos* for the tomb's construction, while the initial use of Irish court tombs has recently been modelled as *starting 3700–3570 cal BC* (95% probability: Schulting *et al.* 2012, 27). This estimate was based on 47 determinations from 12 court tombs, two of which lie nearby: Ballyglass Ma. 14, 230 m to the south, and Behy, 6.4 km to the west, so is likely to be representative of activity in the area (although as mentioned above, dates from Ma. 14 may be problematic). With Irish Early Neolithic houses currently modelled as *ending 3640–3605 cal BC* (95% probability: Cooney *et al.* 2011) or *3640–3620 cal BC* (95% probability: Whitehouse *et al.* 2014), we are presented with a scenario of Ballyglass Ma. 13 appearing towards the end of the estimated range of court tomb use. In this regard, it is interesting to note that the pottery retrieved from Ballyglass Ma. 13 was almost exclusively Middle Neolithic in style, thought to represent a phase of re-use when the original tomb contents were cleared out (Roche n.d.; Fig. 11.5). However, it may in fact reflect the shifting pottery styles of the 36th century BC communities that erected the monument.

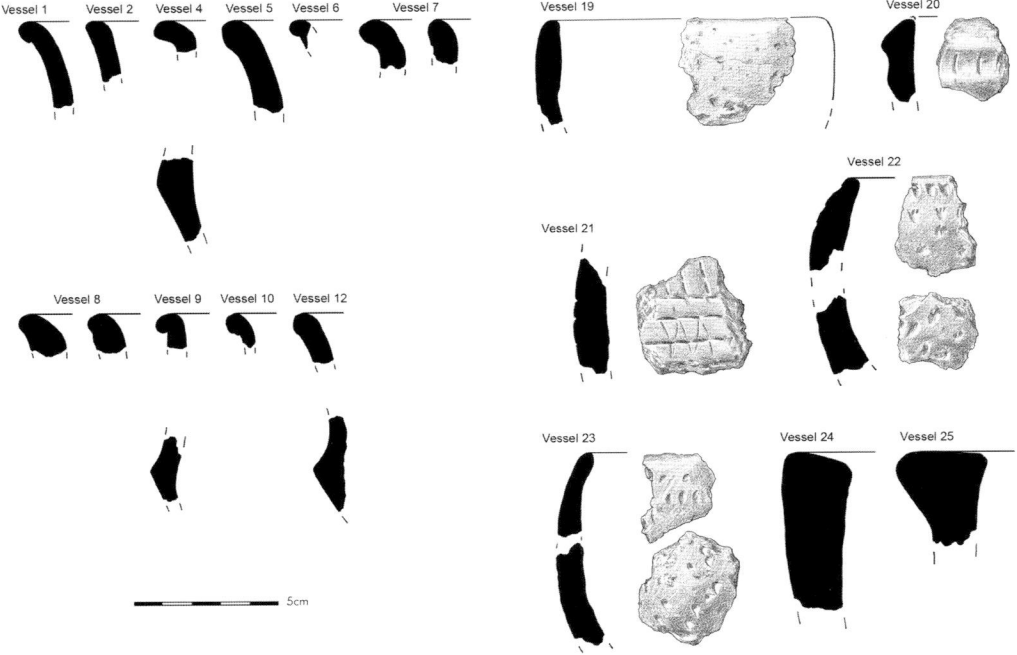

Fig. 11.5: Examples of Early Neolithic Carinated Bowl pottery from the Ballyglass house and Middle Neolithic globular bowls from the court tomb above (illustrations by Ursula Mattenburger).

THE CONNECTION BETWEEN HOUSE AND TOMB

The activity taking place at Ballyglass while the house was standing, before the court tomb was erected, certainly fits wider patterns of form, function and practice seen at similar Early Neolithic sites (Smyth 2014). While the relatively small area investigated prevents us defining the full extent of the settlement, there are examples of both single houses and small clusters of buildings being built during this period and Ballyglass could have developed in either way (Smyth 2014, 25). It is also important to note that activity associated with the house going out of use is not necessarily connected to the positioning of the later tomb. In addition to the episode of burning in the eastern wall mentioned above, postholes in the house seemed to have been deliberately filled with stones and soil, presumably after the posts had been removed, with some postholes covered by a layer of daub (Ó Nualláin 1972, 54–5). Ó Nualláin concluded that the house was intentionally demolished to make way for the tomb, but the large number of houses excavated since the early 1970s show that deliberate acts of destruction or decommissioning are common. Intense burning, dismantling and infilling, the digging of pits and purposeful deposition occurs on many sites that never saw the superimposition of a funerary monument and is more likely to be related to practices tied up in the lifecycle of the house (Smyth 2014, 59–69).

So why did Ballyglass take this trajectory, changing from a domestic space to one associated with mortuary ritual? It may be useful to first unpick the idea of a 'house of the living' being transformed into – or directly referenced by – a 'house of the dead', which is perhaps too simplistic to explain the process at Ballyglass. Significantly, house and tomb do not share the same orientation and, while there is certainly a stratigraphic relationship, the court tomb is not centrally placed on the house. Indeed, the main orthostatic structure avoids the earlier house completely, sited just to the east (Fig. 11.2). This spatial relationship is very similar to that observed on Early Neolithic settlements with multiple houses, *e.g.* at Monanny, Co. Monaghan, where buildings rarely share an identical orientation and are virtually never superimposed (Smyth 2014, 22–7). Interestingly, House B at Monanny was intensely burnt at one section of its southern wall and appears to have been deliberately dismantled, while House C, located less than 3 m away and interpreted as the final building on the site, was burnt down *in situ* (Walsh 2009). Like other settlements, there may have been a stage at Ballyglass where both structures lay side by side, the footprint of the house, discernible through burnt and disturbed patches in the soil, nearly abutting the newly erected megalithic settings. However, the Ballyglass house was eventually subsumed by the monument, although not fully covered or erased. The south-eastern half of the building was buried under the cairn, with hints that this was done carefully with a memory of what lay beneath. The stones of the south-western kerb were placed along the line of the southern/south-western house wall and during excavation it was noted that within the cairn itself, composed of angular sandstone slabs, nine large rounded granite boulders up to 1.5 m in height had been set into the cairn material overlying the south-eastern section of the rectangular house. This is the portion of the house that saw intense burning and also the area from which the deposit of cremated human bone was recovered. Caveats about bone preservation notwithstanding, if there was a point of divergence in Ballyglass' history from that of an 'ordinary' Early Neolithic settlement to megalithic monument, it may have been rooted in the marking or memorialisation of this cremation deposit rather than the house itself.

Another consideration in assessing the 'house of the dead/house of the living' model is the fact that Ballyglass Ma. 13 effectively comprises two 'houses of the dead' – the galleries that run in opposite directions from the central court. The design of central court tombs like Ballyglass Ma. 13 has been discussed by Powell (2005, 15), who speculates on the presence of a 'local community built around an alliance between two unrelated lineages', the alliance reflected in the single shared court and their lack of shared ancestry reflected in two galleries with their backs at opposite ends of the monument. If this were the case at Ballyglass – and Ó Nualláin (1976, 108) was confident that the monument was conceived as a single design – then a straightforward translation of timber house into megalithic house is problematic. How do we reconcile the apparent difference in social units across house and tomb? Might the occupants of the house have comprised one of Powell's lineages, and from where might the second group have come?

The landscape around Ballyglass also brings an important dimension to the site and interpreting its trajectory. Ballyglass forms part of an extraordinarily dense cluster of 30 court tombs spread across an area approximately 20 km east–west by 10 km north–south (Fig. 11.1). The fact that these tombs are located on moderately elevated land, largely on the sides of river valleys, and on relatively thin and well-drained soils, suggests they map onto the settlement pattern of the communities that built them (de Valéra and Ó Nualláin 1964, 114–6). Likewise, density of tomb distribution is presumed to mirror density of settlement, reflecting the quality and carrying capacity of land in that particular area (Darvill 1979, 316) as well as the accessibility of the terrain relative to other places along the north-west coast (de Valéra and Ó Nualláin 1964, 116). Successive writers have imagined a dynamic landscape around Ballyglass in the Neolithic: an initial 'massive incursion' of sea-borne farming groups (de Valéra and Ó Nualláin 1964, 116) creating a contested space negotiated through court tomb design, construction and ritual practice (Ó Nualláin 1976; Darvill 1979; Powell 2005). Competition within and between local groups is also suggested to be a driver of the land enclosure – the Céide Fields complex – recorded across this court tomb distribution (Powell 2005; Fig. 12.1), which in places is clearly associated with tomb construction and use (Caulfield *et al*. 2011; Caulfield *et al*. 2013; Warren 2018). In this sense, Ballyglass Ma. 13 is as much a 'tomb for the living' as a 'house for the dead' (Case 1969, 13; Fleming 1973). If farming groups poured into this area in the early fourth millennium BC, it is an episode not recorded in the monument distribution or in the settlement remains in any other part of the island. The unusual sequence of house and tomb at Ballyglass may thus be due to a particular set of social dynamics at play across this small coastal region, where the landscape was marked out in different ways to the rest of the island. Without better chronological resolution of individual court tombs within this north-west Mayo cluster, we cannot tell if the wider Ballyglass landscape was as busy as previous writers have assumed. In the well-dated and modelled Severn-Cotswold region, some 7000 km^2 in area compared to the 200 km^2 here, tomb-building is estimated to span around 400 years, with most dated monuments falling in between 3750–3550 BC (Whittle *et al*. 2007, 137). Of the approximately 120 monuments built over that time period, only half would have been in use at any one time, if a 100-year use life is assumed, or just a quarter of tombs if a 50-year use life is assumed. This tempo of building activity would have left 'territories' of 120 km^2 and 240 km^2 respectively around active monuments, areas perhaps too large for any great degree of social control to be exerted (Whittle *et al*. 2007). While the areas involved at Ballyglass are of course much smaller, with as little as 400 m between some court tombs, we should be careful of uncritically assuming scenarios of heightened competition or tensions between farming groups based solely on monument distribution.

MORE HOUSES BENEATH COURT TOMBS?

Another slant on the Ballyglass sequence is that it provides a lucky glimpse of what was a relatively common occurrence in Early Neolithic Ireland, but something which survey and excavation to date have not been particularly well-tuned to finding. It is something that Ó Nualláin pondered early on, noting the occupation debris recorded underneath previously excavated court tombs, including circular 'huts' beneath nearby Ballyglass Ma. 14 and wondering if '… more extensive investigation in the precincts of court-tombs during the course of excavation might well repay the extra labour involved' (Ó Nualláin 1972, 56). Of the nearly 400 court tombs recorded in Ireland (Jones 2007), approximately 10% have been excavated, most in the mid-twentieth century. Just over thirty years ago, Herity (1987) could list 42 court tombs that had been excavated post-1930. Since then, just two sites have been added to that total: Parknabinnia, Co. Clare, started in the late 1990s as a research excavation (Jones 2019), and Aghnaskeagh 4, Co. Louth, excavated in 2005 along the route of the M1 Dundalk Western Bypass. The excavation of megalithic tombs is these days rarely undertaken in a research context, while within developer-funded archaeology most linear infrastructural developments such as roads and pipelines avoid recorded megalithic remains at the route planning stage. The pre-excavation record for Aghnaskeagh 4, for example, indicated a very ruined monument and when uncovered just 60% of the court tomb – that within the road take – was excavated. The above factors make it very difficult to reconcile settlement remains with upstanding monuments and to speak more confidently about the overlap of house and tomb, and of different realms or spheres of activity, in the Early Neolithic. Might there be additional timber houses lying beneath the approximately 90% of unexcavated Irish court tombs? It is not such a ridiculous question, but one that can only be answered with targeted geophysical survey and open-plan excavation.

HISTORY MAKING IN THE EARLY NEOLITHIC

A final point to make is that we should be cautious in assuming a universal logic to prehistoric built spaces, particularly the idea that a 'house of the dead' should have to mimic or symbolise a pre-existing 'house of the living'. With an increasing corpus of Neolithic settlement sites to interrogate, early and slightly under-baked theories on the long mounds of Atlantic Europe memorialising the LBK longhouses of central Europe (*e.g.* Hodder 1984) have been gradually replaced with more nuanced understandings of historical sequence and time depth in early farming communities, and how they were given expression across a variety of media (*e.g.* Hodder 2013). Indeed, several recent discoveries demonstrate how such processes of 'history-making' could vary across the islands of Britain and Ireland in the Early Neolithic. On Orkney, radiocarbon dating has shown that stone houses such as the Knap of Howar appeared approximately 300 years after the first stalled cairns, upturning long-held assumptions about the tombs mimicking domestic architecture (Richards and Jones 2016). On Anglesey, excavations at Parc Cybi have uncovered a Neolithic timber house on the same orientation to Trefignath chambered tomb, located just 100 m away to the north-north-east and visible from the house through a narrow cleft in the surrounding rock outcrop (Kenney this volume). Recent re-evaluation of the site archive at Doon Hill, East Lothian has also provided compelling evidence for an Early Neolithic timber house (Hall B) erected on top of an earlier and larger timber hall (Hall A) after it had burnt down (Ralston 2019). The Ballyglass sequence incorporates elements from all of these examples and is yet quite different, reminding us to look beyond simple timber-stone and living-dead binaries to a wider and richer repertoire of Neolithic ritual practice.

ACKNOWLEDGEMENTS

Gabriel Cooney, Graeme Warren, Conor McDermott and Rob Sands in UCD School of Archaeology are thanked for their help navigating the Ballyglass archive and related datasets. The lipid analysis reported here is part of a wider Céide Fields project funded by the 2016/17 UCD Seed-Funding Scheme and facilitated by the Organic Geochemistry Unit, University of Bristol, who are also warmly thanked for their support.

REFERENCES

ApSimon, A. (1969) An Early Neolithic House in Co. Tyrone. *Journal of the Royal Society of Antiquaries of Ireland* 99, 165–8.

Bronk Ramsey, C. (2017) Methods for summarizing radiocarbon datasets. *Radiocarbon* 59 (2), 1809–33.

Case, H. (1969) Settlement patterns in the north Irish Neolithic. *Ulster Journal of Archaeology* 32, 3–27.

Caulfield, S., Byrne, G., Dunne, N. and Warren, G.M. (2011) *Excavations on Céide Hill, Behy and Glenulra, North Co. Mayo, 1963–1994*. UCD School of Archaeology/INSTAR2: Neolithic and Bronze Age Landscapes of North Mayo.

Caulfield, S., Byrne, G., Warren, G.M. (2013) The Céide Fields. In G.M. Warren and S. Davis (eds) *North Mayo*, 90–9. Dublin, Irish Quaternary Association, IQUA Field Guide No. 31.

Cooney, G., Bayliss, A., Healy, F., Whittle, A., Danaher, E., Cagney, L., Mallory, J., Smyth, J., Kador, T. and O'Sullivan, M. (2011) Chapter 12: Ireland. In A. Whittle, F. Healy and A. Bayliss (eds) *Gathering Time: dating the Early Neolithic enclosures of southern Britain and Ireland*, 562–669. Oxford, Oxbow Books.

Copley, M.S., Berstan, R., Dudd, S.N., Docherty, G., Mukherjee, A.J., Straker, V., Payne, S. and Evershed, R.P. (2003) Direct chemical evidence for widespread dairying in prehistoric Britain. *Proceedings of the National Academy of Sciences of the United States of America* 100 (4), 1524–9

Darvill, T. (1979) Court cairns, passage graves and social change in Ireland. *Man* 14, 311–27.

De Valera, R. (1951) A group of 'horned cairns' near Ballycastle, Co. Mayo. *Journal of the Royal Society of Antiquaries of Ireland* 81, 161–97.

De Valera, R. (1960) The court cairns of Ireland. *Journal of the Royal Society of Antiquaries of Ireland* 60, 9–140.

De Valera, R. and Ó Nualláin, S. (1964) *Survey of the Megalithic Tombs of Ireland. Vol. II, Co. Mayo*. Dublin, Stationery Office.

Fleming, A. (1973) Tombs for the living. *Man* 8, 177–93.

Friedli, H., Lotcher, H., Oeschger, H., Siegenthaler, U. and Stauffer, B. (1986) Ice core record of the $13C/12C$ ratio of atmospheric CO_2 in the past two centuries. *Nature* 324, 237–8.

Hayes, R.J. (ed.) (1965) *Manuscript sources for the history of Irish civilisation. Vol. 1*. Boston, G.K. Hall and Co.

Hodder, I. (1984) Burials, houses, women and men in the European Neolithic. In D. Miller and C. Tilley (eds) *Ideology, Power and Prehistory*, 51–68. Cambridge, Cambridge University Press.

Jones, C. (2007) *Temples of Stone*. Cork, Collins Press.

Jones, C. (2019) The North Munster atypical court tombs of Western Ireland – social dynamics, regional trajectories and responses to distant events over the course of the Neolithic. In J. Müller, M. Hinz, M. Wunderlich (eds) *Megaliths, Societies, Landscapes: early monumentality and social differentiation in Neolithic Europe*, 983–1004. Bonn, Habelt Verlag.

Ó Nualláin, S. (1972) A Neolithic house at Ballyglass near Ballycastle, Co. Mayo. *Journal of the Royal Society of Antiquaries of Ireland* 102, 49–57.

Ó Nualláin, S. (1976) The central court-tombs of the north-west of Ireland. *Journal of the Royal Society of Antiquaries of Ireland* 106, 92–117.

Ó Nualláin, S. (1998) Excavation of the smaller court-tomb and associated hut sites at Ballyglass, County Mayo. *Proceedings of the Royal Irish Academy* 98C, 125–75.

Ó Ríordáin, S. (1954) Lough Gur excavations: Neolithic and Bronze Age houses on Knockadoon. *Proceedings of the Royal Irish Academy* 56C, 297–459.

Powell, A. (2005) The language of lineage: reading Irish court tomb design. *European Journal of Archaeology* 8 (1), 9–28.

Ralston, I. (2019) Going back in time: re-assessment of the timber halls at Doon Hill, Dunbar. *Transactions of the East Lothian Antiquarian and Field Naturalists' Society* 32, 5–27.

Reimer, P.J., Bard, E., Bayliss, A., Beck, J.W., Blackwell, P.G., Bronk Ramsey, C., Buck, C.E., Cheng, H., Edwards, R.L., Friedrich, M., Grootes, P.M., Guilderson, T.P., Haflidason, H., Hajdas, I., Hatté, C., Heaton, T.J., Hoffmann, D.L., Hogg, A.G., Hughen, K.A., Kaiser, K.F., Kromer, B., Manning, S.W., Niu, M., Reimer, R.W., Richards, D.A., Scott, E.M., Southon, J.R., Staff, R.A., Turney, C.S.M. and van der Plicht, J. (2013) IntCal13 and Marine13 Radiocarbon Age Calibration Curves 0–50,000 Years cal BP. *Radiocarbon* 55 (4), 1869–87.

Richards, C. and Jones, R. (ed.) (2016) *The Development of Neolithic House Societies in Orkney*. Oxford, Windgather Press.

Rieley, G. (1994) Derivatization of organic compounds prior to gas chromatographic–combustion–isotope ratio mass spectrometric analysis: identification of isotope fractionation processes. *Analyst* 119 (5), 915–9.

Schulting, R.J., Murphy, E., Jones, C. and Warren, G. (2012) New dates from the north and a proposed chronology for Irish court tombs. *Proceedings of the Royal Irish Academy* 112C, 1–60.

Smyth, J. (2014) *Settlement in the Irish Neolithic*. Oxford, Oxbow Books (Prehistoric Society Research Papers 6).

Smyth, J. and Evershed, R.P. (2016) Milking the megafauna: using organic residue analysis to understand early farming practice. *Environmental Archaeology* 21 (3), 214–29.

Walsh, F. (2011) Archaeology of two townlands (Part I): from Stone Age settlers to 19th-century farmers at Monanny and Cloghvally Upper, Co. Monaghan. *Clogher Record* 20 (3), 500–20.

Warren, G.M. (2018) The prehistoric archaeology of North Mayo. In P. Boschiero, L. Latini, with S. Caulfield (eds) *The Céide Fields, Ireland: International Carlo Scarpa Prize for Gardens*, 92–107. Treviso, Fondazione Benetton Studi Ricerche.

Whitehouse, N.J., Schulting, R., McClatchie, M., Barratt, P., McLaughlin, T. R, Bogaard, A., Colledge, S., Marchant, R., Gaffrey, J. and Bunting, M.J. (2014) Neolithic agriculture on the European western frontier: the boom and bust of early farming in Ireland. *Journal of Archaeological Science* 51, 181–205.

Whittle, A., Barclay, A., Bayliss, A., McFadyen, L., Schulting, R. and Wysocki, M. (2007) Building for the Dead: events, processes and changing worldviews from the thirty-eighth to the thirty-fourth centuries cal. BC in southern Britain. *Cambridge Archaeological Journal* 17 (1) (suppl.), 123–47.

Chapter 12

Shaky foundations: Romantic nationalism and the development of the 'Irish model' of Neolithic settlement

Andrew Whitefield

With the rise of populism and nativism in modern politics, our attention is increasingly drawn to what distinguishes *Us* from *Them*. It is frequently argued that not since the 1930s has international politics been so divisive (*e.g.* Niklasson and Hølleland 2018; Hogan *et al.* 2015). It is no coincidence that the modern discipline of archaeology emerged in the febrile atmosphere of the interwar years in Europe, as nation-states looked to the distant past for the essence of distinctive cultural identities. Much remains to be done if archaeology is to unpick this legacy (Brück and Nilsson Stutz 2016).

A case in point is the interpretation of evidence for settlement at the time of the first farming communities in Ireland and Britain. Though historically scarce, considerable evidence came to light in Ireland during the second half of the 20th century, and into the new millennium. Around 90 rectangular timber Neolithic houses have been identified in Ireland to date (Smyth 2014). The consensus that has developed in the interpretation of these structures follows the 'classic model' of dispersed, permanent, timber farmsteads that has its roots in the 1930s (Cooney 2000, 68), part of a 'sacred canon of Irish archaeology', which we are 'inclined to defend as Holy Writ' (Woodman 2000, 2–3). McLaughlin *et al.* (2016, 121), identify the continuing influence of the 'Irish model' on the interpretation of Neolithic rectangular timber structures.

The Irish model is often contrasted with that of southern Britain, where, given the general absence for substantial Neolithic 'houses', a less fixed settlement pattern has often been suggested. While more Neolithic timber structures interpreted as houses have come to light in Britain in recent years (see Barclay and Harris 2017), Britain (and most other European countries) have a significant corpus of Neolithic timber structures that are classified as non-megalithic monuments – a classification that, according to Kinnes (1992), archaeologists working in Ireland have generally failed to 'seek or accept'.

Kinnes (1992, 26–7) went on to say that it would be surprising if Ireland were the only megalithic province in Europe to lack a non-megalithic component, arguing there was a 'a clear need for reappraisal and a re-articulation of established traditions'. Other archaeologists developed Kinnes' argument (*e.g.* ApSimon 1997; Darvill 2011; O'Sullivan 2011), but the consensus remains that the majority of rectangular timber structures in Ireland are 'decidedly domestic', part of the 'settlement signature' of Neolithic Ireland (Smyth 2006, 240; 2011, 28; see also *e.g.* Cooney *et al.* 2011, 599).

In what follows, the three principal sites that underpin the Irish model are examined in the context of the development of the modern discipline in Ireland, and its divergence from British archaeology in the 1920s and 1930s. While the British and Irish evidence is frequently considered together in British syntheses, the Irish evidence has often been interpreted from a different (more ethnographic, less outward looking) perspective. This has served to reinforce the idea that Ireland and Britain followed different paths to Neolithisation, despite the ample evidence of cultural interactions during the Early Neolithic, particularly in the 'Irish Sea zone' (Lynch 1990; Waddell 1992).

Of course, British interpretations are not free from cultural bias, and it has been suggested that a colonial approach has in some cases led researchers to apply the 'Wessex model' of the southern English Neolithic uncritically to Ireland and Britain as a whole (Cooney 1997; Barclay 2001).

THE SYMBOLISM OF THE IRISH COTTAGE

At the time of the formation of the Irish Free State, small-scale mixed farmers embodied the values of the nation, representing the 'critical nation-forming class' (Larkin 1975, 1245; Garvin and Hess 2009, 21). Éamon de Valera knew his constituency well. The rural communities of Ireland's western seaboard, furthest from the malign influence of Britain (*e.g.* Richards 2009, 28), lived among some of the best-preserved ancient monuments in Europe. They represented the 'timeless' continuity of Irish rural life and become emblematic of Ireland's cultural independence from Britain. This was famously expressed in de Valera's 1943 radio address to the nation:

> The Ireland that we dreamed of would be…a land whose countryside would be bright with cosy homesteads, whose fields and villages would be joyous with the sounds of industry…whose firesides would be forums for the wisdom of serene old age. The home, in short, of a people living the life that God desires that men should live.

In the decades leading to independence, writers and artists had elevated the rural homestead to the status of national icon, bearing the 'cultural weight' of the ideal Ireland (Nash 1993; Cosgrove 1995). In the spirit of romantic primitivism, the rural landscapes that were evoked were 'emptied' of any indications of hardship (Cusack 2001, 227). No artist contributed more to the symbolism of the Irish homestead than Paul Henry, who along with Jack B. Yeats, formed the Society of Dublin painters in 1920 (Duffy 1997, 67). Henry's simplified, stylised west of Ireland landscapes came to represent the *real* Ireland, such that he was 'almost the official artist of the Free State' (Brown 1985, 76; Sheehy 1980, 180; see Fig. 12.1, below). In *Saorstát Eireann* (Hobson 1932) – the official guide to the Free State – Henry's paintings featured not in the section of contemporary art, but instead as candid representations of Irish rural life (Reid 2007, 937). The *Saorstát Eireann* handbook features 10 illustrations of thatched cottages, along with liberal images of ancient artefacts (Cusack 2001).

Adolf Mahr, the Austrian archaeologist who combined his position as head of the National Museum of Ireland (NMI) with that of leader of county's branch of the Nazi party, wrote the section on Irish archaeology. He set out his view that megalithic monuments were introduced to Scandinavia (where he believed farming in Europe began) from Spain via the staging post of Ireland (Mahr 1932, 212). Mahr saw the small-scale farming communities of Ireland's

Fig. 12.1: Paul Henry (1876–1958), A Connemara Village, *1930–1933. Oil on wood panel, 76.2 × 91.4 cm, NGI.4734. National Gallery of Ireland Collection. Photo © National Gallery of Ireland.*

Atlantic seaboard the 'most important continuum by which the archaeological past and the present society are connected in an unbroken succession' (quoted in Wallace 2007, 198).

The peasant house had become a central fixture of openair folk museums in Scandinavia, Germany and Central Europe in the early 20th century (Stoklund 1999). It was a means by which the urban middle classes could experience the material culture of traditional farmers, and the essence of the authentic *Volk* (Nic Craith 2008). At the invitation of the Irish Folklore Commission, founded by de Valera's government, with Mahr a Board member – a 'Swedish Folk Culture Mission' carried out a survey of Irish rural houses in the mid-1930s (O'Dowd 2012; Carew 2018).

Mahr accumulated a substantial folklife collection at the NMI, elements of which he began to display alongside archaeological material. President Éamon de Valera opened the 1937 exhibition on the Irish farmhouse at the NMI, which had been organised by Mahr to celebrate the work of the Swedish mission. In the summer of that year, the exhibition travelled to Edinburgh, where it was displayed at the Congress of the International Association of European Ethnology and Folklore. The Irish delegates described the theme as 'the Irish farmhouse, and the cultural landscape and the rural life which formed its ethnological background' (O'Dowd 2012). The rural cottage was the metaphor that enabled farming life in modern Ireland to be projected back into the mists of antiquity. What was lacking was an ancient archaeological example of an Irish house which was comparable to the cottages observed by the Swedish mission in the west of Ireland. The task of finding such evidence would fall to Mahr's successors.

Mahr left Ireland in the spring of 1939, having secured eight weeks' leave from the NMI to attend the International Congress of Archaeology in Berlin, and to attend prearranged meetings with fellow Nazis at the Nuremberg Rally (Mullins 2007, 90–1). He did not return to Ireland. Mahr was arrested for war crimes and imprisoned by British soldiers in Germany in 1946.

Nevertheless, Mahr ensured his archaeological legacy in Ireland by establishing the NMI, *not* the universities, as the 'academy of the future', (O'Sullivan 2009; Carew 2018, 34). The leading archaeologists of the next generation mentored by Mahr included Joseph Raftery, future Director of the NMI, whose son, Barry, later become Professor of Celtic Archaeology at UCD. Barry Raftery's predecessor at UCD was Rúaidhrí de Valera (son of Éamon) who also spent time at the museum under Mahr (Mullins 2007, 66). Likewise, Michael Duignan, who became professor of archaeology at University College Galway (now NUI Galway), and later registrar and deputy president of the university. Mahr's most influential protégé, however, was Seán Ó Ríordáin, who would become professor of archaeology at University College Cork, before replacing R.A.S. Macalister in the Chair at UCD.

Ó Ríordáin took the lead in the search for archaeological evidence of the antiquity of Irish settlement traditions while still at the NMI. His first candidate for a prehistoric Irish homestead was discovered during excavations at the site of a cluster of conjoined ringforts (medieval settlement enclosures) at Cush, Co. Limerick. The excavations revealed several Bronze Age urn burials in the interior of a ringfort which also incorporated a souterrain. Despite being unable to present supporting stratigraphical evidence, Ó Ríordáin was convinced the urn burials represented the final use of the site. Given that the urns were Bronze Age, this conflation led to a belief among some archaeologists that the origins of Irish ringforts and souterrains were to be found in the Bronze Age (Waddell 2005, 210, see Ó Ríordáin 1942, 2).

At Lough Gur, also in Co. Limerick, Ó Ríordáin went on to direct the first large-scale programme of archaeological excavations in the newly independent Ireland (Waddell 2005). Here, between 1936 and 1954, he discovered what he believed to be Ireland's first Neolithic rectangular house, one of the few known in Europe at the time, providing what he felt was evidence of contact with Germany and Scandinavia during the Neolithic (Ó Ríordáin 1954, 305–6). Ó Ríordáin's work at Lough Gur established the paradigm of Irish settlement archaeology: dispersed farmsteads, comparable to modern rural Irish cottages (Ó Ríordáin 1979, 4; see below).

ANACHRONOUS ICONS OF NEOLITHIC SETTLEMENT

The chronology which Ó Ríordáin developed for Lough Gur, placing the rectangular 'house' known as Site A at the start of the Neolithic, relied on a pottery sequence that saw flat-bottomed 'Class II' pottery as contemporary with (earlier Neolithic) carinated bowl pottery (Cleary 1993). Ó Ríordáin reported 'Class II' pottery at the 'lowest levels' of his excavations, and thus 'belonging to the earliest occupation of the site', the Early Neolithic (1954). Doubts concerning Ó Ríordáin's attribution of Class II pottery to the Early Neolithic first emerged in the 1950s (E. Evans 1953). Sheridan (1995, 15) argued that 'shallowness of the deposits and the shortcomings of the excavator's recording system' at Lough Gur meant new evidence was required before any 'house' structure at the site could be considered Neolithic. Cleary and others (1993; 1995; Cleary et al. 2003) have demonstrated that the 'Class II' pottery from Lough Gur is in fact diagnostic of the later Bronze Age (see also Sheridan 1995, 17). The radiocarbon dating of structural remains accords with this determination (Cleary 1995; Cleary et al. 2003).

It is a measure of Ó Ríordáin's success in establishing Lough Gur as the template for future understanding of Irish *Neolithic* settlement that the evidence that Site A was misdated has had a limited impact on the consensus narrative among archaeologists in Ireland (e.g. Cooney 2000; 2007; Grogan 2002; McSparron 2008). A recent major review of Neolithic settlement in Ireland noted that most of the settlement remains at Lough Gur have been re-dated to the Bronze Age, but maintained that Sites A and B 'are still considered to be Early Neolithic, mainly because of the similarity in shape to the early rectangular houses from elsewhere in Ireland and the Continent (Smyth 2014, 74). Based on 'little more than educated guesswork', the Site A rectangular 'house' has been linked to a nearby Neolithic burial, and thus assumed to date to the mid-fourth millennium BC (Smyth 2014, 78–9).

Cush and Lough Gur demonstrate the potential for misinterpretation where excavations are undertaken with strongly held preconceptions. Similarly, the dating of the Céide Fields, the other foundational exemplar if the Irish settlement paradigm (Smyth 2006; *cf.* Cooney 1997), may owe much to conflated stratigraphies and the weight of disciplinary tradition. (See Whitefield 2017; 2015, Chapter 3, for detailed critique).

Early surveys on Céide Hill indicated the discovery of a 'Celtic' field system of the type found in many parts of Europe (Caulfield 1974; 2014, 41). The excavation of a Neolithic court tomb on the hill during the 1960s revealed that a section of a stone boundary was constructed on top of the court tomb's covering cairn (Herity 1971, 262; Warren et al. 2009, 5; Caulfield 2014, 28). It followed that the boundary post-dated the monument, perhaps by millennia in the view of two of the excavation directors (Ó Nualláin 1979, 7; Caulfield 2011, 19; 2014, 28). The other excavation director, however, took the view that peat covered field boundaries might offer a means of redressing the imbalance in evidence between monuments and settlement evidence from the Neolithic and Early Bronze Age.

By the late 1970s, the Céide Fields had been attributed to the Neolithic, and described as the oldest field system in Europe (Caulfield 1978). Given the relative lateness of Ireland's Neolithisation, it has been assumed that the fields were laid out by 'immigrant farmers with an already established [N]eolithic economy' (Caulfield 1983, 205). There is, however, overwhelming evidence which continues to accumulate (e.g. Nielsen et al. 2017) demonstrating that 'Celtic' field systems across Europe are a phenomenon beginning in the Middle Bronze Age (mid-second century BC), and continuing to be constructed into the early centuries AD (Whitefield 2017). Indeed, there is no reliable evidence for field systems of any kind, anywhere in Europe (or the rest of the world) during the fourth millennium BC.

The evidence from the limited archaeological excavations at the Céide Fields supports a Late Bronze Age/Iron Age (first millennium BC) date. A pollen core extracted from the downslope edge of a field wall – the only source of radiocarbon dates in direct association with a field wall on Céide Hill – returned three later Bronze Age/Iron Age dates

(Molloy and O'Connell 1995, table 2; Cooney *et al.* 2011, table 12.6). According to the analysts, the core provided 'particularly strong' evidence for sustained cultivation in the Late Bronze Age/Early Iron Age (Molloy and O'Connell 1995). Infill material from apparent plough-marks in the subsoil beneath the peat similarly returned a Late Bronze Age/Iron Age radiocarbon date (Molloy and O'Connell 1995). The plough marks run parallel with the southwest–northeast alignment along the long axial field walls, in keeping with the interpretation that this feature of many 'Celtic' field systems allowed a plough-team an uninterrupted progression (Harding 2000; Johnston 2013).

But in the absence of evidence for arable farming at Céide Fields during the hypothesised Neolithic occupation, the assumption was that the land must have been cleared to create open pasture (*e.g.* Caulfield 1978; 2014; Cooney *et al.* 2011). As Cooney *et al.* (2011, 625) acknowledge, there is no practical reason why the management of herds should require the complex of stone boundaries (see also Caulfield 2013, 98–9). Open woodlands, heaths and wetlands are perfectly suitable for cattle and other grazing animals (Molloy and O'Connell 2016; Bickle and Whittle 2013). Exposed sections of the boundaries are broad, low spreads of stone (Molloy and O'Connell 1995, 222). It is accepted that they were never effective stock barriers (Caulfield 1983, 200). Neither are there structural indications, in the form of droveways or stock-handling facilities, nor even gateways between the fields. There is no direct evidence for pastoral farming, and even if the boundaries were somehow augmented to control animals, the question remains: *why*? Cooney *et al.* (2011, 625) speculate that the boundaries may have represented 'a distinctive way of signing the land, an expression of regional identity or identities, a means of aligning people with the substance of the earth and its mythic properties, and a medium through which community could be assembled and tied to place'. An alternative interpretation is that the field boundaries are linear clearance cairns, clearing the way for the plough-team.

Caulfield (1974) explained: 'Unlike the tombs or well-known prehistoric objects which can readily be identified as ancient, these walls are given an antiquity solely because of their position below the bog'. Caulfield *et al.* (1998) set out to try to age a vast area of bog covering much of north County Mayo by obtaining radiocarbon dates from pine stumps/trunks that had been preserved in peat. A total of 44 samples were identified across hundreds of square kilometres of bogland, having been exposed by natural erosion or the hand-cutting of turf for fuel. Just three of the samples came from Céide Hill (Caulfield *et al.* 1998, 630; see Whitefield 2017, fig. 12.1). The uncalibrated radiocarbon dates for the preserved timbers clustered around the Neolithic-Chalcolithic transition, leading Caulfield *et al.* (1998, 639) to conclude: 'Much of Céide Fields and other Neolithic pre-bog field systems in North Mayo were abandoned and already covered by shallow peat by 4500 BP.'

There is no doubt that localised pockets of peat bog began to accumulate in north Mayo during the Neolithic, and that in some cases *Pinus sylvestris* (Scots pine) trees – which can grow on peat – were preserved in the waterlogged peat. But these events are separate, both in time and space, from stone boundaries. The pine samples were not selected on the basis of their archaeological significance and, are for the most part at a considerable remove from any known stone boundaries. Indeed, very little is known about the sampled pines, as precise details – photographs, drawings, measurements, circumstances of recovery, context, whether waterlogged or desiccated, inferred stratigraphic relationship, soil conditions, slope, topography: no such information was recorded. What does seem clear is that the sampled timbers were generally large (trees with more than 100 rings) (O'Connell and Molloy 2001, 102). It follows that they were preserved in relatively deep pockets of peat.

Caulfield *et al.*'s (1998) methodology assumes a more-or-less synchronous 'fossilisation' of large tracts of north Mayo in blanket peat during the Neolithic (*e.g.* Caulfield 1978, 142–3; 1983, 195–6; 2014, 34). But there was no 'Pompeii-style' event in Neolithic north Mayo (O'Brien 2009, 6). Blanket bogs comprise a complex of different mire types. The 'blanketing' of the landscape, which disguises the complexity of the underlying topography, is the final stage of a process can be drawn out over millennia (*e.g.* Charman 2002, 81–3; Lawson *et al.* 2007, 26). The accumulation and survival of blanket peat is highly variable, in accordance with myriad factors including slope, aspect, microtopography, hydrology, underlying soil, vegetation, exposure to weathering, and the actions of animals and people (*e.g.* Edwards and Hirons 1982; Evans and Warburton 2007).

The Céide Fields are situated on the lower and middle slopes of Céide Hill. Water running over and through the peat renders it inherently unstable (Edwards and Hirons 1982; M. Evans and Warburton 2007). The intense hydrology at the interface between the peat and the mineral soil is a major contributary factor to the gradual gliding of the entire peat mass downslope (Moore and Bellamy 1974, 40–41). Mass movements such as peat slides and bog bursts are well attested to in the locality (*e.g.* Kneafsey 1995; Guttman-Bond *et al.* 2016). As Edwards and Hirons (1982) caution, estimations of the age of blanket peats based on extrapolating data from a small number of atypically deep deposits is inherently unreliable. The initialisation of pockets of peat growth during the later Neolithic is entirely compatible with the major *extension* of peat growth taking place in the first millennium BC (Chambers 1982, 38). Warren *et al.* (2011, 139) acknowledge that, '… in several places within [the main Céide Fields] system archaeological dates are now showing that the landscape was free of bog into at least the Bronze Age, if not the Iron Age'. As at Lough Gur, strongly held prior expectations appear to have led to the conflation of archaeological evidence from difference periods.

While none of the dating evidence from the Céide Fields is entirely satisfactory, a late-second/early first millennium BC date for the establishment of the field system seems the logical working hypothesis.

DEFINITE HOUSE?

The Céide Fields complex is the archetype of the Irish model of Neolithic settlement. The traditional interpretation, however, conflates the Bronze Age/Iron Age field systems (where the ancestors worked) with a Neolithic court tomb (where the ancestors worshipped), and (absent) houses (where the ancestors lived) (MacConnell 1990; Caulfield 1992, 11). No credible evidence of a Neolithic house has been identified among the Céide Fields. Excavations at a large circular enclosure did produce a small quantity of possible-Neolithic pottery and lithics, but these were in upper 'debris layers' of uncertain location (Caulfield *et al.* 2009, 8). Despite the acknowledged absence of evidence for a 'classic' Neolithic house (Caulfield and Warren 2011, 72; Caulfield 2014, 29), a 'typical' pattern of dispersed settlement is envisaged (*e.g.* Caulfield 1992; 2013; Cooney 1997; 2000; Lucas 2010). The narrative that ties the Céide Fields into the Irish settlement model draws on evidence from elsewhere in Co. Mayo where the remains of a rectangular timber structure were found beneath an excavated court tomb at Ballyglass (*e.g.* Cooney 2000; Lucas 2010, 2; Smyth 2013). This 'definite house' (Grogan 2004) was among the first post-Lough Gur Neolithic timber structures to be excavated in Ireland (Ó Nualláin 1972; see Fig. 12.2).

Described by the excavator as 'roughly the same dimensions as the houses of small farmers now living nearby', the Ballyglass rectangular timber structure measures 13 m by 6 m (Ó Nualláin 1979). The principal structural components were discovered beneath the western end of the cairn of the court tomb and, comprise foundation trenches (*c.*20 cm deep), which incorporated postholes (Ó Nualláin 1972). The line of the cairn follows the western wall trench of the timber structure. The excavator speculated that the earlier structure was 'intentionally demolished to make way for the construction of the tomb' (Ó Nualláin 1972).

Few artefacts can be unequivocally associated with the timber structure because of the 'lack of reliable stratification' (Ó Nualláin 1972, 55). Sherds of Carinated Bowl were recovered from wall trenches and postholes, but this is routinely found in both presumed-domestic and presumed-ceremonial/mortuary contexts. A small number of

Fig. 12.2: Conjectural reconstruction of the Ballyglass 'house' at the Céide Fields visitor centre, Co. Mayo. The information panel submits: 'The rectangular house with large central room is strikingly similar to the traditional house of the region' (photo: the author).

lithics were found within the footprint of the structure, while pits in front of the court area of the tomb yielded 'numerous implements, with concave scrapers predominant'. The excavator proposed that 'it may well be that these pits should be associated with the occupation of the house rather than the period of tomb construction' (Ó Nualláin 1972). It is not clear why this should be the case. Lithics would have been required in the construction of the timber structure (whatever its future purpose) but, may equally have had a role in activities associated with the stone monument. Nevertheless, the excavator (Ó Nualláin 1972; 1979) and contemporary syntheses were emphatic: 'The [Ballyglass] house yielded Primary Neolithic pottery with pointed rims, and a flint assemblage similar to that in the centre Court Cairn above. Though a relatively long span of habitation, say even a century, is implied in the permanence of such a well-built house, there is no need to regard it as other than the house of a family of Neolithic A [Early Neolithic] farmers, the most extensive evidence for which so far is the thirty Court Cairns in the area, show them to have been well-organized stock raisers and agriculturalists' (Herity and Eogan 1977, 47; see also Ó Ríordáin 1979, 4).

It is not inconceivable that the timber structure at Ballyglass was some form of domestic structure, but certainly no 'smoking gun' is in evidence. Against this, the role of the court tomb as a mortuary structure and ceremonial monument is uncontroversial. Setting aside the choice of primary construction materials, there are many parallels between chambered megalithic monuments (such as court tombs and portal tombs) and segmented timber structures, particularly some of the larger, multi-chambered 'houses' such as Ballyglass (ApSimon 1997; *cf.* Sheridan 2006). Following Kinnes (1975, 19–21), Powell (2005) suggests that court tombs, particularly the more complex examples such as Ballyglass (which is effectively two conjoined monuments), were 'modular', having been modified over many generations (*cf.* Sheridan 2006).

In addition to the division of the internal space, several of the larger 'house' examples, including Ballyglass, appear to have been at least partially open at one end, having post holes but no slot trench (see Whitefield 2015, 368–70). Tankardstown 'House 2', Co. Limerick, is another large (15 m by 7.5 m) example with three chambers, and 'two stout corner posts' that apparently define an open end (Gowen and Tarbett 1988; 1990). Like most other rectangular timber structures in Ireland, Tankardstown 'House 2' was largely devoid of artefacts and ecofacts. This contrasts with its near neighbour, Tankardstown 'House 1' which, though much smaller and roughly square in shape, yielded a cache of cereal grain. Cereal grain in meaningful quantities (*i.e.* more than low single figures of possible cereal grains) is extremely rare. The discovery at Tankardstown has led to this atypical 'house' being substantially over-represented in interpretations of Neolithic timber structures in Ireland (McClatchie *et al.* 2009; Whitehouse *et al.* 2014; Whitefield 2015, chapter 4).

At Dooey's Cairn, Co. Antrim, where a timber structure (which was burnt down) was incorporated into a later court tomb, the excavator suggested there may have originally been a forecourt, similar to the 'crescentic facade of upright timber posts' identified at Lochhill cairn in Kirkcudbrightshire, southwest Scotland (Collins 1976; see also Masters 1973). At Shanballyedmond, Co. Tipperary, the excavation of the court tomb revealed a U-shaped setting of 34 postholes which enclosed the cairn (O'Kelly 1958; 1989, 89–91). In other examples, the use of 'post and panel' oak planks and timber posts has parallels in the use of orthostats with drystone walling in court tombs (Sheridan 2006). Unless timber features have been complemented or replaced by stone features, excavation in Ireland is historically unlikely to have covered a sufficiently extensive area to detect them.

Timber screens are a feature of some of the Scottish Neolithic rectangular timber structures, including Eweford West in East Lothian (MacGregor and McLellan 2008; Thomas 2015, 1083). Some of the larger Irish rectangular structures have curving walls at one end which may have functioned similarly (see Simpson 1996; Smyth 2011). It is interesting to contrast the interpretation of the rectangular timber structure at Cloghers, Co. Kerry, with the ostensibly similar evidence at Eweford West. What is interpreted as a 'possible fence line' at Cloghers linked with domestic/farming activity (Smyth 2006, 241), is remarkably similar to the 'timber screen' at Eweford, which is interpreted as shielding aspects of mortuary practice from view (MacGregor and McLellan 2008, 25). Both fences/screens are *circa* 10 m long, constructed of post and stakes in a trench, and appear to have been burnt down (MacGregor and McLellan 2008; Kiely 2003, 185).

Smyth (2006, 245) identifies the deliberate burning as a 'practice bound up with houses in early Neolithic Ireland'. Many 'linear zone' rectangular timber mortuary structures in Scotland similarly appear to have been deliberately burnt down (see also *e.g.* Barclay *et al.* 2002, 120; Sheridan 2006; 2010). These include those at Eweford West and Pencraig Hill, East Lothian (MacGregor and McLellan 2008). Lochhill and Slewcairn in Kirkcudbrightshire (Masters 1981), and Dalladies, Aberdeenshire (Piggott 1972). At Inchtuthil, Perth and Kinross, the 'ditched enclosure' (foundation trench in Irish model?) contained a 'timber fence' which was 'burnt down and replaced' (Piggott 1972; see Barclay and Maxwell 1991). Again, it is difficult to imagine anything other than a domestic function being assigned to such a structure, had it been excavated in Ireland.

There are ample grounds to consider alternatives to the domestic paradigm in the interpretation of some Neolithic timber structures in Ireland. Wooden components beneath megalithic monuments, including examples at the Boyne Valley, would be a logical place to start (O'Sullivan 2011).

CONCLUSION: IMAGINED COMMUNITIES OF NEOLITHIC IRELAND

Archaeology in Ireland, in common with its counterparts in all other countries, has helped shape and, has been shaped by the nation's image of itself (*e.g.* Díaz and Champion 1996). Archaeologists have cultivated the myth of timeless continuity in rural settlement, influencing the wider portrayal of ancient Ireland (Fig. 12.3). Most archaeologists would nevertheless maintain that their interpretations are grounded in scientific neutrality and are value-free (*cf.* Cooney 1995).

Ireland's small community of research archaeologists faces an overabundance of prehistoric antiquities in need of interpretation. The modern discipline in Ireland diverged from its nearest neighbour at the beginning of the 20th century and followed the ethnographic approach of Germany and Scandinavia. Syntheses of Irish archaeology have tended to be highly convergent (Fontijn and Van Reybrouck 1999), focused on presenting new discoveries within interpretive paradigms that were established in the first half of the twentieth century (Cooney 1995, 269). Most new discoveries are made in the context of development-led excavations. Where these do come to publication, they are likely to

Fig. 12.3: Front page of travel supplement to British newspaper The Guardian, *16 March 2019. (Reproduced with kind permission of Guardian News & Media Ltd.)*

be interpreted within disciplinary norms. A reluctance to challenge established archaeological interpretations has been observed in other countries where the influence of German archaeology has been especially strong (*e.g.* Cornell *et al.* 2008; *cf.* Cooney 1995).

Research by Irish archaeologists has tended to focus on Irish evidence. A sometimes insular approach has led to interpretations which can seem out of step with developments in Britain and elsewhere in Europe. British syntheses typically include Irish evidence, but have limited access to the underlying excavation data, so often incorporate anomalies as indications of regionality. Legitimate concerns about smothering diversity and creating normative accounts can give way to retrospective nationalism (Geary 2002) – losing sight of the fact that, as Macalister (1949, xii) observed: 'in Ancient Europe there were no "nations"'. What is abundantly clear from the architecture (whether wood or stone), and portable artefacts such as pottery and lithics, is that the Irish Sea connected the communities around its shores during the Early Neolithic, and was likely to have been an important conduit in the Neolithisation of both Ireland and Britain (*e.g.* Sheridan 2017).

The Céide Fields are not a unique occurrence of a Neolithic 'Celtic' field system, laid out more than 2000 years before such field systems appear widely elsewhere in Europe. There is a corollary between the apparent ubiquity of rectangular timber houses in Ireland and the apparent absence of timber funerary structures: some of the buildings that are interpreted as houses may have been mortuary structures. Both the Céide Fields and the corpus of Neolithic rectangular timber 'houses' have been interpreted within the paradigm of the Irish model of Neolithic settlement.

'Terminology', as Kinnes (1985, 26) pointed out, is often 'formative to both perception and expectation'. In an influential edited volume on Neolithic timber structures in Ireland, Armit *et al.* (2003, 146) cautioned that: 'In the view of the obvious differences in both scale and layout of these buildings, it would clearly be simplistic to assume a single or uniform function for Neolithic rectilinear structures. […] It should probably be expected…that such large and complex buildings will have served a range of functions, and this range of possibilities is beginning to be explored'.

Archaeology's image of itself as an objective discipline grounded in scientific method is frequently at odds with the image it projects to scholars in related disciplines, where the speculative and politicised nature of some longstanding archaeological narratives is well understood (Cooney 1995). The historian Clare O'Halloran (2007, 188) describes the development of archaeology in Ireland as 'slow and halting; its progress shaped and, at times, stunted by nationalist ideology and by the cultural legacies of colonialism'. These distorting influences can, nevertheless, allow for simple and attractive narratives that make the distant past seem comfortably familiar. Despite the weight of tradition that underpins it, the Irish model of Neolithic settlement does not constitute an unassailable truth which can be uncritically incorporated into new research. Rather, the Irish model is a hypothesis in need of (rigorous) testing. Any such hypothesis is 'always tentative, incomplete and open to challenge' (Smith 2017, 521).

ACKNOWLEDGEMENTS

I am grateful to the College of Arts, Social Sciences and Celtic Studies at NUI Galway for research support funding which enabled my participation in the London conference. A friend and colleague who wishes to remain anonymous provided an invaluable critique of an earlier version of this paper.

REFERENCES

ApSimon, A. (1997) Wood into stone: origins for the Irish megalithic tombs. In A. Rodríguez Casal (ed.) *O Neolítico Atlántico e as Orixes Megalitism*, 129–40. Santiago de Compostela, University de Santiago de Compostela.

Armit, I., Murphy, E., Nelis, E. and Simpson, D. (2003) Irish Neolithic houses. In I. Armit, E. Nelis and D. Simpson (eds) *Neolithic Settlement in Ireland and Western Britain,* 146–8. Oxford, Oxbow Books.

Barclay, A. and Harris, O. (2017) Community building: houses and people in Neolithic Britain. In P. Bickle, V. Cummings, D. Hofmann and J. Pollard (eds) *The Neolithic of Europe: papers in honour of Alasdair Whittle*, 222–33. Oxford, Oxbow Books.

Barclay, G. (2001) 'Metropolitan' and 'parochial'/'core' and 'periphery': a historiography of the prehistory of Scotland. *Proceedings of the Prehistoric Society* 67, 1–18.

Barclay, G. and Maxwell, G. (1991) Excavation of a Neolithic long mortuary enclosure within the Roman legionary fortress at Inchtuthil, Perthshire, *Proceedings of the Society of Antiquaries of Scotland* 121, 27–44.

Barclay, G., Brophy, K. and McGregor, G. (2002) Claish, Stirling: an Early Neolithic structure in its context. *Proceedings of the Society of Antiquaries of Scotland* 132, 65–137.

Bickle, P. and Whittle, A. (2013) LBK lifeways: a search for difference. In P. Bickle and A. Whittle (eds) *The First Farmers of Central Europe: diversity in LBK lifeways*, 1–27. Oxford, Oxbow Books.

Brown, T. (1985) *Ireland: a social and cultural history, 1922 to the present*. London, Cornell University Press.

Brück, J. and Nilsson Stutz, L. (2016) Is archaeology still the project of nation states? An editorial comment. *Archaeological Dialogues* 23 (1), s. 1–3.

Carew, M. (2018) *The Quest for the Irish Celt: the Harvard archaeological mission to Ireland, 1932–1936*. Newbridge, Irish Academic Press.

Caulfield, S. (1974) Agriculture and settlement in ancient Mayo. *The Irish Times*. 23 December, 3.

Caulfield, S. (1978) Neolithic fields: the Irish evidence. In H. Brown and P. Fowler (eds) *Early Land Allotment*, 137–44. Oxford, British Archaeological Reports British Series 48.

Caulfield, S. (1983) The Neolithic settlement of north Connacht. In T. Reeves-Smith and F. Hamond (eds) *Landscape Archaeology in Ireland*, 195–215. Oxford, British Archaeological Reports British Series 116.

Caulfield, S. (1992) *Céide Fields, Ballycastle, Co. Mayo*. [Fieldguide. Publisher and place of publication omitted].

Caulfield, S. (2011) History of archaeological and related research in north Mayo. In S. Caulfield, G. Byrne, N. Dunne and G. Warren (eds) Neolithic and Bronze Age landscapes of north Mayo: report 2011, 106–16. Unpublished report, UCD School of Archaeology.

Caulfield, S. (2013) Céide Fields: Europe's oldest surviving dairy fields? In M. Jebb and C. Crowley (eds) *Secrets of the Irish Landscape,* 95–100. Cork, Cork University Press.

Caulfield, S. (2014) Céide Fields and Belderrig Valley: four score years of research. In G. Moran and N. Ó Muraíle (eds) *Mayo History and Society: interdisciplinary essays on the history of an Irish county*, 25–44. Dublin, Geography Publications.

Caulfield, S., O'Donnell, R. and Mitchell, P. (1998) Dating of a Neolithic field system at Céide Fields, County Mayo, Ireland. *Radiocarbon* 40 (2), 629–40.

Caulfield, S., Warren, G., Rathbone, S., McIlreavy, D. and Walsh, P. (2009) Archaeological Excavations at the Glenulra Enclosure (E24): stratigraphic report. Unpublished report, UCD School of Archaeology.

Caulfield, S. and Warren, G. (2011) Excavations at the Glenulra enclosure 1970–1972. In S. Caulfield, G. Byrne, N. Dunne and G. Warren (eds) Excavations on Céide Hill, Behy and Glenulra, north Co. Mayo, 1963–1994, 52–73. Unpublished report, UCD School of Archaeology.

Charman, D. (2002) *Peatlands and Environmental Change*. Chichester, Wiley.

Cleary, R. (1993) The later Bronze Age at Lough Gur: filling in the blanks. In E. Shee Twohig and M. Ronayne (eds) *Past Perceptions: the prehistoric archaeology of south west Ireland*, 114–20. Cork, Cork University Press.

Cleary, R. (1995) Later Bronze Age settlement and prehistoric burials, Lough Gur, Co. Limerick. *Proceedings of the Royal Irish Academy* 95C (1), 1–92.

Cleary, R., McKeown, S., Tierney, J., Hannon, M., Anderson, E., Cahill, M. and O'Shaughnessy, J. (2003) Enclosed Late Bronze Age habitation site and boundary wall at Lough Gur, Co. Limerick. *Proceedings of the Royal Irish Academy* 103C (4), 97–189.

Collins, A. (1976) Dooey's Cairn, Ballymacaldrack, County Antrim. *Ulster Journal of Archaeology* 39, 1–10.

Cooney, G. (1995) Theory and practice in Irish archaeology. In P. Ucko (ed.) *Theory in Archaeology: a world perspective*, 263–77. London, Routledge.

Cooney, G. (1997) Images of settlement and the landscape. In P. Topping (ed.) *Neolithic Landscapes,* 23–31. Oxford, Oxbow Books.

Cooney, G. (2000) *Landscapes of Neolithic Ireland*. London, Routledge.

Cooney, G. (2007) In retrospect: Neolithic activity at Knockadoon, Lough Gur, Co. Limerick, 50 years on. *Proceedings of the Royal Irish Academy* 107C, 215–25.

Cooney, G., Bayliss, A., Healy, F., Whittle, A., Danaher, E., Cagney, L., Mallory, J., Smyth, J., Kador, T. and O'Sullivan, M. (2011) Ireland. In A. Whittle, A. Bayliss and F. Healy (eds) *Gathering Time: dating the Early Neolithic enclosures of Southern Britain and Ireland. Volume 2*, 562–669. Oxford, Oxbow Books.

Cornell, P., Borelius, U., Kresa, D. and Backlund, T. (2008) Kosinna, the *Nordische Gedanke* and Swedish archaeology: discourse and politics in German and Swedish archaeology 1900–1950. *Current Swedish Archaeology* (15–16), 39–59.

Cosgrove, M. (1995) Paul Henry and Achill Ireland. In U. Kockel (ed.) *Landscape, Heritage and Identity: case studies in Irish ethnography*, 93–116. London, Routledge.

Cusack T. (2001) A 'countryside bright with cosy homesteads': Irish nationalism and the cottage landscape. *National Identities* 3 (3), 221–38.

Díaz-Andreu, M. and Champion, T. (1996a) Nationalism and archaeology in Europe: an introduction. In M. Díaz-Andreu and T. Champion (eds) *Archaeology and Nationalism in Europe*, 1–23. London, University College London Press.

Darvill, T. (2011) Megaliths, monuments and materiality. In M. Furholt, F. Lüth and J. Müller (eds) *Megaliths and Identities*, 35–46. Bonn, Dr Rudolf Habelt.

De Valera, E. (1943) *St Patrick's Day 1943 Address*. Raidió Teilifís Éireann radio broadcast. 17 March. Available at: http://www.rte.ie/laweb/ll/ll_t09b.html (accessed 21/032011).

Duffy, P. (1997) Writing Ireland: literature and art in the representation of Irish place. In B. Graham (ed.) *In Search of Ireland: a cultural geography*, 64–83. London, Routledge.

Edwards, K. and Hirons, K. (1982) Date of blanket peat initiation and rates of spread – a problem in research design. *Quaternary Newsletter* 36, 32–7.

Evans, E. (1953) Archaeology in Northern Ireland, 1921–1951. *Ulster Journal of Archaeology* 16, 3–6.

Evans, M. and Warburton, J. (2007) *Geomorphology of Upland Peat: erosion, form and landscape change*. Oxford, Blackwell.

Fontijn, D. and Van Reybrouck, D. (1999) The luxury of abundance: syntheses of Irish prehistory. *Archaeological Dialogues* 6 (1), 55–73.

Garvin, T. and Hess, A. (2009) Gustave de Beaumont: Ireland's Alexis de Tocqueville. In S. Ó Síocháin (ed.) *Social Thought on Ireland in the Nineteenth Century*, 9–26. Dublin, University College Dublin Press.

Geary, P. (2002) *The Myth of Nations: the medieval origins of Europe*. Princeton, Princeton University Press.

Gowen, M. and Tarbett, C. (1988) A third season at Tankardstown. *Archaeology Ireland* 2 (4), 156.

Gowen, M. and Tarbett, C. (1990) Tankardstown South. In I. Bennett (ed.) *Excavations 1989: summary accounts of archaeological excavations in Ireland*, 38–9. Bray, Wordwell.

Grogan, E. (2002) Neolithic houses in Ireland: a broader perspective. *Antiquity* 76, 517–25

Grogan, E. (2004) The implications of Irish Neolithic houses. In I. Shepherd and G. Barclay (eds) *Scotland in Ancient Europe: the Neolithic and Early Bronze Age of Scotland in their European context*, 103–14. Edinburgh, Society of Antiquaries of Scotland.

Guttmann-Bond, E., Dungait, J., Brown, A., Bull, I. and Evershed, R. (2016) Early Neolithic agriculture in county Mayo, Republic of Ireland: geoarchaeology of the Céide fields, Belderrig, and Rathlackan, *Journal of the North Atlantic* 30, 1–32.

Harding, A. (2000) *European Societies in the Bronze Age*. Cambridge, Cambridge University Press.

Herity, M. (1971) Prehistoric fields in Ireland. *Irish University Review* 1, 258–65.

Herity, M. and Eogan, G. (1977) *Ireland in Prehistory*. London, Routledge.

Hobson, B. (ed.) (1932) *Saorstát Eireann: official handbook*. Dublin, Talbot Press.

Hogan, J. and Haltinner, K. (2015) Floods, invaders, and parasites: immigration threat narratives and right-wing populism in the USA, UK and Australia. *Journal of Intercultural Studies* (36) 5, 520–43.

Johnston, R. (2013) Bronze Age fields and land division. In H. Fokkens and A. Harding (eds) *The Oxford Handbook of the European Bronze Age*, 311–27. Oxford, Oxford University Press.

Kiely, J. (2003) A Neolithic house at Cloghers, Co. Kerry. In I. Armit, E. Nelis and D. Simpson (eds) *Neolithic Settlement in Ireland and Western Britain*, 182–7. Oxford, Oxbow Books.

Kinnes, I. (1975) Monumental function in British Neolithic burial practices. *World Archaeology* 7 (1), 16–29.

Kinnes, I. (1985) Circumstances not context: the Neolithic of Scotland as seen from the outside. *Proceedings of the Society of Antiquaries of Scotland* 115, 15–57.

Kinnes, I. (1992) Balnagowan and after: the context of non-megalithic mortuary sites in Scotland. In N. Sharples and J.A. Sheridan (eds) *Vessels for the Ancestors: essays on the Neolithic of Britain and Ireland in honour of Audrey Henshall*, 83–103. Edinburgh, Edinburgh University Press.

Kneafsey, M. (1995) A landscape of memories: heritage tourism in Mayo. In U. Kockel (ed.) *Landscape, Heritage and Identity: case studies in Irish ethnography*, 135–54. Liverpool, Liverpool University Press.

Larkin, E. (1975) Church, state, and nation in modern Ireland. *American Historical Review* 80 (5), 1244–76.

Lawson, I., Church, M., Edwards, K., Cook, G. and Dugmore, A. (2007) Peat initiation in the Faroe Islands: climate change, pedogenesis, or human impact? *Earth and Environmental Science Transactions of the Royal Society of Edinburgh* 98 (1), 15–28.

Lucas, B. (2010) *Tentative Submission to World Heritage Centre: the Céide Fields and north-west Mayo boglands*. Wexford, Department of the Environment, Heritage and Local Government.

Lynch, F. (1990) Wales and Ireland in prehistory: a fluctuating relationship. *Archaeologia Cambrensis* 138, 1–19.

Macalister, R. (1949). *The Archaeology of Ireland*. Second revised edition. London, Methuen.

MacConnell, S. (1990) Uncovering the secrets of the Céide Fields. *The Irish Times*. 22 September, 3.

MacGregor, G. and McLellan, K. (2008) A burning desire to build: excavations at Eweford West and Pencraig Hill (3950–3380 BC). In O. Lelong and G. MacGregor (eds) *The Lands of Ancient Lothian: interpreting the archaeology of the A1*. Edinburgh, Society of Antiquaries of Scotland.

Mahr, A. (1932) Archaeology. In B. Hobson (ed.) *Saorstát Eireann: official handbook*, 212–32. Dublin, Talbot Press.

Masters, L. (1973) The Lochhill long cairn. *Antiquity* 47, 96–100.

Masters, L. (1981) Chambered tombs and non-megalithic barrows in Britain. In C. Renfrew (ed.) *The Megalithic Monuments of Western Europe*, 97–112. London, Thames and Hudson.

McClatchie, M., Whitehouse, N., Schulting, R., Bogaard, A. and Barratt, P. (2009) Cultivating societies: new insights into agriculture in Neolithic Ireland. In M. Stanley, E. Danaher and J. Eogan (eds) *Dining and Dwelling: proceedings of a public seminar on archaeological discoveries on national road schemes, August 2008*, 1–8. Dublin, National Roads Authority.

McLaughlin, T.R., Whitehouse, N., Schulting, R., McClatchie, M., Barratt, P. and Bogaard, A. (2016) The changing face of Neolithic and Bronze Age Ireland: a big data approach to the settlement and burial records. *Journal of World Prehistory* 29, 117–53.

McSparron, C. (2008) Have you no homes to go to? *Archaeology Ireland* 22 (3), 18–21.

Molloy, K. and O'Connell, M. (1995) Palaeoecological investigations towards the reconstruction of environment and land-use changes during prehistory at Céide Fields, western Ireland. *Probleme der Küstenforschung im südlichen Nordseegebiet* 23, 187–25.

Molloy, K. and O'Connell, M. (2016) Farming impact in Ireland from the Neolithic to recent times with particular reference to a detailed pollen record from east Galway. In M. O'Connell, F. Kelly and J. McAdam (eds) *Cattle in Ancient and Modern Ireland: farming practices, environment and economy*, 27–43. Newcastle upon Tyne, Cambridge Scholars Publishing.

Moore, P. and Bellamy, D. (1973) *Peatlands*. London, Elek Science.

Mullins, G. (2007) *Dublin Nazi no. 1: the life of Adolf Mahr*. Dublin, Liberties Press.

Nash, C. (1993) Embodying the nation: the west of Ireland landscape and Irish identity. In M. Cronin and B. O'Connor (eds) *Tourism in Ireland: a critical analysis*, 86–114. Cork, Cork University Press.

Nic Craith, M. (2008) From national to transnational: a discipline en route to Europe. In M. Nic Craith, U. Kockel and R. Johler (eds) *Everyday Culture in Europe: approaches and methodologies,* 1–18. Aldershot, Ashgate.

Nielsen, N., Holts, M, Gadd, A. and Holtz, K. (2017) The layout and internal development of Celtic fields: structural and relative chronological analysis of three Danish field systems. *European Journal of Archaeology* 21, 1–26.

Niklasson, E. and Hølleland, H. (2018) The Scandinavian far-right and the new politicisation of heritage. *Journal of Social Archaeology* 17, 138–62.

O'Brien, W. (2009) *Local Worlds: early settlement landscapes and upland farming in south-west Ireland*. Cork, The Collins Press.

O'Connell, M. and Molloy, K. (2001) Farming and woodland dynamics in Ireland during the Neolithic. *Proceedings of the Royal Irish Academy* 101B (1–2), 99–128.

O'Dowd, A. (2012) Bygones and relics and museum acquisitions: some thoughts on the Irish Folklife Collection in the National Museum of Ireland. In S. Ó Síocháin, P. Garvey and A. Drazin (eds) *Exhibit Ireland: ethnographic collections in Irish museums*, 105–26. Dublin, Wordwell.

O'Halloran, C. (2007) Review of 'Foundation myths: the beginnings of Irish archaeology by John Waddell'. *Journal of the Galway Archaeological and Historical Society* 59, 188–90.

O'Kelly, M.J. (1958) A horned cairn at Shanballyedmond, Co. Tipperary. *Journal of the Cork Historical and Archaeological Society* 63, 37–72.

O'Kelly, M.J. (1989) *Early Ireland: an introduction to Irish prehistory*. Cambridge, Cambridge University Press.

Ó Nualláin, S. (1972) A Neolithic House at Ballyglass near Ballycastle, Co. Mayo. *Journal of the Royal Society of Antiquaries of Ireland* 102 (1), 49–57.

Ó Nualláin, S. (1979) The Megalithic tombs of Ireland. *Expedition* 21, 6–15.

Ó Ríordáin, S. (1942) *Antiquities of the Irish Countryside* (1st edn). Cork, Cork University Press.

Ó Ríordáin, S. (1954) Lough Gur excavations: Neolithic and Bronze Age houses on Knockadoon. *Proceedings of the Royal Irish Academy* 56C, 297–459.

Ó Ríordáin, S. (1979) *Antiquities of the Irish Countryside* (5th edn). London, Methuen.

O'Sullivan, M. (2009) The life and legacy of R.A.S. Macalister: a century of archaeology at UCD. In G. Cooney, K. Becker, J. Coles, M. Ryan and S. Sievers (eds) *Relics of Old Decency: archaeological studies in later prehistory. Festschrift for Barry Raftery*, 521–30. Dublin, Wordwell.

O'Sullivan, M. (2011) Megalithic tombs and storied landscapes in Neolithic Ireland. In M. Furholt, F. Lüth and J. Müller (eds) *Megaliths and Identities*, 53–66. Bonn, Dr Rudolf Habelt.

Piggott, S. (1972) The excavation of the Dalladies long barrow, Fettercairn, Kincardineshire. *Proceedings of the Society of Antiquaries of Scotland* 104, 23–47.

Powell, A. (2005) The language of lineage: reading Irish court tomb design. *European Journal of Archaeology* 8 (1), 9–28.

Richards, S. 2009. The playboy of the western world. In P. Mathews (ed.) *The Cambridge Companion to J.M. Synge*, 28–40. Cambridge, Cambridge University Press.

Reid, B. (2007) Creating counterspaces: identity and the home in Ireland and Northern Ireland. *Environment and Planning D: Society and Space* 25, 933–50.

Sheehy, J. (1980) *The Rediscovery of Ireland's Past: the Celtic revival 1830–1930*. London, Thames and Hudson.

Sheridan, J.A. (1995) Irish Neolithic pottery: the story in 1995. In I. Kinnes and G. Varndell (eds) *'Unbaked Urns of Rudely Shape': essays on British and Irish pottery for Ian Longworth*, 3–22. Oxford, Oxbow Books.

Sheridan, J.A. (2006) A non-megalithic funerary tradition in Early Neolithic Ireland. In M. Meek (ed.) *The Modern Traveller to our Past: festschrift in honour of Ann Hamlin*, 24–31. Southport, DPK.

Sheridan, J.A. (2017) Interdigitating pasts: the Irish and Scottish Neolithics. In P. Bickle, V. Cummings, D. Hofmann and J. Pollard (eds) *The Neolithic of Europe: papers in honour of Alasdair Whittle*, 298–313. Oxford, Oxbow Books.

Simpson, D. (1996) The Ballygalley houses, Co. Antrim, Ireland. In T. Darvill and J. Thomas (eds) *Neolithic Houses in Northwest Europe and Beyond*, 123–32. Oxford, Oxbow Books.

Smith, M. (2017) Social science and archaeological enquiry. *Antiquity* 91, 520–8.

Smyth, J. (2006) The role of the house in Early Neolithic Ireland. *European Journal of Archaeology* 9 (2–3), 229–57.

Smyth, J. (2011) The house and group identity in the Irish Neolithic. *Proceedings of the Royal Irish Academy* 111C, 1–31.

Smyth, J. (2013) Tides of change? The house through the Irish Neolithic. In D. Hofmann and J. Smyth (eds) *Tracking the Neolithic House in Europe: sedentism, architecture, practice*, 301–28. London, Springer.

Smyth, J. (2014) *Settlement in the Irish Neolithic: new discoveries on the edge of Europe*. Prehistoric Society Research Paper 6. Oxford, Oxbow Books.

Stoklund, B. (1999) How the peasant house became a national symbol. *Ethnologia Europaea* 29 (1), 5–18.

Thomas, J. (2015) What do we mean by 'Neolithic societies'? In C. Fowler, J. Harding and D. Hofman (eds) *The Oxford Handbook of Neolithic Europe*, 1073–92. Oxford, Oxford University Press.

Waddell, J. (1992) The Irish Sea in Prehistory. *Journal of Irish Archaeology* 6, 29–40.

Waddell, J. (2005) *Foundation Myths: the beginnings of Irish archaeology*. Bray, Wordwell.

Warren, G., McIlreavy, D., Rathbone, S. and Walsh, P. (2009) Archaeological Excavations at Behy (E747): stratigraphic report. Unpublished report, UCD School of Archaeology.

Warren, G., Caulfield, C., Byrne, G. and Dunne, N. (2011) The chronological development of the Céide Hill landscape in prehistory. In S. Caulfield, G. Byrne, N. Dunne and G. Warren (eds) Excavations on Céide Hill, Behy and Glenulra, north Co. Mayo, 1963–1994, 132–40. Unpublished report, UCD School of Archaeology.

Whitefield, A. (2015) Sustainable Change: settlement, environment and the temporality of Neolithic western Ireland. Unpublished Ph.D. thesis, National University of Ireland, Galway.

Whitefield, A. (2017) Neolithic 'Celtic' Fields? A reinterpretation of the chronological evidence from Céide Fields in north-western Ireland. *European Journal of Archaeology* 20 (2), 257–79.

Whitehouse, N., Schulting, R., McClatchie, M., Barratt, P., McLaughlin, T., Bogaard, A., Colledge, S., Marchant, R., Gaffrey, J. and Bunting, M. (2014) Neolithic agriculture on the European western frontier: the boom and bust of early farming in Ireland. *Journal of Archaeological Science* 51, 181–205.

Woodman, P. (2000) Hammers and shoeboxes: new agendas for prehistory. In A. Desmond, G. Johnson, M. McCarthy, J. Sheehan and E. Shee Twohig (eds) *New Agendas in Irish Prehistory: papers in commemoration of Liz Anderson*, 1–14. Bray, Wordwell.

Chapter 13

Structure, metaphor and funerary practices in Neolithic Scotland

Alison Sheridan

As noted elsewhere in this volume, the argument that Neolithic funerary monuments in Britain echo the design of the houses of the living, and acted as houses for the dead, was proposed by Ian Hodder in the 1980s (1982; 1984), developing an idea regarding long barrows earlier articulated by Gordon Childe (1949). Hodder drew parallels between the trapezoidal shape of many long barrows and that of earlier houses belonging to the Linearbandkeramik (LBK) culture on the Continent; between stalled cairns and earlier Neolithic houses in Orkney; and also between the cruciform shape of Maeshowe-type passage tomb chambers and that of Late Neolithic houses at Skara Brae, also in Orkney. This model has been influential and has been discussed, revisited and reworked by several subsequent commentators (*e.g.* Bradley 1996; 2019, 54–62; Richards 1992; Richards and Jones 2016, 40).

While attractive in its simplicity of concept, this model is not without its problems, not least as regards the significant chronological gap between British long mounds and the LBK houses that are supposed to have inspired their shape, as discussed by Alasdair Whittle elsewhere in this volume. This contribution offers a critical review of the relationship between house design and the design of funerary monuments in Neolithic Scotland, set within the broader picture of the full range of funerary practices there. This task has been greatly facilitated by the increase in the number of houses (including the large 'halls') and of radiocarbon-dated sites in Scotland over the last 20 years, particularly as far as Orkney is concerned (Bayliss *et al.* 2017) – although, as will be seen, many more houses and dates will be required if we are to refine our narrative.

THE EARLY NEOLITHIC, TO *c*.3600 BC

The earliest evidence for Neolithic funerary practices in Scotland belongs to two discrete traditions (Sheridan 2010a; 2018). One relates to the arrival of farming groups from the Morbihan area of Brittany in the west of Scotland at some point between 4300 BC and 3900 BC (probably around 4000 BC: *cf.* Cassen *et al.* 2009 for the dating of the corresponding Late Castellic 'culture' in Brittany). These people brought a tradition of building megalithic closed chambers and simple passage tombs (Fig. 13.1); the latter stand at the beginning of a long tradition of passage tomb construction in Scotland, spanning up to a millennium (*contra* Whittle *et al.* 2011 and Bayliss *et al.* 2017; see Sheridan 2016 for an exploration of the ceramic evidence supporting this long chronology). The other relates to the arrival of 'Carinated Bowl Neolithic' groups from Nord-Pas de Calais probably during the 39th century BC, bringing a non-megalithic funerary tradition (Fig. 13.2) (*cf*. Whittle *et al*. 2011, 804–40 on dating this phenomenon). The latter groups seem to have arrived along Scotland's east coast, before spreading west and south across Scotland and into north-west England, the Isle of Man and Ireland. Early Neolithic cave burial is also attested, on the west coast of Scotland (in the Macarthur, Distillery and Raschoille caves, Oban: Bonsall *et al*. 2012; Armit *et al*. 2016); its possible cultural affinity is discussed below.

That we can confidently talk of traditions that have been introduced by immigrant communities – as has long been argued by this author on the basis of the archaeological evidence (*e.g.* Sheridan 2010a) – is due to the results of recent DNA analysis of Mesolithic and Early Neolithic human remains, which confirm that the latter have genetic signatures not hitherto represented in Britain (Brace *et al*. 2019). There is much that still needs to be done to 'flesh out' our picture of these movements of people: above all, the undertaking of more total genome analyses of individuals in north-west and northern France dating to the centuries around 4000 BC, even though in Brittany the task is complicated by the paucity of surviving Neolithic human remains in the acidic environmental conditions. Suffice it to note here that the 'Iberian' genetic signature found in some of the British Neolithic individuals does *not* indicate any Early Neolithic movement from Iberia to Britain, contrary to some geneticists' claims (*e.g.* Sánchez-Quinto *et al*. 2019); 'Iberian' elements are attested among Neolithic individuals in northern France.

Regarding the groups who arrived from Brittany, we can currently say nothing about the shape of their occupation structures and whether there was any architectural homology between these and the small closed megalithic chambers and simple passage tombs in which they deposited their dead, because no clear settlement evidence has yet been found. Indeed, in the landscape of western Scotland and the Hebrides, where rough grazing predominates, it would be hard to seek out and find settlement sites. In Brittany, settlement sites belonging to the Middle Neolithic II Late Castellic 'culture' are sparse (Cassen 2000a), but nobody has suggested that the closed chambers and simple passage tombs found in Brittany offer a close match for the design of structures for the living. In other words, there does not seem to have been a literal translation of the houses of the living into the houses of the dead – even if the funerary monuments may well have been regarded as places where the dead resided.

Some valuable insights into the belief system that informed the design of closed chambers and passage tombs in the Morbihan area of Brittany have, however, been provided by Serge Cassen (2000b). In his detailed examination of the closed chamber in a barrow at Lannec er Gadouer, Erdeven, he explained how the design and construction of the chamber, the choice of materials used to construct the mound that enveloped it and the iconography of the objects buried in the chamber (or otherwise associated with the monument) all underlined the deceased's passage into the Otherworld and separation from this world. The accessibility and collective nature of the passage tombs of the Morbihan was contrasted with this closed monument form, as representing a 'living architecture' as opposed to an emphasis on the dead body, separated from this world; and elsewhere, Cassen (with Christine Boujot) had suggested that the design of passage tombs evokes the form of a womb, and was associated with a concept of female fertility (Boujot and Cassen 1992). It seems likely that this world-view was what informed the decision to build first a closed chamber, and then a simple passage tomb, at Achnacreebeag on the west coast of Scotland (Ritchie 1970); this

Fig. 13.1: Achnacreebeag, Argyll and Bute: left, plan of the closed megalithic chamber and simple passage tomb, and section through the cairn at the closed chamber; top right, view of closed chamber; bottom right, Late Castellic bowl from the simple passage tomb. Images: drawing: Crown copyright, reproduced with permission of Historic Environment Scotland and the Society of Antiquaries of Scotland; site photo: the late Graham Ritchie; pot: National Museums Scotland.

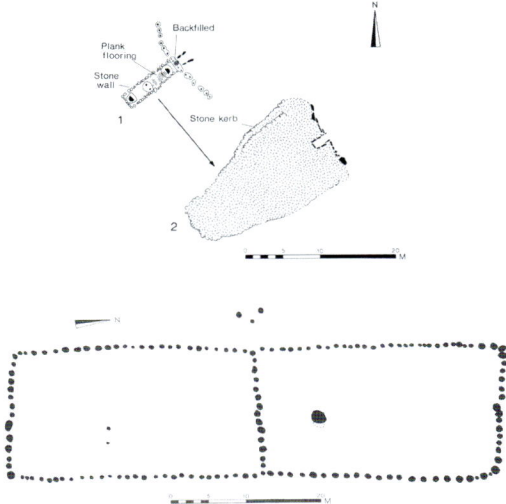

Fig. 13.2: Examples of CB Neolithic funerary monuments: top, timber 'linear zone' mortuary structure and façade, subsequently covered by a trapezoidal cairn and stone chamber, Lochhill, Dumfries and Galloway; bottom: putative 'mortuary enclosure', Douglasmuir, Angus. From Kinnes 1992a, reproduced with permission.

monument would have been constructed at a time when both chamber forms were in use in the Morbihan. This suggestion gains support from the fact that the Late Castellic bowl associated with the simple passage tomb at Achnacreebeag bears the 'rainbow' motif as found on Late Castellic pottery in Brittany, and also that a fragment of rock crystal – a material that produces a 'rainbow' effect when held up to the light, and which is associated with Breton funerary monuments – was found in the passage. The significance of the rainbow as something that links the world of the living to that of the gods (and hence can help the dead to pass over from this world to the Otherworld) was discussed by Cassen (2000b, 724–7).

The stark contrast between this way of dealing with the dead and that relating to the contemporary fisher-hunter-forager communities on Oronsay, who laid out their dead on their shell middens so that their remains could rejoin the natural world, has been discussed elsewhere (Sheridan 2010a; 2018) and needs no underlining here.

Before turning to the funerary practices relating to the Carinated Bowl (CB) Neolithic, it should be noted that the practice of depositing the dead within caves, communally, in the west of Scotland finds no obvious parallel either in the Morbihan or in the Nord-Pas de Calais region of France (from where the CB Neolithic immigrants appear to have come). This is not surprising, given the absence of caves in these regions. Nor had this mode of dealing with the dead featured in the funerary tradition of the indigenous fisher-hunter-forager groups in Scotland, in contrast to other parts of Britain (Bonsall *et al.* 2012; Brace *et al.* 2019). Unfortunately, no pottery or other diagnostic artefacts have been associated with the individuals in question – an arrowhead found in Raschoille Cave was sadly lost – and so it is hard to assess whether it was the Breton immigrant farmers who chose to bury people in caves, as well as in their megalithic monuments. All one can say is that the caves in question are within a few kilometres of Achnacreebeag, and are far from the areas where CB Neolithic funerary traditions are found, and so the practice is most likely to be associated with the Breton immigrants. What is clear, from the results of DNA analysis, is that the individuals in these caves were indeed incomers; and there are two examples, from Raschoille Cave, of inter-mixing between the incomers and the indigenous community (Brace *et al.* 2019).

As for the funerary tradition associated with the CB Neolithic immigrants (Fig. 13.2), this involved a variety of practices, and where monumental structures were involved, these were initially non-megalithic (Kinnes 1992a; 1992b). The megalithic monuments of the CB Neolithic tradition, which are mostly restricted to the south-west and west of Scotland, constitute a translation into stone of the timber structural forms as outlined below. The range of attested CB Neolithic funerary practices can be summarised as follows:

1. Deposition of a small number of corpses within a rectangular 'linear zone' mortuary structure, usually made by splitting a large oak trunk in two to define its front and back, and sometimes including a third post mid-way along, presumably to support a platform. Simpler box-like structures are also known. These mortuary structures can be associated with a monumental façade and some are set within a long rectangular or trapezoidal timber enclosure. After decomposition of the bodies, these mortuary structures were usually burnt, and sometimes, as at Eweford West, East Lothian, successive examples were built then burnt (Lelong and MacGregor 2007). A final act, in many cases, was the erection of a long rectangular or trapezoidal mound, although in the case of Pitnacree (Perth and Kinross), a round mound covered the mortuary structure (Coles and Simpson 1964; Sheridan 2010b). The megalithic versions of the 'linear zone' mortuary structure and associated features in west and south-west Scotland began with the simple box-like chambers surrounded by round, then trapezoidal, mounds at Mid Gleniron I and II, Dumfries and Galloway (Henshall 1972, 535–7), and the box-like chamber, antechamber, façade and long mound at Cairnholy I, Dumfries and Galloway (Henshall 1972, 438–9); the Clyde cairn tradition can be seen to develop from the latter. Greatly elongated variants of the long mound were later constructed at a few locations in Scotland, with the 342 m-long bank barrow at Auchenlaich, Stirling, being by far the longest; here the very long cairn may well have been added to a pre-existing monument of Clyde cairn affinities (Foster and Stevenson 2002). At Cleaven Dyke, Perth and Kinross, a very narrow mound 1.82 km long was constructed, perhaps next to a pre-existing funerary monument

(Barclay and Maxwell 1993). Whether the Auchenlaich and Cleaven Dyke monuments were built before, around or after 3600 BC is unclear, however.
2. Presumed deposition of corpses within long rectangular timber 'mortuary enclosures' (*e.g.* at Douglasmuir, Angus and Inchtuthil, Perth and Kinross, the former arguably sharing some design features with the Cat's Brain structure, Wiltshire: Kendrick 1995; Barclay and Maxwell 1991). It is assumed that, following decomposition, the bones were removed for deposition elsewhere. It has to be admitted that the function of these structures as mortuary enclosures has not been proven, even though it is clear that they are ceremonial, monumental constructions; the funerary interpretation is guided by their close resemblance to the long enclosures around some 'linear zone' mortuary structures, and to long barrows. Just as long mounds found a later expression in greatly elongated forms, these rectangular 'mortuary enclosures' seem to have been succeeded, in parts of Scotland during the second quarter of the fourth millennium, by long, rectangular, timber or earthen cursus monuments (*e.g.* Holywood and Holm Farm, Dumfries and Galloway: Thomas 2008).
3. Open-air cremation of several individuals, followed by burial in a pit (at Duns, Scottish Borders: Anderson 2018) or being covered by a round mound (as at Boghead, Moray: Burl 1984) or a ring mound (at Midtown of Pitglassie, Aberdeenshire: Shepherd 1996).

What unites many of the non-megalithic CB Neolithic monuments is the fact that once the mound was constructed, the human remains therein would be inaccessible – or rather, only accessible by dismantling parts of the mound. In other words, these served to memorialise a small number of people, and were not designed for long-term successive use. What happened to the bodies of the vast majority of the CB Neolithic population is unknown; it may be that deposition of human remains in modest (and hard to spot) pits, as seen at Duns, was the norm.

How, if at all, can these funerary structures be related to the houses of the living? Luckily we have a number of Early Neolithic large houses ('halls') and smaller houses with which to compare the funerary monuments (Fig. 13.3; Sheridan 2013). It is clear that these structures for the living do not offer a close formal or structural parallel for the 'linear zone' mortuary structures, for the mortuary enclosures or for the long mounds (and certainly not for the round mounds). The only points of comparison are in the use of wood, including some impressively large timbers in the 'halls'; in the large size of both the 'halls' and the mortuary enclosures and long mounds; and in the generalised rectangular shape of the various structures. Had the builders of the funerary monuments wished to reproduce the design of the 'halls' and smaller houses faithfully, one would have expected to see roughly parallel-sided structures with convex ends.

That said, one cannot rule out the possibility that the funerary monuments were indeed regarded as idealised houses for the dead. Whether or not their shape harked back to a by then very ancient Continental house design will no doubt remain a topic for debate, as will the apparent chronological gap of several centuries between long mounds along the southern fringe of the Channel (*e.g.* at Colombiers-sur-Seulles, Normandy: Marcigny *et al.* 2007) and those in Britain. What is arguably less in doubt is the role of the monumental constructions as expressions of community identity and as prominent materialised statements of land ownership. By choosing to memorialise certain individuals by sealing them within mounds that would have required a considerable amount of communal effort to build, these groups may

Fig. 13.3: Examples of Early Neolithic Scottish 'halls': top, artist's impression of one of the Doon Hill 'halls' being burnt down when the inhabitants 'budded off' to live in individual farmsteads (Crown copyright, reproduced with permission of Historic Environment Scotland); bottom, ground plans of: a) Crathes Warren Field, Aberdeenshire; b) Balbridie, Aberdeenshire; c) Claish, Stirling; d) Doon Hill A, East Lothian; e) Lockerbie Academy, Dumfries & Galloway (showing alternative interpretations of plan, as one and as two structures); from Sheridan 2013.

effectively have been designating these people as founding ancestors for the community, whose authority and power could be invoked by later generations. If the mounds were regarded as the abodes of the ancestors – and if by building them, communities were perpetuating and manipulating a tradition that stretched back several centuries on the Continent – then it should not matter whether or not they mirrored the shape of contemporary houses.

As for the massively elongated monuments referred to above (and see Bradley 2019, 71–3), these may express community identity on a larger scale. While the rationale for undertaking such vast constructions (and the subsequent burning down of timber cursūs) may well have been to honour and commemorate the dead, arguably the most important aspect of these projects was the bringing together of considerable numbers of people – a whole tribe, perhaps, if they self-identified in such terms – to work communally, thereby deepening their sense of belonging to a large social group. Perhaps, indeed, the very long mounds were regarded as the metaphorical houses of the dead of an entire tribe.

FUNERARY PRACTICES AND HOUSE STRUCTURES, *c*.3600–*c*.2500 BC

As in the Early Neolithic, a considerable variety of funerary practices and monuments are attested in Scotland for the millennium or so following *c*. 3600 BC. The passage tomb tradition, with its round mounds, continued in parts of the west, north and east of Scotland including Orkney, where a specific and complex regional trajectory of chamber tomb construction between *c*. 3600 and *c*. 2900 BC, not all of it connected with passage tombs, can be traced. Burial in caves and similar locations in the west continued, at the Oban caves, at Creag nan Uamh cave, Inchnadamph, Highland (Saville 2005) and at the rock shelter at An Corran on Skye (Saville *et al.* 2012). In east-central Scotland, during the second half of the fourth millennium, large timber exposure platforms whose ground plan echoes those of Early Neolithic 'halls' were built at Littleour, Perth and Kinross (Barclay and Maxwell 1993) and at Balfarg Riding School, Fife (Barclay and Russell-White 1993). And on the Scottish mainland, a Late Neolithic practice of cremation and of (generally) individual burial in pits with Grooved Ware pottery is attested (*e.g.* at Stoneyfield, Raigmore, Highland: Copper *et al.* 2018).

Space does not permit a detailed exposition of the specific monument forms, but it may be noted that an interplay between elements of different funerary traditions can be seen in the choice of mound shape. In the former county of Caithness, for example, a process of monumental aggrandisement, poorly dated but probably occurring around 3600 BC or 3500 BC, seems to have involved imposing the long cairn format of the CB Neolithic tradition – in the form of huge trapezoidal horned cairns – onto pre-existing round-cairn passage tombs, whose ultimate origin can be traced back to the Breton strand of Neolithisation. A good example of this can be seen at Camster Long, where two such passage tombs were incorporated within a horned cairn (Fig. 13.4; Davidson and Henshall 1991, ch. 5). This can be interpreted in two ways: either it represents a cultural appropriation and 'rebranding' of ancient monuments belonging to one group of people by a different group, expressing their CB Neolithic affinity; or else it expresses the acculturation of the descendants of passage tomb builders to a CB Neolithic identity. Either way, it represents a significant investment of communal effort to enhance the abodes of the ancestors, quite possibly as part of a process of competitive conspicuous consumption.

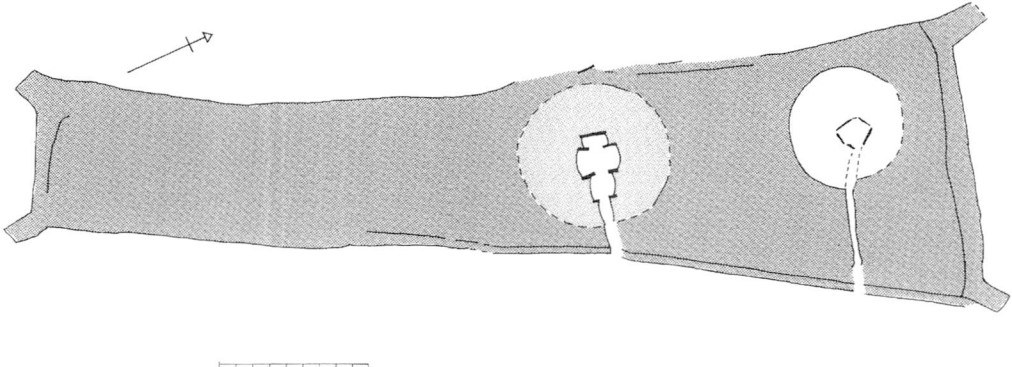

Fig. 13.4: Camster Long, Highland (formerly Caithness): two formerly free-standing passage tombs with round mounds incorporated within a long horned cairn. From Davidson and Henshall 1991, reproduced with permission.

As for the degree to which any of the post-3600 BC funerary monuments mirrored contemporary house design, the archaeological record is frustratingly patchy, with very few house structures surviving (but suffice it to note that there is none that resembles a horned long cairn). Where the shape of houses can be made out, there is generally no read-across to the design of the local funerary monuments: on North Uist, for example, the design of the islet house on Eileann Dòmhnuill (Armit 1998) does not echo that of the passage tombs (Henshall 1972, 111–57) that had already been standing for at least a century, to judge from the ceramic evidence (Sheridan 2016).

It is only on Orkney where, thanks to numerous recent house discoveries (Richards and R. Jones 2016) and a growing number of radiocarbon dates (Bayliss *et al.* 2017), it is possible to interrogate this question of design homology in some detail – and even then, the dating of the various kinds of chamber tomb still needs to be improved. Here, the recently-discovered timber houses, such as the two sub-circular examples and one rectangular house at Wideford Hill (Richards and A.M. Jones 2016, fig. 2.6), do not provide any particularly close *comparanda* for the stalled cairns that were built, in various formats and sizes, during the second half of the fourth millennium, although some stone houses (such as Knap of Howar) do possess the stall-like internal divisions as seen in the tombs and there does indeed appear to be some homology in the design (Fig. 13.5). The question of which came first – stalled cairns or the houses that resembled them – has been addressed through Bayesian modelling of all the available dates, with Richards and A.M. Jones (2016, 40) and Bayliss *et al.* (2017) concluding that the stalled format started in the funerary monuments, and was then evoked in the design of houses. (The question of how, and why, the stalled chamber form may have evolved from the tripartite structure of earlier Orkney-Cromarty type passage tombs cannot be explored here.)

It may be, then, that the convergence of tomb and house form in Middle Neolithic Orkney offers the first reasonably convincing example of this design homology – of a read-across between contemporary houses for the living and houses of the dead. While earlier funerary monuments could have been regarded as metaphorical houses of the dead, now the metaphor was being expressed in an unambiguous manner. And just as a process of competitive conspicuous consumption – rationalised as the desire to build bigger and better houses for the dead – may have driven the imposition of huge horned cairns onto passage tombs in Caithness, a similar process could well lie behind the construction of increasingly large stalled cairns, and in particular the massive examples on Rousay at Midhowe and the Knowes of Lingro and Rowiegar (Davidson and Henshall 1989, 134–8, 146–8).

This same competition between groups of (presumably fairly prosperous) farmers in Orkney is likely to have motivated the long-distance voyaging, by certain individuals, to the Boyne Valley to visit the magnificent huge passage tombs at Newgrange, Knowth and Dowth that were constructed from *c.* 3200 BC (Schulting *et al*. 2017), and to participate in the seasonal ceremonies there. Knowledge of these tombs and cemeteries will have spread along the pre-existing network of contacts that linked Orkney with the Hebrides (as shown in the sharing of the Unstan Bowl ceramic form: Sheridan 2016), and the Hebrides with Ireland (as shown, for example, in the presence of a porcellanite axehead from Co. Antrim at Shulishader on Lewis: Sheridan 1992). As argued elsewhere (*e.g.* Sheridan 2014), one powerful idea that was brought back as a result of this 'cosmological acquisition' was the cruciform design, long passage and solstitial alignment of the Newgrange passage tomb, along with the use of sacred symbols on passage tombs. All these elements, in varying combinations, can be seen on the Maeshowe passage tombs of Orkney, which will have 'trumped' all previous passage tombs there in their size and in the complexity and sophistication of their construction. (Note that as for the pre-3200 BC dates for some of the human remains from Quanterness passage tomb [Schulting *et al*. 2010], these could easily relate to remains that had been transferred from an older monument elsewhere; they do not, *contra* Bayliss *et al*. [2017, 1184], prove that the tomb was built as early as 3400 BC, or that this constituted the earliest passage tomb architecture in Orkney or in Britain and Ireland more generally.)

Regarding the question of whether there was a convergence in the design of houses (and other structures) in Orkney from the time when Maeshowe-type passage tombs appeared, there does indeed seem to be some read-across, with the non-funerary structure design being influenced from the passage tomb chamber design, rather than *vice versa* (Fig. 13.5). It is most clearly seen in the use of recessed walling to create divisions in structures at Barnhouse, Ness of Brodgar and Skara Brae (Phase 2) – divisions that are reminiscent of the recessed side-cells leading off the main chamber in Maeshowe-type passage tombs. But clearly there was not a slavish copying: the Phase 1 houses at Skara Brae (Shepherd 2016) do not have this feature, and the piered walling within the massive structures at Barnhouse (Richards *et al*. 2016) and Ness of Brodgar (Card *et al*. 2017) echoes not only the cellular design of Maeshowe-type passage tombs but also the stalls in stalled cairns. Within this vibrant society, where a new world order and a new cultural identity were being forged (*e.g.* in the use of Grooved Ware as a novel, Orcadian style of pottery), domestic and ceremonial architecture was clearly one arena in which aspects of design could be appropriated and amended, and where the houses of the dead offered one, but not necessarily the only, source of inspiration.

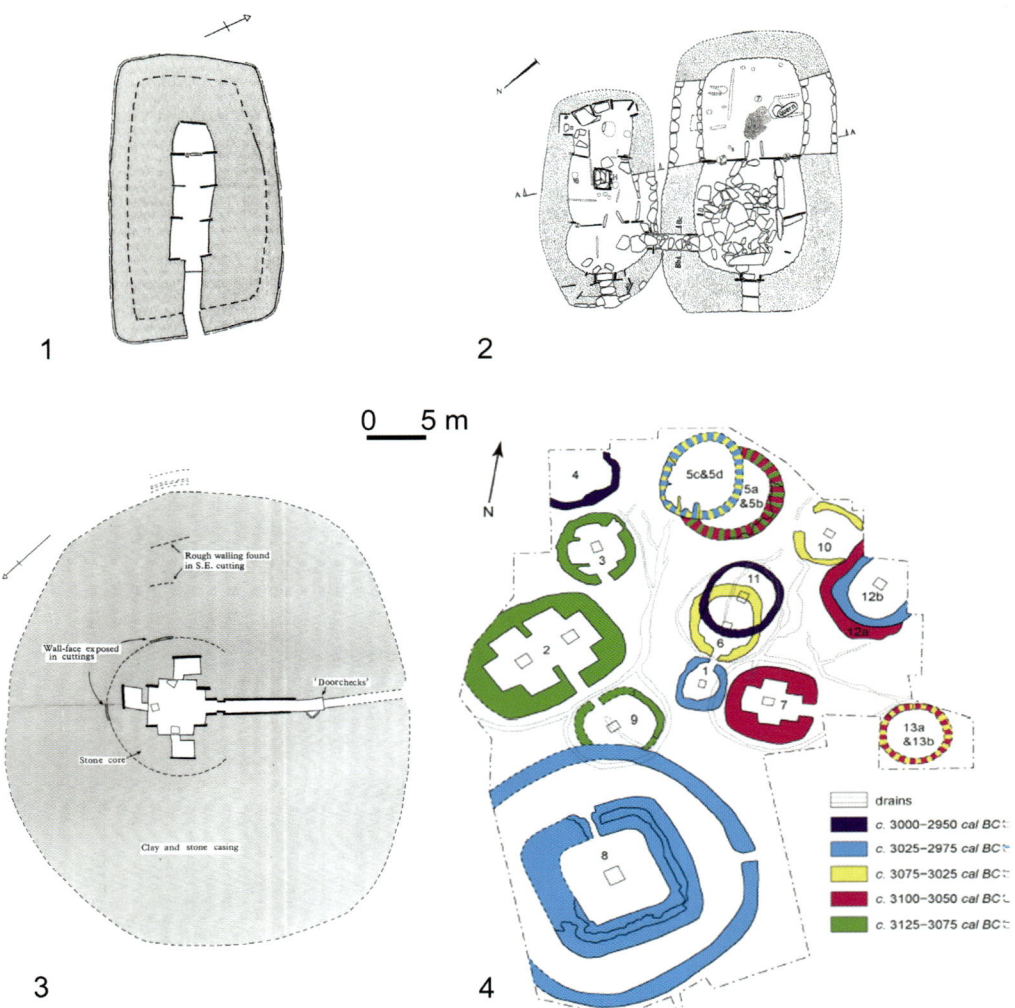

Fig. 13.5: Comparison between Orcadian chamber tomb forms and domestic and ceremonial structures: 1. Stalled cairn, Knowe of Yarso, Rousay; 2. Knap of Howar houses with 'stall' divisions, Papa Westray; 3.Maeshowe passage tomb; 4. Structures at Barnhouse that may echo or evoke the chamber design of Maeshowe. Images 1 and 3 from Davidson and Henshall 1989, with permission; 2 reproduced with permission from Anna Ritchie and the Society of Antiquaries of Scotland; 4 from Richards et al. 2016, reproduced with permission.

CONCLUSIONS

It is hoped that this rapid review will have highlighted the variability of funerary practices in Neolithic Scotland, and the rarity of the instances where an unambiguous design connection was made between the houses of the living and the houses of the dead. The imposing monuments of the Early Neolithic may indeed have been regarded as houses for the dead, but without underlining the metaphor by designing them to match the contemporary houses of the living (or *vice versa*).

Instead of focusing on how closely the design of funerary and non-funerary structures were aligned, it seems to this author that a more fruitful way to approach the archaeology of death in Neolithic Scotland would be to explore how the deceased were treated and how their monuments reflected concerns about their identity and that of the wider social groups to which they belonged. This relates to questions of how traditions were either maintained or transformed. Such an approach might help to account for the 'vocabulary' of funerary monuments and the nature of its changes over time.

REFERENCES

Anderson, S. (2018) A prehistoric cremation burial at Duns Law Farm, near Duns, Scottish Borders. *Proceedings of the Society of Antiquaries of Scotland* 147, 29–47.

Armit, I.A. (1998) *Scotland's Hidden History*. Stroud, Tempus.

Armit, I., Sheridan, J.A., Reich, D., Cook, G., Tripney, B. and Naysmith, P. (2016) Radiocarbon dates obtained for the GENSCOT ancient DNA project, 2016. *Discovery and Excavation in Scotland* 17, 195–8.

Barclay, G.J. and Maxwell, G.S. (1991) Excavation of a Neolithic long mortuary enclosure within the Roman legionary fortress at Inchtuthil, Perthshire. *Proceedings of the Society of Antiquaries of Scotland* 121, 27–44.

Barclay, G.J. and Maxwell, G.S. (1993) *The Cleaven Dyke and Littleour: monuments in the Neolithic of Tayside*. Edinburgh, Society of Antiquaries of Scotland.

Barclay, G.J. and Russell-White, C.J. (1993) Excavations in the ceremonial complex of the fourth to second millennium BC at Balfarg/Balbirnie, Glenrothes, Fife. *Proceedings of the Society of Antiquaries of Scotland* 123, 43–210.

Bayliss, A., Marshall, P., Richards, C. and Whittle, A. (2017) Islands of history: the Late Neolithic timescape of Orkney. *Antiquity* 91, 1171–89.

Bonsall, C., Pickard, C. and Ritchie, G.A. (2012) From Assynt to Oban: some observations on prehistoric cave use in western Scotland. In K.A. Bergsvik and R. Skeates (eds) *Caves in Context: the cultural significance of caves and rockshelters in Europe*, 10–21. Oxford, Oxbow Books.

Boujot, C. and Cassen, S. (1992) Le developpement des premières architectures funéraires monumentales en France occidentale. *Révue archéologique de l'Ouest, supplément* 5, 195–211.

Brace, S., Diekmann, Y., Booth, T.J., van Dorp, L., Faltyskova, Z., Rohland, N., Mallick, S., Olalde, I., Ferry, M., Michel, M., Oppenheimer, J., Broomandkhoshbacht, N., Stewardston, K., Martiniano, R., Walsh, S., Kayser, M., Charlton, S., Hellenthal, G., Armit, I., Schulting, R.J., Craig, C.E., Sheridan, J.A., Parker Pearson, M., Stringer, C., Reich, D., Thomas, M.G. and Barnes, I. (2019). Ancient genomes indicate population replacement in Early Neolithic Britain. *Nature Ecology and Evolution* 3, 765–71.

Bradley, R.J. (1996) Long houses, long mounds and Neolithic enclosures. *Journal of Material Culture* 1 (2), 239–56.

Bradley, R.J. (2019) *The Prehistory of Britain and Ireland* (2nd edn). Cambridge, Cambridge University Press.

Burl, A. (1984) Report on the excavation of a Neolithic mound at Boghead, Speymouth Forest, Fochabers, Moray, 1972 and 1974. *Proceedings of the Society of Antiquaries of Scotland* 114, 35–73.

Card, N., Mainland, I., Timpany, S., Batt, C., Bronk Ramsey, C., Dunbar, E., Reimer, P.J., Bayliss, A., Marshall, P. and Whittle, A. (2017) Formal chronological modelling for the Late Neolithic site of Ness of Brodgar, Orkney. *European Journal of Archaeology*, 1–47.

Cassen, S. (2000a) Les modèles d'habitations dans l'Ouest au Ve millénaire. In S. Cassen with C. Boujot and J. Vaquero (eds) *Éléments d'architecture*, 425–6. Mémoire XIX. Chauvigny, Association des Publications Chauvinoises.

Cassen, S. (2000b) Architecture du tombeau, équipement mortuaire, décor céramique et art gravé du Ve millénaire en Morbihan. À la recherche d'une cosmogonie des premières sociétés agricoles de l'Europe occidentale. In S. Cassen with C. Boujot and J. Vaquero (eds) *Éléments d'architecture*, 717–35. Mémoire XIX. Chauvigny, Association des Publications Chauvinoises.

Cassen, S., Lanois, P., Dufresne, P., Oberlin, C., Delqué-Kolic, E. and Le Goffic, M. (2009) Datations sur site (Table des Marchands, alignement du Grand Menhir, Er Grah) et modélisation chronologique du Néolithque morbihannais. In S. Cassen (ed.) *Autour de la Table. Explorations archéologiques et discours savants sur des architectures néolithiques à Locmariaquer, Morbihan*, 737–68. Nantes, Université de Nantes.

Childe, V.G. (1949) The origin of Neolithic culture in northern Europe. *Antiquity* 23, 129–35.

Coles, J.M. and Simpson, D.D.A. (1964) The excavation of a Neolithic round barrow at Pitnacree, Perthshire, Scotland. *Proceedings of the Prehistoric Society* 31, 34–57.

Copper, M., Sheridan, J.A., Gibson, A.M., Tripney, B., Hamilton, D. and Cook, G. (2018) Radiocarbon dates for Grooved Ware from mainland Scotland arising from the project *Tracing the Lines: uncovering Grooved Ware trajectories in Neolithic Scotland*. *Discovery and Excavation in Scotland* 19, 214–7.

Davidson, J.L. and Henshall, A.S. (1989) *The Chambered Cairns of Orkney*. Edinburgh, Edinburgh University Press.

Davidson, J.L. and Henshall, A.S. (1991) *The Chambered Cairns of Caithness*. Edinburgh, Edinburgh University Press.

Foster, S. and Stevenson, J.B. (2002) The Auchenlaich long cairn. In G.J. Barclay, K. Brophy and G. MacGregor, Claish, Stirling: an Early Neolithic structure in its context, 114–9. *Proceedings of the Society of Antiquaries of Scotland* 132, 65–137.

Henshall, A.S. (1972) *The Chambered Tombs of Scotland*. Volume 2. Edinburgh, Edinburgh University Press.

Hodder, I. (1982) *Symbols in Action*. Cambridge, Cambridge University Press.

Hodder, I. (1984) Burials, houses, women and men in the European Neolithic. In D. Miller and C. Tilley (eds) *Ideology, Power and Prehistory*, 51–68. Cambridge, Cambridge University Press.

Kendrick, J. (1995) Excavation of a Neolithic enclosure and an Iron Age settlement at Douglasmuir, Angus. *Proceedings of the Society of Antiquaries of Scotland* 125, 29–67.

Kinnes, I.A. (1992a) *Non-megalithic Long Barrows and Allied Structures in Britain*. London, British Museum.

Kinnes, I.A. (1992b) Balnagowan and after: the context of non-megalithic mortuary sites in Scotland. In N.M. Sharples and J.A. Sheridan (eds) *Vessels for the Ancestors: essays on the Neolithic of Britain and Ireland in honour of Audrey Henshall*, 83–103. Edinburgh, Edinburgh University Press.

Lelong, O. and MacGregor, G. (2007) *The Lands of Ancient Lothian: interpreting the archaeology of the A1*. Edinburgh, Society of Antiquaries of Scotland.

Marcigny, C., Ghesquière, E. and Desloges, J. (2007) *La Hache et la Meule: les premiers paysans du Néolithique en Normandie (6000–2000 avant notre ère)*. Le Havre, Muséum d'histoire naturelle du Havre.

Richards, C. 1992. Doorways to another world, the Orkney-Cromarty chambered tombs. In N.M. Sharples and J.A. Sheridan (eds) *Vessels for the Ancestors: essays on the Neolithic of Britain and Ireland in honour of Audrey Henshall*, 62–76. Edinburgh, Edinburgh University Press.

Richards, C. and Jones, A.M. (2016) Houses of the dead: the transition from wood to stone architecture at Wideford Hill. In C. Richards and R. Jones (eds) *The Development of Neolithic House Societies in Orkney*, 16–40. Oxford, Windgather Press.

Richards, C. and Jones, R. (eds) (2016) *The Development of Neolithic House Societies in Orkney*. Oxford, Windgather Press.

Richards, C., Jones, A.M., MacSween, A., Sheridan, J.A., Dunbar, E., Reimer, P., Bayliss, A., Griffiths, S. and Whittle, A. (2016) Settlement duration and materiality: formal chronological models for the development of Barnhouse, a Grooved Ware settlement in Orkney. *Proceedings of the Prehistoric Society* 82, 193–225.

Ritchie, J.N.G. (1970) Excavation of the chambered cairn at Achnacreebeag. *Proceedings of the Society of Antiquaries of Scotland* 102 (1969–70), 31–55.

Sánchez-Quinto, F., Malmström, H., Fraser, M., Girdland-Flink, L., Svensson, E.M., Simões, L.G., George, R., Hollfelder, N., Burenhult, G., Noble, G., Britton, K., Talamo, S., Curtis. N., Brzobohata, H., Sumberova, R., Götherström, Storå, J. and Jakobsson, M. (2019) Megalithic tombs in western and northern Neolithic Europe were linked to a kindred society. *Proceedings of the National Academy of Sciences of the United States of America* 116 (19), 9469–74.

Saville, A. (2005) Archaeology and the Creag nan Uamh bone caves, Assynt, Highland. *Proceedings of the Society of Antiquaries of Scotland* 135, 343–69.

Saville, A., Hardy, K., Miket, R. and Ballin, T.B. (2012) An Corran, Staffin, Skye: a rockshelter with Mesolithic and later occupation. *Scottish Archaeological Internet Report* 51, www.sair.org.uk.

Schulting, R., Sheridan, J.A., Crozier, R. and Murphy, E. (2010) Revisiting Quanterness: new AMS dates and stable isotope data from an Orcadian chamber tomb. *Proceedings of the Society of Antiquaries of Scotland* 140, 1–50.

Schulting, R., Bronk Ramsey, C., Reimer, P., Eogan, G., Cleary, K., Cooney, G. and Sheridan, J.A. (2017) Dating Knowth. In G. Eogan with K. Cleary (eds) *Excavations at Knowth Volume 6: the passage tomb archaeology of the great mound at Knowth*, 331–79. Dublin, Royal Irish Academy.

Shepherd, A. (1996) A Neolithic ring-mound at Midtown of Pitglassie, Auchterless, Aberdeenshire. *Proceedings of the Society of Antiquaries of Scotland* 126, 17–51.

Shepherd, A. (2016) Skara Brae life studies: overlaying the embedded images. In F.J. Hunter and J.A. Sheridan (eds) *Ancient Lives: object, people and place in early Scotland. Essays for David V Clarke on his 70th Birthday*, 213–32. Leiden, Sidestone.

Sheridan, J.A. (1992) Scottish stone axeheads: some new work and recent discoveries. In N.M. Sharples and J.A. Sheridan (eds) *Vessels for the Ancestors: essays on the Neolithic of Britain and Ireland in honour of Audrey Henshall*, 194–212. Edinburgh, Edinburgh University Press.

Sheridan, J.A. (2010a) The Neolithisation of Britain and Ireland: the big picture. In B. Finlayson and G. Warren (eds) *Landscapes in Transition*, 89–105. Oxford, Oxbow Books.

Sheridan, J.A. (2010b) Scotland's Neolithic non-megalithic round mounds: new dates, problems and potential. In J. Leary, T. Darvill and D. Field (eds) *Round Mounds and Monumentality in the British Neolithic and Beyond*, 28–2. Oxford, Oxbow Books.

Sheridan, J.A. (2013) Early Neolithic habitation structures in Britain and Ireland: a matter of circumstance and context. In D. Hofmann and J. Smyth (eds) *Tracking the Neolithic House in Europe*, 283–300. New York, Dordrecht, Heidelberg and London, Springer.

Sheridan, J.A. (2014) Little and large: the miniature 'carved stone ball' beads from the eastern tomb at Knowth, Ireland, and their broader significance. In R.-M. Arbogast and A. Greffier-Richard (eds) *Entre archéologie et écologie, une préhistoire de tous les milieux. Mélanges offerts à Pierre Pétrequin*, 303–314. Besançon, Presses universitaires de Franche-Comté.

Sheridan, J.A. (2016) Scottish Neolithic pottery in 2016: the big picture and some details of the narrative. In F.J. Hunter and J.A. Sheridan (eds) *Ancient Lives: object, people and place in early Scotland. Essays for David V Clarke on his 70th Birthday*, 189–212. Leiden, Sidestone.

Sheridan, J.A. (2018) The Neolithisation of Britain and Ireland: the arrival of immigrant farmers from Continental Europe and its impact on pre-existing lifeways. In N. Sanz (ed.) *The Origins of Food Production*, 226–45. Mexico City, UNESCO.

Thomas, J. (2008) *Place and Memory: excavations at the Pict's Knowe, Holywood and Holm Farm, Dumfries and Galloway*, 1994–8. Oxford, Oxbow Books.

Whittle, A., Healy, F. and Bayliss, A. (2011) *Gathering Time: dating the Early Neolithic enclosures of southern Britain and Ireland*. Oxford, Oxbow Books.

Chapter 14

The state of play

Frances Healy

PARTITIONED THINKING?

To think in terms of houses of the dead as opposed to those of the living may be a misjudged starting point. Penny Bickle's conclusion (this volume) that it is 'challenging to separate out life and death as two distinct areas of social and material concern in the LBK' extends to virtually all of the scattered and diverse societies touched on in this volume. Those who lived among known and remembered burials in a Linearbandkeramik or Brześć Kujawski culture settlement – and probably witnessed some of the interments – would have an immediate familiarity with the defunct. So would those taking part in the repeated re-working of progressively disarticulated human bone and in the associated rites in the Xagħra hypogeum.

In Britain, the progressive rearrangement of skeletal remains in tombs, and their placement in often repeatedly recut enclosure ditches, would have given at least some sections of the community intimate experience of corpses in the process of decay as well as of intact and dismembered skeletons. This would have instilled a working knowledge of skeletal anatomy, glimpsed in the assembly of bones from two individuals into a simulacrum of a single skeleton in bone group D at Fussell's Lodge, Wiltshire (Ashbee 1966, 10–12; Brothwell and Blake 1966, 51).

Whether people lived their daily lives among graves (and decayed houses) or engaged with human remains at all stages of disaggregation at ceremonial sites, the dead would have been a regular part of the lived experience. These circumstances could encompass the architectural interplay proposed by Jane Kenny (this volume) between an intervisible house and tomb on Holy Island, Anglesey. Living with the dead seems to have been a more frequent Neolithic experience than confining them to a separate sphere.

LONGHOUSES AND LONG MOUNDS

Like most generalisations, the decades-old notion of an origin for long burial mounds in ultimately Linearbandkeramik longhouses becomes fragmented, complex and questionable on closer inspection and with the accumulation of evidence. It remains most plausible in the Polish lowlands where Joanna Pyzel (this volume) describes a possibly uninterrupted transition between post-LBK Brześć Kujawski culture longhouses, built almost up to the end of the fifth millennium, and eastern TRB long barrows built from the start of the fourth, to a comparable plan but with a different dominant orientation. Elsewhere intervals are longer and inspiration questionable. Philippe Chambon (this volume) emphasises the amount of time that would have elapsed between the abandonment of LBK longhouses at Balloy, Seine-et-Marne, and the placement over them of mid-fifth millennium Passy-type burial monuments: the mounds formed by the decayed houses would have been ancient rather than immediately ancestral. He also emphasises how exceptional the Balloy superimposition is, against the growing number of excavated LBK settlements and Passy-type monuments in the Paris basin. The citation of Balloy by at least two other contributors to this volume reflects the absence of alternatives.

Within a much shorter timeframe, the triple house-to-long-barrow succession at Dorstone Hill, Herefordshire (Ray and Thomas this volume), may prove to be equally *sui generis*. Jessica Smyth (this volume) underscores the less than symmetrical and direct relation between house and court tomb at Ballyglass, where the occupied and then dismantled house was eccentric to the tomb and on a different alignment, and may have been beside the megalithic setting before the cairn was built over part of it. At Gwernvale, Powys, what may, with hindsight, have been a single rectangular structure made up of bedding trenches under the north horn of the tomb and post rows in the forecourt area, perhaps extending under the south horn, was similarly at an oblique angle and eccentric to the partly overlying tomb (Britnell 1984, 51–5, figs 13–14).

There is a case for viewing these diverse relationships in the context of a much wider, diachronic, European transition from investment of resources in substantial houses to their increasingly frequent investment in substantial burial monuments, highlighted by Philippe Chambon (this volume; *cf.* Last 2013, 278). This is not to deny a measure of continuity. It is noteworthy that Ballyglass and Gwernvale are among the very few Irish and British houses to incorporate human remains: a small amount of cremated human bone in a charcoal spread in the former, and human skull fragments in a bedding trench and associated posthole of the latter (Britnell 1984, 52). With changing practice and belief, a single location could remain the focus for a community's gatherings and ceremonies, a mark of its attachment to land, and the site of the occasional cohesion of shared labour – it is important to remember how much of a long barrow or cairn consists of mounded earth and/or stone, far in excess of what would have been needed to cover the contained burials. From this perspective, the scarcity of human remains in some such monuments and their occasional absence from others is no surprise: it rather reflects multiple roles and emphases, as do non-funerary deposits and the occasional absence of human remains in early Bronze Age round barrows built and used more than a millennium later (Healy and Harding 2007).

SHAPE AND SIZE

Timber structures in or beneath British long barrows and cairns tend to fall into two classes. Some, including rare rectangular buildings, form part of occupation traces beneath the mounds, where, as Alasdair Whittle points out (this volume), there are sometimes demonstrable, although short, intervals between occupation and construction. These may mark the initiation of lastingly significant locations. Others were integral to the monuments and were only sometimes freestanding. Of these, linear zones, often delimited by massive timbers, are clearly mortuary structures, in some cases demonstrably freestanding during the successive placement in them of burials, like the Wor Barrow 'box'. Some may well have been roofed and remained accessible once mounded, like the chamber of the Haddenham long barrow (Evans and Hodder 2006, 101), as did chambers in stone cairns.

Larger timber settings, while they evidence the same skill set as roofed rectangular buildings, have generally little in common with their architecture. They are often larger than all but the largest British houses, which currently have a maximum length of just over 20 m and a maximum width of just over 10 m (Sheridan 2013, table 12.1); are often of trapezoid or ovoid rather than rectangular plan; and lack features that might have been internal roof supports (*e.g.* Kinnes 1992, fig. 2.4.3). While these are habitually called 'mortuary' enclosures, Roy Loveday's argument (this volume) for most, if not all, of them having been revetments is a cogent one. He provides the valuable reminder that the trapezoid plans and tapering profiles of many British long barrows and cairns do not echo preceding and contemporary rectangular buildings – trapezoid houses, after all, emerged considerably later in the local Neolithic. He also argues convincingly that many of the structures preserved in them are unlikely to have been freestanding or roofed, especially given the practical problems of roofing an unsupported span of more than a few metres with available technology. A trapezoid structure in a trapezoid mound is strongly suggestive of revetment, analogous to stone kerbing, an interpretation which Loveday argues on stratigraphic grounds for the substantial example at Fussell's Lodge, Wiltshire. On a comparable scale to the $c.40$ m × 12 m of Fussell's Lodge is the $c.50$ m × 10 m of the Raunds long barrow in Northamptonshire, where surviving waterlogged oak revetment timbers set in a slot of tapering plan were pushed outwards by the spreading mound which also seemed to have been reveted with turf blocks inside the timbers (Bradley 2007). Smaller, less robust instances occurred at Haddenham, Cambridgeshire, where the slight, fence-like revetment of the sides of the ovoid first mound appeared contemporary with it (Evans and Hodder 2006, 74). Richard Bradley's decades-old interpretation of the 'mortuary enclosure' beneath Wor Barrow as the revetment of the first mound (1973) is repeatable at many other sites.

Vertical, contained sides on an earthen monument my suggest an attempt to replicate the profile of a stone-built structure. Alasdair Whittle's proposal (this volume) that large rectangular buildings could have contributed to the development of British long barrows, as models for imitation and memorialisation, underestimates differences of geometry and size. The skills applied to and developed during house construction would be applicable to the timber elements of long barrow building, but it is difficult to see imitation rather than the application of the technology current in a single society, adumbrating Philippe Chambon's emphasis on the extent to which similarities between structures may reflect restricted ranges of plans, materials and building techniques. Memorialisation of already significant places, occasionally the sites of pre-existing rectangular buildings, is far more persuasive than deliberation replication of house forms. Similarly, Andrew Whitefield's contention (this volume) that some Irish rectangular timber structures were mortuary enclosures ignores the lack of morphological resemblance between them and the rare examples of timber structures in Irish funerary monuments which he cites. It also ignores the rather consistent range of apparently domestic artefacts and food remains from the Irish houses.

The Cat's Brain structure seems to have been freestanding, on the evidence of the differing vegetation reflected by the mollusca from the structure and the ditches and of its substantial construction, and to have been extended before it was mounded over. The trapezoid plan is unlike those of early fourth millennium houses but like those of many long barrows. The span of up to just over 10 m is, by Roy Loveday's criteria, wide for unsupported roofing; and the slightly concave wider end, with a possible entrance and more massive timbers than the rest of the structure, is a feature found recurrently in long barrow façades (*cf.* Kinnes 1992, fig. 2.4.4), and only less frequently in rectangular buildings. The near-absence of food remains and artefacts, apart from carved chalk, points to non-residential use. This writer agrees with the editors that the structure, roofed or not, may have been a communal focus and meeting place, but this does not preclude its having contained subsequently ploughed-out human remains.

ELONGATED ENCLOSURES AND THE HAZARDS OF THINKING IN TWO DIMENSIONS

The 'long mortuary enclosure', in the sense of an elongated, parallel-sided area defined by a ditch, figures in several papers here, despite the absence of evidence for any funerary function in most excavated examples. It is significant that Denise Drury and Tim Allen have found that, when sectioned, some continuous-ditched cropmark long barrows in Lincolnshire have much slighter ditches than local excavated earthwork long barrows and are unlikely to have been of any great height. It could suggest that some of these monuments were ditched and banked enclosures, the slight surviving spread earthworks deriving from banks rather than mounds, in other words than plan and dimensions alone need not define a flattened long barrow.

Farther south, in the different environment of East Anglia, several excavated continuous, parallel-sided ditched enclosures with rounded or squared terminals, within the size-range of those documented by Drury and Allen, have provided no evidence for internal earthworks in their ditch fills, and/or have had ditches too slight for the construction of anything more than a bank. They have also tended to yield few or no finds (Healy 2012, table 3). Scarcity of finds and elongated plan could both place them at the small end of a continuum which extends to cursus monuments, in the period of altered monument forms and use which followed the *floruit* of long barrows and causewayed enclosures. This possibility is enhanced by their frequent association with cursus monuments and ring ditches in monument groupings of Roy Loveday's Barford-like complex (2007, 65–67, fig. 33) in the river valleys of eastern England and the Midlands. Cleanliness makes the dating of these elongated enclosures problematic. At least one example, however, can be placed around the turn of the fourth and third millennia cal BC: the long enclosure at Raunds, with a modelled construction date of *3350–2890 cal BC (95% probability*; Harding and Healy 2007, 98).

DICHOTOMY? – TOO SIMPLE

The rectangular 'houses' and 'halls' of the early fourth millennium cal BC in Britain and Ireland undoubtedly had multifarious meanings and uses. Nonetheless their defined chronological horizon – shortest in Ireland, but still relatively tight in Britain – marks these structures out as epitomising a particular convergence of circumstances. Less conspicuous, perhaps more ephemeral, forms of settlement existed alongside them and continued long after their demise. Chronological overlap with the earliest long barrows and cairns, with their longer collective currency and sometimes longer individual histories, reflects a transition to a society in which the focus of communal labour and communal gatherings shifted to monuments, some of them funerary. During the emergence of new lifeways among what was probably a growing population, and the transfer of resources and skills to new priorities, it would have been no more than incidental that some structures in and under long mounds resembled the freestanding houses of previous centuries.

REFERENCES

Ashbee, P. (1966) The Fussell's Lodge long barrow excavations 1957. *Archaeologia* 100, 1–80.
Bradley, P. (2007) The long barrow. In J. Harding and F. Healy, *The Raunds Area Project: a Neolithic and Bronze Age landscape in Northamptonshire*, 73–84. Swindon, English Heritage.
Bradley, R. (1973) Two notebooks of General Pitt Rivers. *Antiquity* 47, 47–50.
Britnell, W.J. (1984) The Gwernvale long cairn, Crickhowell, Brecknock. In W.J. Britnell and H.N. Savory, *Gwernvale and Penywyrlod: two Neolithic long cairns in the Black Mountains of Brecknock*, 43–154. Cardiff, Cambrian Archaeological Association.
Brothwell, D.R. and Blake, M.L. (1966) The human remains from the Fussell's Lodge long barrow: their morphology, discontinuous traits and pathology. In P. Ashbee, The Fussell's Lodge Long barrow excavations 1957. *Archaeologia* 100, 48–63.
Evans, C. and Hodder, I. (2006) *A Woodland Archaeology: neolithic sites at Haddenham: the Haddenham Project Volume 1*. Cambridge, McDonald Institute for Archaeological Research.
Harding, J. and Healy, F. (2007) *The Raunds Area Project: a Neolithic and Bronze Age landscape in Northamptonshire*. Swindon, English Heritage.
Healy, F. (2012) Starting something new: the Neolithic in Essex. In N. Brown, M. Medlycott and O. Bedwin (eds) *The Archaeology of Essex: proceedings of the Chelmsford conference*, Transactions of the Essex Society for Archaeology and History 4th ser. 3, 1–25.
Healy, F. and Harding, J. (2007) A thousand and one things to do with a round barrow. In J. Last (ed.) *Beyond the Grave: new perspectives on Barrows*, 53–71. Oxford: Oxbow Books.
Kinnes, I. (1992) *Non-Megalithic Long Barrows and Allied Structures in the British Neolithic*. British Museum Occasional Paper 52. London, British Museum.
Last, J. (2013) The end of the longhouse. In D. Hofmann and J. Smyth (eds) *Tracking the Neolithic House in Europe: sedentism, architecture and practice*, 261–82. New York, Springer.
Loveday, R. (2007) *Inscribed Across the Landscape: the cursus enigma*. Stroud, Tempus.
Sheridan, A. (2013) Early Neolithic habitation structures in Britain and Ireland: a matter of circumstance. In D. Hofmann and J. Smyth (eds) *Tracking the Neolithic House in Europe: sedentism, architecture and practice*, 283–300. New York, Springer.